A RENAISSANCE TAPESTRY

A
RENAISSANCE
TAPESTRY

The Gonzaga of Mantua

KATE SIMON

1817

HARPER & ROW, PUBLISHERS, NEW YORK

Cambridge, Philadelphia, San Francisco, Washington
London, Mexico City, São Paulo, Singapore, Sydney

For Stella Enright

FIRST EDITION

Copy editor: Marjorie Horvitz
Designer: Barbara DuPree Knowles
Indexer: Sydney Cohen

Library of Congress Cataloging-in-Publication Data

Simon, Kate.
    A renaissance tapestry.

    Bibliography: p.
    Includes index.
    1. Gonzaga family.   2. Mantua (Italy)—Civilization.
3. Italy—Civilization—1268–1559.   4. Renaissance— Italy.
DG975.M32S58   1988   945'.2   87–45669
ISBN 0-06-015847-6

88 89 90 91 92 HC 10 9 8 7 6 5 4 3 2 1

CONTENTS

* * *

CONTENTS

Illustrations follow page 182

ACKNOWLEDGMENTS

*　*　*

I would like to express my thanks to Prof. Dott. Adele Bellù, Archivista di Stato, Mantua, and to her staff, who eased Latin and early vulgate into comprehensible Italian for me. Many thanks, also, to Prof. Caterina Forni of the Accademia Nazionale dei Lincei in Rome and to the advisers, checkers, and deliverers of books at the Biblioteca Nazionale in Florence, at the British Library in London, at the Library of Congress in Washington, and at several branch libraries in New York. Returning to Mantua, I must express my gratitude to the Biblioteca Comunale and its cooperative staff under the direction of Dott A. Schizzerotto, and to several book dealers, highly informed gentlemen, of Mantua, as well as the enthusiastic and helpful tourist office of the city. And back home again, thanks to my editor, Hugh Van Dusen, and his assistants for valor and patience through the years of shaping this book.

THE GONZAGA

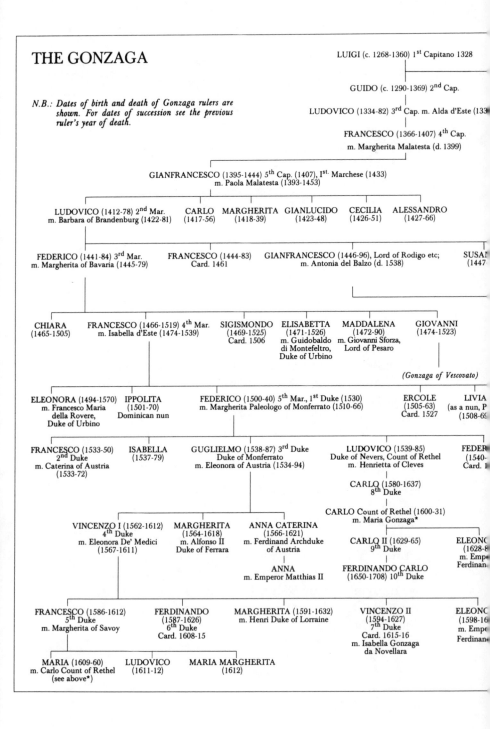

N.B.: Dates of birth and death of Gonzaga rulers are shown. For dates of succession see the previous ruler's year of death.

LUIGI (c. 1268-1360) 1st Capitano 1328

GUIDO (c. 1290-1369) 2nd Cap.

LUDOVICO (1334-82) 3rd Cap. m. Alda d'Este (133

FRANCESCO (1366-1407) 4th Cap.
m. Margherita Malatesta (d. 1399)

GIANFRANCESCO (1395-1444) 5th Cap. (1407), Ist. Marchese (1433)
m. Paola Malatesta (1393-1453)

LUDOVICO (1412-78) 2nd Mar.
m. Barbara of Brandenburg (1422-81)

CARLO (1417-56)

MARGHERITA (1418-39)

GIANLUCIDO (1423-48)

CECILIA (1426-51)

ALESSANDRO (1427-66)

FEDERICO (1441-84) 3rd Mar.
m. Margherita of Bavaria (1445-79)

FRANCESCO (1444-83) Card. 1461

GIANFRANCESCO (1446-96), Lord of Rodigo etc; m. Antonia del Balzo (d. 1538)

SUSAN (1447

CHIARA (1465-1505)

FRANCESCO (1466-1519) 4th Mar. m. Isabella d'Este (1474-1539)

SIGISMONDO (1469-1525) Card. 1506

ELISABETTA (1471-1526) m. Guidobaldo di Montefeltro, Duke of Urbino

MADDALENA (1472-90) m. Giovanni Sforza, Lord of Pesaro

GIOVANNI (1474-1523)

(Gonzaga of Vescovato)

ELEONORA (1494-1570) m. Francesco Maria della Rovere, Duke of Urbino

IPPOLITA (1501-70) Dominican nun

FEDERICO (1500-40) 5th Mar., 1st Duke (1530) m. Margherita Paleologo of Monferrato (1510-66)

ERCOLE (1505-63) Card. 1527

LIVIA (as a nun, P (1508-69)

FRANCESCO (1533-50) 2nd Duke m. Caterina of Austria (1533-72)

ISABELLA (1537-79)

GUGLIELMO (1538-87) 3rd Duke Duke of Monferrato m. Eleonora of Austria (1534-94)

LUDOVICO (1539-85) Duke of Nevers, Count of Rethel m. Henrietta of Cleves

FEDER (1540- Card. I

CARLO (1580-1637) 8th Duke

CARLO Count of Rethel (1600-31) m. Maria Gonzaga*

VINCENZO I (1562-1612) 4th Duke m. Eleonora De' Medici (1567-1611)

MARGHERITA (1564-1618) m. Alfonso II Duke of Ferrara

ANNA CATERINA (1566-1621) m. Ferdinand Archduke of Austria

CARLO II (1629-65) 9th Duke

ELEONC (1628-8 m. Empe Ferdinan

ANNA m. Emperor Matthias II

FERDINANDO CARLO (1650-1708) 10th Duke

FRANCESCO (1586-1612) 5th Duke m. Margherita of Savoy

FERDINANDO (1587-1626) 6th Duke Card. 1608-15

MARGHERITA (1591-1632) m. Henri Duke of Lorraine

VINCENZO II (1594-1627) 7th Duke Card. 1615-16 m. Isabella Gonzaga da Novellara

ELEONC (1598-16 m. Empe Ferdinan

MARIA (1609-60) m. Carlo Count of Rethel (see above*)

LUDOVICO (1611-12)

MARIA MARGHERITA (1612)

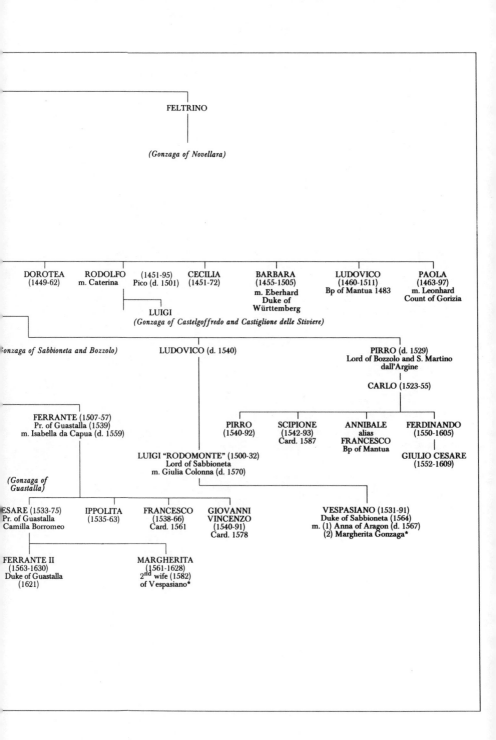

FELTRINO

(Gonzaga of Novellara)

| DOROTEA (1449-62) | RODOLFO m. Caterina | (1451-95) Pico (d. 1501) | CECILIA (1451-72) | BARBARA (1455-1505) m. Eberhard Duke of Württemberg | LUDOVICO (1460-1511) Bp of Mantua 1483 | PAOLA (1463-97) m. Leonhard Count of Gorizia |

LUIGI
(Gonzaga of Castelgoffredo and Castiglione delle Stiviere)

onzaga of Sabbioneta and Bozzolo) LUDOVICO (d. 1540)

PIRRO (d. 1529)
Lord of Bozzolo and S. Martino
dall'Argine

CARLO (1523-55)

FERRANTE (1507-57)
Pr. of Guastalla (1539)
m. Isabella da Capua (d. 1559)

| PIRRO (1540-92) | SCIPIONE (1542-93) Card. 1587 | ANNIBALE alias FRANCESCO Bp of Mantua | FERDINANDO (1550-1605) |

GIULIO CESARE
(1552-1609)

LUIGI "RODOMONTE" (1500-32)
Lord of Sabbioneta
m. Giulia Colonna (d. 1570)

(Gonzaga of Guastalla)

| ESARE (1533-75) Pr. of Guastalla Camilla Borromeo | IPPOLITA (1535-63) | FRANCESCO (1538-66) Card. 1561 | GIOVANNI VINCENZO (1540-91) Card. 1578 | VESPASIANO (1531-91) Duke of Sabbioneta (1564) m. (1) Anna of Aragon (d. 1567) (2) Margherita Gonzaga* |

FERRANTE II
(1563-1630)
Duke of Guastalla
(1621)

MARGHERITA
(1561-1628)
2nd wife (1582)
of Vespasiano*

O * N * E

The small train, its few first-class passengers sitting like Renaissance portraits in their one half of one car, trundles in from Verona, to stop at the usual amiable station with its welcoming big bar, book and newspaper stall, first- and second-class waiting rooms—a curious Italian anomaly considering that many municipalities are Communist governed—and numerous nagging *Partenze*—*Arrivi* signs, which have the voices of stern parents: "I've told you and told you. Now don't you dare be late or lost." The one surprise here is the presence of foreign newspapers at the news stall. Mantua has no university, no great fame for learning like Bologna, "The Learned," nor is it perfumed with aestheticism like Florence, but there are enough small, ardent circles around the redoubtable archives and community library and watchful keepers of old houses full of sonorous echoes to shape a cultivated society that buys foreign newspapers and supports several wide-ranging bookshops. One of the preoccupations of these citizens is not the restoration of old fervid Mantua, as impossible as wrapping Venice in her ancient Persian silks and her airs of spices from the East, but to try to stave off a further slide of the long desuetude the city has suffered. In the late 1960s, there was a despairing local exhibition gathered as "Mantua, a City Worth Saving," and there were other efforts, earlier and subsequently, that tried to revive old glamour, to plaster over blind spaces in gutted palaces, and to sharpen the stone lacework around blank Renaissance windows. (One such recent effort was an exhibition at the Victoria and Albert Museum in London, titled "Splendours of the Gonzaga." Subsidized in part by banking interests of Lombardy and advertised with arresting, ubiquitous posters, the show beckoned not only to its own learned charms but to those of Mantua as well, hoping to attract more than its customary handful of tourists.)

Cook's Guide of 1923 dismisses the city briefly as "of no interest except for art and history," an echo of Dickens's judgment and that of his guide, who said that truly there was not much to see in Mantua. They apparently didn't care much for the art and history, the very attractions that bring visitors to a city that makes no effort to paint itself in the Tiepolo clouds of tourist allure, being generally quite contented to keep itself prosperously busy with the light industry at its outskirts and its much older occupation as an agricultural center. On Thursday, the traditional market day, the city is mobbed with hordes of rural merchants and farmers in stiff city-visit hats, who talk for hours, standing on their resilient Italian legs. The elderly sit interminably in café bars, laughing, growling, gesturing, making deals in grains and wines, vegetables and cheeses. Their sons search for tools and sweaters, a pocketbook for the *fidanzata*, a toy for the baby, in the swollen market of the old city.

As in much of Italy, the summer sun is fat and lethargic, the sky stained with dark, cold patches in the wintertime. Mantua is at her evocative best in the autumn, when she is clothed in the gray mists that rise from her surrounding waters like veils of antique widowhood. The mists wreathe and melt bus lights, diffuse streetlamps and traffic signals, stilling their strong tones to dim whispers. Pedestrians appear and disappear like spirits in old myths. Emboldened by contrast with their gray background, the market flowers shine with startling luminosity. The journey from the railroad station moves through an indifference of automobiles and middle-class shopping to a broad facelessness that bears the heavy stamp of Mussolini. This big Piazza Cavallotti, trailing at one corner an old ribbon of ivied houses rising from the weeds and rushes of a forgotten canal, leads to the deep archways and shops of the Via Roma and the Corso Umberti I—modest, bucolic miscellanies of ropes and pails alternating with high-style clothing, pharmacies that dispense medicines for cows and hogs sitting next to worldly jewels—which express a rural prosperity that takes its finances to banks whose names are variations of *Agricola*.

At the meeting of the Via Verdi with the Via Broletto, the face of modern enterprise changes to resume ancient masks, now vibrant with the optimistic pride of the Renaissance, now brooding and shadowy, smeared with medieval blood. A burst of fanfare calls from the facade of the church of Sant'Andrea, the latest structure on a multilayered site. Mantua, which holds its history dear, says there was once a temple dedicated to Diana here. Early Christianity replaced the temple with a hospice, which sheltered Longinus after his long wanderings, carrying a vial of the blood of Christ he had drawn with his lance, that vial to become the most sacred possession of the city-state, honored with an annual procession. The hospice gave way to an early church, whose Gothic tower remains to soar above a later church designed (but not completed) by Leon Battista Alberti in the 1470s, the idealized classicism of its facade more discreet and contemplative than its prototypes, the triumphal Roman arches that swarmed with the noisy symbols of conquest. A few paces to the right of Sant'Andrea is the imponderably old partner of churches, the market, which flows into subterranean cellars each afternoon at one o'clock, leaving only its flowers to sing in the emptied square. On another side of the market sits the Romanesque church of San Lorenzo, low and round in its earth like a setting red hen, built late in the eleventh century. Adjoining the medieval church stands a handsome clock tower erected to accompany Alberti's improvements in this core of the city. A low, strong building of deep arcades and swallowtail crenellations, built in the mid-thirteenth century and later restored, once served as a Palace of Justice, the seat of tribunals and the keeper of the city's archives. Its gaunt, medieval neighbor is the Tower of the Cage, a box of metal bars where malefactors were put to starve and freeze in the cold, as sure a way of death as hanging but slower.

Back of the market square, a niche, the sort that served as street chapels for a breath of holiness in the swift run of earthly matters, shelters the bust of a man in a Gothic cap. He also wears a beamish smile; his hands rest on a book. He is Virgil, born near Mantua, and her most cherished son. The square toward which he beams is the heart of Mantua's history, the Piazza Sordello, named for an Italian-born singer of Provençal songs, himself sung by Dante and by Robert Browning. Long, broad, and now muted, the Piazza Sordello was the stage for battles and galas, ceremonies and chivalric tourneys. With the exception of the cathedral and the Bishop's Palace, of a later period, the square is a repository of late-medieval palaces built and held by the ruling Bonacolsi family before they were routed by the Gonzaga in 1328. In the hooded complex on the right (as one faces the cathedral), with its confusingly awesome expanses of salons, apartments, gardens, chapels, courts, and armories, the Gonzaga schemed, breathed easily and uneasily, grew fat with power and lean in fear of its diminution, danced, sang, entertained kings and emperors, clad themselves now in hubris, now in humility. The vast compound, the Palazzo Ducale, is not as large as the Vatican or Spain's Escorial, but considering that the court of Mantua had neither the wealth of the Papacy nor the New World silver and gold gathered by Philip II, it makes a respectable rival.

Resisting, postponing for a while the challenge of the Palazzo Ducale, one wanders the Piazza Sordello to admire the wealth of books and postcards by which Mantua hopes to be admired and remembered, and to rub shoulders with a citizenry that names one bar Gonzaga, another for the great court painter Mantegna, and a street for Rubens, who was a longtime protégé of the court. Even comestibles commemorate Mantua's luminaries: a flat, wholesome Gonzaga cake, butter wrapped in the name of Virgil. A short walk past Virgil's grinning niche brings one to the Via Ardigo, the street of the extraordinary Gonzaga archives and, in a wide-halled, steep-staired palace, the Biblioteca Comunale, itself replete with archival material translated and collated from the elderly material next door. Beyond the far end of the Piazza Sordello there is an attractive old house, whose small front garden sports the figure of a humpbacked jester. Recently refurbished and adorned, the building is dubbed "Rigoletto House" to commemorate Verdi's opera, this house the setting of the last tragic scene. (The rake who initiated the tragedy by seducing Rigoletto's daughter is usually identified with the most dazzling and uninhibited of the dynasty, the fourth duke of Mantua, Vincenzo I.)

Off the nearby Piazza Virgiliana a wide park full of grandmothers and grandchildren surrounds a large neoclassic monument to the poet as a young man, in a toga and Roman sandals, on his head a wreath. The expanses of white marble cannot resist the antique Italian craft of scoring graffiti into classical expanses; it makes lavish backgrounds for red hammers and sickles and exhortations to shoot down the Fascists. Politics has no room for

expression on the frenetic facades of the houses designed by Giulio Romano in another part of town, nor has it entered the se-
cretive, graceful house of Andrea Mantegna, or touched the ec-
centricities of the Palazzo del Te, a short distance from the
painter's house.

* In its earliest times, the Palazzo Ducale was a rather simple
entity of court and fortress in clearly defined large space, that
space filled, razed, refilled, manipulated, and remanipulated by
successive Gonzaga, and by the Austrians who ruled after them,
into a confusion of five hundred rooms, not all of them yet thoroughly studied. The endless palace that once rang with music and
showed master paintings and unique antiquities is now depleted,
left with little but incomprehensible passages. An exhibition gallery substitutes blankness for paintings gone; a tourney court surrounded by twisted columns and Gonzaga symbols makes no
sound. Inescapably, one comes on still-extant classical galleries,
dedicated to Troy, the stage for dramas of the Trojan horse, for
Ajax as he is killed by Athena, for the dream of Hecuba and the
judgment of Paris, all painted in the agitated mannerist fashion.
A spread of late-Renaissance panels depicting incidents in Ovid's
Metamorphoses (a popular source of subjects) brighten a few chambers, while a broad, ornate ceiling that once looked down on
tapestries and treasures of the goldsmith's art stares at a few dour
busts and the ubiquitous Roman sarcophagus. And there are other
ceilings: carved, inlaid, worked as puzzles, painted as sky, as zodiacal charts.

Continuing on to the edges of the not very large city, one
comes on trails of canal that touch on discarded palaces, on vague
reminders of dock streets once undoubtedly lively with port business, and a few irregular jumbles of modest houses brandishing
flags of laundry. On such a walk one encounters more clearly the
shape and position of the city: surrounded by the waters of three
lakes formed by the river Mincio, born of the mighty Po. In early
years, her waters could help protect Mantua, as when they were
loosed to flood the roads taken by invading troops. When later
armies massed larger bodies of troops, which could avoid the
flooded roads, when warfare became more sophisticated and the
greed for empire among warrior popes and foreign powers more
voracious, the lakes were of little use. Now slow and quiet, they

serve to float fog and mists and old dreams of splendid barges that once brought royal visitors and their bejeweled girls to offer as brides.

* An unexpected doorway leads out to one of a number of small gardens and a view of a serene early-Renaissance palace designed by Luca Fancelli, Alberti's assistant and the gifted resident architect to the court. A ramp here, a turn there, brings one to the Hall of the Princes and one of the remaining wonders of the palace: sections of turbulent, vivid frescoes by Antonio Pisanello, entombed for centuries and recently rediscovered. Highly esteemed for his work with Gentile da Fabriano for the doge in Venice and the Pope in Rome and later alone in Verona, Pisanello was invited by the Este lords to work in Ferrara. In the course of several years in the late 1430s and into the 1440s, he made for them superb medals of a quality never seen before and rarely after, as well as several paintings, one of them an exquisite portrait of Leonello d'Este. In a practice common between the houses, Mantua borrowed Pisanello for several working visits. Letters mention the painter at work in Mantua in 1439, very probably shaping his medals of Gianfrancesco Gonzaga and other members of that court. Precisely what other work he did in Mantua at that time we do not know. We do know, however, that he became involved in a disastrous military action of the Gonzaga against Venice. Not only were the Gonzaga routed, but the painter, accused of "rebellious acts" and threatened with having his tongue cut out, had to remove himself to the safety of Ferrara. Although some scholars suggest that the murals were painted in short, clandestine trips to Mantua during the fugitive years, it is likely that they were painted at a later, safer time, 1446–48, when Pisanello probably also executed the medals of Gianfrancesco's daughter, Cecilia, her brother, Ludovico II, who had recently become ruler of Mantua, and their old tutor, Vittorino da Feltre.

In the absence of documented information and given the fact that the Gonzaga could not leave their walls untouched or their spaces at rest for any length of time, there is no sure knowing the original context for which the frescoes were meant. Or did Ludovico obliterate portions of the murals, hoping to redecorate the room in the more fashionable "Florentine style" rather than live with the outmoded International Gothic of Pisanello? Whatever Ludovico's intentions, bad masonry took a deciding hand.

A letter dated 1480 from the architect Luca Fancelli to Federico, then marquis of Mantua, informs him of the collapse of a wall in the "Sala del Pisanello." The responding letter urges the rescue of whatever can be saved. Precise information stops there, but it is conjectured that in several Gonzaga changes of apartments and their decorations, Pisanello was obliterated to a substantial degree. Of what was a prolific production throughout Italy, comparatively few of Pisanello's paintings remain. Thus, with the rediscovery of the remaining frescoes, Mantua has become a major repository of extant Pisanello work.

Over the centuries, there have been intermittent attempts at investigating the Sala del Pisanello. Nineteenth-century scholars explored a collection of uncannily alert drawings in the Louvre— it was Pisanello's practice to sketch from life rather than, as was the common habit, from other studies—which hinted at preliminary work for a large composition, a fresco perhaps. Continued exploration found that the ceiling of the Sala had been lowered in the nineteenth century, and bands of neoclassic foolishness were added to adorn the new ceiling, a further complication in the job of removing layers of accretion in which the murals were buried. Bit by bit, painstaking chipping and brushing began to reveal decorative bands, flowers, and animals that shared the virtuosity of the Louvre drawings. In 1966, after more than five centuries of damage, dust, and asphyxiation, fairly extensive remains of the frescoes came to effulgent life. Much has been destroyed by vandal hands—one sees the acts of gouging and scratching with chisels; some sections were never completed, remaining as sketches and afterthoughts; some portions are fully colored, others still await their color; here and there a hard black is touched with delicate red to heighten the drama of chiaroscuro or to indicate potential change.

Pisanello's subject matter, based on an Italian version of the Arthurian legends gathered as La Tavola Rotonda, appears to concentrate on the rivalry of Lancelot and Tristan in their quest for the Holy Grail. The competition grows to enmity, exploding in a great battle that culminates in the death of many warriors and finally in man-to-man combat between the heroes. Tristan emerges the absolute victor. Familiar as they were with these stories, the Gonzaga might easily have identified themselves with Tristan, not he of the love potions and yearnings but, as here, the valiant and victorious. With important areas of the murals gone, it is not absolutely certain that the frescoes actually depict a Tristan-Lancelot conflict, a matter of scholarly interest but of no great importance to the viewer, who is immediately absorbed by the composition's compelling power and soaring imagination. Surrounded by boiling clouds of battle, each armored figure, each horse, is masterfully drawn and there are a few portraits, especially of a black knight and a blond woman, that are extraordinarily elegant and moving. Art historians have named the lovely woman with the banded riches of blond hair "Isolde" and the blond head she appears to be addressing they call "Brangaene," her handmaiden. Or is one of them Lancelot's Guinevere? The viewer finds himself eagerly ready to accept any of the magical names; no lesser women will do for such loveliness.

* The eccentric miscellany of the Palazzo Ducale continues in its wanderings to the famous small apartments where Isabella d'Este-Gonzaga kept her private collections (to be explored more fully in a later chapter). It pauses under a blue and gold maze of ceiling that bears the name of her great-grandson Vincenzo Gonzaga, fourth duke of Mantua and second duke of Monferrato, etched in regal letters and a motto: *"forse che si, forse che no"*— maybe yes and maybe no—signifying the quickness to move in any expeditious direction that was generally characteristic of the family. Then the surprise of a hanging garden, a hall of soft-fleshed river gods taking their ease under vines and trellises; a playful room probably meant for light music now surrounds a meticulously rendered bust of the forceful and extremely plain empress Maria Theresa of Austria, who ruled Mantua in the eighteenth century.

An Exhibition Gallery presents the oddly coarse, strong features of Isabella d'Este's husband, Francesco, and a painting by Domenico Morone, all steely armor, flashing spikes and shields, gorgeous white horses, soldiers in red hose and doublets fighting the battle that forced the then ruling Bonacolsi family from Mantua, leaving the Gonzaga in power. Not far from this painting of Gonzaga triumph is a disconcerting patchwork of a once-large painting by Rubens, ordered by the Gonzaga who were his patrons during eight of his youthful years. The canvas, which clearly lacks a wide middle section and side portions, is the *Adoration of the Holy Trinity*, whose worshipers include the duke Guglielmo, the son he despised, Vincenzo, and their respective wives, the older dressed like a nun, the younger in a gold-embroidered mantle and a huge, stylish ruff, suitable to the Medici heiress she was. Rubens scholars have identified scattered small portraits of children of the house as once having been part of the canvas, which, in its present rigid rearrangement, begs for touches of Rubenesque buoyancy.

Beyond the crippled Rubens is the most famous glory of the Palazzo Ducale, the Camera Picta (more popularly known as the Camera degli Sposi), with its frescoes by Andrea Mantegna, court painter for three Gonzaga generations. Sections have disappeared and others been restored since an eighteenth-century guidebook written by a Mantuan painter reported that major stretches of the room were disfigured and asked the "gentle visitor to mourn with him the great loss of this marvelous work, falling every day into greater desuetude." In spite of the loss and possible distortions of restoration, what remains is, in its own idiom, a superb companion to Pisanello's frescoes.

Here are the Gonzaga of the fifteenth century, large, dignified, and confident, richly dressed, graced by elegant pages and courtiers, blooded horses and keen dogs, as Mantegna bound them in immortal lines and colors. It has been argued that since Mantegna was a slow painter, having begun the frescoes of the family group about 1465 and not been ready with them until sometime in the 1470s, the panels place the family personages in confusing time frames. Two figures who appear forced into the composition surrounding the young Francesco just returned from Rome as a cardinal are generally identified as King Christian of Denmark and the emperor Frederick II, who actually visited Mantua at separate times. Is the girl identified as daughter Barbara actually Margherita of Bavaria, come to marry Federico, Ludovico's heir? Whoever they were, and when, Mantegna's chronology makes its own immutable truth, as irrefutable as Giotto's howling women and angels who mourn Christ's death. Here too are flesh, blood, character, gesture, sound, vividly expressed by Mantegna in the painting tenets of his time.

One striking invention in the then fascinating game of perspective was that of having the viewer look up rather than straight on ("foreshortened from below," as Vasari put it), which serves to create a respectful distance from the exalted family. Curtained space suggests a room and then opens to broad landscape; a knight in bicolored hose dissolves by his presence the wall division before which he stands; putti fly and garlands swing with no regard to the limitations of doors and walls. In the ceiling, an engaging and daring piece of perspective has fat cherubs teetering on a round, garland-hung balustrade, laughing women peering down at the dignified assemblage below, while a peacock disdainfully picks its way among the women, the whole merry piece of illusionism a pioneer that led off a thousand imitations.

In the panel of the family group, Rome, the apogee of all noble cities, and a suggestion of what Mantua must become, is remembered in a distant, creamy landscape, and again in the marble screen that echoes Augustan palaces and forms a distinguished background for the family. The dominant, purposeful plain man at the left of the fresco is dressed in a round red hat, soft leather shoes, and the full loose robe worn by accomplished elderly gentlemen. This is Ludovico, second marquis of Mantua, ruler from 1444 to the time of his death, in 1478. His responsibility as prince, politician, and warrior is symbolized by the note in his hand and the turn of his head as he speaks to his secretary; unlike the rest of the family, he is not dressed formally but prefers to be painted in the act and costume of seeing to state affairs. Next to him and a bit lower sits his German wife, Barbara of Brandenburg, wearing a beautifully patterned gown of cut velvet or brocade (the centuries have erased definition). Her face is quite unattractive under its winged coif of fine veiling. Like Flemish portraitists, Mantegna was apparently not required to flatter. (A later generation of vainer Gonzaga disapproved of Mantegna's portraiture, perhaps for that reason.) Fine clothing and backgrounds that speak of boundless domains, the solid air of "Here I am, here I remain," were quite enough. Ideal beauty was for the Virgin, for blond saints, for ladies of classical mythology.

Not all the legitimate children were represented and certainly not the illegitimate, but several identifications seem to be generally agreed upon. The plump young man between his parents, ripe face and ripe body proclaiming one of the family debilities, obesity, is Federico, to be in time the third marquis of Mantua. The boy with the ascetic profile, whose shoulders Federico holds, is his brother Ludovico, and before him, leaning toward their mother as if offering a piece of fruit, is sister Paola, oddly pretty, oddly pale, the curve of her back rather too full. The excessive curve and her large gaunt eyes point to another family frailty, the malformation that made humpbacks, Ludovico and Barbara's sickly girl especially afflicted. Behind the marquesa Barbara stands another grown son, Rodolfo, a soldier of dark temperament, his fine-nosed, square-jawed swarthiness echoing the virile faces of the Roman soldiers Mantegna had painted earlier in a church of his native Padua. To Rodolfo's right, shadowed in the brocades and velvets of the princelings, is a somber, learned old gentleman who might have been a tutor or mathematician—his inclusion in the group portrait points up the family's respect for learning— and to Rodolfo's left, dressed as richly as her mother, her hair bound in classic Greek fashion, sits peach-faced, nubile daughter Barbara. Half hidden in the folds of the marchesa's train, yet sharply conspicuous, stands a fashionably dressed female dwarf, arrogant little features pinched into a broad, implacable face, a common personage in court paintings and inescapably reminiscent of the dwarf in Veronese's *Convito in Casa di Levi* and the squat, domineering figure that guards Velázquez's *Meninas*. (Although there is mention of a court dwarf-buffoon in Mantua a century before, this type of entertainer-servitor must have disappeared for a while. A letter from a churchman to the marquis's sister, Cecilia, compliments the family for not housing dwarfs and buffoons, but the older Barbara, who was brought up under the same tutelage as Cecilia and Ludovico, succumbed to the demands of courtly fashion and again gathered the funny little people.)

Francesco, of the accompanying panel, was the first in a long line of Gonzaga cardinals, leading off a design to ease rivalries between the firstborn son and the second, who often led an equally princely life, with fewer responsibilities. Although his father's adroit diplomats had been politicking for quite a time and spreading gold in the right places to achieve the cardinalship, the large, heavy boy of seventeen is greeted as if he had just brought great, unexpected honors to his family. His father salutes him with a gesture of reverence, the large-nosed profile of the father repeated as that of another son and, as if it were a visual leitmotiv, in yet another filial profile. Before their cardinal uncle stand two enchanting small boys, Francesco and Sigismondo, the sons of Federico. They are both dressed in the particolored hose of young knights, the ribbons that flow from their sleeves very much like those that decorate the short loose coats of their elders. Francesco's flattened little nose and pouting lips give promise of the adult's sensual, vigorous face. His prettier younger brother, someday himself to be a cardinal, holds the hand of his young uncle Ludovico, who, in turn, holds the hand of his cardinal brother. The garland of clasped hands and embraced shoulders might easily have been dictated by the marquis, eager to show the world sturdy family bonds and to provide a homily for his sons and grandsons and their sons. And though there were lapses and rifts, the dynasty lasted for almost three centuries, family unity often one of its binding factors.

The frescoes—dedicated, on a broad banner held by the most winsome of putti, to "the best of princes and his incomparable wife" by "Suus Andreas Mantinia"—though wearied by time and vandalism, have lost neither the classical quality of an ancient frieze nor the free experimentation of the early Renaissance, qualities that caused the poet Ariosto to link Mantegna with Leonardo and Giovanni Bellini as the three greatest painters of Italy.

There were richer marquises and, later, dukes, a number equally accomplished and fruitful, but rarely again such a full circle, so Roman a father and mother, so stalwart a stand of sons and grandsons. Ludovico, brought up in Greek and Latin and a lover of the works of Virgil, would inevitably have seen himself the way Mantegna suggested him, as the wise and responsible paterfamilias. His wife, sent to Mantua as his betrothed at the age of ten, must have enjoyed seeing herself as the trustworthy, steady helpmeet she actually was. The young bucks hold their heads up confidently, like the peacock above them, aware of their positions and worth. They have looked back and are looking ahead to a history that glistens with blood and jewels, a history manipulated by skillful tightrope walkers and listless fools, by the cautious and the reckless, by the licentious and the steady (most of them confident of their hold on the luck that seemed to smile broadly on them, intimidating superstitious enemies)—a multicolored line which, by the mid-sixteenth century, exerted wide influences that belied the size of its state, hardly more than a city with limited environs.

Plague

In spite of valiant efforts by a few professors of medicine to study the plague in those places where they were permitted to perform autopsies—at least one, a famous physician of Perugia, to die of the disease—and attempts to isolate patients in such sophisticated cities as Venice and Florence, studies of the plague were, obviously, almost impossible. It attacked and killed with ferocious speed. Touching the garments of a stricken person was considered fatal; pigs rooting in a dead man's clothing dropped dead almost immediately after, it was said. Nor was there much time for calm study. In the latter half of the fourteenth century, bubonic plague struck at least four times, staying for several years at a time, to become a constant of European life for decades. One half to two thirds of populations died; Venice and Florence reported the loss of 100,000 inhabitants in each of their territories, their city streets taken over by vermin, wolves, and vultures. To repopulate their cities, they were forced to lower standards for citizenship. Venice invited Germans to settle, empty Padua and Verona declared their prisoners free citizens in order that they might provide labor, start turning the wheels of commerce, and produce future generations. (As the bouts of plague abated, midwives and physicians began to report unusually large numbers of multiple births, nature's feeble apology for the cruelties of the plague.)

The most common measure against the plague was to gather up long processions that carried images of the powerful foes of the catastrophe: Saint Roche, Saint Sebastian, and several miracle Virgins. By their crowded passage from place to place, however, they increased the number of plague victims. To assist the saints, old folk remedies were brought to use. Bits of magic metal, wood, and stone came out of their pagan hiding places, to be carried in one's clothing or worn around one's neck. Small sacks of arsenic and snake venom were common amulets, considered particularly efficacious on the principle that these poisons would cancel out the effects of the plague's poisons. Snake venom was especially promising, since it was the snake who had unleashed original sin and was probably now ready to atone by lending his venom for the benefit of mankind. Those with the strength to stand placed themselves at the sides of tanneries to breathe in their curative airs; others inhaled the odors of latrines. One's own urine (a constant in folk medicine, lately publicized by an Indian politician who drank it every day), taken straight or reduced to its salts, sometimes eaten on bread or mixed with oil as a body lotion, was highly regarded as preventative and cure. One envoy from London favored hot English treacle, which, though it saved his life, he said, ruined his innards forever. Other desperate improvisations tore up gardens and fields. Trees, shrubs, citrus leaves, handfuls of herbs and spices, were burned along with sulfur and camphor—and tobacco when that was later brought from the Americas—to clean the poisoned air. Flowers and aromatic leaves were used to make incense and gathered as bouquets to hold to one's nose. ("Ring around the rosy, a pocketful of posies . . . all fall down" was clearly a plague song.) Apples rose in price, sought after because their odor was considered cleansing and restorative. Herbs steeped in oils became unguents and potions. One such mixture, put together as a plague cure toward the end of the seventeenth century by an Italian living in Germany, gave us eau de Cologne.

✳ A physician's life, if he stayed alive, was exceedingly precarious in such times. The few who made keen guesses as to sources of infection—body lice, contaminated water, damp, rotting garbage in the streets—might have been better off if they remained silent. The Church contended with them vigorously for credit for cures; they were imprisoned, their money taken from them, on charges of manslaughter and profiteering; they were accused of spreading disease so that their practices might increase. Jewish doctors, generally respected, suffered with their coreligionists the accusations of poisoning wells, of deliberately spreading the plague, and were consequently killed. Nor did the alchemists and the astrologers acting as physicians fare much better. They too were accused of money grubbing and helping the Jews spread the plague.

Psychological handling of the plague brings us of course to Boccaccio's *Decameron*, which describes pleasures to dispel the black clouds of 1348–52. The author mentions several styles of conduct. Some chose moderation, almost asceticism, in isolation.

Others, like his group of young men and women who removed themselves from Florence to a country villa, apparently took "the opposite view, and maintained that an infallible way of warding off this appalling evil was to drink heavily, enjoy life to the full, go round singing and merry-making, gratify all of one's cravings whenever the opportunity offered, and shrug the whole thing off as one enormous joke." This popular cure, then and during later onslaughts of the disease, inspired heavy gambling and "bestial" amusements, among peasants and lords, among nuns and priests, among bishops and cardinals and their courtesans and boys. There were religious sects that proclaimed homosexuality no sin and incest no grave matter. At least one lively pope, who cursed and swore by the penis, defended it and its activities as the father of all, including saints. The *Decameron* became extremely popular not only for its stories but as a jolly how-to book, a source of encouragement to death-defying pleasure. During the plague of 1586, ready sensualists formed "academies of love," where, between sessions of lovemaking, the members gambled and told each other stories.

(No one, not even cool Machiavelli, was free from the fervid eroticism heated by the terror and the intense masochism of processions of black-hooded flagellants, tearing blood from their bodies with spiked ropes. After observing the streets of Florence in 1527, bathed in plague stench, its streets almost entirely empty of passersby, he fell deeply in love, he writes, with a woman at a church service, seeing her in terms of the goddess of unbridled appetites, Venus, her slender fingers clearly capable of rousing the dying appetites of the oldest of men, men like himself, near sixty and shortly to die, as he did that same year.)

Like hoi polloi, the rich devotees of sequestered abandon died, even those who were infected with syphilis, which was recommended by a number of physicians as an effective prophylaxis against the plague. It is claimed that the "gather ye rosebuds" eroticism spurred on by the frequent visitations of the plague affected not only poetry and song in Italy but the increasingly dazzling exhibitionism in clothing. The sleek, bright hose, the tight short coats of young men, telling ornaments and symbols, colors that advertised amorous tastes and conquests, were invitations as clear as those signaled by women whose breasts were pushed up as necklines were pulled down to near nudity, women who blazed with jewelry and startled the eye with broad, curly wigs of yellow hair. The delicacy of courtly love and the softness of its verbiage disappeared into the broad sensuality and heated words of dance songs.

Gathering nosegays and singing hearty songs, looking gorgeously inviting, have their somatic uses, as everyone knows, but it was not until one or another powerful physician insisted that streets be cleaned, houses painted, putrid wells drained, patients' clothing burned and they quickly isolated in shelters away from the central town—injunctions with palpably good results—that we have the beginnings of epidemiology in Italy. With the anatomic studies of Vesalius and William Harvey's study of the circulation of the blood, and these findings widely studied, medicine began to take on more solid purpose, including prevention and amelioration in times of epidemics. No longer was the physician limited to tact and wise somber looks, advice that the patient sleep much or little, drink much or little, eat nothing cooked in rainwater, eschew vegetables but not fruit, avoid sexual intercourse but relax, thinking pleasant thoughts. The need for improvisation, with frequent unfortunate results, diminished considerably and continued to dwindle as the famous medical universities, Padua and Bologna important among them, deepened and widened their studies.

T * W * O

Mantua's history, like that of most Italian cities, flows back and back into myth. The story begins with Tiresias, for a time a woman, for a time a man, blinded by Hera but consoled by Zeus with the gift of prophecy; it was he who revealed to the horrified Oedipus his overwhelming transgression, lying with his own mother. Tiresias had a daughter named Manto, also a prophet, who came with a band of followers to this marshy place.

After a long, silent space of time, the Etruscans settled themselves next to the Mincio and built a noble city several hundred years before there was a Rome. The town that grew on the Etruscan ruins, purportedly protected by its waters and its potent relic of the "Precious Blood," was yet vulnerable to invasion from the north; to Gauls, Goths, Huns, Lombards; to the Holy Roman Emperors (Charles the Bald, who had appointed himself king of Italy, was believed to have been mortally poisoned in Mantua). Later centuries saw invasions of French, Spanish, and German troops, and later still, the Austrians, then Napoleon and the Austrians again.

Concentrating their control in cities that they used as the tacks for holding lines of trade and produce, as exchanges of learning, arts, and moneys, as positions for wheeling and dealing—"civilization," in short—northern Italian rulers during the fourteenth century actually devised small republics on the concept of the commune, rarely as democratic, however, as the words "republic" and "commune" might suggest. The ruling committee was the *signoria*, a body composed of merchants, guildmasters, and landholders, who saw to the smooth functioning of the state and its economy. It imposed taxes, paid salaries, decided on embellishments for its palaces and churches, and imposed military service on citizens who had little say in the matter. Among the shrewd and powerful members, estates were quickly accumulated and expanded by clever marriages. The struggles for dominance left few contenders and fewer still, until one family—the Medici, the Gonzaga, the Este, the Bentivogli—held its own city-state as a private fief, retaining a number of "commune" rules to mask the fact that their domains had become private treasuries.

The most aggressive rivals of the Bonacolsi, who owned Mantua in the late thirteenth century, were the Corradi of Gonzaga, a village near the city. The Gonzaga had come into prominence a century before, burgeoning in property and influence by virtue of their close connection with the dominant monastery of San Benedetto of Polirone, whose vassals they were. As early as 1209, one of them, Guido, was an ambassador for Mantua and host to the emperor Otto IV. While the Bonacolsi ruled, the Gonzaga (no longer called the Corradi but, like nobility, naming themselves for the seat of their terrain) waited and planned, characteristically avoiding partisanship with either the Guelphs or the Ghibellines in the endless confusion of battles between popes and emperors. Their sights were on amassing power and wealth, and they brooked no distractions. They knew that Can Grande della Scala, the ruler of Verona, was eager to use his strong hand against the Bonacolsi and hoped for the help of the Gonzaga, with whom he was willing to share the ensuing loot. Verona supplied one thousand men, who were greeted, when they arrived in Mantua, by a mass of Gonzaga supporters prepared for the event. The surprised Bonacolsi leaders, who might have been celebrating Ascension Day that August of 1328, rode out into the piazza before their fortress-palace, to meet defeat and death. Possessed of a fortune accumulated in a few driving decades, the family that had been vassals became lords, the bold and clever Luigi their captain, their leader. On claims legitimate and some not quite, they were ceded large properties by the monastery of San Benedetto (one of them to become in time an immense country retreat, Marmirolo); the sizable clan of brothers, sons, nephews, and grandsons became owners of fruitful estates, which they brought to high yield. Advantageous marriages were carefully arranged and their holdings further expanded with the collaboration of those Bonacolsi who, for a share in the profits, helped them force other Bonacolsi into exile, the confiscated lands and houses to be stamped "Gonzaga." There had been no need to share with Can Grande of Verona, who died in 1329, a timely event cited as one of the examples of Gonzaga luck.

The luck and prosperity held, not without persistent problems. Working the lands for constant profitability meant the close supervision of peasants, of tax collectors, of bailiffs, and coping with a restless floating population of farm workers. Former serfs had become tenants and sharecroppers, each man bound for no longer than one contractual period to one strip of land. When his share of the yield fell from a stipulated one half to one third or less, when the Church demanded increased tithes, when days had to be given up without pay to soldiering or the improvement of fortifications, when a landowner was slow or reluctant to supply essential tools, the tenant would move on to greener fields, which often proved to be as gray and sere as those he had left. So he wandered, joining masses of the poor who went from farm to farm, from city to city, searching for employment—an army of bones, as it was often called, which received only sporadic succor from the Church, since poverty was often interpreted as punishment for original sin. But judicious distribution of stored millet to the poor in hard times, intelligent supervision of workers, plus the benefits of ample water, kept the wheat, the oats, and the barley growing.

A flourishing merchant class, adopting sophisticated habits of bookkeeping and training their heirs in commerce, warranted surveillance by the Gonzaga rulers. And there was need for constant wariness against both internal enmities and the dangers inherent in Mantua's geographic and political situation between the two mighty states of Milan and Venice. To cope with potential threats from her formidable neighbors, to find out what papal and imperial powers might be planning, Mantua became a pioneer in the fine Italian art of diplomacy. At an early stage, she kept ambassadors in foreign courts, primarily informants but often skilled diplomats. In *Renaissance Diplomacy*, Garrett Mattingly points out that the Gonzaga had, even before the mid-fourteenth century, a representative in the imperial court and probably also in Ferrara. A few decades later, there was a Mantuan agent in Milan and a Milanese agent in Mantua, an arrangement terminated by the triumphant predator's march of Gian Galeazzo Visconti, readying to take Mantua but stopped by the plague of 1402—nurtured by the supernatural Gonzaga luck, they said—which killed him.

* As the family wore out its wives and mistresses in rages of fecundity, there were inevitably a number of young daughters to evaluate for their marriageability into useful places. In 1335, Luigi established a long-lasting alliance with the Este of neighboring Ferrara by having his niece Barbara marry Niccolò d'Este, an early link in a chain that would come to high luster in the marriage of Isabella d'Este and Francesco Gonzaga a century and a half later. The boys' marriages too were directed by serious, practical concerns, even the threat of death. In spite of pacts and proclamations of brotherhood and eternal fidelity, uneasy news came seeping out of Verona, now ruled by Can Grande's nephew, Mastino della Scala. He, informants reported, was planning to take over Mantua by the simple expedient of assassinating the senior members of the Gonzaga clan. The swiftest countermeasure was to arrange the marriage of Mastino's sister, Verde, to Ugolino Gonzaga, Luigi's grandson; this did not provide absolute safety but served, at least, as a useful pause.

When Verde died a year after her marriage, Ugolino married a woman of an influential Tuscan family, who lasted only a few years longer than Verde. During the passages of brides, the family reassessed its position vis-à-vis its powerful neighbors and concluded that a tie with Milan should be advantageous. Ugolino took for his third wife Caterina, niece of Barnabo Visconti, who with his brother Galeazzo II, held Milan and an awesomely large portion of Lombardy. (As with the Este, the tie with Milan, now tight, now tenuous, lasted through much of Gonzaga history.)

By one means or another they leaped, from wire to wire, these gifted, acrobatic Gonzaga, holding their footing, shaky as it might be, in their small, vulnerable terrain. In the rare intervals when wariness could be somewhat suspended, the Gonzaga began to mold a court, to gather a reputation as lovers of arts and letters, the sort of distinction enjoyed by their neighbors and relatives in Ferrara. Petrarch, crowned poet laureate in Rome, came to Mantua in 1349 and was treated with high favor and courtesy. He was offered a variety of entertainments: feasting on meats enlivened with herbs and spices from the East; the caprices of human

anomalies—the court records of 1345 list a giant called Gugliel-
mone, a dwarf-buffoon whose name was Frambaldo, and a female
miller, Rizza, who displayed extraordinary, virile strength. For
more suitable, intellectual entertainments, there were declama-
tions of poetry, musical interludes, and flourishes of oratorical
praise. Petrarch's act of homage and thanks was to dedicate his
translation of the *Romance of the Rose* to Guido Gonzaga.

Captain Luigi Gonzaga's chief aides were Guido, Filippo, and
Feltrino, the sons of his first wife. When she died, Luigi married
Caterina Malatesta, of the ruling house of Rimini, and fathered
Corrado, Alberto, and Federico. On the death of Caterina, Luigi
was married for a third time, at the age of seventy-two, to Fran-
ceschina Malaspina. His wedding and those of his son Corrado
and of his grandson Ugolino, son of Guido, were celebrated simultaneously. The assembled brides led off a procession of knights
on gallant horses, followed by servitors bearing carved and
painted *cassoni* filled with gold, gems, plate, furs, the gathered
splendors accompanied by the music of four hundred musicians.

The Gonzaga were ready to be recognized as one of the dominant houses of Italy. They were solidly in control of Mantua,
they had the pride and money to arrange princely displays not
only to honor noble guests but, as well, to celebrate themselves
and their position.

Although their coffers held gold and jewels, Luigi, his sons,
and his grandsons lived in medieval sparseness. Their beds were
straw-filled, as were their chairs, when those were not made altogether of wood; chests held clothing and also served as benches,
a number of them attractively carved, as were the wooden tables
that were moved about to serve impromptu purposes. Interlacing
the squares that opened before the palace and the church were
threadlike streets, easily closed against invasion or internecine
quarrels between families. On these streets lived artisans and minor merchants, whose small houses were divided into workshops
and selling counters at the street level, and upper spaces for sleeping. The toilet was a hole in the kitchen; its waste joined garbage
and offal in the street, which then met the drinking water supplied by a well on a local corner. (Prosperous families dug private
wells in their courts or gardens.) Mantua, like the rest of Europe,
was consequently extremely hospitable to the Black Plague,
which arrived with the rats of Constantinople in 1347, killing a
vast number of the 25,000 to 30,000 population; most of those

spared were driven off by the paralysis of agriculture and trade. Crop failures and consequent famine made heavy demands on traditional relief moneys; in addition, there was an army to support. The tribe managed, in spite of vicissitudes, to keep its cool head and ambitious strengths, profiting from the plague by absorbing the properties of the dead rich. Their biographer Giuseppe Coniglio, once head of Mantua's abundant archives, calls them "cold men, calculating, wise diplomats . . . alert to the fact that they were vases of fragile clay among vessels made of iron." Though some Gonzaga were reportedly more liberal and generous than others, no one personality, the historian adds, made Gonzaga political policy. The family "struggled in every way to maintain that which it had acquired, and the cynicism, the indifference, and the lack of scruples attributed to the first Gonzaga belonged to the group."

Luigi died in 1369, at the extraordinary age of ninety-two. His successor was his son Guido, elected unanimously by the Council of the Commune, Guido's eldest son, capable Ugolino, to be his assistant. Ugolino, admiring his wife's uncle Barnabo Visconti, carefully studied his shrewd political maneuvers and was pleased to feel protected by him. Venice, which viewed with unremitting suspicion her rival Milan, looked on the friendship with a sour eye. The relationship also infuriated Ugolino's brothers, Francesco and Ludovico, who resented Ugolino's position and the respect in which their father held him. Probably prompted, or at least supported, by Venice, his brothers assassinated Ugolino while eating his bread and drinking his wine at his table. With the assistance of the bishop of Mantua and the possible sprinkling here and there of lordly gifts, they persuaded the Pope to pardon them. The rivalry among the brothers was not, however, assuaged by one death; there were still two eager for the captaincy their aging father, Guido, would leave, perhaps shortly. Ludovico was swiftest; Francesco died. A year later, in 1369, after the death of his embittered father, Ludovico became head of the court and the family.

Although he tried to emulate Ugolino in his administration of the court and his treating with Milan, Ludovico lacked his brother's quicker talents. Becoming a steady and rather upright man, he displayed skill in maintaining peaceable local rule and improving the financial stability of the state. After liquidating his grandfather Luigi's debt to Verona, he established an orderly organization of money flow through the city and its terrains. He strengthened fortifications and, with tact and purpose, solidified his own position in court. To firm an old alliance, he had married Alda d'Este, daughter of the marquis of Ferrara, a girl of whom he was genuinely fond; in time, he contracted for the betrothal of their son, Francesco, to Agnese, the daughter of Barnabo Visconti. The marriage assuaged Barnabo's eagerness to attack Mantua (ostensibly to avenge Ugolino's death) and suited his dream of creating a federation of Italian states, an ambition of several early Italian statesmen but not realized until the nineteenth century.

The marriage of Francesco and Agnese took place in 1380, the fourteen-year-old bride, in cloth-of-gold stiff with gems, conducted to Mantua by her scarcely older bridegroom. A party of Milanese nobles entrusted with her dowry of fifty thousand gold florins. Two years later, another stately ceremony: Ludovico had died and Francesco, now sixteen, paced the traditional rites of succession as captain of Mantua. Followed by knights marching to the fanfare of massed trumpets, the young man rode through the streets toward the cathedral, where he received the staff that symbolized his rule of the Commune. Soon after came the essential state visit to vainglorious Venice, where Francesco was well received and given the honor, cherished by later Gonzaga, of being included among the nobility of "La Serenissima." With decisions still in the hands of the Council of the Gonzaga-controlled Commune, Francesco was learning and showing promise in the demanding craft of being a Mantuan lord.

In 1395, seemingly quiet, intellectual, religious Gian Galeazzo Visconti, son of aggressive Galeazzo II and coruler with his uncle Barnabo, trapped Barnabo and two of his five sons and threw them all in prison, where Barnabo ultimately died of poison. With bribes and promises and the help of well-paid mercenaries, Gian Galeazzo became the one and only overlord of Milan. Francesco's wife, Barnabo's daughter Agnese, had proved to be no great asset; she was unappealing and frail, and she loudly hated her triumphant cousin. With Gian Galeazzo in the ascendant, troublesome Agnese's voice asked to be silenced. It was bruited about the court that she was organizing an anti–Gian Galeazzo cabal in Mantua, using as her chief aide, messenger, and spy one Antonio da Scandiano, who loathed the Gonzaga. Indiscreet Agnese and her lieutenant were imprisoned, the chief witness against the pair a girl who testified she had seen them in lascivious couplings. Agnese, then twenty-five, lost her head, and her knight probably lost his. Her little daughter was sent off to Ferrara, to be brought up by Este relatives.

In spite of marriage ties and gifts of arms, Galeazzo had no great interest in sparing Mantua. One destructive Milanese plan involved diverting Mincio waters so that they might swell Verona's Adige River and starve out Mantuan agriculture. As Galeazzo tore on, ultimately controlling much of northern and central Italy, Francesco Gonzaga courted Venice, Ferrara, and Bologna for support. The responses were discouraging, but he already had on his side, he hoped, the warlord of Rimini, Carlo Malatesta, twice his brother-in-law, by virtue of Carlo's marriage to Francesco's sister, Elisabetta Gonzaga, and by his own marriage, after Agnese Visconti's beheading, to Margherita Malatesta. Another field to scour for possible aid was France, with whom the Gonzaga had some tentative connections. For having opened the door to a foreign power, however, and a disobedient one at that, the Pope excommunicated Mantua, its lords and plebes. Not excessively troubled (it was a common papal act), Francesco made his gesture of contempt for Milan by having the Visconti serpent excised from the Gonzaga insignia, the unity once seemingly assured by Visconti marriages and a mingling of the bloods and heraldic symbols scornfully nullified.

✳ The opening of the fifteenth century was a time of frenetic activity: conquests, counterconquests, alignments, counteralignments, treaties scribbled and torn up almost daily. Mantua had a short rest when, in addition to struggling with the exigencies of conquest and colonization, Milan found herself in serious difficulties with influential imperial powers, German nobles who were berating the inept Holy Roman Emperor for having made dangerous concessions to Milan. Gian Galeazzo was not ready to give up the favors he had bought and the territories he had taken, and sent streams of ambassadors and his keenest *oratores* to the imperial court to protect his interests, to little avail. The Gonzaga watched, and when Milan's position seemed especially shaky, hired themselves out to Venice, whom they helped to recover Padua and Verona from Milan.

As *condottieri* for Venice, the leaders of her troops and the bands of mercenaries they hired, the Gonzaga earned substantial sums, moneys augmented by later generations of the dynasty, who continued to serve as captains of Venetian troops. Francesco put much of his earnings and his superb early-Renaissance energy into embellishing his city. It was he who commissioned the toppling of ineffectual towers near the river and substituted the handsome Gothic Castello San Giorgio, which served specifically as a fortress, constantly replenished with horses, soldiers, arms, and stores. The living quarters in the houses farther inland were redesigned as small pleasure palaces and apartments. The version of the Church of Sant'Andrea that left its medieval campanile to sit with Alberti's later version was initiated by Francesco, as were a scattering of small churches and the large sanctuary of Santa Maria delle Grazie, a few kilometers from the center of town. It had from early medieval times been a thanksgiving shrine for miracles, the goal of Assumption Day pilgrims who came to worship an image of the Virgin painted by Saint Luke. Francesco rebuilt the shrine to commemorate the passing of one of the frequent visitations of plague. (It was later transmogrified, expanded, stuffed with ex-votos, and fitted with niches rather like theater boxes, to house large figures of persons about to be hanged, macerated, imprisoned, drowned—all at the moment before a miraculous rescue; around the boxes of the tortured, bands of plaster hearts, hands, and breasts. This bizarre orchestration of the elements of the church redesigned by Franciscan monks of the sixteenth and seventeenth centuries evokes the same entertaining odor of perversity as does the *angoisse voluptueuse* of Bernini's Saint Teresa in the church of Santa Maria della Vittoria in Rome. To add amusement and bafflement, a dried crocodile—meant to represent a medieval dragon?—hangs among the Venetian chandeliers of the ceiling.)

Under Francesco, the city became a well-organized urban unit, large and complex enough to be divided into *contrade* (boroughs) headed by responsible citizens. Francesco's building programs were efficiently accomplished primarily because his engineers and masons were paid well and promptly, not a common practice, as we know from the notes that wail out of numerous city archives. He continued to observe and correct his judicial system to make it more workable, spurred religious "companies" whose charge was the care of the poor and the sick to wider activity; encouraged the weaving guilds to reexamine their practices and regulations and thus helped expand the industry. In spite of some local doubts and fears, Francesco invited nobles and merchants, either in exile or unhappy in their own cities, to bring their knowledge, skills, and money to Mantua, an act that inevitably broadened and improved trade. From their sturdy financial base, Francesco and his wife Margherita were able to buy jewels, brocades, velvets, and the services of skilled decorators and painters, and to expand the court library to some four hundred books, an unusually large number for a layman's library in the days before printing. Among the finely bound and illuminated books, at least seventy were devoted to the French romances, a reflection of the taste for chivalric thought and manners that would last for several generations.

* It was in Francesco's time that a colony of Jews established themselves in Mantua, with his consent and that of the Pope. The first Jewish loan bank was founded in 1390. With the arrival of more Jews, the number of bankers reached a dozen, all committed by regulation to a limit of 20, then 25, percent interest on their loans, considerably less than many Christian bankers and goldsmiths asked, in spite of the interdicts of the Church against usury. The laws set down for the Hebrews in Deuteronomy instruct that they not ask interest of their tribesmen but allow them to charge outsiders. Since the whole Christian world was a tribal agglomerate, it would appear that Christians following the old laws were not to impose interest rates on their fellow coreligionists. Communities that adhered in the main to the biblical rule and were in need of loan services asked that the Pope authorize the colonization of Jews in their cities. They protested the later expulsion of Jews, which came with the establishment by the Franciscans of their pawn houses, the *monti di pietà*, ostensibly established to help the poor but quickly involved in gainful business with heads of guilds and propertied clerics.

A merchant class that was becoming increasingly numerous and prosperous established its own rules. A Christian banker might atone for his usury by building a hospice for the indigent or an expiatory chapel. (The wondrous Giotto panels of the lives of Christ and Mary in Padua derive from usury: The son of the Scrovegni who was condemned by Dante to Hell because he had amassed the largest fortune in Padua on high-interest loans built the chapel to rescue the soul of his father.) Other non-Jewish usurers paid annual fines to the treasuries of their communes, a satisfactory arrangement all around and one that allowed northern Italian banking houses to earn high gains as they proliferated throughout Europe, one group still remembered as Lombard Street in the banking area of London. The increasing complexity of banking services, the employment of currency experts in far-flung branch offices, defaults by debtors, occasional losses in foreign exchange, all required, in time, that the ancient rules be altogether suspended. Faint waves of anti-Semitism appeared, one of them fostered by the *monti di pietà* Franciscans, who claimed that the interest they collected covered general overhead costs and was not usury. But Christians denying their debts, fanatics whipping up fanatics, expulsions, executions, burnings, the despoiling of Jewish property—rarely as brutal in Italy as elsewhere in Europe—were yet to come. In the late fourteenth century, the flourishing colony lived peaceably, protected by the spendthrift court that needed its services.

* Though Jews had too much history for total serenity, they were not as troubled in their beliefs as were a good number of thinking Christians. The effects of the Black Plague, followed by lesser plagues and periods of famine, led to disturbing questions, posited by Renaissance elitist thinkers and beginning to trickle down into more common lives and minds. In the court, in the marketplace, in the guild houses, someone would put forth an unanswerable proposition: If plagues were the work of the Devil, where was the opposing God? If plagues were God's work, why? If God designed them to drive out man's sins or punish him, why attack innocent children and the holy people who attended the sick sinners? The Christian passivity of the Middle Ages no longer served well enough, and another system of faith took a serious blow as well. Gian Galeazzo Visconti had been promised by his astrologer that he would rule all of Italy, and though he conducted his life and politics with consummate faith in the prophecy, it proved shockingly false; he died before he could attack Florence, a major goal of his campaigns.

After a long pause to consider the reliability of his own astrologers, Francesco Gonzaga turned his attention to a nagging preoccupation, the matter of a title. The uncrowned and soon deposed Emperor Wenceslaus had sold Visconti the title of duke for a neat sum of money; Francesco felt that he was rich and important enough to deserve something better than "count," which Pope Boniface IX had dubbed him. Wenceslaus had been eager to sell him "marquis" but demanded too high a price. The matter was left suspended but not forgotten. Francesco turned his attention to strengthening his fortresses, checking on the crops of each harvest, and tutoring his heir, Gianfrancesco, in the statecraft the boy would need to hold on to that which was, and must stay, his. The training came none too early; when the boy was twelve his father died, having barely entered his forties. Under the practiced eye of his uncle Carlo Malatesta and the more distant yet sharp watchfulness of the Venetian Council to which Francesco had entrusted his son as ward, the boy entered a dangerous time, a time that required a thousand eyes of Gonzaga watchfulness, a time of stringent controls.

Malatesta saw to everything while Gianfrancesco, a keen boy, looked on. Harsh laws to diminish corruption were instituted and enforced; old alliances were to be reconfirmed and political alliances carefully examined before tighter knots were tied; Venice was to be respectfully heeded when she spoke. Uncle Carlo also arranged a marriage for his nephew, to Paola Malatesta, the daughter of the lord of Pesaro and Fossombrone, a bright and pretty girl, according to contemporary reports, but touched with a deformity that would twist the backs and lives of several of her descendants. The couple, both sixteen, took off for an extensive honeymoon, the boy instructed to observe the habits and practices of his host courts, while Uncle Carlo, the elders of the Commune, and representatives of Venice saw to Mantuan affairs. The return of the young people in January of 1410 launched twelve days of feasting, dancing, and tourneys. The gifts sent from the guardians in Venice, the courts of Tuscany, and prosperous relatives were of dazzling luxury. Paola had brought with her a full, showy entourage and the promise of a dowry of five thousand ducats plus territories and their castles, to be turned over at some future time. The dowry was never paid, however, and the territories never delivered, because Paola's father died, leaving heavy debts. Worth infinitely more than her dowry, according to historians, was Paola's quick intelligence, which helped guide Gianfrancesco during the long absences of Carlo Malatesta, off fulfilling contracts as a *condottiere*.

Immediately after he reached maturity and became sole lord of Mantua, Gianfrancesco voiced considerable displeasure with the activities and organization of the court controlled by his uncle

Carlo. He mistrusted the military affiliations that paid his uncle and he began to measure with malevolence Carlo's leading aides. The Conti dei Prato were Tuscans who had for many years served in Mantua, holding key positions; they managed local government as well as foreign affairs. The seemingly smooth collaboration between the Conti dei Prato and the Mantuans was ripped apart when the Tuscans suggested that Mantua join with the emperor Sigismondo in a foray against Pandolfo Malatesta of Brescia. Gianfrancesco wanted peace with Pandolfo and, furthermore, refused to help an emperor who, in his turn, demanded an exorbitant sum for the title of marquis. Gianfrancesco had the Conti dei Prato and their friends arrested on charges of treason; their extensive holdings and moneys were confiscated and they were exiled. Having proved that he was independent and ruling from his own strengths, Gianfrancesco went on to Venice, to remind her that he was a favored son. The occasion he used was the election of a new doge, the celebration enhanced by a Mantuan procession of two hundred splendidly accoutred knights, who acquitted themselves outstandingly in the jousting, cheered on by thousands of Venetians and their guests. (These games of combat were often mock jousts. Although the armor was martial and authentically aggressive, the lances were frail and blunted, easily smashed before they could inflict much damage. There were injuries—Henry II of France was struck in the face, perhaps his eye was pierced, during the tourneys that were part of marriage celebrations, and died soon after—but not many were grave.)

Though valued for her good sense, and aware of it, Paola was still afraid that her deformity might cause her to be put aside or, worse, caged in a manufactured plot and killed. She spent a good deal of time in curative baths near Siena and, for spiritual balm, visited and revisited a number of favored shrines. Gianfrancesco spent time away from Mantua as Supreme Commander of the Venetian Armies, accumulating with each successful battle a large sum of money, an extensive piece of property, a fine palace on the Grand Canal. He strode from one show of success and grandeur to another. He could now afford to dispense out of his own earnings and the accumulations of his thrifty ancestors the sums needed to astonish his peers and to make his one of the first cities of Europe, a city in which popes and antipopes of the Great Schism (late fourteenth century into the fifteenth) might take their ease from the gnarled intricacies of papal games in Rome and Avignon. And, finally, he could easily pay the twelve thousand florins required by the emperor Sigismondo to make him the first marquis of Mantua. It was an occasion for solemn rites and overwhelming splendor. The formal investiture by the emperor took place on September 22, 1433, surrounded by gestures and symbols heavy with meaning. The Gonzaga coat of arms, to stress an intimacy with the Empire, now carried four spread-winged imperial eagles. For a yet closer tie with the emperor and influential German courts, the marquis affianced his firstborn son, Ludovico, to the emperor's niece, the very young and plain Barbara of the noble and impoverished house of Brandenburg.

Carried by his triumphs to a disdain for councillors, Gianfrancesco led himself into a serious error. In a chivalric dream of extraordinary feats, he believed he was ready to challenge Venice, then at the height of her powers, her ships and piers loaded with merchandise from the East and from mercantile Europe, her banks rich in funds, her armies strong. Gianfrancesco was not altogether mad; this venture was to be made in collaboration with almost equally powerful Milan, still concentrated on taking lands in the Veneto. The resulting defeat cost Gianfrancesco the services of Pisanello (for a while, at least), four thousand gold ducats handed over to Venice, and the loss of strongholds he had earlier been granted.

He died at forty-nine in 1444, a diminished lord of a vulnerable yet still imposing court. Like all the Gonzaga, he had built feverishly: the fortress of San Giorgio completed; new churches planned; decorative, protective arcades built over the streets— some of the work a relief program to lighten the effects of a severe crop failure. To improve the quality and reputation of Mantuan weaving, he had imported Flemish craftsmen to help establish the first Italian ateliers devoted to tapestry-making. His will was a carefully balanced document that left a sizable sum to his servants and provided the city with a center of learning that, while not quite equal to Bologna's or Padua's, was promising enough to attract accomplished scholars. His division of lands among his heirs (we see Paola's hand here) would cause difficulties later but was a clear attempt at judicious distribution.

There had been two acts in his life that were curiously advanced for his era. In 1430, Gianfrancesco addressed himself to a group of citizens of Mantua, asking for suggestions that might improve the well-being of the community. It was not a signal of democracy as we know it—unthinkable in a time when peasants and small merchants had no public voice—but it was a call for the participation of leading citizens in discussions of the economy of the region. Of the twenty-two men called, a few were lawyers, a number were landholders, and the rest members of long-established mercantile firms. They were questioned for ideas concerning improvements in techniques and increased earnings from the leading industry, the *arte di lana*, wool-weaving. Would they also reexamine the tax situation and find a way to make it more workably profitable without imposing unfair burdens? How might agricultural yields be made larger? What was a fair share to be apportioned a farm worker, a share that might keep him from straying? Perhaps increased salaries and better housing for weavers would improve their morale and output. We don't know whether Gianfrancesco was trying to appease members of the rich old families who felt overtaxed and slighted as advisers or was actually making tentative steps toward reestablishing something that might resemble the old Commune, possibly as it existed in early-fourteenth-century Siena, the city that Ambrogio Lorenzetti idealized in his mural *Good Government*. It may be that behind the call for a conference was Gonzaga's fear of the contagion of a peasant revolt, as in Ravenna, or an uprising of the weavers, who, like the Ciompi of Florence, might, in their furious numbers, take over the government. Whatever his purposes and fears, Gianfrancesco's petition for advice was answered sparsely and timidly; we know of no concrete results.

A more fruitful pioneer move had been to appoint—again we see Paola's intelligent hand—Vittorino da Ramboldini da Feltre, one of the most quietly luminous characters in Renaissance history and venerated into the present, as tutor to the Gonzaga children. Vittorino's was the first court school, the school that shaped the man Ludovico Gonzaga ultimately became and, through him, the city-state universally admired for its culture and beauty.

Vittorino da Feltre

Vittorino Ramboldini, known in history as Vittorino da Feltre, for his native village in the hills north of Venice, was born of a poor family in 1378. He picked up whatever learning he could as he made his way to Padua, there to expand his studies and work as assistant to established scholars. Having mastered Latin and advanced skills as a mathematician, he moved on to Venice to study Greek with Guarino da Verona, later linked with Vittorino as one of the great Renaissance educators. A taste for teaching and the need to earn a living sent Vittorino back to Padua, dense with students and would-be students, where he opened a school, working at first as a medieval "pedagogue," a sort of crammer, and gradually refining and broadening the educational principles that made him, according to historians, "the founder of modern education" and "the greatest educator of the Renaissance." His growing fame as an educator and as a gently persuasive moral force among unruly students earned Vittorino the chair of Rhetoric, a concentration on Latin oratory and prose, at the University of Padua.

Paola Gonzaga, searching for an ethical man devoted to Christian as well as classical ideals, and Gianfrancesco, eager for a distinguished addition to his court and a teacher sufficiently adaptable to make of his sons cultivated princes and agile warriors who would strengthen the house of Gonzaga, asked the advice of Guarino, who recommended Vittorino. Inclined to the religious life and contemplating joining an order, Vittorino hesitated. Marriage was not for him, and when he was urged to marry and to have children, with whom he was so affectionally influential, he pointed to his students and said, "These are my children." Attracted to a service that might demand as much, and more, of him as the religious life, he finally accepted the Gonzaga offer, suggesting that since his work was with the total individual, and that meant the individual's environment as well, he hoped he was entering a decorous, serious court. For himself, he could not work in an atmosphere that was in any way morally ambiguous.

Reassured, and promised a free hand with his pupils, the slight, somberly dressed scholar prepared a house in one of the gardens of the Castello, until then a pleasure house, La Zoiosa, designed for dancing and dalliance. He renamed it La Casa Giocosa—The Joyful House—and had its walls muraled with studies of children at play. In this first boarding school in Europe, he lived and taught the court children, among them the girls Cecilia and Margherita and the little German Barbara, not yet ready for marriage to Ludovico Gonzaga.

The fame of the innovative school and its principles, the range of the education, the obvious pleasure of the children in mastering difficult subjects, the care and respect with which the children were handled, the meticulous selection of teaching assistants, attracted the attention of other courts, which would, in time, imitate Vittorino's school. In the meantime, they sent their sons to Mantua: from Venice, from Padua, from Faenza, from as far away as Turkish Trebizond, once controlled by the Greeks and the last stronghold of Hellenistic learning. These students became an extraordinary group of gifted leaders in the Church and among the laity, the most notable of them Federico da Montefeltro, the duke of Urbino, a connoisseur of arts and letters, a *condottiere* and politician who could walk his night streets unguarded, a stellar example of the "enlightened Renaissance Prince."

Some of the gilded children presented a number of problems. As an infant, the rich Renaissance child was a darling putto, a Cupid, and at the same time the sacred Bambino sitting in the lap of the Virgin. Once out of the mess of swaddling clothes, immediately after the conquests of speech and locomotion, he became a miniature adult. Although there were injunctions about not touching or molesting children, about separating them from each other and from adults in bed, they wandered freely in farm villas, in ateliers, in courts, to observe, to pick up salacious quips, and to avoid or lend themselves to gropings by a people who were, according to the Victorian Matthew Arnold, ferociously violent in their obsessed sexuality. A child like Federico Gonzaga, later in the dynasty, was sent notes by ladies of his mother's court, expressing longings to kiss him here, there, anywhere he liked, as they had done before he left Mantua for Rome. As in revered old Rome, incest and incestuous gestures and the sexual uses of little boys were quite common, unremarked except as gossip and pasquinades. A pubescent court boy, early addicted to gaming with dice and cards and to whoring, might already be pained and worried about his first syphilitic chancre, or proud of it.

Clearly, not everyone who applied to the school of Vittorino was accepted; some were already too spoiled, others had little eagerness to learn. The sons of ambitious merchants destined for mercantile and banking careers, better taught in business apprenticeships, were also tactfully rejected. There were lesser difficulties with the children admitted. What could one do with youngsters who ate rich food almost constantly, it seemed to the abstemious Vittorino, out of richly colored, costly platters from Faenza? Or those who strutted about superbly and stiffly dressed, accompanied by perfumed, quarrelsome courtiers? Now and then the schoolmaster was tempted to resign, to give up what might prove to be a dubious project and retire to the modest order of life in a monastery. But it was difficult to leave, to give up his vision of the ideal school; he liked the court children and was grateful to their parents, who were sincerely interested in what he was doing— particularly Paola—and boundlessly generous, instructing their functionaries to give the tutor whatever he needed without question, including his request that the Gonzaga library be expanded and opened to scholars.

To keep court sycophants away, he had guards placed at the school doors and forbade the children to leave without his permission. Meals became moderate and dress increasingly simple. Taming came with reasoning, with affection and imagination. Meals for Ludovico, an obese boy, were gradually reduced, and because he enjoyed music, music was often his only dinner. Carlo, his brother, was thin and encouraged to eat as much as he liked. His disciplines established and working, Vittorino brought in poor boys ("for the love of God," says Vespasiano, the Florentine bookseller and biographer), who lived with the princes and were often clothed by Vittorino out of his stipend and the extra allowances given him by Paola. All that was asked of the poor boys, at times as many as seventy, was decent behavior and enthusiasm for study. These boys were the test and proof of a basic Vittorino tenet: ability anywhere, everywhere, should be given the opportunity to flourish. Whatever other moneys he had, Vittorino spent on the sick poor, on dowries for their daughters, on the homeless indigents he found during his walks through the city. It was also his Christian duty, he felt, to have those unjustly imprisoned released and to free the slaves bought from traders in

North Africa and beyond the Adriatic to be sold to prosperous Italian households. With his unwavering ethics and quiet independence, he became a significant figure in Mantua.

The overall educational aim was high: a harmonic blend of physical, mental, and moral development. The curriculum was demanding: riding, wrestling, archery, fencing, swimming, along with mathematics, Latin, Greek, history, philosophy, theology, music, and drawing. And time was made for dancing and outings, like those of Latin poets, to admire the countryside. In this house one had always to watch his bearing and his speech; tempers had to be controlled, complaints suppressed. If it was cold and a young hand ached in the icy damp of the Mantuan winter, a future soldier-ruler or cardinal must learn to endure it. Though it seemed exigent in its expectations (students had to learn some Greek, although it was difficult to work from the limited and fragmented texts then available), the school was admirably malleable and considerate in practice. The poor boys, often overwhelmed by the threat of scholastic demands, were assured that in the beginning, they might learn at their own pace. No boy was punished for not completing a task; he was simply asked to study while his friends were at games. Quiet little Alessandro Gonzaga, clearly born to be a scholar, was allowed to work prodigiously at his Latin and Greek, leaving the wrestling and swordplay to the more eager athletes. Gianlucido, his next elder brother, weak and slightly deformed, was given to Vittorino when he was four, and he too was excused from vigorous exercises so that he might concentrate on writing Latin verse and in time memorize all of Virgil. Federico of Urbino was an energetic, physical boy in whom, the master pointed out to his father, keenness of intellect would have to be developed, as it clearly was. When he left Mantua in his late teens, as well educated as he might have been at a university, Federico was ready to exemplify the ideal melding of body, mind, ethics, and manners for which the Casa Giocosa was designed.

The ground bases for the curriculum was Latin literature touched with Greek and strengthened with the basic precepts of Christianity, not so much as doctrine but as spirit. A revitalized interest in the Roman classics, with their portraits of strength and virtue, stood well with Renaissance Italians, themselves eager to live heroically in bright frames; on the example of these forebears who had created a Golden Age they would build their own

Golden Age. Vittorino's teachers had already paved the way for induction of the young into this old-new world, by translating ancient treatises on education. Guarino, for one, had translated Plutarch's views on the education of the young. His contemporary Petrus Paulus Vergirius, a Greek scholar, a physician, and a keen observer of children, reintroduced an antique tract of considerable importance to the Romans and to later humanist teachers: *The Education of the Orator*, by Quintilian, an educator and a consul under Vespasian and quite possibly the teacher of Tacitus. The term *oratori*, most frequently used in the Renaissance for the quickest-thinking, smoothest-tongued ambassadors (a class apart, to judge from their clustered separateness in a Bellini painting of a Venetian processional), was applied by Quintilian to a well-educated man who could present his knowledge and ideas forcefully. Within the broad picture, there were specific requisites: complete sincerity and utter truthfulness and recognition that knowledge must be put ultimately to use for the public good. As an echo and extension of the idea, we have Vittorino's statement that though not everyone has the capacity or opportunity for a leading role in the social fabric, everyone, as a social being, is responsible for the personal influence he exerts.

Vittorino's own influence was not limited to his boys, rich and poor, or to the many recipients of his charity. His long tenure, the regard and affection he had earned in his role as something of family priest, something of wise grandfather, called him into serious family disputes. Alessandro, everyone's courteous, gentle friend, had no difficulty turning from Greek and Latin to sacred studies. His sister Cecilia, an equally gifted classics student and also eager to turn her talents to the Church, met with a hard rebuff. Her father, Gianfrancesco, insisted she marry the loathsome Oddantonio di Montefeltro of Urbino. Her impressive knowledge of Virgil, every line, didn't matter, nor did her command of Greek, and so what if she could explain the propositions of Euclid? Her vocation was marriage. Cecilia, brought up by Vittorino to know her worth and supported by the teacher, who was especially fond of her, refused and refused again. One of Vittorino's arguments in support of the girl was to point out to her father that such "perseverance and strength in a girl was not without the special disposition of heaven; to counter it would be prideful and impious," a statement of the quintessential Vittorino, devout Christian, defender of the young, and compelling *oratore*. A few face-saving paternal storms continued and than abated, ending in the dissolution of the marriage plans. (Not too long after, the putative bridegroom was assassinated, supposedly by a congeries of citizens whose wives had been raped and their sons menaced by this youth "violently bent on the libidinous," accompanied by fierce gangs of night raiders.)

On their tutor's death, at a peaceable though penniless old age, Ludovico and his wife, Barbara, arranged a funeral befitting a great man, though no monument, on Vittorino's request, marks the end of his fruitful life. Ludovico's respect, it is said, was such that he would not, even as prince of his realm, sit in the presence of his old master; he always rose. This, too, was a mark of an education that stressed manners and bearing, inner grace and grace in addressing the world, as exemplified and taught by the man of whom John Addington Symonds wrote: "Few lives of which there is any record in history are so perfectly praiseworthy as Vittorino da Feltre's; few men have more nobly realized the ideal of living for the highest objects of their age; unspotted by the vices of the world around them."

T·H·R·E·E

The fraternal rivalries that had killed Ugolino Gonzaga in 1362 threatened again during Gianfrancesco's rule. The marquis was dissatisfied with his stout, awkward heir, Ludovico. He clearly preferred Carlo, the second son, who was bright and musical, who handled a horse and a sword with impressive skill, who was handsome and graceful. In his own mind already a great soldier, Carlo immersed himself in the exploits of Roman heroes whose lives he had translated from the Latin in Vittorino's classes. Ludovico was plain and physically slow; his father found him embarrassing on horseback. The father, though himself obese, was a swift hunter and horseman, as a warrior and nobleman should be, and so bitter was he over the blow fate had dealt him that he petitioned the emperor to name Carlo his heir after his death. Uncertain of his future in Mantua, Ludovico left the court and offered himself as *condottiere* to Milan. It was at about this time that Gianfrancesco, with son Carlo as his aide, staged his futile foray against Venice, where Carlo was briefly imprisoned. Reluctantly reconciled by the efforts of Paola and, very likely, Vittorino, the brothers and their father returned to Mantua. On the succession of Ludovico as marquis (with no interference from the emperor) in 1445, Carlo left to settle on one of the holdings he had inherited, Viadana, and let it be known that his respected military skills were for hire, independent of family commitments. Younger brother Gianlucido, a gifted Latinist and mathematician, removed himself from the troubled court by entering the religious life, after ceding much of his property to Ludovico. Paola and her accomplished daughter Cecilia entered convents, supplied with the means for good works by Gianfrancesco's bequests. Paola, whose health had never been robust, died within a few years, further worn by the enmity between her eldest sons.

* Mighty Milan was dwindling; territories she had once taken from Venice were back in the control of the Queen of the Adriatic, a situation exacerbated by the tension between the duke of Milan, Filippo Maria Visconti, and his daughter's husband, Francesco Sforza, who was blatantly eager to become his successor, one way or another. Visconti sent to Mantua for military help, offering a contract for one year, renewable for a longer period if there was need. Ludovico, who in spite of his father's criticism (or because of it) had become a respected warrior, responded with an offer of seven hundred horsemen and three hundred foot soldiers, who were to be paid by Milan. A separate sum of six thousand ducats was to be paid Ludovico as leader; and, as always, there was the promise of conquered lands. Gonzaga aid was hardly enough, however, against the Sforza, who had already conquered impressive portions of the Marches, near the Adriatic, and might turn back to take Milan. Visconti quickly arranged a fragile alliance against Sforza with Pope Pius II, with Alfonso, the king of Naples; Florence; and, for the time being, Venice. Reluctant to waste her money and her men, Venice forced a tentative peace, to wait out potential developments.

In 1447, Filippo Maria Visconti died, and Milan's leading citizens formed the short-lived Ambrosian Republic. In early 1448, with the fate of the new Milanese republic quite uncertain, Ludovico Gonzaga decided to join with a solid Venice and an exceedingly wealthy Florence against Milan, as captain general of troops he gathered for them. On the opposing Sforza side was his brother Carlo Gonzaga, who had been promised Asola, Lonato, and Peschiera, important points of defense at the borders of Mantuan terrain, if his army captured them. Sforza had little interest in the Ambrosian Republic; he wanted Milan as his dukedom, an ambition that did not sit well with Venice. She made a proposal: The central portion of the extensive Milanese lands was to remain as a republic, the rest to be divided between Sforza and herself. Sforza rejected the plan and, with the support of the Florentine Cosimo de' Medici (who had canceled his earlier al-

liance with Venice), took over the Milanese republic, which offered little resistance to its new duke.

Ludovico stayed with Venice and with Alfonso of Naples, who
had put him in command of mercenaries within striking distance
of Milan. For its time, Ludovico's expanded army was sizable: 900
lancers and 900 foot soldiers, whose pay, including that of their
leader, would amount to 45,000 florins. Then came a wooing by
Sforza, who had the need and the wealth to buy an outstanding
leader for his large armies, and Ludovico found himself in a characteristic Gonzaga dilemma: Remain with Venice and Naples? Or
could he do better under Sforza and assure himself of the right—
something of a Holy Grail to his dynasty—to fight for the three
local strongholds that had earlier been promised his brother
Carlo? He finally decided for Sforza and Milan in late 1450, and
in the next ten years—with intervals for plagues and inclement
weather—fought with Sforza against Venice, earning substantial
sums. Carlo Gonzaga not unexpectedly crossed over into the orbit
of Venice and began to threaten areas close to Mantua. After a
bloody conflict, Ludovico put him to flight. Carlo took refuge in
Ferrara, the home of his wife, Lucia d'Este, and his sister Margherita, where his cultivation and high spirits faded to despair
and death in 1456.

Sforza had turned his interest, in the meantime, to the fragmented kingdom of Naples and invited the French, who had long
claimed Naples for the house of Anjou, to join him in trying for
a foothold in the south. The French came down in the winter of
1453, alarming not only Naples but Venice, already shocked by
the threat to her trade and power with the fall of Constantinople
to the Turks earlier that same year. These concerns did not,
however, prevent her from raiding in the west, moving into Mantuan lands. Ludovico and Sforza forced Venice back and were
attacked in return, the continuous zigzag destroying fruitful lands
and reducing the peasantry to starvation and flight. After some
destructive months, the scholarly, conciliatory Pope, Nicholas
V, called the major Italian powers—Milan, Venice, Florence,
Naples, and representatives of the Papacy—to Lodi, near Milan,
where they signed yet another ephemeral pact of which a major
stipulation required that northern Italian states aid the kingdom
of Naples if she was attacked.

Ludovico was obligated by a clause in the pact to return to
his brother Carlo properties confiscated earlier; nor had he gained

the villages of Asola, Lonato, and Peschiera. His contracts with Milan remained highly lucrative: 36,000 ducats in peacetime and 80,000 in times of war, that sum increased to 81,000 when his eldest son, Federico, joined him. There was, however, no expansion of lands or power and not likely to be. His children were growing up; there were daughters to marry off and sons to direct and place in favorable situations. Their mother was devoted and capable and encouraged her court in its flourishing, but he was tired of battle and wanted to take a decisive hand in local matters. When Pius II who became Pope in 1458, offered him an enormous sum to head papal forces that might hold back the French, Ludovico claimed regretfully that he was too ill to serve.

The French threat, which would return fearsomely a few decades later, faded away; it was the Turks, moving westward with terrifying speed, who had now to be stopped. In 1459, Pius II, only few months a pope, called on the emperor and on France, England, Poland, Austria, the Italian states, and leading prelates, for representatives to plan action against the infidel Turks. The site of the conclave was Mantua, the host, Ludovico Gonzaga. As if he had already gathered his cohorts and their supporting moneys and armies, as if he had already routed the Turks, Pius II entered the conclave like a Roman conqueror. According to his own report, when he transferred from a boat of the Este to a boat of the Gonzaga to complete his voyage on the river Po toward Mantua, "trumpeters filled all the surrounding valley with an extraordinary din. They displayed a whole forest of banners tossing in the wind. The inhabitants, seated along the banks, implored the Pope's benediction and when he blessed them, they shouted 'Viva.' " When he entered Mantua late in May, a few days before the congress opened, it was as part of an endless, awe-inspiring procession. Twelve white horses, who bore no riders but were nevertheless resplendent with gold saddles and bridles, were followed by three banners, on the first of which shone the sign of the Cross; on the second, the keys of the Church; on the third, the five crescents which are the arms of the Piccolomini (Pius's family name). "Then came a golden tabernacle borne on a white horse under a silk canopy and surrounded by many tapers, in which was the Eucharist, that is, the sacred Host of our Savior. Next rode Galeazzo of Milan and the Marquis Ludovico, then the venerable order of cardinals and finally the Pope himself raised high on his throne, wearing the papal robes and the miter blazing with precious gems." He was then given the keys to the city gates by Ludovico, an act of courtesy and respect proffered in all the towns Pius had traversed except defiant Siena and Florence, which, "though under the heel of a popular tyranny, wished to make a show of freedom by keeping the keys."

When the congress opened on June 1, Pius looked across a meagerly populated assembly hall. Where was Duke Borso, who governed Ferrara as a fief of Rome and had promised to appear in Mantua? He sent excuses: His astrologer had said the stars spoke death should he venture a journey to Mantua; he was stricken with a fever (informants said he was on a hawking expedition at the time); he would come when he recovered and in the meantime would send a contribution to the war chest. None came. Borso was not unique in his indifference, as acknowledged in an opening address of disappointment and anger by Pius: "Our brethren and our sons, we hoped on arriving at this city to find that a throng of royal ambassadors had preceded us. We see that only a few are here. We have been mistaken. Christians are not so concerned about religion as we believed . . . no one can say the time was too short, no one can plead the difficulties of travel. We who are old and ill have defied the Apennines and winter. . . . Not without danger we left the patrimony of the Church to come to the rescue of the Catholic Faith which the Turks are doing their utmost to destroy." However, many of the cardinals were critical of the Pope's futile gesture. "They said that Pius had been foolish to come to Mantua, that very few representatives of princes had assembled there and still fewer were likely to come; the place was marshy and unhealthy; the heat was intense; they did not like the flat wine or any of the other things necessary to sustain life; most of them were sickening; very many were catching fever; nothing was to be heard except the frogs."

✻ Those who came stayed, and congratulated themselves on their own fortitude and resilience. Though an increasing number of bridges shortened some journeys, the trip from Rome, for instance, took several days on horse, and for those who crossed the Alps, an endlessness of time and hazard. Those with papal and imperial credentials that proved them important personages found shelter in the great abbeys and palaces along the way; lesser agents had to make do with inns of miscellaneous quality. Some supplied food for men and horses, and nothing else. Others were elaborate establishments, equipped with bedrooms, stables, and eating rooms large enough to provide space for business meetings. There were inns whose management was careful to keep out beggars, the sick, the criminal. In others, watchfulness was the responsibility of the visitor; if he was robbed or killed, it was his own careless fault. To protect himself from infestations of lice and other vermin, the traveler was often advised to carry his own linens and an extra supply of clothing. Whatever category of inn he chose, he rarely had—nor did he demand—privacy, a modern virtue. His bed might not have been as large as the Bed of Ware mentioned in *Twelfth Night* and now a wondrous presence in the Victoria and Albert Museum of London, but he was sure of at least one or two bed companions.

Nor was there much privacy when visitors arrived in Mantua and were distributed among court apartments and the palaces and villas of friends and relatives. As often as not, they were bedded with the head of the household and his wife. But to ease the exhaustion of travel, they were bathed and massaged by a maid or a female slave, and the Mantuan bed in which they slept was no battered straw thing, as in some inns; that was good enough for the servant's pad at the foot of the big bed or beneath it. In Ludovico's house, the bed would have had silk canopies held by carved posts, the sheets would have been of linen or silk, the mattress and comforter of goose down. The salons in which the dignitaries met and spoke shone with mirrors and the gleam of gold vases; one might pick up a recently discovered manuscript in Latin or Greek or examine a bronze miniature that might be authentically Roman. The table at which one dined faced a huge credenza glowing with plates and cups of precious metals. Tapestries, many borrowed for the occasion, warmed those walls not adorned with murals; rugs woven in the East and large, warm animal skins decorated and warded off the chill of stone floors.

To relieve the rather desultory policy discussions during the Pope's congress, there was a busy schedule for feasting and entertainment. A star humanist, Francesco Filelfo, made a long, graceful oration, and there was music. Most important, there was the hunt. Ludovico had become a master huntsman, proud and careful of his reserve, and he found it necessary to warn his keeper of possible damage that might be inflicted by the heedless Spanish cardinal, Roderigo Borgia (later Pope Alexander VI). The one pastime that lacked was jousting. Ludovico would permit no clashing of arms, which reminded him of his long *condottiere* years and of his inept childhood under the critical eyes of his father.

* If the congress achieved little as a war council, it served to show members of other courts the splendors of Mantua and to convince the Pope that Ludovico's second son, the adolescent Francesco, was ready to become a cardinal. The ailing Pope, carrying the meager gains of a few promised ships and small supplies of arms and men, dragged his large entourage out of Mantua. Ludovico went off to the baths near Siena, where his mother and father had frequently gone, to ease his arthritic pains and to rest after the demanding duties of hosting the fruitless congress. Returned from Siena, he spent much of his time writing letters that he hoped would keep his presence and interests fresh in the minds of lords he respected; he wrote distant relations to strengthen ties and to extract information that filled a wide gamut of fashions in art and dress, of gossip and political conjecture and warnings. The giant strides the Ottoman Empire was taking to claim vast territories, the dizzying shifts of position from enemy to partner, partner to enemy, among the major Italian powers, required more and more agents in more and more places to sense out inimical strategies and to warn the home office. Ludovico's ministers, ambassadors, secretaries, advisers, and informers became a large force culled from the best-educated, most tactful courtiers of Mantua.

Rarely far from his mind in these nonbelligerent pauses was the constant concern to embellish his court and his city. Rome was of course the ideal, and reports from Rome giving details of the fervor of rebuilding there were carefully heeded, to inspire similar activity in Mantua. Although improvements in the look of Rome, which for centuries had been a sinkhole, had been going on for some time, it was Pope Nicholas V, the first of a line of humanist popes, who devoted himself to recreating the look and tone of the city as it was, supposedly, under the Caesars. A cultivated, knowledgeable man, he gathered Piero della Francesca, Fra Angelico, Benozzo Gozzoli, and Leon Battista Alberti to adorn his city and bought many books and manuscripts from Vespasiano da Bisticci, the Florentine bookseller and biographer. Nicholas also hired illuminators, copyists with the most comely handwriting, and translators of Greek texts. His thousands of manuscripts became the core of the Vatican Library, the most extensive of its time, and it was he who guided the scholarly

Federico of Urbino in collecting the books that formed the extraordinary Urbino library, second only to that of the Medici and the Vatican.

Gonzaga could rival neither Nicholas nor his old schoolmate, but he did add a distinguished gathering of rarities to his father's collection. Pricked by complaints about the mud in his streets voiced during the papal conclave, he had them paved, with financial cooperation from the owners of adjacent properties. Bartolomeo Manfredi, a Mantuan mathematician and astronomer, was appointed to put together the complicated works for the great town clock.

The carefully nurtured wool-weaving industry now had a partner, silk-weaving, introduced with the growth of mulberry trees, both trades encouraged to brighten the city's streets with displays of their wares. Effective engineering to hold back floodwaters and direct canals to the young mulberry trees and to the rice also recently brought to Lombardy was an urgent need. Who better to give advice than Brunelleschi, the genius of the dome of Santa Maria del Fiore in Florence? Ludovico petitioned the *signoria* of Florence to allow the architect-sculptor-engineer to come to him. "And so Filippo [Brunelleschi] was sent thither by them, and designed the dikes to hold in the Po . . . and some other things in conformity with the prince's desire, who made much of him," Vasari reports.

No *condottiere* in the killing trade could consider himself thoroughly devout, but Ludovico was religious within the forms of his position and his epoch, and responsive to the exigencies of the local clergy. Church attendance had become casual and the church fathers, with the tacit consent of the marquis, insisted on the renewal of formal baptisms, on regular attendance for confession and communion—and long hellfire sermons. The adoration of the Virgin, painted in a thousand touching ways, and the lives of the martyred saints, graphically painted on church walls for those many who couldn't read, created a mounting fervor, urged on by the clergy. Mantua was soon the home of a sizable populace of those on their way to sainthood as *beatos* and *beatas,* who, in their zeal, induced the marquis to forbid Christians to buy meat from Jewish slaughterhouses, apparently a common practice. It was probably the *beatos* who insisted that some of the Precious Blood, the city's most sacred possession, be returned after it had been carelessly allowed to stray elsewhere. (It was purportedly brought back shortly after Ludovico's death and placed in an appropriately awesome reliquary in the cathedral.) The recrudescence of religious passion necessitated church building and rebuilding (commented on favorably by Pius II), and Ludovico complied, using the outstanding talents of his architects and master masons. He also gathered the small medieval hospices and primitive cure houses of the locality into a large, efficient Ospedale Maggiore, placing one of the capable women of his family in charge of its functioning. In these as in other matters, Ludovico had the close cooperation of his wife, Barbara, with whom the arranged marriage had grown into an affectionate partnership. Although the family's genealogical tree lists several natural children along with the impressive number of legitimate offspring that Ludovico fathered, Barbara did not protest; in fact, she saw to their welfare. Her place was secure and her major concern was the misshapen backs, inherited from their paternal grandmother, afflicting too many of her children.

The costs of creating his handsome city, of supporting a lavish court, of entertaining popes and their retinues of hundreds, of devising splendors to surround the emperor on his visit, and to refurbish apartments, with the help of Mantegna, for the king of Denmark and his queen, Barbara's sister, were prodigious. The moneys owed to Ludovico as *condottiere* were often slow in coming, as he suggests in his apologetic letter to his court painter, Mantegna, who growled when he was not paid on time. Yet in spite of unpaid debts, in spite of recurrent floods and epidemics, Mantua prospered, accruing new fertile land by purchase and inheritance. After Carlo's death, the emperor Frederick III conceded his considerable lands to Ludovico, who thereafter supported his brother's widow and his children, apparently illegitimate, since no claims were made for them as heirs. When brothers Gianlucido and Alessandro died, the first in 1448, the second in 1466, their remaining holdings became part of the marquisate.

The economy of the state was meticulously managed. All Mantuan earnings, rural and urban, were subject to carefully controlled taxes in carefully kept books. Rural taxes were higher than those in the city, a cause for dissension and the abandonment of some lands, but not markedly enough to cause major disturbances in the economy. In addition to the taxation (with some concessions for essential services, such as the milling of grain), each community was required to offer days of free labor, usually on local roads and protective walls, the number of workers determined by the size of the community. If beasts of burden and wagons were required, they were considered part of the free-labor obligation.

Ludovico had wavering relations with his Jewish community, now sizable and in the main affluent. He banned usury from all of his domain, then changed his mind and put a limit of 25 percent interest on loans, appointing a committee to watch out for violations. One cautious loophole in his early ban on usury was permission for the Jew Leone Norsa to establish a loan bank, a privilege that cost Norsa a large sum, part of it supplied by his coreligionists.

* As he grew older, an imposing figure experienced in war and politics, Ludovico was sought out as elder statesman to settle disputes outside his court. Late in 1476, Galeazzo Maria Sforza of Milan, a well-educated, capable, dissolute, and cruel man, was assassinated by a group who were not so much incensed by his brutality as, according to one historian, inspired by Renaissance revivals of the annals of heroic Romans who had fought and died for liberty. The would-be heroes had no popular support, and most of them were captured, while their leader fled to refuge in Florence. An uneasy rule was taken over by Galeazzo's unpopular wife, Bona of Savoy, acting as regent for their young son, Gian Galeazzo. The major port of Genoa defected from Milanese control, invasion threatened from the north, and Ludovico Sforza clearly meant to take his sister-in-law's dukedom. Bona appealed to Ludovico Gonzaga, still nominally captain of her army, to come, with his son Federico, to her aid. Gonzaga treated with Ludovico Sforza and his brothers, who allowed themselves to be persuaded that an annual grant of twelve thousand ducats each, to be provided by Bona's treasury, was not a bad deal, for the time being. Another threat to Bona and her son came as a suggestion by the emperor that Gonzaga lead the imperial armies for a takeover of Milan, whose frailty at the time inspired covetousness from several directions. Such an enterprise promised major effort and problems, and the rewards were uncertain, so Ludovico declined the job, turning instead to a pleasing, aesthetic matter—cooperating with Bona's masons in the design of a tower in her castello.

The marquis's tactful handling of a complicated imbroglio among Lucca, Pietrasanta, and a powerful religious company of Genoa again brought him to the favorable notice of the emperor, who was additionally pleased with the family when Federico— "hump-backed, well-mannered and amiable"—was married, in 1463, to Margherita of the German duchy of Wittelsbach.

* Before his marriage to Margherita, Federico was the hero of a romantic, largely apocryphal story that recounted chivalric wanderings in inimical lands and the fidelity of knights serving a wounded lord who suffers the pangs of true, unattainable love— basic elements of immortal tales. The story begins with the return from Rome of Francesco Gonzaga, the young new cardinal, accompanied by three hundred knights, to fervid acclaim by his family and the citizens of Mantua. Honors rendered and festivities over, attention turns to the marriage contract arranged for brother Federico. But the young man is profoundly in love with a local girl of humble origin and will not submit to life with an elderly— she was already eighteen—and unattractive foreigner. His father insists that he be imprisoned until he comes to his senses, but his mother helps him escape, under the protection of six servants. On their way to shelter at the court of Naples, the band is robbed and the prince becomes very ill. The servant-knights sequester Federico in the house of a peasant woman, whom they help with rough farm work for their keep. His mother, having had no word for a worrisome length of time, sends messengers throughout Mantua and beyond to try to find her son and also enlists the help of the king of Naples, who has search parties scout his lands. The six knights are ultimately found but will not state their names or their business. They are recognized, nevertheless, and in time reluctantly tell their story. Federico is taken to the palace of Naples to be cared for, while his mother is apprised of his whereabouts and pitiable condition. She begs her husband, as she had before, to bring their son back under peaceable terms. Ludovico, once himself an exile from his father's house, again refuses. When she insists that he read the letter from Naples, he yields dourly, telling her merely to do what she thinks best. Federico returns with his faithful men and begs pardon of his father. It is granted, as in all sentimental stories, and the devoted knights are generously rewarded. They become gentlemen of means, spoken of as

"The Faithful," the ancestors of the long, honorable Mantuan family line of Fideli.

Although, in reality, there was no reason for Federico to give up a lady love for a bride—lady loves were one of his privileges—he must have been taken aback by the girl with whom he would have to, at the very least, make children. She was described by court reporters as short, pale, and fat-faced; she spoke not a word of Italian and was coarsely dressed, like a rich peasant. In spite of his tendency to obesity and the family infirmity that pulled one of his shoulders high, Federico was an attractive young man of fine education. He had come under the personal influence of his father's teacher, Vittorino, and had been taught for some years by a student and disciple of the old master. At least one of his sisters, Barbara, had the taste and style—convincingly elegant and aristocratic, as Mantegna painted her—to complement her fine looks. His aunt Cecilia was a distinguished scholar, while his delicate, well-educated sisters Susanna and Dorotea were gracious, intelligent girls. How could he live with this dumpy German rustic? But Federico, trained as a politician and a disciplined warrior, finally accepted her. The marriage was celebrated in June of 1463, in the manner expected of princely houses. Led by Federico's brothers Rodolfo and Gianfrancesco, a gallant band of over one hundred knights in silks and velvets set out for Bavaria to fetch the bride, whom they escorted back to Mantua. A short distance outside the city proper, she was greeted by her new husband, her new father-in-law, and nobles of several courts, accompanied by a multitude of horsemen, as many as three or four thousand, if one can credit contemporary adulatory reports. Ludovico had called together his weavers and decorators to embellish a special apartment for the newlyweds, the Camera degli Sposi, on whose walls would appear the Mantegna family portraits a decade or so later. The palace courts were prepared for games and races, cheered on by ornamental ladies ablaze with gems. In the tapestried halls, concerts and dances were staged, and the tables heaped with delicacies.

There is interestingly little mention of church ceremonies in these accounts of marriages; the rituals that have since become the binding elements of a marriage were of minor importance. Although there was an elaborate body of canon law on the subject, including considerations of pulchritude and sexual willingness on the part of the girl, the signing of a contract and the days of jubilant show *were* the wedding. A marriage consummated before the official celebrations was, if a contract had been agreed on, by that very act considered sealed and binding. It was not until the Council of Trent, which stretched over several years and covered many doctrinal matters in the mid-sixteenth century, that there was set down, sharply and specifically, the obligation to perform the sacrament of marriage in the Church.

✳ The satisfactions of having a young cardinal son and close ties with the emperor were some compensation for bitter earlier humiliations suffered by Ludovico, Barbara, and two of their girls. In 1450, a marriage contract had been written to join the very young Susanna Gonzaga with the young heir of Milan, Galeazzo Maria Sforza. The contract was reviewed in 1454, one caveat stressed: if the child developed soundly. By 1457, Susanna appeared distinctly malformed and the contract was changed to bear the name of Dorotea, her younger sister, a thoroughly satisfactory arrangement agreed to by Galeazzo Maria and his family. The revised marriage paper carried the same stipulation for Dorotea as it had for her sister: Should she be too ill to marry and bear children, the contract would be canceled.

In late 1458, wife Barbara accompanied one of Ludovico's illegitimate daughters, Gabriela, to Cremona, to settle her into a marriage with a local nobleman. She then went on to Milan with Dorotea, to stay for two weeks. From all reports, Dorotea and Galeazzo enjoyed each other. He sent her affectionate letters after she returned to Mantua and acted the attentive fiancé on his visits to her house. Thus matters stood for a long while. A few months after Federico's wedding, in 1463, the marchioness received the duke of Milan's confidential secretary, who delivered an eager, romantic note from Galeazzo to Dorotea and then reminded the mother that the girl was approaching fourteen and should soon be ready for a full matrimonial life. His duke suggested, added the secretary, that before her birthday, the girl submit to a medical examination, limited to shoulders and back, her breasts to be kept modestly covered, to determine whether she was becoming humpbacked, as was bruited about in Milan's court. Everyone knew that humpbacks bred humpbacks, who gave birth to lepers as well. (Whether a young prince was psychotic, syphilitic, or the carrier of hereditary deformities was rarely questioned.)

When the indignant refusal by the Gonzaga to have Dorotea examined—hadn't Galeazzo been with her and touched her many times? hadn't doctors already seen her?—was reported in Milan, the boy's father answered that he considered the rejection of his proposal a sign that he was free to search elsewhere. Galeazzo vowed that he wanted the girl, but his father insisted that she first be examined. Ludovico, not easily discouraged, sent his wife to Milan to persuade Sforza that Dorotea was healthy; it had to be made known in Milan and other courts that his girl was ready and suitable for marriage, a judgment echoed by a Milanese ambassador, who enthusiastically reported that she was quite fit. But Barbara's mission failed and Ludovico resigned from the captaincy of the Sforza troops. The response was conciliatory letters from Milan, written while the duke hatched alternative matrimonial plans. The duke of Savoy, backed by France, which was still eager for a wedge into Italy, had offered the Sforza one of his daughters, Bona (who was later a suppliant for help from Ludovico). There was as yet no marriage contract signed with Savoy when Dorotea and her brothers, accompanied by three hundred fifty horsemen, set off for Reggio to attend a reception for the prince of Naples. Knowing that Galeazzo Maria would undoubtedly be there too, Barbara sent her daughter a letter instructing her to make herself pleasing and yet conduct herself as a member of a great house; Dorotea was to betray neither eagerness nor hurt in her encounters with the princeling. Nothing came of the meeting; the matter appeared to be entirely closed. Among the letters that flew between members of the Gonzaga family, there is one written by Barbara to her daughter Susanna, who had entered a convent. It described in sadly dignified terms the rejection of Dorotea, and elicited a moving response. Susanna's letter opens with a bow to the will of God, which everyone knows must be obeyed because, thus, everything will be for the best. The tone then moves beyond gentle piety: "I must say that my flesh hurts, I have wept bitterly for her whom I have loved and continue to love so that all pains and tribulations I feel as my own, and for the disgrace to our house." Dorotea died at the age of eighteen, early in 1467, her marriage contract not yet annulled. Some chose to see in her death the violent hand of Galeazzo Maria (assassinated at the age of thirty-two); they said he had her poisoned to clear the way for marriage with Bona, using a slow-acting venom secretly administered by a Mantuan servant in the employ of Milan. Closer to the truth may be the fact that a not too robust, deeply humiliated girl might have been assailed by one of the many diseases that were incurable in her time, from malaria to tuberculosis.

No longer captain of Milanese troops, his family severed from Milan, the 42,000 ducats owed him in back pay not forthcoming, Ludovico turned to listen to the blandishments of Venice. She would not, however, agree to the return of Mantuan border areas the family had long wanted, and no deal was made. At this time, son Federico was treating with Naples for leadership of both the Neapolitan and the Milanese armies, the salary to be paid by both states. Milan and Mantua were in partnership once again, preparing with Naples for assaults on the Veneto. While these seesaw alignments were arranged and rearranged, the court at Mantua continued to flourish singularly.

The young cardinal Francesco was becoming a collector of art and antiques and a connoisseur of music. One of his companions was another worldly cardinal, Roderigo Borgia, who, along with other sybarite cardinals, frequented antiquarians, artists, and lovely women, suavely pacing a life that evoked unheeded criticism from Pius II. An Italian historian, the nostalgic envy dripping from his lines, finds the whole of Francesco's life beautifully harmonious and aesthetic, a life designed on the Renaissance ideal of *grazia* as Castiglione and Vasari defined it. Their luxuriant ease floated on "an atmosphere of art, of letters, of love for beautiful rare things flowing almost into nature toward the beauty of an attractive, responsive female body, combined with the sensual pleasures of colors, of velvet, of fine statuary, to make a life that was more *palpitante.*" This "throbbing" life called for Francesco to be a fine huntsman of game, sex, antiquities, and anything else that met his tastes. In 1472, he asked his father to send him court musicians and a fellow antiquarian, Mantegna, to judge his collection of bronzes, medals, and other fascinating bits and pieces that were being pulled from the Roman earth.

Ludovico, his father's namesake, the keenest of the children and the wittiest, with a highly developed taste for literature and the classical theater, became yet another sort of Renaissance prelate. As bishop of Mantua, he had available to him, and enjoyed, pliant women, but he insisted that the amorous games at his little inherited court at Gazzuolo be conducted discreetly, while he retired, from time to time, to games of the mind. As for amassing bright shining things, like a jackdaw, it was not for him, with his light, amused cynicism.

Pretty, robust Barbara, who had been rejected, along with her sisters, by the Sforza, was later affianced to Everardo, count of Württemberg, who actually admired and loved her. The brilliance of the wedding celebrations of 1474 was matched by an extravagant dowry of five thousand ducats' worth of silver and hangings, four thousand in a wardrobe and jewelry, twelve thousand in cash, and credit for four thousand on deposit in a Venetian bank. She took with her books and pictures, and promises that more would be sent her by her family. She kept herself informed about what was going on among the painters, writers, philosophers, and musicians in Italy and shed the borrowed brightness on her influential new court, with the ready acquiescence of her husband. This second German marriage further pleased the emperor, who continued to hold the Gonzaga in high esteem. Paola, the youngest of the children and markedly deformed, could not expect such a marriage, nor would she enter a convent, like her sister Susanna. The marriage field from which her father could choose for this pale, meager child was so limited he settled on the gross, stupid count of Gorizia. Paola was accompanied to his palace by her brother Ludovico, who tried to comfort her when she ran from the savage conjugal bed. She could not return to her home— few girls could in the circumstances—but she saved herself from too many encounters with her husband by dying young.

At home, the steady stream of entertaining and stimulating people continued to enliven the court. Acclaimed foreign *improvvisatori* came, to be clamorously applauded and well paid. The accomplished of various parts of Italy, including intellectually gifted Florentine protégés of the Medici, visited, and some stayed on to enjoy the courtesy and generosity of the court. Mantegna continued to cover the walls of the central palace and the outlying villas, complaining while Ludovico praised, soothed, apologized, and sold family jewels to appease his painter. Distinguished visitors were dazzled by this glowing world of stately palaces hung with paintings in the "new" style, by the new Palace of the Commune and the lordly new guild house of the weavers, by the luxuriance of dress and ornament, by the searching minds and wit of fellow guests. In the course of their tour, the visitors would have been shown the printing press that Ludovico acquired in 1455, shortly after the new German machine was introduced into Italy; a manuscript copy of Virgil, Ludovico's favorite poet; and masterfully illustrated editions of the founding trio of Italian literature—Dante, Petrarch, and Boccaccio. Several of the books they would examine were inevitably treatises on the rearing and care of horses, a normal interest of *condottieri* and huntsmen, and a passion among the Gonzaga. A broadening world of early scientific knowledge was symbolized in five volumes devoted to the animals of the earth. They were dedicated by Pietro Candido Decembrio to the marquis, who had asked that the volumes be illustrated by "the hand of a good craftsman." The craftsman must have been quite gifted, since Dürer's famous engraving of a hippopotamus strongly suggests that during one of his sojourns in Italy, he took a long look at the drawing in Mantua.

Ludovico's last years were a quiet triumph. The warrior whose ferocity had earned him the sobriquet "Il Turco" was now a Solon. It was noted in richer courts that in spite of comparatively limited finances and several setbacks, he supported the most distinctive talents and had arranged marriages for his children that were envied by larger states. His reputation for benevolence stemmed also from the extraordinary fact that he did not have his brother Carlo—his enemy—killed, although fifteenth-century mores would have justified the act. Thoughtful and in many ways enlightened, he was not so enlightened as to tolerate more than a shadow of democratic rule, no more than his coequals did. He cut and tightened the waning powers of the *podestà* and other civic bodies. Although he gave grants to improve the agricultural yield of Mantuan lands, they stayed under the court's supervision. It was not in his politics or in his character, which had struggled through a despised youth for its strengths, to ask advice, as his father had, of his citizens. In the pattern of his peers, he was a tyrant-ruler, whose absolute power was mitigated by foresight and balance.

His distinguished city had grown to a population of forty thousand; the guild records of the Arte della Lana (Wool) showed lively, widespread sales; his heirs would inherit more lands than he had. In 1477, he was accorded a crowning honor. The Pope sent him the delicate golden rose customarily presented to the royal families of Europe. Like the wise kings of old stories, Ludovico had built a rich, reasonably contented, reasonably solid kingdom. Full of satisfactions and honors, he retired to Goito, a favorite hunting seat, to rest and to escape yet another visitation of the plague. But in 1478, when eighteen thousand Mantuans died of the plague, Ludovico Gonzaga was among them.

Words and Thought

When Rome of the marble temples of Augustus, of an empire that reached northern England, pierced Asia, and took its grain from Africa, became, for the Renaissance, the best of all possible worlds, her language, as well as her matter and manners, was reexamined, restudied. Popes took to themselves titles like "Optimus Maximus" and addressed their cardinals as "Senator." Certain popes earned their position, according to contemporaries, with their command of Latin: Nicholas V, the collector of books, scribes, and writers, for his cadenced eulogy on the death of Eugene IV, and Pius II for the Latin ornaments that embroidered his speeches and documents. A command of eloquent Latin became essential to biographers and ambassadors, who brightened the dross of dullness with Ciceronian gold. In the main, however, Latin as used in communications among courts and seats of the Church was distorted and lame, according to scholars who took pleasure in pointing out the errors and awkwardness of the classic tongue as burbled by courtiers and church fathers. For them, and because he was a witty man, the humanist Lorenzo Valla wrote a Latin thesaurus that encompassed lessons in fine, graceful usage. The book had wide circulation, elevating to high style obscene insults, a poem on syphilis, spates of elegant name-calling, as well as ornate sycophantic praise.

According to the Latinist snobs, the Italian of Petrarch, Dante, and Boccaccio was a tongue for the ignorant, useful only for dealing with tradesmen and servants. The irrepressible "vulgar" language nevertheless insisted on making itself felt and was used in increasingly wide areas. A telling example of the change to the vulgate—at times an uncertain mixture of Latin, Italian dialects, and borrowings from the French and Spanish—appears in the chancellery records of Mantua, those of the first years of the fifteenth century predominantly Latin, those of the 1440s, with few exceptions, in the vulgate. By the opening of the sixteenth century, Italian on the Tuscan model became an established language in several European courts, although Latin was still used for communications with the Church. Within a century, Italian had become the language of international communications. There may have been a taint of nostalgia in it, but "Pietro Paulo Rubens" was the signature the painter used in his correspondence with patrons in several courts.

Most of Alberti's overwhelming literary production was expressed in Italian, for whose general use he campaigned enthusiastically. Vespasiano da Bisticci wrote his 105 biographies of famous men in Italian, and Piero della Francesca's pioneer work on perspective, as well as Leonardo's uncanny observations, used the "vulgar tongue." The popular old stories of the Paladins of Charlemagne, of Tristan and his two Iseults, of King Arthur and his knights, wandered into Italy speaking popular tongues. Their passions and magics, made large and iridescent by Boiardo's *Orlando Innamorato,* could hardly have played out their gorgeous fantasies in stately Latin, and furthermore, court ladies lacked sufficient Latin to follow their favorite stories in that inappropriate language. Francesco Guicciardini, the author of the masterly *History of Italy* and as cold-eyed as his contemporary Machiavelli, warns his fellow citizens in forceful words not to be distracted by hopes of reviving a world long gone, language and all: "We are not Romans," but Italians of here and now, who must concentrate on their own present good. However, fine Latin stayed an elitist instrument of scholars expressing part of the intellectual verdure of the Renaissance. Marsilio Ficino (1433–99), taken into the household of Cosimo de' Medici as a promising youngster, learned Greek in order to translate Plato into Latin and revived the thought of the Roman philosopher Plotinus, the father of Neoplatonism, so that he might meld them with Christian theology.

One of the several startled judgments of Victorian historians of the Renaissance stresses rather repeatedly "the value attached in this age to pure scholarship, in spite of moral considerations" (Symonds). A prime example of learning and loathsomeness was Francesco Filelfo, born near Ancona in 1398. A vicious man given to vindictive letters and ready swordplay, he was yet welcomed with honors in many courts, among them that of Ludovico in Mantua, where he was asked to make the Latin oration that welcomed Pope Pius II to the congress of 1459.

At eighteen, already a professor of Latin literature and rhetoric, he was invited by Venice to teach there and, after two years, was sent to Constantinople as secretary to the Venetian consul general. He remained there for seven years, studying Greek and improving his position in the consulate. He returned to Venice with a thorough knowledge of Greek and a large number of Greek texts, letting it be known, far, wide, and repeatedly, that there was no one who could meet his command of classical literatures; for the 1420s, he may have been right, and was bitterly resented. The plague in Venice forced him to Bologna and then on to Florence, where he gathered enmities among scholars and a sword slash across his face. The contest for learned men was fierce among courts and universities, and in spite of his reputation as a contentious, unpleasant man, he was invited to adorn many places. "By fair means or foul," according to one biographer, he managed to become a star. Naples honored him with a knighthood, and courteous welcomes came to him from Ferrara, from Rimini, and, as mentioned, from Mantua. His longest stay was in Milan, under the Sforza, until Francesco Sforza, his patron, died. By then an old man, Filelfo responded to earlier invitations to teach in Rome and, should there be a vacancy, become a member of the Church Chancery. His haughtiness and bad temper, expressed in brutally termed letters burning with invective, forced him back to Milan briefly and then again to Florence, where Lorenzo the Magnificent invited him to teach Greek literature. He arrived in time to succumb to the dysentery that threatened every traveler, dying at the rare old age of eighty-three. Other than his indisputable learning, the many letters that mirrored the personages and events of his time, and his contribution to Italy of theretofore unknown Greek texts, Filelfo was not a major force in the development of humanist thought but served rather as an example of the respect, tinged with acquisitive upmanship, granted learned men by fifteenth-century princes and prelates.

* Lorenzo Valla, whose life spanned the years 1407 to 1457, was another contentious man, although mainly intellectually so. He distinguished himself early as a Latin scholar and later as a fierce enemy of papal distortions of history, of papal greed and ruthlessness, and, always, of bad church Latin. Among his translations from the Greek into Latin there was an infuriating study of Epicurus, defending pleasure as a life-giving principle, opposed to the cold strictures of Stoicism and the fleshlessness of monastic thought. His translations and analyses, philologic and philosophical treatises, became, by 1431, the six volumes of *De Elegantia Latinae Lingue*, a model for elegant Latin style and one of the causes of dissension with other scholars in the University of Padua, where Valla taught rhetoric. Six years after the publication of *De Elegantia*, he was invited by Alfonso of Naples to be his poet laureate, his private secretary, and the voice of Alfonso's dissension with the Papacy, which challenged his right to the throne of Naples. Treated with esteem, well kept, and encouraged by his patron, Valla sent forth blasts against the small minds of the clergy, against the barbaric prose they habitually used, and, as climax, issued an accusation that an eighth-century document, known as the "Donation of Constantine," supposedly based on a proclamation by Constantine, giving the Papacy supreme control of the Western world was a forgery. He also let it be known that, after careful study, he could not accept, nor could any conscientious scholar, the traditional assertion that the Apostles' Creed had been composed by a committee of twelve. Critical blasts called "Invectives" busied the air between Naples and Rome. Then came the Inquisition, to whom Valla reported that he was a believer in most of the principles of a church that knew nothing. Protected by Alfonso, he was not taken or further molested.

It is one measure of the humanist pope Nicholas V that so iconoclastic a writer, given to praising (always on philosophic grounds) pagan joys, a harsh critic who accused the Church of forgery, extortion, and every sort of dishonesty, could find favor with the Papacy. Valla was taken on as Apostolic Writer, to be housed and fed exceedingly well. Nicholas knew that Valla's *Donation* exposé was in spite of its rational strength a futile exercise; the Church would continue to amass territories where and when she could. Quite possibly Nicholas was stimulated by the intellectual furies Valla whipped up with his talent for disturbing entrenched values. While translating Herodotus and Thucydides into Latin, Valla found time to criticize the monastic vows of obedience, chastity, and poverty, since they carried with them no understanding of their true meaning and no sense of real devotion. In his treatise *De Voluptate*, he attacked again the misunderstood, misused ideal of chastity. A final blast from the dissident who lived in a handsome house with his mistress and their three children, supported by several Church benefices, roared out of the Church of Santa Maria Sopra Minerva in Rome. Assigned to speak the praises of Thomas Aquinas during an anniversary celebration, he tore the saint's tenets to shreds and, in the process, attacked—inevitably—his execrable Latin style. Shortly thereafter, Lorenzo Valla died, casting a long shadow into the future Reformation, leaving an indelible image for such independent thinkers as Erasmus to admire.

* Of a less showy cast of dissent, and ultimately, like Valla, a recipient of support and honors from the Church, was Bartolomeo Platina (1421–81), who chose a classical name to supplant the parental Sacchi. In his youth a pupil of Vittorino da Feltre and for a short while tutor to the children of the Mantuan court, he brought from the experience a report on the life and methods of the old teacher and a lifelong connection with the Gonzaga. Later he joined an academy in Rome that dedicated itself to Roman literature and history and to exploring the city's catacombs. Members addressed each other by classical names and marked their days according to the Roman calendar. As were their peers in Florence, who lived as close to Plato as possible, the Roman academicians were accused of thinking and conducting themselves as pagans rather than Christians. Encouraged by a generous patron, Cosimo de' Medici, the Platonic Academy in Florence could indulge itself in being as Greek as it liked, to the degree of observing as a sacred holiday the day of Plato's birth. In Rome, a suspicious Papacy feared that its academy was plotting a return to Roman republicanism in the style of Cola di Rienzo, who had made the attempt a century before. Charging them with heresy, abominable practices, and Satanic beliefs, the Pope had Platina and his colleagues thrown into prison. After hearings that produced no proofs against them, the group was released. Sixtus IV, the begetter of the Sistine Chapel, was not a man to waste available talent of a high order; he commissioned Platina to write an authoritative *Lives of the Popes* and appointed him Keeper of the Vatican Library, a distinction commemorated by Melozzo da Forli in a painting of the Pope greeting a grave, distinguished scholar. As an established savant and connoisseur, Platina was petitioned by ambitious courts for suggestions on expanding their growing libraries. One visit to Mantua, as the friend and guest of Ludovico and his son Federico, produced an impressive list of wanted titles and an eager search for them. Platina made a later and probably last journey to Mantua to deliver a funeral oration at Ludovico's death. Comfortably and honorably ensconced, his prickly super-classicism smoothed away, Platina remained a major functionary and intellectual ornament of the Vatican until his own death, at sixty.

* Of all the humanist scholars, Giovanni Pico della Mirandola leaves the most incandescent, romantic image. His courage to follow his adventurous mind into conflict with the Inquisition, his extraordinary gifts, and his death at thirty-one foreshadow another supreme rebel and romantic, Percy Bysshe Shelley. According to Angelo Poliziano, the author of the play *Orfeo* (himself an ill-favored man): "Nature seemed to have showered on this man, or hero, all her gifts. He was tall and finely molded; from his face a something of divinity shone forth. Acute, and gifted with prodigious memory, in his studies he was indefatigable, in his style perspicuous and eloquent. You could not say whether his talents or his moral quality conferred on him the greater lustre. Familiar with all branches of philosophy, and the master of many languages, he stood on high above the reach of praise." Allowing for Renaissance adornments, we are yet in the presence of an extraordinary personage. Pico, born in 1463, was an aristocrat, the count of Mirandola, his father the prince of a small, prosperous court near Modena. By the time he was fourteen, he was ready for the University of Bologna, where he mastered whatever it could teach him of philosophy, mathematics, rhetoric, logic, and Oriental languages. Then on to Paris for a broadening of his achievements, facilitated by a capacity to absorb everything on a page in one reading, though that page might be in a recently acquired language. His reputation as a polymath and the possessor of an awesome library, as a beautiful prince with a racing, prolific mind, soon reached Florence, and he was invited to become a member of the Platonic Academy.

By the time he was twenty-four, he was ready to challenge, in Rome, the leading ecclesiastical minds of all Europe. For debates with these savants he brought nine hundred theses, and as prelude to the debates, an address, his *Oratorio*. The underlying thrust of his theses followed a basic humanist tenet that all knowledge and religions could be reconciled to create one universal system. Impressed with his learning, a preliminary meeting of the erudite of the Church nevertheless found the samples of Pico's thought unacceptable. Although he rejected astrology, his inter-

Kate Simon

est in Orphic mysteries (a secret religion that worshiped Dionysus and at times Eros; that believed in the transmigration of souls and a strict purity of conduct and rites, which would lead to immortality), his defense of prophecies in dreams and the flights of birds, his references to the mysterious practices of the ancient Chaldeans, his approval of the Greek unities of love, beauty, and pleasure, his intimacy with Hebrew thought (especially the awesome Cabala, which, he insisted, supported Christian doctrine), led to inevitably harsh judgments. If he wasn't an outright witch, said the Church, he was certainly a heretic; a few of his ideas were worth exploring, the rest were a bundle of abominations. Pico offered a bold rebuttal, defending a number of his proofs and suggesting that the men who had judged him might themselves be accused of heresy. And, of course, their Latin was execrable. A papal edict prohibited the universal meeting of scholars Pico had hoped for, then prevented the publication of his propositions and swiftly pointed the Inquisition his way. Wherever he fled it followed, until the powers of Florence intervened to offer him shelter and the untroubled leisure to continue his studies of Aramaic, Chaldaic, and Hebrew. The Inquisition continued to peck at him, to be stilled by a pair of widely contrasted forces: The Borgia Pope Alexander VI called for a halt, while Savonarola's burning spirit, which ruled Florence with threats of hellfire and destruction, induced Pico to become a Dominican monk. He died shortly after entering the order, "exhausted by study and insufficient rest," deploring voices said.

The attractiveness of Pico's mind lay in the confidence and learning not only to challenge the Church but to do intellectual battle with his fellow philosophers as well. Although humanist thinkers tended to dismiss medieval thought as primitive, feeble in the new studies and uses of philology and rhetoric, Pico, in line with medieval scholarship, insisted that philosophy was more important than verbal dissections, although he conceded that philosophy might gain from philologic studies. Since he spoke from extraordinary knowledge, from reading in the original of Plato and the Platonists, from explorations of the Old Testament as it was written, from the "mysteries of the ancients" as he knew them beyond the knowledge of other men, he was difficult to vanquish in argument.

In spite of his admiration of the spiritual passion of Savonarola, he refused to accept the monk's view of man as prisoner of his own corruption. Man as the most significant of entities, his soul the core of the universe, striving with intellect and will toward godhood, was a concept expanded by Pico, most fervently in his essay *The Dignity of Man.* God, after the creation of the earth, the waters, the firmament, and the beasts, addresses Adam: "Neither an established place, nor a form belonging to you alone, nor any special function have we given you, O Adam, and for this reason, that you may have and possess, according to your desire and judgment, whatever place, whatever form and whatever functions you shall desire. . . . You, who are confined by no limits, shall determine for yourself your own nature, in accordance with your own free will, in whose hand I have placed you." Man, created neither mortal nor immortal, possessed of limitless free will, can make of himself whatever he prefers: "you shall be able to be reborn out of the judgment of your own soul into the high beings, which is divine." Man can be and therefore is potentially a god.

Phenomenal in his lifetime, Pico became legendary after his death, extolled for his beauty and elegance, his grace and courtliness (as Castiglione sketched him in *The Courtier*), and for the depth and breadth of his learning. England, already engaged in its long love affair with Italy, closely examined Pico's thought; Sir Thomas More was sufficiently impressed to translate some of his work into English. Pico's matter caused difficulties in Germany, however. Led on by the young Italian reputed to be the first Christian scholar to examine the ancient books and the mysticisms of the Cabala, German savants also delved into the archaic texts to explore incantations against evil and symbols that might grasp the radiance of total knowledge. In its suggestions that man's soul was eternal and might enter a body to do mischief or, if it was pure, could overcome evil forces, in its promise of revealing secrets of the universe, the Cabala was whispering, as Pico had insisted, half-hidden Christian tenets. One German work on the Cabala evoked accusations of heresy, and soon there was issued an interdict that covered all Hebrew learning. The mischief was out, though. Hebrew studies were never completely suppressed and, when combined with Greek study and profounder examination of "pagan" enlightenments, stimulated renewed philosophic conjecture in Germany and beyond. Ultimately the Church decided that Hebrew texts were essential as background for Christian theology, a practice that lapsed from time to time, reinforced through the centuries by scholars like Matthew Arnold, who stressed constantly the need of theologians for a full knowledge of Hebrew thought and its implications.

The practice might be considered one of Pico's lasting legacies, his prime legacy being the radiance of his humanistic mind and being, which continue to light the centuries.

F*O*U*R

The reign of Federico il Gobbo—the Humpback—was short and difficult. Much of it was spent, now that his strong father was gone, in guarding against court plots and in maintaining his military commitment to Milan, as leader of her troops. The respect he enjoyed at home for being reasonable and *cortese*—courteous— was enhanced by his reputation for not molesting women, or boys. He continued his father's support for and patience with Mantegna and commissioned Luca Fancelli to work on the reconstruction of a large area, the Nova Domus, in the palace compound.

Federico was not an especially cultivated man, but he had picked up the tastes that surrounded his youth. He collected antiques and continued to commission scholars to search out manuscripts for his library. Besides these and similar expenditures, there was the cost of the marriage of his daughter Chiara to Gilbert, count of Montpensier, of the noble house of the Bourbons. The dowry, adornments, and celebration consumed over thirty thousand ducats.

Over these pleasures hovered clouds of distress. Federico's sister Susanna died in her convent in 1481. His cardinal brother, Francesco, a warm support and an important link with the Church, died two years later.

Following a sinister common pattern (echoed in Shakespeare's "Murder of Gonzago"), his brothers Rodolfo and Gianfrancesco had attempted to poison him and his son, but were foiled by another brother, Ludovico. Rodolfo repeated another not uncommon act: He had his wife, Antonia Malatesta, beheaded for having been unfaithful, a fair possibility. It is also likely that she was both instrument and victim of court schisms that flourished in Federico's long campaign absences. Since Federico's wife, Margherita, was a limited woman and not to be trusted in governmental matters, political matters were turned over to Eusebio Malatesta, local affairs to Francesco Secco d'Aragona and to Evangelista Gonzaga, a natural son of Federico's uncle Carlo. It was in the web of pulls among them that Antonia Malatesta lost her life.

Milan was at this point aligned with Ferrara and Venice against the Pope and Naples. To relieve a siege imposed by papal forces on Milanese territory, Federico acted with notable skill and speed. His contract was renewed, for a salary of thirty thousand scudi in times of peace and twice as much in times of war. Ercole d'Este of Ferrara was put in charge of the anti-papal forces, while Federico Gonzaga's next assignment was to force back the Neapolitan armies which had reached Tuscany. While he was in Tuscany, Federico received news that his wife, long ailing, was mortally ill. Tired of quarrels, especially with d'Este, about leadership and strategy, he eagerly returned to Mantua and stayed there through his wife's death and for some time thereafter before returning to arms and controversies.

Then again came political shifts, again changes of partners in perilous games. Lorenzo de' Medici, il Magnifico, a man devoted to the ideal of collecting inimical fragments of Italy to create unity, sued for peace with Naples—a former enemy—and the Pope and achieved it briefly in 1480. But Sixtus IV could not let matters rest. He was a curious man of whom much had been expected, those expectations hampered by the contradictions in his interests and passions. He welcomed the Inquisition, but when the Dominican fathers paid him no heed regarding regulations and limitations, he opened Italy to Jews expelled from Spain. He rebuilt sections of Rome, expanded the Vatican Library, and had the Sistine Chapel decorated, with the help of the finest artists of his time. These were avocations, however, intervals in his political quarrels, which involved furious controversies with the French Church and court. He was also driven by fierce nepotism, insistent that his nephews Girolamo Riario and Giovanni della Rovere take control of fecund territories, preferably in the environs of Ferrara. Equally eager for Ferrarese territories, Venice decided to join the Pope. Florence, Bologna, Ferrara, and Mantua remained on the side of Milan, with the duke of Urbino as general of troops.

War broke out in the spring of 1482, soon followed by incursions of Venice into lands near Mantua and directed toward Ferrara. Federico Gonzaga relieved Ferrara by impeding the advance; he flooded the Venetian line of march by cutting into the confines of the Mincio, loosing its waters. The Pope, in one of his erratic changes of heart and mind, began to look sourly on his ally Venice and nimbly leaped to the support of the former opposition. Though somewhat impeded by the loss of the papal forces, Venice went on foraging. In the summer of 1483, Sixtus IV excommunicated the republic, its doge, its councils, and its citizens. La Serenissima remained unimpressed and belligerent.

In the continuing campaigns, a new Gonzaga *condottiere* came to the fore. His siege and conquest of elusive Asola was a short-lived triumph since the town was retaken, but while it lasted it was a glorious experience for Francesco, the eldest son of Federico, a valiant, showy young warrior who bent his full energies and courage into trying to hold off Venice. She was stronger and inflicted considerable damage on the peripheries of his city. Lands depleted, himself exhausted by perfidy and disagreements, Francesco's father, the marquis Federico, for some time ill, went home, to die on July 14, 1484, at the age of forty-two. The exhausted contenders decided to call a halt; the usual evanescent peace treaty, an exercise in exquisite calligraphy on white parchment, bore as one signature that of the new marquis of Mantua, Francesco Gonzaga.

✳ Francesco's first step into immortality was paced for him by Mantegna. The older of the two solemn little grandsons of Ludovico II, he is painted standing close to their uncle the new cardinal, in the Camera degli Sposi fresco. Though he is in profile, one can see the short wide nose and the full lips that would later, when his hair had grown crisp and bushy, give him a vaguely African look.

When Francesco was barely in his teens, he was betrothed to Isabella, the daughter of Duke Ereole d'Este, still a little girl. This arrangement had been made during the ceremonies that bade farewell to Chiara Gonzaga, Francesco's elder sister, who was about to depart for the country of her bridegroom, cousin to the king of France. Isabella was already sought after, for her brightness and accomplishments and for the prominence of her house. The most luminous rival over whom Francesco triumphed was Ludovico il Moro, the Sforza, newly ruler of the important state of Milan, who contented himself with taking Isabella's younger sister, Beatrice. (Beatrice was instantly much richer and could command Leonardo da Vinci to design gowns, interior decor, and magical theater effects. But she grew fatter sooner than her sister and had to countenance the attention and money her husband lavished on two exquisitely beautiful and talented mistresses, both painted by Leonardo.)

After the customary exchange of wedding portraits, Isabella's painted by her father's court painter, Cosmé Tura; after visits, gifts, and poetic little missives written by Mantuan poets for Francesco; after tactful notes from Isabella's mother, Leonora, holding the importunate suitor off because she felt her daughter was not quite ready for marriage; after long months of preparation, the marriage ceremonies and fetes finally took over Ferrara. According to Julia Cartwright's biography of Isabella d'Este, the Ferrarese painter Ercole de' Roberti was sent to Venice for a wealth of gold leaf, with which he painted the thirteen wedding chests the bride was to take to Mantua, along with an elaborate marriage bed, a chariot, and a gilded boat presented to her by her father. Tapestries that shone with gold thread, part of the dowry brought by Eleonora, the daughter of the king of Naples, when she married Ercole of Ferrara, illumined the Este palace walls; the dishes for feasting were designed by Tura. When the bride, her brothers, her parents, and their entourage stepped off the gilded barge and set foot on Mantuan soil, they entered a world of garlands, song, pageantry, and dancing. Vivid banners hung from every window; the fountains ran wine, and sweets were distributed to everyone, anyone. The Gonzaga court was young, both parents were dead, and the festivities were unbridled, running to tourneys as shows of strength and horsemanship, indefatigable dancing, and roaring through the midnight streets. The more decorous indoor shows were ornamented with tapestries and fine rugs, with silver and gold vessels and lengths of Oriental silks—as in Ferrara, some of the objects borrowed from friends and relatives, a not uncommon practice for displaying the most resplendent *bella figura*.

The cold February days of celebration were propitious ones according to the astronomers of the Este court, in a propitious year, 1490, according to the historian Francesco Guicciardini: "Italy had never enjoyed such prosperity, or known so favorable a situation as that in which it found itself so securely at rest in the year of our Christian salvation, 1490, and the years immediately before and after." Huge tracts of land in Lombardy and Emilia were producing millet, which could be stored for long periods and used in times of crop failure, plagues, and invasions. Rice was grown extensively and profitably, and rice flour, also capable of lasting, milled. Agriculture was becoming an industry, with steady large work forces, extensive investments in lands, and the profits to carry them. Mantuan weaving was strongly protected by the Arte della Lana guild, whose craftsmen were courted by northern industrialists like the Fuggers (originally themselves weavers).

The unbridled merriment in prosperous streets in prosperous, peaceful times outsang the discord and dispelled the shadows that would come to affect the complex lives of the couple, sometimes lightly, often balefully touched by a galaxy of forces both Italian and foreign: the Sforza of Milano, the Montefeltro and della Rovere dukes of Urbino, the Medici of Tuscany, the senates and doges of Venice. And a line of French kings: Charles VIII, Louis XII, Francis I, as well as King Alfonso of Naples, King Ferdinand of Aragon, plus a procession of popes—Alexander VI, Pius III, Julius II, Leo X, Adrian VI, Clement VII, Paul III—and the emperors Maximilian and Charles VI.

Besides practical considerations, there was a special distinction in marrying an Este girl. The Este were not only richer than the Gonzaga but of a much older and more cultivated house. Of ancient Lombard descent, the Este were well ensconced as leaders of the Guelph (papal) party by the twelfth century, and connected by marriage to leading families in Italy and Germany. With the aid of the Church, the Este took over Modena and Reggio and began to establish the accoutrements that an imposing city such as their Ferrara should have: an extensive castle-fortress, a highly esteemed academy, an effective army. In short, the Este were a presence that other states were forced to recognize and deal with as foe, friend, intermediary.

Of Ferrara, and of Mantua as well, Denys Hays writes in *Italian Renaissance in Its Historical Background*: "The reception of Renaissance values in Italy should begin not with the great princes but with the little princes. The first clear adoption of humanist assistance in the arts and graces of life and the day-to-day administrative machine is to be found in the small tyrannies." The gentle, learned "little prince" Leonello—he of the ascetic face as sculptured in medallions by Pisanello and rendered in a telling portrait by the Flemish painter Rogier van der Weyden—managed to have the school founded by the tutor Guarino Veronese designated by the emperor as a university, and it soon became one of the leading seats of learning in Italy. Its widespread fame attracted such scientists as Paracelsus, Copernicus, Vesalius, such scholars as Pico della Mirandola and Erasmus; Leon Battista Alberti and Piero della Francesca were friends and advisers on matters of architecture and art. Leonello's brother Borso, who became ruler in 1450, continued to pursue vigorously the goal of making himself and his Ferrara notable in every way. He managed to persuade—for how much?—the emperor to dub him duke of Modena and Reggio, and from Pope Paul II he received the title of duke of Ferrara. An odd, vainglorious, good-natured fat man, Borso left his most significant mark in the murals he ordered of Francesco Cossa and Ercole de' Roberti, assisted by Cosmé Tura, to adorn the palace called Schifanoia—roughly, "Sans souci." They depict a series of months, focused on Borso as huntsman and kindly lord. Whatever the month, the murals live in an eternal spring: Everyone is blond and juicy and dressed in velvet and brocade. The horses and dogs are studies in eager grace; there is much kissing and music-making in the presence of several adorable rabbits touched by affectionate breezes. These enchanting murals, often referred to as a "glory of Italian painting," exemplify an ideal Renaissance as it liked to see itself and as it possibly was for a man like Borso. He maintained the image by organizing ravishing spectacles with himself always at the center, gathering around his plump, beaming self hundreds of men in silver and gold cloth, their horses cloaked in embroidered velvets edged with silver bells.

Borso was followed by his half-brother Ercole, who consolidated Ferrara's status not only by marrying into the house of Aragon, which then ruled Naples, but by placing his children well and effectively into other useful marriages. On principles propounded by Leonello's friend Alberti, Ercole remade a portion of his city into broad, symmetrical streets, which bordered massive palaces and extensive gardens; it is still cited as one of the earliest successful experiments in city planning. (Leonardo recommended that his patron Ludovico Sforza do likewise, to rectify the overcrowding, the ugliness, the stench, and the wells of pestilence in crowded Milan, but Sforza saw no virtue in the idea.)

The Este were musical and most of them played an instrument or two and sang well. For new music they invited Europe's leading composers, but they had a special fondness for Provençal songs of courtly love, which paralleled their enthusiasm for French romances, whose atmosphere of gallantry, heroism, and obsessed love made Ferrara the appropriate seminal ground for the great vernacular epics of Boiardo, Ariosto, and Tasso, which in turn inspired the literature of the rest of Europe. The theater was a passion of Duke Ercole, Isabella's father. He had relics of Greek plays translated by court scholars, Roman plays redone in the Italian vernacular, and he also staged sacred plays—all sorts of drama, whose costumes and scenic effects he supervised carefully and on which he lavished large sums.

Much of the theater fervor in Ferrara was described by Isabella, a frequent visitor and an assiduous correspondent. We learn from her, as well, the attributes and interests of her brother Alfonso. He plays the violin reasonably well, he is an inventive ceramicist and is clever at devising deadly and deadlier cannon. His gentler proclivities attract him to the curious paintings of Dosso Dossi, to whom he acts as generous patron, as he also does to the king of painters, Titian. He is the builder of one of the loveliest pleasure palaces in Ferrara, the Belvedere, situated on an island in the river Po. Surrounding its marbles and frescoes of playful nymphs, he plants gardens and woods full of exotic fauna and flora.

All the elements that went into the intellectual and aesthetic style of the court were paid for with moneys earned by the Este as *condottieri* and by the astute commercial acumen that sent Alfonso, for one, into the trade centers of northern Europe to observe banking and business practices that might advantageously be used at home.

Wearing the multifaceted tiara emblazoned "Este" and "Aragon," for the eminent court in which her mother was born, the sixteen-year-old Isabella knew her worth as ornament and hostess, as chatelaine and sophisticated observer of political mazes. These were to be the major roles of the marchesa of Mantua. Practical and efficient, she quickly learned the financial management of the court. Francesco gave her a generous allowance and properties that yielded increased incomes under her supervision. She soon knew how much was due her from taxes and tolls and the rents of her estates, and the cost of feeding dozens of servants and of keeping herself in a brilliance of jewels, silks, and furs so awesome that Louis XII of France suggested that his wife, Anne of Brittany, stay out of Italy because the superb Italian princesses, particularly the Este women, would shame her. Isabella and Francesco were a couple assiduously watched, not only for their curious politics (they often seemed to shout at each other from opposite sides of a political fence) and extravagant temperaments but for their style, the cultural riches of their court, and their élan. His horses were coveted by Henry VIII of England, who sent an ambassador to buy a number of the prized Gonzaga breed. Her fashions were copied in several European courts, her designs, her recipes for perfumes and cosmetics, frequently solicited. (The "Mantua makers" of English cloaks in the Italian style may have derived their designs from one of Isabella's models.) The ornate plump caps, frequently jewel-studded, that were worn in many Renaissance courts were devised by her. She kept herself apprised via correspondence and agents of what musical instruments were available in Venice, who was painting what and the prices being asked, which banking houses would make long-term loans, what books were being printed and sold, what the silk weavers and goldsmiths were creating, and what exotica might be expected of the lands beyond the Adriatic.

* By the time Isabella settled into Mantua, the young court had been diminished by the departure of Chiara, Francesco's eldest sister, and the death of Maddalena, the youngest. This left Sigismondo, who was to become a cardinal and in his limited way helpful in later years, and the youngest brother, Giovanni, who was the same age as Isabella and always a pleasant, trusted companion. Her favorite by far of the family was Elisabetta, three years her senior and the wife of Guidobaldo da Montefeltro, who had returned from her duchy of Urbino to greet her new sister-in-law in Mantua. From all contemporary reports we hear of Elisabetta's gentleness, her generosity and accomplishments. Castiglione's The Courtier was written in homage to her memory. "And if my mind be troubled with the loss of so many friends that have left me in this life, as it were in a wilderness full of sorrow, yet with how much more grief do I bear the affliction of my dear

lady's death, than of all the rest; since she was more worthy than all, and I more bounden to her." Pietro Bembo, guardian of Italian letters and secretary to Pope Leo X, had to say of Elisabetta: "I have seen many excellent and noble women, and have heard of some who were as illustrious for certain qualities, but in her alone among women, all virtues were united and brought together. I have never seen or heard of any one who was her equal, and know very few who have even come near her." Allowing for Renaissance hyperbole, we are still left with a remarkably admirable woman.

Her husband, Guidobaldo, was a gifted scholar in both Greek and Latin—he died with Virgil's lines on his lips—and, like his father, Federico, a judicious, humane ruler. He had several physical afflictions; he suffered from gout and probably arthritis, and most important, he was impotent. Elisabetta's reception into Urbino as the new duchess was a lyrical show of classicism, with women and children walking down the hills of Urbino carrying olive branches, while a chorus sang a cantata composed for the event. There were nymphs, and a goddess of Mirth, who offered the good wishes of the whole assemblage.

According to Isabella, who visited Elisabetta, the palaces at Urbino and Gubbio were "furnished in the most sumptuous manner; with vases of silver, rich draperies of gold and silk, and other rare and splendid articles. To this was added a great collection of statues and busts in bronze and marble, and of the most excellent pictures; but the prize of the palace and the envy of other princes was the superb and copious collection of books in Greek, Latin and other languages, with which the library was adorned, enriched with ornaments of silver and gold." Still, Elisabetta, who was quoted as asking a young relative, "Isn't it nice to lie with a man?" had no man with whom to lie. She was fond of Guidobaldo, respected him, and had no wish to hurt him; in any case, infidelity was not her style, forbearance was.

She kept in constant touch with her family, visiting Mantua frequently and for long periods. Francesco was especially fond of her, concerned about her health and safety, and when her court fell in their mature, troubled years, saw to her well-being and that of her family. (He was probably especially grateful for the care and affection Elisabetta showed his daughter Leonora, more motherly to the troubled girl than was her own mother.) When she came to Mantua to celebrate her brother's marriage, she was still mourning the loss of her sister Maddalena, who had died in childbirth, as well as mourning her own enforced infertility, and yet she did not neglect to bring her brother some of the Urbino gold plate and silver to adorn his palace. She stayed on for months after the wedding festivities, her spirits mending to the point where she and Isabella could take outings, spending days singing, walking, and dancing at the villa of Porto, which Francesco had built. They rode, they boated, they fished and hunted. They released falcons and petted small dogs and gamed lightly. They read and talked. They talked about the dwarf who was due to deliver soon and which relative deserved the tiny baby (assuming the new-born would also be dwarfed) everyone seemed to want. They talked about rare cats imported from the East and how much Isabella would enjoy having a few. They planned feasts, Isabella to serve the especially good breads of her kitchens. There was, they agreed, plenty of cheese in the larder and olive oil for cooking. It would be best not to use butter for frying; people said it caused leprosy. If beef wasn't available, what about game birds or geese stuffed with sweetened cheese? The wine recently brought in from Marmirolo should be drunk soon; it was not the kind to age well. And maybe more goblets should be ordered, so that each guest had his own cup; it was inelegant and probably unwholesome to have several people drinking from one large vessel, too common and vulgar a practice.

As young women and later, as matrons, the two also spoke of popes and emperors, of Milan and Venice as political friends or foes, and they spoke a good deal about art and architecture: refurbishing palace apartments, collecting paintings and objects to adorn them. Isabella, younger, more tempestuously avid—she spoke of herself as a greedy person and impatient to have what she wanted *now*—was the more talkative and the more competitive. Her sister-in-law had gone as a bride to a state furnished with many beauties, among them the magnificent Ducal Palace and the superb art collected by Guidobaldo's father, Federico da Montefeltro. Her young sister, Beatrice, had married into the Sforza wealth that hired Bramante as architect and supported Leonardo for eighteen years in his bewildering array of explorations, from the painting of *The Last Supper* to the design of tanks and flying machines. And there were her cousins in Naples and her brothers in Ferrara to emulate; she and Mantua were to be no less than any of them.

A woman of unusual vigor, Isabella made time between her extensive journeys, her duties as hostess, her intricate political maneuvers, her nonstop correspondence, to ask that ambassadors and agents traveling to and from Mantua, Ferrara, and Venice order or bring costly articles—not always paid for and a number ultimately returned. Beatrice had a stunning belt of semiprecious stones and she asked that a copy be sent her; a Ferrarese agent was to bring from Paris fine French linen and whatever else that was Frenchly elegant he thought she might fancy. Clusters of diamonds, silks from the East, pearls, rubies, figurines, a silver lute, and from a master organ-maker a clavichord like that of her sister Beatrice. As "la prima donna del Mondo" she would brook no delays; she threatened a slow painter, a too contemplative goldsmith, a hesitant carver of medallions, with imprisonment in freezing dungeons. It was her brothers' way with recalcitrant craftsmen, why not hers? Although she was an enthusiastic, and usually admiring, customer of the Aldine Press in Venice, appreciating the intelligently made and comparatively low-priced Greek and Roman classics produced for a widening spectrum of readers, she begged to differ, often severely, with Aldus Manutius, the publisher: He had not used the papers she had ordered, his prices were too high, and back on the next convoy of carts and mules the overpriced books would go.

Her busiest negotiations were with painters, the painter-decorators who designed settings for her collections, and the scholars who programmed the paintings for symbolic and allegorical meanings. As she had known in Ferrara and observed in Urbino, collectors' showrooms of favored paintings, miniature museums, were arranged as someone or other's *studiolo* and *grotta*, the latter usually the place for statuary. Isabella's *studiolo*, though sacked and ruined, is now one of the enchantments of the strange Palazzo Ducale. It is a place of small, jewel-like rooms decorated here with a fine grotesque on a white ceiling, there with an elegant marble insert in a door, and on several walls, exquisite panels of inlaid wood designed as views; and as if to stress Isabella's living presence and its enthusiasms, musical instruments. Occult symbols that suggest the musical or the privately superstitious enlace the rooms that adjoin a "secret garden." From these rooms there came her letters, issued by a royal "we," to painters and craftsmen: polite, cajoling, at times imperious, at times didactically heavy with instructions. Her frenetic searches for art acquisitions have earned her a reputation as an influential connoisseur, as an avaricious magpie, as having the tastes of a rich provincial who ventured only in the safeties of established reputations. There were in her elements of all these possible characters, as there were in collectors before and after Isabella. Her precise instructions to artists, giving them little leeway, were only partially urged by her willful character and commanding position. For centuries, the Church, the greatest patron of painting, very carefully described just what it wanted: The Virgin must wear a flowing blue robe, the child must hold a bird or a pomegranate or some other telling symbol in his legend; Saint Sebastian must be young and full-fleshed, to support his arrows most effectively; Saint Jerome always a starved old ascetic. Such precise stipulations had moved to a different provenance, that of the court classicists who invented flattering schemes out of Greek and Roman stories. Mantegna, long practiced in working for the Church and the Gonzaga, seemed to have had little difficulty, especially as he himself was an ardent, well-educated classicist. Perugino struggled for a long time with "you may do only this, you may not make other changes." From the Bellini, the leading painters of Venice, Isabella received apologies for delays and more delays; ultimately she received from them a couple of urban maps, made by their old father, Jacopo.

* Isabella did not, could not, program a number of the paintings that were supposedly portraits of herself. Quite early, she was painted in her father's court by Cosmé Tura. Some time later, while she was still young and in her father's court, she was painted by Giovanni Santi, Raphael's father. These youthful portraits were unquestionably authentic. As the reigning lady of Mantua she sat for Mantegna, whose painting displeased her; she dismissed the work as that of an inept portraitist. When Ludovico Sforza was taken by the French, in 1500, Leonardo returned to Florence by way of Mantua, where he was induced, in the most flattering terms, to do two sketches—one now gone, the other, in the Louvre, generally accepted as a fairly authentic portrait of Isabella in her mid-twenties. The profile view, with little coloring, shows her light-eyed and light-haired, strong-featured and alert, attractive but not especially good-looking. She was eager to have the sketch become a full Leonardo painting, but he was soon too busy with other matters, first as military consultant to Venice, then as Architetto Ingegnere Generale for Cesare Borgia.

As she approached forty and worried about her looks, she commissioned portraits done at long distance, often pastiches of old retouched paintings. Francesco Francia, with whom she disputed the color of her eyes, worked from verbal descriptions and an undistinguished extant portrait. Francia's painting is gone, but we have a woman with dark eyes painted by Rubens after a lost Titian, and a richly dressed woman wearing one of Isabella's famous turbans, as painted by Giulio Romano; both possibly Isabella and probably not. Lorenzo Costa, official painter in Mantua after the death of Mantegna, painted at least one portrait, which was, for a time, claimed by Bernhard Berenson to be an authentic image. There is in Hampton Court a *Lady* by Perugino that is suspected of being Isabella, and so is another by Parmigianino. There is no certainty that any of these were actual portraits. It is a sad and ordinary paradox that a woman who displayed herself so handsomely and effectively was driven by vanity and fear of age and obesity to avoid faithful, direct portraiture. We are left with one possibly sound image, selecting as a true portrait Leonardo's Louvre sketch—and that retouched—not necessarily for its verity but for our faith in his genius.

The most steadily reliable character portraits derive from her correspondence, her dealings with a world of people, craftsmen to popes, and her political minuets. She had observed political adroitness in her father's court. Strength and valor she had absorbed from her mother, who had defended the fortress at Ferrara when it was under attack and the duke Ercole elsewhere. She had been trained in decorum and discipline along with the arts of elegant address, and yet, as we know, could cut sharply and loudly when she was vexed by disobedient artists or hurt, especially by Francesco.

Her husband respected her confidence, her style, her connoisseurship, and seemed to have loved her, in his fashion, during the early years of their marriage. His fashion, which became increasingly careless over the passage of years, was not enough for her. Never the patient Griselda, she protested, eliciting from him the complaint that she was excessively quarrelsome. In one terse, bitter letter, she responds that there would be no contention between them if she had any proofs of his love, but for some time past there had been little, a fact obvious not only to herself but to members of both their families and to the courts in which he displayed his mistresses. It was a courageous, futile struggle against the very nature of things, endured also by her sister, her sisters-in-law, her mother, her cousins, her daughters-in-law.

Mantegna and Alberti

Andrea Mantegna, born in 1431, probably could not remember a time when he didn't draw or paint. At the age of ten, he was adopted by Francesco Squarcione and taken into his teeming atelier in Padua. He was set to copying paintings, casts, and casts of casts on Greco-Roman subjects, training that, according to Bernhard Berenson, imprisoned the painter's native genius for most of his life. The apprenticeship with Squarcione was only one strand in the education of an intelligent, gifted, and ambitious youngster responding to the fervor for art and learning in Padua. Established in the early thirteenth century, its university was becoming world renowned in the fifteenth, with scholars flocking to be taught from its extensive list of courses and with painters joining or establishing its many workshops, one of them the studio that produced, late in the fourteenth century, Cennino Cennini's *Libro dell'Arte*, a handbook of precise instructions in several techniques, the first study that began to pull away from the precepts of medieval painting. (It was Cennini who pointed out, long before Leonardo did, that painting a panel was a "gentleman's job, for you may do anything you want to with velvets on your back.")

From the classicists and their dream of life in a "New Rome" grew the classicism of Mantegna's work and a lifelong passion for antiquities—an enthusiasm shared by other prosperous artists: Brunelleschi, Donatello, and Ghiberti—that made him a respected connoisseur and kept him in constant debt. The young Andrea must have learned something of the emotive power of painting from Giotto's Scrovegni Chapel in Padua, although Giotto may have appeared somewhat too Byzantine to his Rome-centered eye. Donatello was in Padua for some years, leaving the city his equestrian statue of the *condottiere* known as "Gattemelata," a superb example of the monumental inextricably fused with the human. Excursions with friends into Tuscany may have taught Mantegna the naturalist strength of Masaccio's murals in Florence, the pioneering architecture of Brunelleschi and his dome, the flow of figures in Ghiberti's doors. In Siena he may have studied the works of the Lorenzetti, both well advanced in perspective, and observed in Pietro Lorenzetti's *Birth of the Virgin* the spacing of full-bodied, speaking figures moving freely through a canvas.

By the time Mantegna was seventeen, he had already, according to Vasari, accomplished "a picture worthy of a mature and experienced craftsman," which was placed on the high altar of the Church of Santa Sofia in Padua (gone by the late seventeenth century). When Squarcione was commissioned to paint the chapel of Saint Christopher in the Eremitani Church of Sant'Agostino, he entrusted the frescoes to Mantegna and Niccolò Pizzolo, a gifted painter and a Renaissance roisterer who lived with a sword and many animosities. Pizzolo was killed after he had finished a few impressive sections, and the rest was left to Mantegna, then eighteen. Though much was destroyed during a World War II bombardment, enough remains of the *Martyrdom of Saint James* to astonish with its daring perspective and the "Romanness" of the scene: the massive decorated arch, the armor of the soldiers, and, above all, the heroic figures in a convincingly imagined ancient Rome.

When the Bellini—father Jacopo, sons Gentile and Giovanni—left Venice for more promising Padua, a center of Italian art then rivaled only by Florence, they looked hard at young Mantegna's growing achievements and invited him to work with them, one of the lures Niccolosia Bellini, Jacopo's daughter, who was accompanied by a respectable dowry. Never casual about money or fame—and the Bellini had the edge over Squarcione in both—Mantegna married the girl in 1453, when he had just entered his twenties. Squarcione was loud and bitter about the loss of his stellar assistant, his adopted son. He attacked the work in the Eremitani church, ten years in the painting, with a complaint reiterated by other critics, saying, according to Vasari, "that they were inferior work since when he did them Andrea imitated marble statues." He would have done better to paint them as if they actually were of marble, "seeing that his figures resembled ancient statues and such-like things rather than living creatures." Vasari agrees, claiming that Andrea found ancient statues more sublime than nature's forms, and Berenson joins them in his judgment that at times Mantegna "painted, so to speak, in Latin . . . labouring to reconstruct the world as seen by an imperial Roman and to reconstruct it in Roman visual language." But Berenson adds that, on the whole, Mantegna owed more to Donatello and other Florentines than he owed to the antique. In addition, there was the exchange of painting gifts between the Bellini and their new in-law: their observation of landscape and living flesh for his lessons of sculpturesque dignity, particularly impressive to Giovanni.

With increasingly important commissions and the friendship of renowned scholars, with whom Mantegna made lyrical journeys, wandering with the Muses and searching out archaeological inscriptions, came an invitation to work in the court of Mantua. Ludovico Gonzaga, always eager to make his city as notable as any in Italy, first wrote the painter in 1456 and then sent an agent, his sculptor-architect, Luca Fancelli, to make generous offers; there would be a good stipend, comfortable lodgings, wood to burn against damp cold, wheat to feed the family, now six, and a boat for the journey. Mantegna was in no hurry to enclose himself in Mantua, away from his friends in Padua and the animation of its university and the ateliers. In the manner of his artist contemporaries who were beginning to know their worth as the coveted prizes of princes, Mantegna played hard to get, using the quite legitimate reason of commissions yet to complete. He needed time for the altarpiece for the church of San Zeno in Verona, at least six months, and a commission for the *podestà* of Padua would take additional time. Gonzaga, a seasoned politician, knew how to wait while he pursued the painter with subtle tenacity.

The Mantegna family settled into Mantua near the end of 1459, but there are no records of work done for Gonzaga until 1463, when mention is made of the painter's stay at Goito, a vast country palace then being decorated. Other works of this early time were a triptych painted for a small palace chapel described as "containing many small but most beautiful figures"; the *Death of the Virgin*, set against a view of Mantua and its waters; a *Saint George* that echoes Donatello. Also of these years, the *Dead Christ*, a culminating study in perspective yet horrifyingly of the flesh, a painting Mantegna would not part with in his lifetime; it was sold by a son to settle his father's debts after he died.

Life with Mantegna was not easy, no more than it was with Michelangelo, Leonardo, the Bellini, and other esteemed artists before and later. "Not now, maybe later"; "What happened to my meager stipend?" they would say in varying tones of tact, or no tact at all. Ludovico took it, as his children and grandchildren did, with generosity and grace. The first extant letter between patron and painter follows the deeply trodden path first marked out by the artists who adorned Egyptian tombs and the Assyrians who engraved on the walls of their temples the deeds of their warrior kings: Mantegna complains that his money is trickling in too erratically. Ludovico, himself often short of funds, admonishes his treasurers to be more prompt in their disbursements to the painter. Another letter asks for money to make the painter's house more livable and attractive, befitting an artist whose skills, it was said, rivaled those of the great classical artists, even Alexander's "sublime" Apelles. Ludovico had an ample sum sent. He gave his artist a country property for the family's summer use and patiently interceded in the quarrels that "our delight," as the marquis addressed him, stirred up and kept boiling. There was trouble with a gardener, with a tailor, with ill-spoken neighbors, with engravers whom the artist had assaulted, insisting that the men had stolen his plates. A country neighbor, a member of an upstanding old Mantuan family, had stolen, the painter insisted, five hundred—no more, no less—quinces from his most beautiful tree. The neighbor complained in court, pointing out that irascible Mantegna was then involved in five lawsuits with various neighbors.

But he was, as he kept pointing out, enormously industrious, though admittedly slow, in designing decorations and ornaments (among them tarot cards), producing paintings, designs for tapestries, and engravings (he was one of the first engravers of his time), whose number and quality attracted connoisseur visitors and wider fame and praise. Leonardo came in 1483, as interested in Mantegna's effects of perspective and trompe l'oeil as in the antiquities the painter kept amassing. There were pressing invitations from other courts, which Mantegna rejected—one such refusal handled by the marquis himself, who apologized for his rude painter (in the immortal terms "you know how temperamental these artists are"). After the death of Ludovico and the early death of his son Federico, who had had a serious interest in all the arts and antiquities, Mantegna, as always carrying a heavy load of debts, became edgier than usual and appealed for patronage to Lorenzo de' Medici, whom he met when the Florentine prince came to explore Mantua and its art. Affairs in Mantua proved less difficult, however, than his fears had projected, and with the marriage of the marquis Francesco to Isabella of the Este, for whom the painter had worked briefly, he felt as secure again in Mantua as he ever could feel.

In the mid 1480s, Mantegna turned again to the ancient Rome he had revered and studied all his life, to create a set of large panels concerned with a triumph of Julius Caesar and, by implication, the triumphs of the family of *condottieri* whom the painter served. Planned to adorn yet another palace in the growing complex, the monumental project was interrupted by a summons from Pope Innocent VIII, demanding that Mantegna join with other painters in decorating the Belvedere Villa in the Vatican. Francesco Gonzaga knighted Mantegna, granted him a valuable tract of land, and sent him off to spend two years, 1488 to 1490, on frescoes that were ultimately erased, along with the works of several fellow artists, in later Vatican changes. Mantegna predictably didn't like fifteenth-century Rome; he was probably not sufficiently honored in the company of other honored painters; he was homesick, worried about his family, worried about the care given his unfinished "Triumph"; and he complained that the Pope gave him no assistants and, suffering the disease of all patrons, paid too slowly. Francesco, who had known the painter all his life and treated him rather like a vexing but awesome old uncle, promised to see that the "Triumph" would be well taken care of, pledged he would find employment for one of Andrea's sons, and urged him to take care of his health.

The Roman exile ended with compliments and money and a warm welcome in Mantua, where there was the important task of finishing the "Triumph" (only nine of the planned ten were completed). The monumental work was painted in tempera on canvas, each section nine feet tall. As in the Eremitani church, the scenes disclose not only a scholar's knowledge but an uncanny, immediate involvement: We stand with the artist in the Roman Forum, observing and hearing the sounds that come from trumpeters and standard bearers, the bearers of captured spoils and images of foreign gods; the elephants, the pretty boys, the priests, the train of captives, the jesters. Finally, the great Caesar himself, about to be crowned with a laurel wreath by Victory, the supreme accolade of worshipful thanks for his conquest of Gaul. The animation and freshness (in spite of "restorations" by several maladroit hands) stem from a stunning melding of scholarship, imagination, and consummate skill. "The study of the antique supplies form, nature gives moment and the last touch of life," said Goethe, analyzing the strengths of the panels.

Except on occasions when they were used as stage decorations for Roman comedies, the "Triumph" paintings remained in their original palace space for over a hundred years, much visited and admired, their fame and beauty widely spread throughout Europe by way of the engravings Mantegna made from them and the series of woodcuts produced by Andrea Andreani more than half a century after the painter's death.

The marquis Francesco, quite contented with the symbiotic relationship that gave his painter lands, money, and honors, and himself stature as patron of that painter whose "virtue is known to the world," tried to ease the declining years of the quirky old man. He saw to it that his debts were reduced and his old quarrels settled, gave one of his sons a position in the court, and consented to add another son to the art payroll as one of his father's assistants. The complaints were fewer now; old age and high prestige spread a calm only occasionally disturbed by accusations of thievery by neighbors. Francesco's wife, the marchesa Isabella, ambitious from her youth to have her own private *studiolo* hung with art works, commissioned Mantegna, Perugino, and Costa to create for her the exquisite retreat she had for years envisioned. At first she petitioned the services of Leonardo and of Giovanni Bellini in her search for the unrivaled best, but Leonardo, absorbed in his variety of scientific studies, was not interested, and Bellini resented the many strictures—specific allegorical theme, size of canvas, size of figures—and produced little for Isabella. Mantegna's notable contributions to the miniature gallery were two allegorical paintings, now in the Louvre. Based on subjects proposed by a court classicist, they suggest views of herself that Isabella found pleasing: *The Expulsion of the Vices* has a windy, helmeted Minerva chasing grotesques into a quagmire, the drive assisted and adorned by cloudlets of butterfly-like putti. The *Parnassus* is a painting of the Muses (the pregnant lady in the center said to be Isabella herself) dancing and singing to Apollo's lyre. Off to one side, Mercury and a velvety-winged, bejeweled Pegasus; on the crest of an earth bridge stand armored Mars and nude Venus, and nearby, Amor, the inspiration for love and music—the whole an airy, musical composition.

Another masterwork, the *Madonna della Vittoria*, has a distasteful provenance, an episode in one of the anti-Semitic manias that spotted Mantuan history. Daniele Norsa, a Jew, bought a house in 1495 whose facade was decorated with a painting of the Madonna. Norsa asked permission of a local bishop to remove it. Permission was granted. Nevertheless, the house was attacked during celebrations of Ascension Day by zealots stirred to a frenzy by a fanatic friar. In spite of the bishop and an appeal to the marquis, a body of Mantuan elders judged the Jew a despoiler of a most sacred image, sentenced him to build a new church on the site and to commission Mantegna to paint another Virgin. At the time of these events, Francesco was engaged in battle with the French. In the course of the battle he committed himself to the care of the Virgin and promised her a new church. Daniele Norsa's money paid the major expenses; the elaborate ceremony, processionals, and stage management that accompanied the painting from Mantegna's studio to the church were paid for by Francesco, immortalized by his painter as a valiant knight in shining dark armor, kneeling in thanks to the Virgin who helped effect his triumph.

Mantegna's was a remarkable career—one of the most admired and studied of Italy's painters, he spent over forty years under the protection of princes who dealt openhandedly with him. His old age was still artistically fruitful, his children were grown and comfortably established; he was the owner of property and coveted rarities. He might have been fairly contented, but he could not keep up with his commissions and his ever-mounting debts. Eager for more properties, as always, he took yet another house, for which he was to pay in three installments. When he was pressed for payments he couldn't make, he appealed to Isabella, offering to sell her the dearest of his antique treasures, a bust of one of the two empresses named Faustina. Her response was to instruct an agent to bargain hard for the piece, to offer the painter less than the one hundred ducats he wanted. The dickering continued while the creditors pressed, but the old man got his price, giving up Faustina "with great reluctance, recommending it to my care [wrote the agent] with much solicitude and with such demonstrations of jealous affection that if he were not to see it again for six days I feel convinced he would die." He was dead within six weeks, in the fall of 1506. Neither Isabella nor Francesco mourned deeply, although good-natured Francesco kept the two Mantegna sons in his employ as a payment of his debt to the artist, who had ennobled his court and had painted him as a hero. It was fellow artists who felt the loss; Dürer, on his way to visit Mantegna on the day he died, spoke of it as the saddest day of his life.

A memorial chapel in the Church of Sant'Andrea, appropriately close to Alberti's classical facade, had been paid for and the handsome decorations designed by the painter himself. The laurel-wreathed bust in the chapel may be a self-portrait. If so, it is one of the most merciless views into a mirror of any artist until we meet Rembrandt and Goya. The heavy features in the worn face speak of barely contained anger; the tight-lipped mouth is shut in a line of discontent; the eyes, coldly skeptical, speak of the irritability and displeasure in a life he himself filled with worries and obstacles. Or does the face reflect his creative struggle to combine the revered antique with living, breathing humanity? He seems to have resolved the melding brilliantly in the "Triumph," in the Camera degli Sposi murals, in his Muses dancing on Parnassus. Possibly he felt that the achievement was not—as it rarely is—altogether compatible with the vision. Nor does the unconsoled face betray the satisfaction of having directed the brushes of numerous painters in a long, imposing list: Signorelli, Cosmé Tura, the Bellini, Caroto, Costa, Raphael, as well as the many anonymous artists who studied Mantegna's engravings, and, on the other end of the artistic scale, the apogees, Dürer and Leonardo. Though his prominence waned over the years, we still find references to his work in much later periods, as in a recent small show at the National Gallery of London, which pointed up the unmistakable link of a Degas composition to one designed by the old Mantuan.

* When Roberto Rossellini prepared his didactic film series on the Italian Renaissance, his commentator, the ideal "Man of the Renaissance," was a slight-figured Leon Battista Alberti—who would not have used the phrase, unknown in his time, but who would certainly have agreed with its definition; his assessment of himself included all the essential "Man of the Renaissance" ingredients, and a few more. Alternating "he" and "I" in a self-portrait as the universal man, Alberti begins with the obvious statement that "he" must be well educated and zealous for fame, a goal unabashedly pursued by all achievers. His skills must encompass the handling of horses and arms, of musical instruments and "other most strange and difficult things." A capacity for painting and modeling is essential and a study of letters, and when these tire him, he may turn to wrestling, javelin throwing, and war games, hurling the lance with absolute accuracy and shooting an arrow so that it can pierce the thickest iron breastplate.

The scrim of the third person is pulled aside and we are soon given a chronological autobiography. Concentration on the study of civil and canon law impaired Alberti's health, so he turned to writing a play, *Philodoxeos*, issued as an original creation until someone pointed out that it was merely a rediscovered antique. (That the upright Alberti did not put the record straight was not startling to his contemporaries; plagiarism was no sin—if it was done with discretion and taste—and the faking of "discoveries" was common, the most famous example the *Sleeping Cupid* of the young Michelangelo, who presented the figure he had made as a piece of Roman antiquity.)

While the Alberti clan, a family of merchants and bankers, were in exile, Leon Battista's father died and all the wealth was absorbed by an uncle, who left his nephew destitute. Plagued by poverty and illness, the young man nevertheless studied mathematics and wrote verses and "works on love of such a kind as to inculcate good habits in those who studied them and to foster the quiet of the soul," probably the "erotic works" mentioned by Vasari. Since Alberti had lived in exile in his youth, his native Tuscan was inelegant, but that was remedied by persistent study, an achievement exquisite enough to be imitated by fellow intellectuals and conducive to formulating a grammar, written in 1443, the first of its kind in Italy. When Alberti was about thirty, he wrote for his relatives a group of books—in his perfect Tuscan—called *On the Family,* which he completed in ninety days.

Substantial sections of the work, examining the family's several aspects—as a unit of parents and children, as a clan, as a group related to the state—bring us back to Vittorino da Feltre. Like that master, Alberti knows that the body, "the noblest and most graceful of living things," is to be well cared for and used with consciousness of its strong beauty. He agrees with Vittorino that an elementary knowledge of writing and numbers, the basic equipment of most Florentine boys, essential in that commercial center, is not enough. Poetry, painting, music, the history of heroic Roman deeds, are not only enhancements of life but in a profound way round out the well-functioning man, whether he is destined to become a lawyer, a merchant, or a leader of troops. Where Vittorino was enlightened in his attitude toward women, eager to help them strive toward the farthest reaches of their capacities, Alberti felt they should rely on the judgment and will of the "masters," who were advised not to make wives privy to business secrets or give them access to records and strongboxes.

In spite of envious foul-speakers and his own tendency to "wrath and bitterness of spirit," Alberti disciplined himself to patience and gentleness. He did not court the princes who respected him, since he "detested all forms of ambition and adulation," but he did watch his general comportment in order not to displease anyone, stressing, as Castiglione did in his *Courtier*, the important art of appearing artless: "art should be added to art lest anything seem to be done artfully when one is walking about the city, riding a horse, or speaking"—an important ingredient of *grazia*, elegance and harmony. He was happiest among the friends with whom he discussed literature and practiced writing, and whose portraits he painted or modeled in wax as he dictated his little essays. When alone, he painted and modeled himself so that "he could be more easily known to strangers approaching him." Inevitably, he wrote on sculpture and painting in keen and adventuresome treatises, many of his observations derived from a "camera oscura," a device which diminishes and enlarges figures, opens to broad landscapes, and helps refine studies of perspective.

This awesome man of many skills became a prophet when he foretold disasters that would visit his city of Florence and events that would affect the Papacy in years to come. At the same time, he continued to work on his own perfection, constantly practicing tolerance of pain and cold and conquering a violent revulsion to garlic and honey. He asked questions of cobblers and masons and bricklayers, examined gems and the faces of old men, and delighted in the wonderful things that men can achieve.

Through this maze of interests and achievements ran one steady thread: a profound interest in and knowledge of architecture, the core of his concentration being the work of the Roman authority Vitruvius, whose ten volumes on building, the engineering of waterworks, designs for military defenses, machines for construction, and elements of city planning, were most influential in molding Renaissance architecture. Vitruvius guided Alberti's approach to architectural commissions and to the ten volumes on architecture he himself completed in 1452. In spite of his admiration for cobblers and poor old men, Alberti remained the aes-thete and aristocrat, concentrating on the places for "pleasure and delight" that were built by the rich, their villas to follow the scheme of palaces, with forecourts large enough to allow for horse racing and inner courts large enough for swimming, walking, and taking the fresh air. From room to room he goes, describing the uses and arrangements most appropriate to each. Since the Greeks kept their women segregated, the women of Alberti's contem-poraries should be kept in palaces "dedicated to religion and chastity," although he must have known that privileged Italian women were not inclined to live out their lives in chapels. To allay the dangerous boredom of young women and virgins, their rooms were to be fitted up in the "neatest and most delicate manner." The husband and wife must have separate chambers, so that "when she lies in" he will not be disturbed. The mistress of the family should have an apartment from which she can hear all the activities of the house, while her old mother lives in a remote room, equipped with a fireplace to comfort and cheer her. Allotting logical spaces to other members of the family, their servants and visitors, Alberti continues with an observation that swallows, young and old, are meticulously careful that their nests not be fouled. "Since nature has given us this excellent instruc-tion, I think we ought by no means to neglect it," an engaging example of Alberti's verbal grace and a reminder of how dirty and odoriferous the fifteenth century could be.

By the time Alberti became closely involved with Ludovico Gonzaga, to whom he presented a copy of his volumes on archi-tecture, he had advised Pope Nicholas V in the rebuilding of sections of Rome, had built the prestigious Rucellai palace in Florence, and had transformed a church of Sigismondo Malatesta, lord of Rimini, into a bold, handsome Roman temple, a temple of love dedicated to a favored mistress. Ludovico, who had suc-cessfully lured Mantegna to Mantua, was equally eager to use the talents of this widely respected font of knowledge and skill. As assistant, to supervise his ambitious building program—some of it never realized—Ludovico hired a capable, responsible stone-mason from Florence, Luca Fancelli, on whom Alberti relied to see to the completion of the buildings he designed. Ludovico himself became well educated in architecture and developed a reputation for being a connoisseur of building "in the ancient style." At times, Mantuan projects appeared to be creations of a committee of three: the master architect, Alberti; the superintendent of works, Fancelli; and their disciple, pupil, critic, and sponsor, Ludovico. Ludovico, though breezily friendly with the devoted Fancelli, treated Alberti as an honored guest whose designs he defended against other members of his family, to whom he gave financial advice, and for whom he set aside a rural palazzo for undisturbed work and leisure.

The two monuments Alberti left in Mantua are incomplete, although Federico Gonzaga continued to have work done on them after his father's death. The Church of San Sebastiano, the first Renaissance church built on the Greek cross plan, was too "modern," too non-Gothic, to please the family, who said it looked like anything but a church. It was built, as churches dedicated to Saint Sebastian often were, to guard against the plague, but before it was finished, plans were changed; the building was neglected for a long while and centuries later remodeled. Only the crypt and the exterior arches show the distinctive Alberti eye and hand. Sant'Andrea too underwent modifications, but the basic scheme of inner arches and the noble facade, work that required twenty years of Fancelli's attention, speak eloquently of the architect and his style.

In spite of the cynicism and occasional dark pessimism of his time, Alberti believed, like his fellow humanists, in the perfectability of man, and to that perfectability, as writer, as educator, as architect, he directed himself, balancing instructions from the Roman past with inquiry into the new. This melding of the rediscovered and the exploratory left a long influence on Italian architecture, the Rimini and Mantua churches being frequently remembered in schemes of subsequent buildings. It is difficult to measure the effect of Alberti's books on painting and sculpture, nor can we be certain that he actually redesigned family life, but as an influential presence, he pressed forcefully the more optimistic humanist tenets of his age. Let the ignorant swing helplessly on the wheel of fortune; Alberti's man was mightier, the source of his own fortune and misfortune, nor should he ever "conclude that the power of gaining praise, wealth and reputation should be attributed to fortune rather than ability." "Man can accomplish all he wishes to," Alberti said, offering his own person and achievements as convincing proof.

F * I * V * E

By the time he was married, Francesco Gonzaga had been the lord of Mantua for five years by imperial investiture, not as secure a position as it might seem. Along with his rule, Francesco inherited two uncles, Stefano and Francesco Secco, who had acted as regents after Federico's death, ostensibly to protect the boy from being victimized or even destroyed by two others uncles, Rodolfo and Gianfrancesco Gonzaga. From Milan, Ludovico Sforza continued, as he had during Federico's time, to dictate the job requirements and rewards due his new captain, Francesco Gonzaga. A renewed contract stipulated that should there be war between Milan and Venice, Francesco's spoils would be Verona, Vicenza, Brescia, Bergamo, and the trio, Asola, Lonato, and Peschiera, should he win them. The same contract called for an alliance that would last for ten years.

Four years later, in 1490, the year of his marriage, Francesco, spurred by suspicion of Sforza's erratic politics and by concern for his own security, signed on with Venice. Though he and Francesco Secco had their difficulties with each other, a momentary peace sent them out together to the Veneto in 1491. When they reached Verona, a spate of accusations and counteraccusations exploded. Francesco accused his uncle of setting his cook and his secretary to spy on him, probably planning his death; he had the two imprisoned. Secco in turn accused Francesco's councillor of spying on him and had *him* taken prisoner. When they reached Venice, a surface reconciliation was forced on them by the doge.

However, Francesco was quite obviously searching for ways to rid himself of Francesco Secco, reduce Stefano Secco's control or put him out of the way also, and, finally, rule Mantua alone. Keenly aware of the way his winds were blowing, Francesco Secco removed himself from responsibility to Mantua, to Milan, to Venice, by becoming one of the heads of Lorenzo de' Medici's army, his station to be Pisa.

Home again after treating with Venice, now lord of his house and of a capable, spirited wife, Francesco devoted himself to pleasant pursuits. Although he had been under the tutelage of a son of the scholar Filelfo, and other skilled tutors, not too much that was intellectual rubbed off on him. He could write a forceful letter, appreciated men of learning, took care of crotchety old Mantegna as his father and grandfather had done, and gave his wife money enough for her to make their court a celebrated font of cultural pleasures. But he preferred hunting and jousting, the breeding of falcons and dogs, and especially the development of an outstanding line of horses. In spite of the fact that leading *condottieri* like himself were given some leeway, there were states that forbade the exportation of horses. Spain, where there was an *oratore* from Mantua, was willing to sell, however, and in spite of the cost and difficulties of shipping, Francesco bought many animals from Spanish stables, and from Sicily and North Africa. Because his agents were expert judges and Francesco paid dealers well, he received the best horses, which, bred with the Gonzaga horses, produced handsome animals fit to be offered as royal gifts, sturdy and responsive enough to be efficient mounts in battle. It was a profitable business-avocation: Large numbers of horses were killed in combat; large numbers were bought to replace them. When he wasn't warring or jousting or supervising his stables, Francesco womanized, at times inspired by the pornography written for him by a nameless Bolognese student of the law.

Along with the physicality there was intelligent curiosity. As early as the time of his investiture, he made a journey with a few friends, all incognito, to know other parts of Italy and to the emperor's court at Frankfurt, observing that which would be handy to know for a prince and a leader of armies. He had a spontaneity that his wife lacked, a ready warmth that prompted affectionate letters to his sisters and an unconventional, good-hearted response to the news that his second child, like his first, was a girl. Their mother was sorely disappointed, especially since her sister Beatrice gave birth to two sons, but he consoled her by giving her a fine bauble and telling her he was quite contented; where there were girls born there would certainly be sons. Although Isabella adored her first son, variously loved the boys that came later, and never quite liked the sad, beautiful firstborn, Leonora—it was her Este grandparents who insisted that the child be painted, not her mother—Francesco loved all his children when he had the time, without selective emphases.

"*Valoroso e magnanimo*," Francesco had a concomitant impulsiveness that edged on irresponsibility; the willful boy in him lasted too long and gathered suspicion as an unreliable ally. Although Venice frowned and even ordered that he not play on enemy ground, Francesco went incognito and without Isabella to Milan to enjoy the wedding festivities that celebrated the marriage of Beatrice d'Este and Ludovico il Moro, recently employer and ally, now nominally adversary, but in this context a friend and relative who arranged tourneys of jousting among the most skillful knights of several courts. Since Francesco's prowess was considerable, the incognito may or may not have held. His wife, a dedicated traveler, an accomplished dancer and singer, like most Renaissance people robustly immodest, also loved displaying her several kinds of high style. The Ferrarese wedding festivities for Beatrice and Ludovico, combined with the celebration of the marriage of the Este brother Alfonso to Anna Sforza, gave Isabella yet another stage. Before a background of triumphal arches, uninhibited Roman comedy, vats of wine, and mounds of food, Isabella and her new sister-in-law led off the dancing, first pacing out polite court measures and then, as the night grew merrier, jouncing about in hearty country dances. In the summer of that same year, Isabella went again to visit her sister in Milan. Heeding reports of grumbling in Venice, Francesco avoided Milan and took off for the *pali* in Lucca and Siena, at that time contests of gentlemen riders.

In spite of Francesco's variety of extracurricular activities, there was no forgetting for long that he was the captain of a major army and that Venice demanded obedience and service for the generous salary she was paying him. The elaborate systems of eavesdropping maintained by Mantua and Venice brought menacing news of invasions soon to speed out of France, news that called for swift preparation. Unfortunately, Lorenzo de' Medici, who strove for concerted action among the principal states of

Italy, died in 1492. While the rest of the Italians continued to contend among themselves, Francesco managed to stay clear of danger with the help of his alert agents and his own nimble skill at his "audacious, dangerous game," as it has been described, a game of feigned loyalties as captain of various troops, changing fealties as it suited his estimate of the safety of his state. One of the advantages he had and used well several times was the right, sanctioned by the Pope, to have steady relations with the Turks. His representatives could send back reports to the Pope on events and plans in the rapidly expanding empire to the east, and his most courtly speakers and reasoners could meet with the sultan in Constantinople, as he himself did in 1492, to present gifts and to arrange a barter of Mantuan woolen cloth and mules for swift Arab horses. Thus Francesco gathered information and the horses he needed for his growing army of mercenaries and for his own subjects, who in threatened times were required to serve as soldiers.

Life with Venice continued in its jumpy course. Because she was rich and her finances well administered, Francesco's pay came regularly. Commercial dealings between the cities remained active and profitable, Mantua now capable of transshipping through Venice vats of oils and wine, cured fish, cereals, cheese, sausage, woven silks and wools. Isabella profited with lavish gifts, the poor and sick of Mantua profited because their care was more generously seen to; the troops profited with the purchase of more and improved crossbows and pikes. But the relationship between Gonzaga and the Venetian senate still trembled with suspicion. If Francesco could leap from Milan to the service of Venice, why should he—a heedless adventurer, as they judged him—not return to Milan's Sforza, a close relative, a man who had promised him Venetian territories, the possibility quite remote yet alluring. On the other hand, Francesco heard rumors that Venice planned with France to dismember Mantua. Actually, it was Il Moro— the dusky Ludovico Sforza—who signed a pact with Charles VIII in the spring of 1493 that helped open Italy to invasion by the French, a pact that began the Italian wars and ultimately buried Ludovico. In the meantime, Francesco walked carefully, delicate in his dealings with La Serenissima, full of graceful compliments and expressions of gratitude for the helpful role played by the Venetian ambassador to Rome in trying, if unsuccessfully, to have brother Sigismondo made a cardinal. When Ludovico, hoping to win back Francesco, announced an imminent visit to Mantua, Francesco immediately explained to Venice that he had tried to avoid the meeting, and to sweeten his position, he reported what he knew of Ludovico's plans, already suspected by the alert papal powers and keen Venice.

Between consultations with Venice, Francesco strengthened his fortresses and castles, inspected and improved his roads and waterways, and made tentative, friendly, "just in case" gestures toward Ludovico, toward the French, toward the emperor. On Isabella's—and Francesco's?—orders, Benedetto Capilupi, Mantua's leading statesman and emissary and at times Isabella's secretary, was commissioned to obtain from Beatrice d'Este-Sforza a promise that Il Moro would come to Mantua's aid should she be attacked. To attract ties with the emperor, Capilupi was charged with requesting that the investiture of Francesco be reconfirmed as an official imperial act and that Mantua be given formal permission to establish a *studio*, a small university. The information that dashed from Milan to Mantua and on to Venice, the usual mélange of facts and fictions for Venice to unravel, included a report that Il Moro had lent Charles VIII the colossal sum of 400,000 ducats to pay for yet more mercenaries and artillery.

When feeble Gian Galeazzo Sforza died in late 1494, of "excessive coitus"—a not uncommon diagnosis, though poisoning was not excluded in the gossip, since he was a virtual prisoner in Milan—Ludovico had for some time been in possession of the treasures, the troops, the bastions, the government of the dukedom. He *was* the duke; only official acknowledgment was lacking. For the solemn rituals that made him indisputably duke of Milan, Ludovico rewarded the emperor with the hand of his niece Bianca Maria Sforza, who was accompanied by 400,000 ducats in gold and 40,000 in jewels. After busying himself with consolidating his domestic position among a people who did not much like him, by erasing some taxes, easing others, and paying long-standing debts, he sent tactful, conciliatory messages to Venice and continued to direct the strategies of France.

Diligent in forwarding to Venice information gathered, among several sources, from agents close to the French armies, Francesco, however, continued to stay away from Milan. When the Gonzaga were invited to attend the baptism of Ludovico and Beatrice's firstborn, Massimiliano, excuses were invented for not attending: an important meeting in Venice: no suitable horses to bring with him for the jousting; recent entertainments had so depleted his treasury that there was no money for an appropriate gift for the child. Isabella went, not only to celebrate the birth of her nephew but to help cool differences between Ludovico and Beatrice, who could not brook rivalry with favored ladies of Sforza's court. (The enchanting Cecilia Gallerini, painted by Leonardo as *The Lady with Ermine*, was the rarest of mistresses: of an aristocratic family; a gifted writer in Latin and of Italian poetry; knowledgeable in music, philosophy, and the arts, with which she enriched Sforza's court; graceful, ineffably beautiful. Protests from Beatrice and her father forced Il Moro to marry her off after acknowledging her child as his. This stopped the succession of major involvements until a year before Beatrice's death, when he raised Lucrezia Crivelli to the position once held by Gallerini, had a son by her as well, and commissioned Leonardo to paint the lovely woman, who may have lived on, although the matter is in dispute, as *La Belle Ferroniere* in the Louvre.)

As a reward for his concern and patient care when a Venetian fuctionary became quite ill in Mantua, Francesco was earnestly warned by the man to watch out for the Venetian senate, which disliked the meetings of the Este-Sforza-Gonzaga tribe, often disguised as gatherings for hunting and gaming in Ferrara. Also, Francesco and his relatives were to keep a close eye on the Borgia Pope Alexander VI, who had designs on the Este and on the court, treasures, and lands of Urbino. To assuage Rome, Francesco sent his best-spoken *oratore*, who, along with his skillful words, carried presents. One gift was a golden necklace to be given the duke's former brother-in-law, Giovanni Sforza, lord of Pesaro, once married to Francesco's dead sister, Maddalena Gonzaga, and now about to marry the Pope's daughter, Lucrezia, so dearly loved by her father that the bawdy times whispered loudly of incest. In Mantua, Francesco kept the eyes of Italy and France on remarkable tournaments to which he invited the most valiant knights; one show, arranged on instruction from Venice, called for a review of troops and their commanders in full magnificent regalia. Never parsimonious, Francesco made these events as impressive as he could, the entertainments and martial displays dazzling enough to empty Mantua's treasury. At one point no salaries were paid and the concerted protests almost paralyzed the machinery of government and of commerce. In such situations, Isabella sent a jewel or two, often more, to her pawnbrokers.

* Although young Charles VIII was impatient to prove himself a great conqueror, an obsession inspired by his own recklessness and the advice of corrupt advisers, who had been heavily bribed by Sforza, there were shows of parleying, of alignments that had to be endured while Sforza attempted to sort them out to his own advantage. To confound matters further, the duke of Urbino consented to become a *condottiere* for the French, while the king of Naples managed to convince the Pope—who had grievances, personal and political, against Naples—to sign with him a very secret treaty that they come to each other's defense should it be necessary. According to Francesco Guicciardini, Ludovico now "parried in the most artful manner: now seeming displeased at Charles' Italian claims as perilous for all the Italians, now justifying his actions as necessitated by his ancient alliance with the French ruling house . . . obliging him to take heed of the request which the King [it was said] had made him; and now promising, sometimes to Ferdinand [of Naples] and sometimes to the Pope and Piero de' Medici [Lorenzo's unsure, inept son], to do all he could to cool Charles' ardor. Then he thought it would be possible to lull them all asleep, in the hope that no moves would be made against him before the French were well-prepared and organized; and he was all the more readily believed because the decision to invite the King of France in Italy was judged so risky even for Sforza, that it didn't seem possible that ultimately, considering the danger, he would not have to withdraw from it." In the waiting time, Charles mended a few fences, settling disputes he had with their great Catholic majesties Ferdinand and Isabella of Spain and becoming friendly once more with the emperor Maximilian. Ludovico kept making promises all around, while the Pope decided to separate himself from Naples because King Ferdinand would not meet the Pope's increasingly exigent demands. Charles forced Florence into a reluctant promise of alliance by threatening to shut down trade with Florentine bankers. "In such a state of mind and in such confusion of affairs, likely to lead to new disturbances, began the year 1494—a most unhappy year for Italy and in truth the beginning of those years of misfortune, because it opened the door to innumerable horrible calamities, in which a great part of the world was subsequently involved"

(Guicciardini). It was the year in which France was preparing, in a phrase used by many historians, her graveyard called Italy. Ferdinand of Naples died that year and left as heir the implacable Alfonso, not as amenable to peaceable solutions as his father had been. He approached the marquis of Mantua for military aid. Francesco was eager to help since the wages were good; in addition, Venice gave her consent. The arrangement was to be kept quiet but was soon bruited about (Francesco himself might have babbled proudly and drunkenly), until Venice decided it was best that Francesco cancel the arrangement. The disappointing loss of income might have been shortly remedied by an offer from his sister Chiara's husband, Gilbert de Montpensier, who suggested he become a warrior for France. The possibilities were too risky, and Francesco reluctantly turned him down.

Charles, about to launch his campaign, sent ambassadors to ask for firmer cooperation from Florence. She answered that although she had the greatest admiration for France and wished to remain her friend, there were prior obligations to go to the defense of Naples should she be menaced, and furthermore, Florence could not permit the passage of French troops through Tuscany should they attempt a southward drive toward Naples. Charles expelled all Florentine ambassadors from France and, following Ludovico's advice, closed down Florentine businesses and banks in Lyons, a key commercial center. Venice begged to be excused from helping France, since all her concentration was directed, and had to stay directed, against the Turks.

Alfonso gathered his forces, as did Charles (urged on by Ludovico), so certain of victory that he assumed Alfonso's title, King of the Two Sicilies. While a Neapolitan fleet was trying to make its way northward, French ships arrived and forced them back. Piero de' Medici and the Pope now rushed to the help of Alfonso's land forces on their northward march, but, realizing their vulnerability, Piero and Alfonso also made attempts to treat with Ludovico, who had, however, his own ambitious scheme of things to come: The French would humble Florence and Naples and then return to France, leaving him in a securely powerful position as master of large sections of Italy. When Charles (so ugly that he "seemed more like a monster than a man") entered Asti, in northwestern Italy, early in September of 1494, he was greeted with ceremonious awe by Ludovico, Beatrice, her brother Ercole of Ferrara, nobles of several courts, and a collection of

Milanese beauties. The king was again broke and Sforza gave him more money for the advance of his powerful armies. Besides thousands of well-trained archers and horsemen, the French had brought by ship a frightening supply of sophisticated artillery, rarely seen in Italy. The most effective were bronze cannon, which used iron balls rather than the usual stone and were mounted on horse-drawn carriages so that they were easily maneuverable. "So little time elapsed between one shot and another and the shots were so frequent and so violent was their battering that in a few hours they could accomplish what previously in Italy used to require many days." In addition to seasoned troops and advanced matériel, the French had as leaders of companies patriotic noblemen, neither contentious nor avaricious—unlike, says the aristocrat Guicciardini, the Italian rabble and their hate-filled, brawling leaders, inspired only by vanity and greed. The French and Swiss soldiers were furthermore well organized and kept their formations in battle, while the Italians scattered, sheltering behind trees and in ditches.

In spite of a continuing lack of funds, suspicion of the motives of Il Moro, and terror of the poisons the Italians used so freely, Charles moved on Tuscany, inflicting swift devastation on a number of strongholds, to the shocked horror of many Italians, who were accustomed to combat as courtly, symbolic rites, rather like jousting—something in the style of Barletta, where thirteen Italian knights fought to the death thirteen French knights, thus lifting the siege on their town. As French artillery and huge bodies of efficient Swiss mercenaries approached Florence, Piero de' Medici handed over Tuscany's major fortresses. Thunderous dissent from the merchants and nobles of Florence forced Piero and his brothers Giuliano and Giovanni out of Florence. Charles, having extracted money and acquiescence from Florence, moved toward Rome. Alexander VI assured the king, for a promise of support when he should need it, a number of key fortresses to be held by the French until Naples was theirs. The southward march then continued, so terrifying Alfonso that he fled his court as secretly and silently as he could manage, while the French, after "having given vent to every other kind of savage barbarism, committed the ultimate cruelty of setting the buildings on fire. This method of making war, not used in Italy for many centuries, filled all the kingdom with the greatest terror, because in victory, the farthest point the cruelty of the victors [Italian] had ever gone was to plunder and free the conquered soldiers, to sack the towns captured by assault and take the inhabitants prisoners in order that they would have to pay ransom" (Guicciardini).

After a few feeble attempts to hold its kingdom together, Naples went over to France, while Girolamo Savonarola, the Dominican prophet of the destruction of Florence for its transgressions in the flesh and the spirit, took control of his city. In spite of widely spread largesse, Charles felt himself dangerously out of favor in Naples. Leaving his captains in control of the conquered lands, the king and several other leaders of troops turned homeward. The northward journey was slow, Charles and his captains discomfited by the news that there had been a great celebration to toast a new anti-French treaty between the emperor Maximilian, Venice, Rome, the Sforza of Milan, and Ferdinand of Spain, the latter already in control of Sardinia and Sicily and eager to add Naples to his growing empire. He joined two thousand horsemen to those of the newly allied forces and sent ships to the Adriatic coast to meet with those of Venice. Maximilian pledged to send ten thousand soldiers to prove himself, as he then needed to, a fearsome ruler. The Pope did not want any sort of foreign power in Italy, not even the devout Spanish, but appeared to agree to the anti-French alignment, then vacillated, then fled Rome in fear of Charles.

Magics and Sciences

Every popular magazine and newspaper today must carry horoscopes; horoscopy makes best-sellers; gypsies and fellow "advisers" lay out tarot cards and read crystal balls. The poorer churches of Latin America are hung with tin heads, lungs, ears, eyes, hands, to induce magic cures. Prophets and magicians abound, from the makers of revenge and love potions in the *botanicas* of New York to the *curanderos* in hill caves of Mexico. As answers to immortal needs from immortal times, the magics may never die. In 1980, Florence staged an exhibition of alchemy, astrology and magic in the Renaissance. It was one of a number of simultaneous shows that included art, commerce, book production, science, the religious establishment, the theater. Two weeks of daily comparison proved that the line to the magics was often twice and three times as long as the lines to the other exhibitions, clever and attractive as they were.

✳ When the Babylonians began to record their observations of the related positions of heavenly bodies four thousand years ago, imaginative speculations grew out of the observed patterns and their possible control of men's lives. The Egyptians and the Persians contributed their considerable mathematical skills to the charting and the speculation, which were further enriched and emotionalized when they were melded with the mystery religions of the East. The forceful system proliferated into every corner of the known world, maintaining its power as companion to monotheistic religions when they developed and spread.

Each planet, increasingly personified over the centuries and adorned with symbols, achieved its own stone, its own flower, its own metal. The sun was gold, the moon silver; Venus was copper and Mercury evanescent quicksilver, a useful catalyst. Mars was iron and Jupiter tin, while Saturn was represented by lead, dull and lacking in power. Like man, these astrological rulers were combined of air, fire, water, and earth, their characters determined by the dominance of a particular "humor." According to that dominant humor, their zodiacal symbols were assigned control of specific organs of the human body: Leo the heart, Cancer the genitals, for example.

Astrology, the "serious science" that Sir Isaac Newton declared one of his major interests, was in and out of official favor at various times, often simultaneously. Banned from time to time in ancient Rome, it stubbornly remained in common use. The emperors themselves, choosing to hide the prognosticated outcome of battles and the projected dates of their own deaths, abolished the practice publicly, while they continued privately to consult practitioners, since astrology governed destiny. As in present-day India, an astrological chart was cast at the moment of a child's birth. A merchant consulted his astrologer before setting a ship out to sea; the times for sowing and reaping were determined by astrology. And so was the date of a wedding, the gathering for battle, the breaking of ground for a new building, even by so rational a man as the architect Alberti. As a medical tool, astrology determined the seat and duration of an illness. No less than architects and physicians were popes and princes free of these forces that controlled the world and the need to know how the forces would defeat or exalt them. Although the Papacy forbade it, Paul III consulted the renowned Lucas Guaricus, also adviser to the Gonzaga, paid him handsomely, and was influential in settling on the astrologer the secure benefices of a bishopric. Christina of Sweden had a touching faith in her personal guide through the planets, and an Italian who took the name William Parron for his English practice traced the destinies of nobles in the court of Henry VII.

Interpreters of planetary charts who made mistakes were often severely punished. A nervous warlord who saw his assured triumphs lying about him as rags of defeat might hire a hand swift with the poignard to kill his false prophet. Or a friendly priest might be persuaded to turn the false seer over to the Inquisition as a certified heretic, a warlock in close partnership with Satan. Astrologers also had occasional difficulties with churchly skeptics: Since the Magi were astrologers, could they not have seen and prevented Christ's suffering after the stars had signaled his birth? On the other hand, astrologers were generally credited with having foreseen the disastrous arrival from the New World and into the ports of Italy a malevolent variant of a fairly innocuous old theme, syphilis, caused by a most unfortunate meeting of Jupiter, Mars, and Saturn.

The Counter-Reformation, trying to keep God's hand stronger and the voice of the Church more persuasive than that of the astrologers, placed a strong ban on the practice. The vision of the artist could hardly be constantly controlled, though, and remarkable paintings enlaced Christian devotion with astrology. Cosmé Tura of Ferrara, for one, painted an exquisite Virgin, slender fingers folded prayerfully above the Child in her lap, sitting before an ornamental version of the astrologers' zodiac, while many other artists sent their Christian cherubim and seraphim swirling through the domains of Gemini or Sagittarius. One of Dürer's many astrological engravings depicts the explosive earthquake and black sun of an apocalypse promised by a number of leading astrologers. The Gonzaga Palazzo del Te seethed with astrological symbols, less frightening and more luscious than Dürer's.

* Painters and engravers, dukes and clerics, workers and peasants, were equally occupied with astrology's potent sister science, alchemy, at least as old as astrology. Approximately five thousand years ago, the Egyptians mined considerable quantities of gold. As standards of value were imposed and refining became more complex and sophisticated, the handling of the precious metal became a secret of the priests, who wreathed its qualities in mysteries and ritual. When the Greeks settled in Egyptian Alexandria, they brought with them their pantheon of gods, one of whom was Hermes, the winged messenger. With time and the fusions of arcane religions, he took on the guise of Hermes Trismegistus ("three times greatest"), a legendary king whose rule lasted through millennia. He purportedly wrote thousands of books, of which limited pieces in Greek were said to have survived, expounding philosophical ideas that were a compound of pagan, early-Christian, and Hebrew thought and alchemic formulations veiled in obscure allusions that could be understood only by a chosen few. These guarded secrets and a document called the "Emerald Tablet," supposedly found with Hermes' mummy in one of the great pyramids, became the founding tenets of alchemy. The more philosophic practitioners tried to create a harmonious world of their enlightenments. They described it as

"One Entity," the source of all living, which controls the universe with the balanced aid of father sun and mother moon, the basic androgyne. The goal and the promise was that "when thou wilt separate the earth from the fire, the subtle from the gross, gently and with care . . . by this means thou wilt have the glory of the world," and "all obscurity will flee from thee." What were gold and the sun in man, they asked, but the highest Christian virtue, blessedness achieved as his baser metals were burned away and his pure gold freed—if he possessed the elusive, all-powerful "philosopher's stone."

Not too many practitioners were dedicated to cleansing man of his dross; they sought the tangible gold that would emerge from cheaper, baser metals—significant experiments in early chemistry—and the golden dream of eternal youth, which must surely come with the "elixir" that was another guise of the philosopher's stone. Like the astrologer's, the alchemist's was a walking-on-eggs profession. If the Renaissance alchemist broadcast claims that he had achieved gold as precious metal, he would be prey to princes avid for a monopoly of both man and process. When his proofs failed, he was subject to imprisonment and execution, saved only by the greedy optimism that hoped for a successful next trial, or a next.

Alchemists of learning and imagination could avoid accusations of heresy by quoting enigmatic portions of Scriptures, which masked a scent of paganism. They could invent wondrous allegories that turned Eden's serpent into a benign spirit; feeding the high eroticism of the age, they produced a spate of titillating hermaphroditic spirits and other toothsome symbols that wound themselves appealingly about animals, trees, stars, anything. Greek myths were interwoven with biblical figures; the mighty Jason and rich King Solomon had both been alchemists; Noah managed peace in his Ark because he too had the philosopher's stone. With a light push of the imagination, any ancient figure could be dressed in the alchemist's long robe stamped with mystical signs.

Chaucer looked on all alchemists with a sour eye; his king forbade their practice in England. Venice issued a prohibiting edict; Erasmus found them contemptible. They continued to flourish, their basic philosophic concepts encouraged by a few humanist thinkers who also believed in the perfectibility, the potential pure gold, of man. In their gathering of all learnings and creeds to shape a harmonious whole of the universe, they linked Moses as a prophet of Christian truths with Hermes Trismegistus, who was quoted as an authentic authority. Marsilio Ficino, the leader of the Platonic Academy of Florence, which was supported by Cosimo de' Medici, translated on the request of his patron manuscript bits attributed to Hermes, who was valued as a philosophic coequal to Plato and Pythagoras.

On a less exalted level, alchemy and its partner, astrology, joined with the deathless, colorful varieties of folk magics and superstition. There were few households that did not have a cache of disks, amulets, bracelets, and collars engraved with mysterious, powerful symbols; polished crystal, mirrors, and tarot cards in which to search the future; bits of precious stone to guard against poisons; pendants shaped to please Dame Fortune. For the cure of certain illnesses, besides magical images of the affected parts, there were concoctions of mashed toad and hair covered with graveyard dust, cooked over "burning water" (alcohol).

So numerous a set of fears and cures, linked with the threats of astrology and the promises of alchemy, so rich and varied a field of color and symbols, naturally continued to evoke manifold expressions in art. Dürer's well-known *Melancholy* surrounded by magic numbers represents not only one of the four humors that characterized men and women, but elements of magic that might strongly affect that humor. Dürer suggests, as well, the erotic in black magic, by turning a set of graces into witches both repellent and alluring. One of Signorelli's contributions is a hellish engraving of witches and satyrs pulling a chariot bearing a skeleton; Pontormo painted hideous old witches bent to their repulsive rituals.

Artists not only were obsessed by magics but, like much of the rest of the population, were eager to use them to profitable ends. Parmigianino sank his whole career, according to Vasari, into alchemy, hoping "to enrich himself quickly by congealing mercury (the key catalyst). Thus instead of conceiving beautiful ideas and plying his brush he wasted his days in manipulating coal, wood furnaces and other things." He lost money and assignments. "Had he but put aside the follies of alchemy, he would have been one of the rarest masters of our time."

Court ladies, as well, were fascinated by the possibilities of what they preferred to call "natural magics." The same euphemism was used by their husbands and by exalted leaders, like the

Medici pope Leo X who was an ardent aficionado of alchemy and astrology, as were the Gonzaga and the Este. The pope managed various degrees of discretion and the Gonzaga sequestered their "laboratories" and practitioners to the distant Palazzo del Te. Francesco de' Medici, an avaricious speculator and master banker throughout Europe, also had a dark reputation as a magician, but nowhere near as black as that of his second wife, Bianca Capello, mistress of incantations that brought forth evil incubi and succubi who shrieked and groaned hideously and emitted foul odors. Catherine and Maria de' Medici, who married French kings, were loudly suspected of black magic, the proof a conspicuous number of deaths by poison in their courts. The curious girdle of twelve stones bearing zodiacal signs that Catherine often wore proclaimed her, to malevolent eyes, a sorceress.

* Romantic historians have a tendency to claim Mantua as a Prospero's island of enchantments, bright and somber. Had it not been founded by the witch-prophetess Manto, daughter of the androgynous prophet Tiresias? Was not Mantua's most famous son, Virgil, known to have been a great magician? Of white magic only, of course. In spite of its esoteric history, the small state was actually in these respects like most other European communities, constantly stirring with terrifying orgiastic images. Any lingering disease, any swift death, any inexplicable accident, could be attributed to witchcraft. Ready reasons could be found for accusing almost anyone of the black arts, as Henry VIII did after Anne Boleyn did not produce an heir to his throne and stopped pleasing him altogether.

Accounts of Mantuan witchcraft appear not to have been publicized except when the whole community was threatened; records of 1492 report that a witch was accused of causing the banks of the Po to overflow and was consequently burned to death. There is no mention of witchcraft or alchemists in the early Gonzaga court; records were burned by the family precisely because they respected records and wanted no revelations of their dealings with or against their defeated rivals, the Bonacolsi. It hardly seems likely that alchemy had a conspicuous place in the court of Gianfrancesco and his devout wife, Paola, a court whose tone was affected by the virtuous, clear-thinking tutor Vittorino da Feltre. Low-keyed references slipped around Ludovico's wife, Barbara, the Hohenzollern heiress whose father was referred to as "the Alchemist," but there is no reason to believe that she was a devotee. Yet there were other remarkably intelligent people, like the brilliant young humanist Pico della Mirandola, who acknowledged the useful strengths of witchcraft, possibly as part of his gathering of all beliefs—the effort of several humanists—to create one total system.

Whether Isabella d'Este-Gonzaga was her own cosmetician-amateur alchemist or simply director of a small court perfumery and soap laboratory—one of the minor industries of alchemy—her product was highly praised and sought after. When her son Federico, then sixteen, was playing the young gallant in the French court, he wrote his mother to send him, besides gloves for a lady friend, a generous quantity of Mantuan soaps, oils, powders, and scented waters. The Holy Roman Emperor Rudolph II had little interest in such fripperies; he spent his time and money on the search for gold and eternal youth. His contemporary Vincenzo Gonzaga also leaned attentively toward any smooth-talking "philosopher" who would promise him splashing fountains of gold, eternal youth and its sexual freshness. His wife, Leonora de' Medici, an astute woman, suggested tactfully that he had better save his money, and stop appearing a gullible fool, by sending away his expensive gaggle of alchemists, except those, perhaps, who were studying the civet cat and its capacities for producing perfume.

The "natural magics" to produce poisons were not invented in the Renaissance; it was an old business. The Egyptians invented an impressive variety and so did the Greeks. The Caesars' marble palaces ran lively streams of poison, but it was the Italians who brought the confection of noxious potions to a high and subtle science, the legends of their efficacy sparking Italian history and pseudo history, as juicily reflected in Elizabethan plays. There were potions to prevent conception and induce abortion—supplements to the brutal unclean interventions by midwives; there were poisons to inflame the passions, to cause impotence, to inspire unendurable libidinousness, to invite tuberculosis or leprosy. And there was the wide repertoire of quick and slow, sharply painful or gradually wasting killer poisons, to be administered as one drop in wine or as a medicine given in repeated doses, often heavily laced with sugar or pepper, or in compounds of lemon, chicory, fennel, coriander, and bitter almonds, on their own well thought of as digestives.

* One of the most colorful and productive Doctor Faustus of the time, bound to magics yet steadily moving toward the observations and reasonings that were approaches to modern science, was Giambattista della Porta, born in 1538 into an aristocratic Neapolitan family of many gifts. A precocious and omnivorous learner, with a highly developed talent for self-promotion, Giambattista presented himself as a child genius, the author of a great compendium, *Magia Naturalis,* finished before he was sixteen. Since he was prone to reinvent his autobiography when and as it suited him, it is difficult to confirm or deny this proof of astonishing precocity. A later and enlarged edition, however, translated into several foreign languages, discloses the indisputably startling range of his studies, impressive at any age. The *Magia* was an anthology of "science for the layman," which included recipes for herbal medicines, instructions for the concoction of perfumes, the uses of home magics to modify nature's blows, descriptions of his telescopes and their sophisticated lenses, of his studies of light rays as sources of heat. In his discussions of psychological states, he suggests the value of hypnotism, explores magnetism and demonology, and, inescapably, considers the proper alchemic admixture of metals that should produce the philosopher's stone.

Cryptological inventions della Porta devised attracted the Spanish court, which, like all courts, was desperate for one impenetrable code. The attention and honors he accrued enhanced his standing in Spanish-controlled Naples, while his widening reputation as prophet, magician, physician, mathematician, astrologer, alchemist, and philosopher—functions displayed in their full panoply throughout Italy—attracted the Inquisition, which proscribed his activities as medical adviser, soothsayer, and savant to the world. Della Porta took to playwriting, to create, over the years, a good number of naturalistic comedies, unusual in that they featured Neapolitan folk characters whose speeches were delivered in their own zesty dialect.

When the Inquisition stopped pointing its accusing finger at him, he was deluged by invitations to work in this court and that. Duke Vincenzo of Mantua and the emperor Rudolph II, "Prince of Alchemists," contended for the talents that might amass immense quantities of gold to be enjoyed throughout an eternal life. Giambattista decided for the Este of Ferrara, working under the direct patronage of the Este cardinal then in residence at the Villa d'Este at Tivoli, near Rome. Although the physician-alchemist did not distinguish himself in either field, the cardinal took him along when he moved to Venice, and there della Porta began wider studies. He continued to write on optics, claiming that Galileo had plagiarized his telescope (the actual credit for the invention belongs to a Dutch optician); expanded his repertoire of medical ointments and perfumes; continued his examinations of metals and their medicinal properties; and again centered on the philosopher's stone, announcing at frequent intervals that he was imminently close to freeing its stubborn secrets.

Persistent failure, and the information that a German magus who had claimed success in making gold was killed by jealous rivals, turned the aging man to other matters. He produced a book on horticulture, in which he proposed that cross-breeding be used to increase the yield of fruit trees. A book on physiognomy pointed out resemblances between men and animals, such parallels prophetic in character development. The Inquisition found such matter too heavily tainted with the supernatural, and again threatened. Again della Porta narrowed his field. More comedies poured freely from the prolific pen and there was yet another, more advanced, treatise on optics. One new study described something very close to a steam engine and another, on distillation, introduced valuable contributions to early chemistry.

Both afraid and defiant of the Inquisition, Giambattista amused his old age, and the crowds that gathered at his door, by telling fortunes. In private, he continued improving his telescope and tossing off comedies. He died at seventy-seven and his funeral was a solemn public event, homage to a powerful magus, to an entertaining showman, to a man who advanced medicine and the study of optics, leaving fruitful suggestions for others to follow.

* With advances made in botany, illuminated herbals, sometimes more beautiful than useful, gave way to systematizations of botanical knowledge, with emphasis on medical applications. By the mid-sixteenth century, teaching at the bedside of a patient had been firmly established; several common diseases had been differentiated from one another; a number of physicians began to stress the psychological in disease, admitting the power of the

imagination and going so far as to insist that the insane were not willful servants of Satan but victims of mysterious illnesses.

Berengarius of Carpi, Benvenuto Cellini's noted syphilis specialist, had by 1550, the year he died, poisoned a number of patients with experimental cures. He had also performed many dissections, from which anatomical drawings were made that revealed structures and systems hardly known before. The birth of modern anatomy, in part inspired by the Renaissance conviction that man was a divine creature worthy of every sort of study, arrived with Andreas Vesalius, who was appointed professor of anatomy in the University of Padua at the age of twenty-three. With the cooperation of a Flemish engraver who supplied him with meticulous drawings, Vesalius published before he was thirty his landmark volumes, *De Humani Corporis Fabrica,* which pointed up the Greek writer Galen's anatomical errors and emphasized the essential linkage between anatomical observations and surgery, a dangerously ignorant branch of medical practice at the time. Vigorously fought by devout Galenists, Vesalius removed himself from Italy, to become the surgeon for the court of Spain. The inflexible Spanish Church disapproved of both his dissections and his enlightenments and forced him, under threat of death by the Inquisition, to make a penitent's pilgrimage to the Holy Land. He died shortly after, at the age of fifty.

With Vesalius pointing the way, the study of anatomy soared; systems of veins and muscles, unknown tubes and stretches of cartilage, were discovered, insisting on being further studied. Gabriello Fallopio, who gave his name to the Fallopian tubes, traced nerve systems and, as well, studied and described the vagina and the nature and function of the placenta. It is claimed by at least one medical historian that Leonardo da Vinci, sketching from the twenty or so corpses he had dissected, had made an anatomically correct drawing of the uterus. (The fact that painters belonged to the same guild as apothecaries and physicians may have given them particular opportunities for advanced anatomical study.) The eccentric mathematician, physician, astrologer, biologist, and writer Geronomo Cardano had, when he was not in jail for heresy or debt—or glued to a gambling table—developed a respected continental reputation as a physician. Among his lasting contributions to the history of medicine were his imaginative modes of teaching the deaf and blind to reach out of their sequestered worlds. The classification of plants on which Linnaeus later built was initiated by Andrea Cesalpino, professor of medicine and keeper of the botanical gardens at Pisa.

In time, the Church reluctantly gave dispensations to universities, whose dissecting rooms and anatomic theaters became crowded centers of learning. By 1625, several hundred books on medicine had been published. The old four humors no longer sufficed to explain character and behavior; studies in physiognomy and its tentative ties to psychology tried for broader and more subtle explanations. Universities sprang up all over Europe, luring scholars to the amazing world that opened opportunities for inventing new medical tools as well as naval instruments, for advancing mathematical formulae and astronomical observations. Although the Inquisition had silenced Copernicus and Galileo, the German Kepler promoted rethinking of their work and its acceptance. The fervor for the new and improved exploded in every direction, each explosion a catalyst for others, the most driving force the printed book, which poured out of the presses in the tens of thousands, opening wide fields of enlightenment, inspiring study and experimentation, in a steady progress toward modern science.

S * I * X

Charles VIII's progress to the north was hampered not only by the news of what appeared to be a strong coalition but by its vast accumulation of heavy artillery, by wagons on wagons of booty, by the vengeful acts of citizens and peasants of the villages he had earlier ravaged. One immediate goal was to join with French garrisons in Asti and Novara, east of Milan. Considerably to the south and west, a short distance south of Parma, an army of about three thousand men, mainly Swiss mercenaries, found itself surrounded by Italian encampments whose massed strength was overwhelmingly greater than its own, with ditches and ramparts prepared, artillery effectively placed. Francesco Gonzaga, supplied with moneys and logistical aid from Venice, commanded this "flower of the Italian army," a body of five thousand foot soldiers, several thousand horsemen, and a vast band of stradiots—wild, reckless bareback riders imported by Venice from Albania and Greece. His forces also included troops sent by Ferrara and Bologna, a large squadron led by Antonio da Montefeltro of Urbino, and smaller armies of smaller principalities mainly to serve as reinforcements when needed, to straddle the Taro River, a small tributary of the Po, near Fornovo.

An advance guard of two thousand French soldiers reached Fornovo at the end of June 1495 and were instantly assailed by the harrying and howling of the stradiots, which went on through the nights, not a habit of European warriors, whose combat and threats usually broke at nightfall. When the full numbers of the French forces reached their encampment at the Taro, only three miles from the tents of the Italians, it seemed possible that the Italians were doomed by the superior number of their adversaries, by the difficult terrain, and by a violent storm, whose thunder and lightning seemed to prophesy disaster. The river swelled and poured over its weedy, entangling banks, and late-arriving Italian soldiers could not reach their prearranged positions. In spite of this discouraging turn of events, the Italians were confident. Had the king not recently solicited a peace agreement with Francesco? A few days later, early in July, the battle was formally joined, the stradiots were released in their full fury. It was their habit and pleasure to impale conquered heads on their lances and tear back to their leader for the reward earned for each head. Francesco, in a transport of barbaric triumph, gave the first head-bearer a large sum of gold and embraced the savage warmly.

Guicciardini: "It was certain that the Marquis' [Francesco's] charge was most furious and ferocious and was met with equal ferocity and valor, the squadrons entering into the thick of the fray from every side." When their lances shattered, the soldiers took to maces and rapiers; even the horses fought, by "kicking, biting and charging." Francesco, leading a body of specially picked troops, stayed in the forefront, pushing back the French, and encouraged by the capture of a French leader, the Bastard of Bourbon, he went for the king himself. The king escaped, helped not so much by his soldiers, according to contemporary reports, but by his fiery horse, his prayers to Saint Denis and Saint Martin, and the arrival of a fresh French battalion. The battle appeared to be going to the French for a while, especially after one of the most experienced and courageous *condottieri*, Francesco's uncle Rodolfo Gonzaga, was struck by a French dagger when he lifted the beaver of his helmet. He fell from his horse and was trampled. Then fortune seemed to return to the Italians. "But [as everyone knows] the power of fortune is most great in all human affairs, even more in military matters than any others . . . where a badly understood command, or a poorly executed order, or an act of rashness . . . will often bring victory to those who already seem to be defeated." Francesco, who had fought through the death of three horses under him, permitted a gang of stradiots to attack the poorly attended supply wagons of the French. They brought back on the stolen mules and horses gold seals and gemmed altars, relics, armor, everything they could grab. Many others, stradiots and Italians, followed their example, fleeing with their loot, some drowning in the swollen river. Francesco tried to regather his mutinous troops by exhortation and examples of valor, but his army was now in hopeless disarray, most of it in retreat, pursued by the French at one side of the unnavigable river—"an inexcusable shame."

Weariness and losses on both sides stopped the battle, which, since their aim was passage northward and the Italians had not held them, the French might have considered a victory. In the bloodiest and longest battle Italy had ever known, the first encounter of the Italian wars, she lost 3,000 men, among them valued leaders. The French lost their tents, the king's pavilion and its treasures, their supply wagons, and a large number of men, though not as many as the Italians. However, Venice and her allies celebrated their great "victory," celebrated as well in several other states by surviving *condottieri*, who declared themselves heroes of the battle "fought successfully upon the River Taro against Charles, King of France." In the exultation over the peculiar "victory," Francesco's contract as captain general for Venice was renewed at 50,000 ducats in peacetime and 60,000 in times of war. For service already performed, he was to receive a bonus of 2,000 ducats annually, and for his wife there was a gift of 1,000, a windfall that was most welcome to settle her debts to merchants and money-lenders. At home, Francesco, who had managed to arrive as head of a gloriously triumphant military procession, let it be noised about that not only had he made important military and political gains but he had bought back cheaply from his troops booty worth 300,000 ducats and, after having greeted his adversary, the king, as a high-bred cavalier should, had offered the return of some of the conquered treasures. Francesco held on to a few holy objects, to the gold and the horses, magnificent tapestries, chased armor and a book of nude female portraits, supposedly a compendium of Italian courtesans who had pleased the king from time to time. Francesco, feeling expansive, wanted to send some of his loot, a few pieces of royal hangings in gold-shot silk, to his sister-in-law Beatrice. Isabella objected strongly. Her husband had earned these gifts as fruits of the victory he fought for so daringly; they belonged to him and to Mantua. She was quite contented to have Francesco keep the book of nudes, possibly to add to one or two he already had.

* According to Capilupi, her secretary, Isabella was actually pleased with the book, an unremarkable artifact that accompanied the Renaissance taste for the erotic and even obscene. The plays of Plautus and Terence, on which she had been brought up in Ferrara, were hardly chaste little comedies of genteel manners. Isabella's responses seemed to vary according to the stance she felt it appropriate to take at any given time. During the marriage celebrations of her brother Alfonso and Lucrezia Borgia in 1501, she wrote home from Ferrara that the vulgarities of one obscene play so shamed her that she removed herself and her young attending "demoiselles" from the theater. The role of respectable matron might then have suited her, to quell the rumors that she and Ludovico Sforza were lovers, rumors intensified by her strong partisanship of his causes and so insistent that her father, Duke Ercole, felt impelled to present himself to the Venetian Council to assure them that their suspicions of an affair were all lying gossip; the Este, the Gonzaga, the Sforza, were a close-knit, affectionate family, and that was all. (At other times, because it promised political advantages, her demoiselles were dressed, coiffed, and perfumed to entertain influential men, the heat of wine, dancing, and touching meant to cajole and persuade.)

* Francesco, gleaming among his spoils, continued to enjoy the Olympic height of his life, wreathed in phrases like "immortal hero" by the Mantuan worshipful. Master craftsmen were commissioned to strike medals commemorating Fornovo, one of the medals proclaiming Francesco "liberator of Italy." He had been majestically entertained and honored by the doge of Venice, and it was time for Mantegna to memorialize the hero in the full flush of victory. According to the archivist Alessandro Luzio, the original composition of the painting *Madonna della Vittoria* was to include Isabella, kneeling along with Francesco before the Virgin's throne, but she lost out to an elderly woman in modest nunlike draperies, usually identified as Beata Osanna Andreasi. A cult figure of Mantua, closely linked with Isabella and Francesco, she was visited by heavenly visions and had the gift of prophecy. Her prayers were markedly effectual, revered as the heavenly weapons that brought Isabella not only ease from pain but, after ten years of marriage, an heir. To Francesco, she assured protection of his house when he was off to the wars.

After the painting was carried ceremoniously through the streets, to be placed on the altar of the new church dedicated to Santa Maria della Vittoria, and a decree declared that this rite was to be observed annually, like a saint's day, Francesco had to return to the business of being captain of the armies of Venice. Through all the brambles of politics and battles, Venice never lost her clear, covetous view of Adriatic ports, nor did Francesco forget his goal of making his brother Sigismondo a cardinal. Alexander VI had let it be known that he was not averse to raising to the purple the brother of the valiant warrior of the Great Republic. The offer had been suggested before, always attached to a large selling price. Carried away by one promise, Isabella, then visiting her sister-in-law in Urbino, wrote an effusive letter: "One of the greatest desires I have had in this world is to see [our] monsignore become cardinal." She eagerly offered not only her *roba* (jewels and other valuables) in the cause but her blood if that should be necessary. As before and for some time to come, however, Sigismondo didn't make it.

Early in 1496, at the crest of his fame, Francesco decided to handle the matter boldly—no begging, no truckling. He would not go to Rome, not accept the Pope's golden rose, a singular honor, unless his brother was definitely appointed cardinal. A messenger from Venice reassured him that this time Alexander would keep his promise, and slowly, with visits to friends and relatives here and there, Gonzaga made his way to a hero's welcome in Rome. He was greeted affectionately by the Pope, with respect by two young Borgias, Cesare and Lucrezia, accepted the golden rose, but let the matter of Sigismondo rest for the time being and went off to plan further anti-French strategies. It was decided that no overt move was to be made yet; disorder among the French troops—which included an uneasy mixture of Italians, Germans, and Swiss among the French—and shifting loyalties among the allies of France might accomplish destruction on their own. The hoped-for total dissolution of French troops did not appear. Instead, there were frequent inconclusive skirmishes, many bloody and all fruitless. Small campaigns in the southeast, near the Adriatic, were hard on both sides; the Pugliese terrain was unfamiliar and difficult, the replacement of arms almost impossible; food supplies were coarse and limited. (In exchanges of letters that sped with surprising efficiency between the couple, Francesco expressed a yearning for Mantuan food and Isabella managed to send him, by way of a Venetian ship, a supply of sausage and cheese.) The sacked earth and its looted peasants, the exhausted soldiers and their discouraged leaders, called for a halt, a thirty-day truce arranged with Francesco's brother-in-law Montpensier, who led that portion of the French army left in Naples. Francesco was ill of typhoid fever complicated by the syphilis that was to cripple and ultimately kill him. After suffering many uncomfortable stops, he came home to an affectionate, turbulent welcome.

"At this point," according to Giuseppe Coniglio, historian and archivist of Mantua, "there began the descending parabola in the fortunes of Francesco." He was well enough, after a few months of treatment and rest, to proceed to Venice, where there was general approval of his military conduct in the southeast but in other matters, clouds of disapproval and suspicion. Isabella and Francesco were shameless spenders, always in the hands of usurers, and Venice found this profligacy inexcusable. Francesco wanted to free a French hostage who might—although he didn't say so—be useful in times to come. Venice repeatedly insisted, with growing displeasure, that the hostage be held a prisoner in Mantua, in spite of Francesco's rationalization that Venice might profit from such an ally-spy in the French ranks. As always suspecting Francesco of tacit arrangements with France, Venice prevented a member of the Gonzaga court from accompanying Chiara beyond the borders of Italy when she returned to France after the death of her husband, in November of 1496. There were the customary ardent messages of fealty to Venice, and elaborate explanations. How could Francesco's affection for Chiara be held against him, or his concern for her husband, to whom Francesco had naturally sent his own physician and comforting gifts? It did not end there; propelled by conceit and daring, committing a series of boasting indiscretions, Francesco managed to convey the impression that if France invaded again, as she threatened, Gonzaga would protect his lands by standing with the invader—secretly or overtly.

In June of 1497, the senate stripped him of his command, and though he was permitted to keep the honor of Venetian citizenship inherited from his ancestors, he found himself suddenly thrown from his high estate, much poorer and again sick. Like his peers only occasionally a religious man—Beata Osanna took care of interceding for him with God and so did the heads of religious and charitable institutions he supported—he now took his unhappiness directly to God, for whom he had designed a new symbol in the ceiling of his council room: rods of gold ready for burning standing in a crucible, with the accompanying legend "Probasti me Domine"—Try me, Lord.

Having given God his due, Francesco turned for more immediate consolation to his current mistress, Teodora. He showed her off at a tournament in Brescia, where many eyes saw her; she was reported to be magnificently dressed. She was undoubtedly the mother of at least two of his three illegitimate daughters. Her exposure to a fascinated public evoked harsh letters from some of Francesco's associates. One told him, "You are blessed in having a fair, wise and noble wife, a true mother of concord, ever anxious to gratify your wishes, while she prudently feigns not to see or hear these actions of yours which must be hateful to her." Whether designed by Isabella or not, these were justified sentiments; she may have been argumentative and stubborn, but she was generally forbearing and steadfast and guarded Mantua astutely and responsibly. Francesco was grateful for Isabella's devotion to him and their state, but there were other matters besides ill-treated wives and alluring mistresses to be concerned about. Though most of the French army had straggled home, Charles VIII continually threatened to return, frightening all of Italy. The least upset was unconquerable Venice, which enjoyed teasing Francesco by whispering that one of these days he might, as a friend of France, find himself in a Venetian prison. Protests of fidelity to Venice left the doge and the senate unimpressed, while a sharp diminution in wages and the effects of his ravaging disease left Francesco further depressed and desperate. He sent Benedetto Capilupi to sound out the possibility of his being hired as the head of the armies of the emperor Maximilian, who had, on the instigation of the Pope, Sforza, and Venice, in one of their fragile agreements, been marching foolishly up and down Italy. Ludovico Sforza would obviously be responsible for the stipend, since Maximilian was penniless. In midsummer 1498, Francesco took the job as captain of the imperial armies at a salary of forty thousand ducats annually, but the arrangement lacked a formal contract, and furthermore, the prestigious role as head of Sforza's sector of command had been denied him. The humiliations deepened: Ludovico proclaimed it in Venice that Francesco was his minion, and even during a ceremonious visit to Mantua, surrounded as a great power by leading ambassadors, he offered no improvement in position or pay. (The festivities in Ludovico's honor were paid for by a loan of several hundred ducats from Bologna.) Broke, frightened, and troubled by the potential vulnerability of his employers, Gonzaga began again to court strong Venice. She scorned to answer him for a while. He then sent his younger brother Giovanni, whom everyone liked and who had learned to be a tactful negotiator, to prepare the ground for Francesco's visit to the doge to plead for a return to his employ. With difficulty, mainly caused by the objections of members of the senate, Francesco managed to achieve an appointment with the doge in the fall of 1498.

* The volatile politics of Italy accrued additional complications at the end of the fifteenth century. Charles VIII had died in the spring of 1498, leaving as his successor Louis XII, formerly the duke of Valois and Orleans and, through his descent from Valentino Visconti, a claimant to the duchy of Milan. Old treaties were exhumed and new treaties penned, their ultimate effect being to cut Italy into bits. Venice dealt with Louis amicably because part of their new mutual pact promised her the return of old properties, recently held by Milan. The Pope was also interested in being a friend of France, which would help him, for an exchange of favors, to shape a grander role for his son, Cesare, then a cardinal. He dissolved the marriage between Louis and his barren, homely first wife so that the king might marry Anne of Brittany, the more attractive, and impressively dowered, widow of Charles. For his efforts as emissary in the annulment proceedings, Cesare was made duke of Valentois, the "Valentino" he liked to be called. Having received by the offices of his father permission to discard the role of cardinal and the inhibitions it imposed, he was free to marry Louis's choice of a bride for him, Charlotte d'Albert, the sister of the king of Navarre. The emperor had no hand in these negotiations, since he was struggling to subdue the Swiss, who wanted independence and the right to hire themselves out to the French. The Swiss won on both counts and expanded considerably the armies Louis was amassing for his assault on Italy, Milan being in the first line of march. Ludovico Sforza searched for support everywhere, including the Ottoman Empire, the pagan enemy. None came. His fate was sealed—to quote Giuseppe Coniglio—when a vast army, one small segment of it commanded by Cesare Borgia, gathered for its descent in August of 1499.

Francesco was in a situation almost as desperate as Sforza's. He appealed fervently to Venice, which played with him the "maybe yes, maybe no" game he himself had played in more triumphant days. Ludovico hurled furious threats at him and then changed his tactics by offering Francesco seventy thousand ducats a year and his firstborn son in marriage to daughter Leonora if her father would work for him. Afraid of France, afraid of Ludovico's future, Francesco refused and pressed for a quick decision in his favor from Venice. She was, however, treating with King Louis against Milan and would have nothing to do with Gonzaga, who then reluctantly signed a meaningless contract with Sforza. Since there was little, if any, safety in this, he began flirting with Louis, encouraged by his sister Chiara. Louis's response was a salary for some amorphous position or other. At this point, he probably considered Francesco, of no fixed loyalties and with access to several important courts, a useful informer and in times of emergency a useful soldier. An alliance with France now meant renewed ties with Venice. Francesco appealed to her again and was warily accepted. He arranged thus to be sheltered in the arms of both France and Venice.

Bandello and Ariosto

Boccaccio's popular *Decameron* inspired a flood of written stories of cunning tricks and jokes, of cruelties, of impassioned anticlericalism, and—to use that fine anachronistic word—of "lubricity," which made the Italian story universally attractive and an inspiration for the judgment that Italians were a tricky, salacious lot. They also provided plots for Chaucer and Shakespeare.

One collection of such stories, recounting witticisms and practical jokes, frequently involving illustrious names, was written in the last decades of the fourteenth century by a Florentine, Franco Sacchetti—actually not so much stories as lighthearted gossip items. Later, longer tales (*novelle*) concentrated on the vices of priests and the headlong passions of women, most stories trailing little moral tags to mitigate the lewdness. A master storyteller in this genre was Matteo Bandello (1485–1561), whose presence and stories brightened the idle country hours of Isabella d'Este-Gonzaga. She defended his "lewdness"; he, in turn, praised the "heroic house of Gonzaga" and his hostess as a "glorious heroine." He was a monk—a most casual one—who by virtue of a privileged position managed to move around freely and, as he traveled, gathered up story material. He came to Mantua and Isabella after 1515, having fled the French invasion of Milan, which was more or less his home base. He stayed for six years as tutor and entertainer, returned to Milan, and later went on to France, where he lived out the rest of his life.

Because he was a northerner, not bound by the formal Tuscan idiom sponsored by purists, his use of Lombard phrases helped establish a more flexible Italian vernacular. More important, his two hundred and more stories, translated shortly before his death into French and soon thereafter into Spanish and English, suggested the intrigues that reappeared as *Much Ado About Nothing*, the ghost and poison deaths in *Hamlet*, and the doomed young lovers of *Romeo and Juliet*. Not too many of the stories were sad romances or told of madness in high circles; a good number of them followed Boccaccio's lighthearted bawdiness and, when stripped of the embroideries of fiction, proved significant witnesses of Renaissance mores and manners, casting an especially relentless eye on sinful, avaricious priests.

One story tells, with the inescapable fashionable references to Latin history and mythology, of a perfumed, pomaded Neapolitan abbot who "dresses like a young bridegroom" as he acts the flattering lover. He is in pursuit of the daughter of a goldsmith, "feeling within him a hot war between the sensible parts of reason and sensual provocation of the flesh," the eagle of Prometheus tearing at his liver. The abbot pursues the virtuous girl to her father's shop, panting under her window, and instructs his spies to find out when she is likely to leave her house. After a long disquisition on Turks, infidels, and the teachings of Saint Paul, we are returned to the desperate abbot, whom "beauty had made a slave of folly" who is threatening to commit suicide, an unforgivable sin that will be on the head of her who caused the act. Responding to the abbot's messengers, the girl, as prolix as the author himself, finally says, "Let him besiege the fort that is as glad to yield as he to summon." Unpersuaded by her answer, he continues to besiege his chosen fort. Informed by his spies of the plans of the goldsmith and his family to travel to a distant *festa*, he positions himself, with a gang of cohorts, to stop them. (The description of the girl passing near a stream in the light of the warm Neopolitan sun is a delightful passage of sensuality and languor.) When the family is overwhelmed, the girl manages to slash the abbott's face with his own sword and then leaps into the stream, "choosing rather to build her tomb within the belly of some fish or monsters of the sea than to yield the first fruits of her virginity to the polluted image or idol of the Synagogue of Babylon." With God's help, she reaches shore, and the abbot never shows himself again in the streets of Naples. The story ends with a homily on chastity, a frail thing that often needs the help of God, which sentiment rounds back to the opening of the story, where the disappearance of morality in this sinful world was deplored at length.

Embedded in a plethora of digressions among displays of classical learning, among plots of murder and rape and of people who are buried alive, one finds two versions of the Romeo and Juliet story. Both involve nurses, swooning that mimics death, a secret marriage, a threat of marriage to one unloved, a fight between the rejected suitor and a friend of the truly loved. One version has the lovers, supported by the nurse, acknowledged legally married by the Council of Ten in Venice, and everyone lives happily ever after. The second version is basically very much as Shakespeare used it, including the anglicized names of the Montecchi and the Capeletti families of Verona. Juliet does not drink a potion but dies "by checking within her all her vital forces"; Romeo commits suicide; and although peace is established between the feuding families, Bandello, who knew a good deal about family vendettas, concludes the story with the statement that the truce did not last very long.

The stories, hot with Italian passion, blood, and death, attracted all literate Englishmen. "Italian love stories are found in every shop in London," says one commentator. Roger Ascham, tutor to the young Elizabeth and author of *The Schoolmaster*, who approved of the examples set by Castiglione's *Courtier*, judged Bandello's "bawdy books" part of a Roman plot to subvert English morality. "They allure young wits to wantons" and "teach old bawds new school points." If he heard the criticism, the old monk, luxuriating in the pleasures of being bishop of Agen in France, paid it no mind, ending his life in the same lighthearted vein as he had observed, written, and lived it; his farewell to the world was *"Vivete lieti"*—Live merrily.

* Ludovico Ariosto, born in 1474, came early to the court of Ferrara, in whose service he spent most of his life, first under the patronage of Cardinal Ippolito d'Este and later for the duke Alfonso. He had studied law with no enthusiasm, then Latin and a few rudiments of Greek. His major education came from the court itself, where, it was said, poets were as common as frogs in the surrounding countryside. Ariosto's youthful pieces, preparations for that which has been called the most splendid literary work of the Renaissance, were Latin odes and sonnets that recalled Petrarch. The cardinal, contemptuous of Ariosto's poetic efforts, including those written in his praise, sent him on a variety of missions, eliciting the complaint that his patron was turning him from poet to poorly paid messenger boy, a position of enslavement in a court where no one cared whether he lived or died. He exaggerated. The Este cared enough to select him as translator of the comedies of Plautus and Terence they mounted in their lavishly equipped theater, together with one or two of his own plays.

In 1494, Matteo Boiardo, who like Ariosto came of an aristocratic family long attached to the Este court, died, leaving his *Orlando Innamorato* unfinished. Busy with other assignments but weighing suggestions by the respected literati that he continue the epic, Ariosto waited over ten years before he picked up the adventures of Orlando. He used the demanding form of *ottava rima*, a pattern that would shape a good deal of English poetry. When the work began, in 1505, Ariosto was thirty-one; until he died, eighteen years later, he wrote and rewrote his long, extraordinary poem, constantly interrupted by missions for the court. There were theatrical matters to see to and, worst of all, three terrible years as governor of Garfagnana, a nasty, isolated place as snarling as its name. In addition to the onerous jobs and meager stipends, Ariosto was required to remain celibate—a curious demand of a not overly chaste court—and thus forced to keep in hiding for many years a woman to whom he was intensely attached.

Orlando Furioso, based on a mass of chivalric legend, also gathers references from Ovid and a touch of Marco Polo's adventures in the East. Interspersed with wide strophes of adventure, fantasy, and love—love faithful and fickle, love chivalric and earthly—appear hymns of praise to several Este princes, whose lineage Ariosto claims goes back to Troy and whose progeny will create a Ferrarese Golden Age. Duke Alfonso, a pioneer in the improvement of deadly artillery, is clothed in warm praise. The long, hideous imprisonment of his blinded brothers is gently treated. Cardinal Ippolito is heroic and wise, much "the very perfect gentle knight," who nevertheless rewarded his poet with the judgment that his epic was inconsequential nonsense.

When the poet was sent to Mantua to convey congratulations to Isabella on the birth of a child, he stayed to entertain her. She was more gracious than her brother, when he read her stanzas that included: "From your illustrious line there will descend/ One who of every noble enterprise/ Of art of highest learning is the friend;/ Fair Isabella, liberal and wise,/ In whom so many rare endowments blend." She will, the poet adds, live in honorable rivalry with her most worthy husband, "the greatest host and patron of the age" and potentially the savior of Italy in his struggles against the "Gauls' barbaric rage." She is the Penelope to his Ulysses, a lady "endowed with all that is true and good."

Boiardo's *Orlando Innamorato* left off with Orlando, the right-hand man of Charlemagne, already showing symptoms of approaching madness. He is married to Aldabella and in love with Angelica, the siren daughter of the ruler of Cathay, whose mission it is to create disorder in the Christian army. The author leads the faithless Angelica into entrapments and escapes from several perilous places, one of them an island held by a sea monster. Ruggiero, a companion hero of the poem, frees Angelica, who then tracks down the distracted Orlando. After she frees him from an enchanted palace, she again eludes him, to flee to Paris, where there has been a long and brutal battle between the Saracens and the Christians.

After the pagans are routed, the volatile Angelica falls in love with a wounded Moor, Medoro. Disguised as a shepherdess and protected by the powers of a magic ring, she undertakes to cure him and carries him off to Cathay, where he will rule. Orlando, in pursuit of Angelica, finds her name and that of Medoro cut into rocks and trees. "Then in his travail suddenly he knows/ That in this very bed on which he lies/ His love has lain and often, in the close/ Embrace that nothing of herself denies. No drop of all his blood was not on fire/ With hatred, fury, rage and wrath and ire." We turn for a while to explorations of love and battle among several others of the large cast, and then return to Orlando: "He robs, he sacks, he plunders and he slays," and dares only as a madman can. "But Fortune, who takes care of the insane/ Deposited the Count on Ceuta's coast."

We leave him once more, to follow the adventures of other characters, one of them the bright-hearted paladin Astolfo. Riding a hippogriff, he swiftly covers the skies of France, Spain, and Portugal, to come to earth in Ethiopia. Here he is entertained in the luxurious court of Prester John, who, in spite of his limitless wealth, is forever hungry; harpies crowd his table as he approaches it and pollute what they cannot consume, a punishment imposed by God for overweening ambition. Equating the harpies with the foreign invaders who are starving the innocent of Italy, the poet takes us along with Astolfo and his hippogriff to a mountain inhabited by Elijah, the patriarch Enoch, and Saint John the Evangelist. Explaining that Orlando's wits were taken from him because he had sinned, among his sins the passion for a pagan woman, the saint offers to show Astolfo how his friend's wits can be restored.

They ride Elijah's chariot to the moon, passing many wonders, until they arrive at a group of tightly corked vases that contain lost minds, the minds of those too much in love, those enamored of fame, those who hoard paintings and jewels. "Astrologers and sophists by the score/ Have lost their reason, poets too, still more." After sniffing up a bit of the sense he himself has lost, Astolfo disappears for encounters with other personages, to return ultimately to Orlando, pushing his wits back up into his head. "Manlier and wiser" than before, Orlando discovers that he is cured of love and returns to his duties as leader of Christians against the infidels, performing magnificently, as before his attack.

Friend Rinaldo is cured of *his* despairing love of Angelica by a friendly cavalier who dashes the monster symbolic of that love into the Abyss. Eager to join Orlando, Rinaldo gallops fast until he reaches the Po, where he takes his rest in a castle full of remarkable works of art and decorated with magnificent portraits of unmistakably contemporary Ferrarese figures. The first to catch Rinaldo's eye is Lucrezia Borgia, "with all honor names/ Whose loveliness and virtue Rome should prize/ Above her ancient namesake's [the Lucrezia who died for wifely virtue] likewise famed." Obeisance is also done Isabella, Elisabetta Gonzaga, Leonora Gonzaga, and, among the men, "courtly Castiglione."

Among diversions into homilies, discussions of vice and virtue, love attained and love denied, we are informed that the good pagan Ruggiero takes Christian instruction. Welcomed by the emperor Charles, he does triumphant battle in Belgrade and returns to rest among the fair and witty women of Ferrara, Mantua, and Urbino and the lovely girls of Tuscany. After wandering among these pretty flowers, Ruggiero takes us to the end of the epic in a climactic struggle with the Saracen leader Rodomonte, a long fight frenzied with blows, throttling, and blood. But Ruggiero wears a magic helmet and, having Fortune by the forelock, vanquishes "the Mars of Africa," who, with his "insolence and arrogance and pride," is thrust into the pagans' underworld by the newly converted Christian.

These restless bits of outline are the barest framework for a marvelous vivacity of soaring medieval fantasy touched with Renaissance skepticism and irony. The bountiful epic pours forth fancies and sharp insights, the strongly heroic and the imaginatively bizarre, exorbitant waves of love, worshipful and erotic, the whole magicked complex of events and moods held in a finely controlled scheme. Portions of the epic's alluring riches became an English play staged near the end of the sixteenth century, at about the same time that Edmund Spenser published his *Faerie Queen*, a tribute to Queen Elizabeth and a tribute to the Italian poet, whose influence can be discerned in the extravagant English lines. Street-theater groups in Rome still perform sections of the epic; large Sicilian puppets still clatter and clash through "Orlando" battles; concert halls and opera houses frequently present Handel's operatic version of the work.

Although Sir Walter Scott said he read *Orlando Furioso* frequently, the modern reader finds its full great length rather difficult, especially when he is stopped by detailed biography and slavish praise of Este, required in the poet's place and time but wearing to our patience. Taken fifty stanzas at a time, among the thousands, it yet offers enchantments akin to *Gulliver's Travels*, to *The Tempest*, to Wagnerian opera, to space fantasies, and to the multitongued folk and fairy tales that shape our imaginations.

S*E*V*E*N

Francesco strengthened fortifications, tightening the safety of his own lands, which he knew were at hazard should the French, already advanced into Lombardy, take Milan and then advance eastward toward Mantua. He turned away from desperate Ludovico, whose frantic calls were laced with promises of choice tidbits of land. Francesco's judgment that Milan was no place for him to be was justified when, in September of 1499, the simultaneous advance of French troops and Venetian routed Sforza. He fled to Germany, hoping for succor and aid from the inept, bewildered emperor, whose driving concern, however, was to avoid difficulties with France. Though the stay in Germany gave Sforza a short period of safety, he was given little else.

The usual ornate letters vowing devotion and loyalty, the pretty phrasemaking of diplomacy, were exchanged between France and Mantua, some directed to Louis himself, a few to sister Chiara in France. When Louis made his triumphal entry into Milan, early in October, Francesco was a member of the royal entourage, later describing the event fully and zestily in a letter to Isabella. The procession led off with a large number of French and Italian knights on horse, these followed by a thousand foot soldiers, half of them Swiss. The calls of trumpeters and heralds ushered in church and civic officials in their full refulgence, each carrying a golden staff. Then, shaded by a splendid baldachin, came His Majesty, framed by a dignified body of cardinals and princes, among them the rulers of Ferrara and Mantua and Cesare Borgia, the duke of Valentois. The king's private guard of three hundred armored men led off a company of assorted French nobles. Thousands of citizens crammed the streets and crowded every bannered window. During the celebrations of transfer of power, Louis XII conferred on Francesco the insignia of the Order of Saint Michel and promoted him to a responsible command.

He may have been intoxicated by his new honors and his friendship with the king of France; he boasted loudly, he tripped over his own tongue. Venice became distinctly displeased with Francesco once again and withheld a promised advance of moneys. The Gonzaga jewels returned to the moneylenders, and Francesco, wearied by the constant inimical scrutiny of Venice, clung more closely to France, proving his loyalty by refusing to shelter in Mantua anyone named Sforza, even the two natural sons of Gian Galeazzo, who had been destroyed by Ludovico. Ludovico, deprived of aid from the emperor, turned to buying an army of Swiss and German mercenaries. The emperor, also flailing around for support, reminded Francesco that Mantua was feudal territory, pledged anciently to the Empire, and that meant mutual protection. Francesco's response was to report to Louis all the information his agents forwarded about the emperor's plans and movements.

The ruler of Milan, Gian Giacomo Trivulzio, of an old Milanese family and now head of French armies, was fiercely cruel, and he was forced by a citizen's uprising to flee the city. Sforza and his cardinal brother, Ascanio, took advantage of the anti-French disorder to force their way back. On March 21, 1500, Il Moro was again the duke of Milan and again asking for Gonzaga cooperation, hoping that Isabella would move her husband in his direction. Francesco did nothing and continued to do nothing, in spite of pressures from his wife. He remained in Mantua, keeping his troops well equipped, sharp and ready. He did, however, send his brother Giovanni with a token army, not of much use to Sforza but, as events would prove, a serious error. Ludovico's tenure was exceedingly short-lived: He was betrayed by his Swiss mercenaries and turned over to the French in April 1500. Imprisoned in France, he died there eight years later.

Possibly infected by Venetian suspicion and certainly for reasons of her own, France now began to look dourly on her friend Gonzaga. He had made a public gesture, in the person of brother

Giovanni and a band of mercenaries, that proved him a supporter of Ludovico. Urged by Isabella, he had given shelter to refugees from Il Moro's court, among them, it was said, the favorite mistresses, Cecilia Gallerini and Lucrezia Crivelli.

Mantua's shifting loyalties were painted in grave colors by the papal court. If Francesco and Isabella could be proved traitors to France and Venice, the Pope might permit his son Cesare to add Mantua, Ferrara, Urbino, and their friend Bologna to the lands he had already taken in north central Italy. Francesco informed his neighbors and relatives of their mutual danger and implored his sister Elisabetta, duchess of Urbino, in most affectionate words—"by the special love I bear you . . . the good I wish you with all my soul"—not to go to Rome as she planned in that jubilee year. She went and returned unmolested, to receive the news that Isabella and Francesco were celebrating the birth of their first son and heir, Federico, born May 17, 1500. Cesare Borgia was invited to be one of the godfathers, in the hope that he would turn from potential foe to friend. He accepted with pleasure.

Within two years, Louis XII began his campaign to control Italy. An early move was to secure a promise of neutrality from the emperor. Louis then took over a portion of Adriatic Italy abutting on the Venetian state and not too far from Spain's southern Italian domain. Getting wind of a plan hatched among the Pope, France, and Venice to divide Italy among themselves—Mantua to go to France—Gonzaga decided that the safest place for him to be was with the Empire as her captain general, in charge of eight thousand men. Whatever ties he had with Ferrara must, for the time being, be cut. The Este were in their own web of difficulties, destined to be taken by France or fall into the wide, cruel swath being carved by Cesare Borgia. The Pope had a suggestion for Ferrara: arrange a marriage between his daughter Lucrezia and Alfonso, the eldest son of Duke Ercole. The family was horrified. This might mean giving themselves into Cesare's relentless hands altogether, and furthermore, it was a demeaning marriage. The girl had been married twice, her second husband killed by her brother's henchmen; she was reputed to have had numerous sexual encounters, including connections with her brother and her father ("the Pope's daughter, wife and mistress"). The marriage might, on the other hand, protect Ferrara from being swallowed by France, and possibly even protected by the new brother-in-law. After strenuous haggling for an enormous dowry and a threat from Duke Ercole that he would marry Lucrezia himself if Alfonso didn't, the son consented. The dowry amounted to 100,000 ducats in coin, 100,000 ducats' worth of precious objects, and, in addition, a reduction of the large sums Ferrara customarily sent to the Church.

It was clearly not politic for Francesco to attend the nuptial celebrations, nor was it safe. He sent Isabella to Ferrara to help prepare and lead the festivities there, assisted by her pliant demoiselles. It was a costly outing. Detailed reports were pouring into Mantua describing the luxuries Lucrezia had brought with her from Rome; the very mule she rode was clothed in gold-studded velvet. For her own person she had caps and collars of jewels, she had a dress of gold thread and a cloak of silk striped in gold and trimmed with ermine, she had long strings of diamonds and rubies. Her wedding gown would be gold over red satin under a furred mantle of black satin. She would wear a golden cap and a large necklace of pearls with a ruby pendant. Isabella's wardrobe included two new costumes, one of gold-embroidered green velvet and a black velvet mantle trimmed with lynx, another of white shot through with silver, to be worn with a cap of pearls and a pearl necklace.

While the festivities and the displays of high style were going on, Francesco continued to check his fortresses and gates, had the flow of Mincio waters into villages and farms made more effective, bought a fresh supply of long bows, and, to appease the French, rid Mantua of remaining Milanese exiles. Somewhat comforting news came as reports that there was contention among the parties planning his dissolution; they could not decide how and when it was to be done. Francesco wrote cordial letters to every friend and foe, embedding in them discreet bits of information. The correspondence halted when Cesare Borgia took Urbino and everything of value in it. Long streams of wagons and mules descended Urbino's hills, carrying gold, tapestries, bronzes, paintings, books, and antiquities. Duke Guidobaldo fled to Mantua, where his wife, Elisabetta, had already arrived with their nephew and heir, Francesco Maria. The situation was desperate for all, and especially unhappy for Elisabetta. "I have been deprived of high estate, of my home and of fortune, and now I have lost the sister [Chiara had just died] who has ever been to me as a mother." Loved as Elisabetta was by both heads of the house, the Gonzaga had irons in the fire that made sheltering her family an embarrassment, perhaps a distinct danger. In mid-1502, they had negotiated a marriage contract between their two-year-old Federico and the newborn baby girl of Cesare Borgia and Charlotte D'Albret. The baby came with a regal dowry, returnable if the contract fell through. The baby's grandfather, the Pope, promised Sigismondo Gonzaga the long-awaited cardinal's hat for a fee of 25,000 ducats underwritten by a sound bank.

Isabella entered into a brisk, warm correspondence with Cesare, congratulating him on his victories and—in a frequently quoted letter—telling him of the one hundred masks, the products of high local skill, that she was sending to brighten his carnival festivities. Elisabetta, an intelligent and worldly woman, understood the games Mantua was playing but was still appalled by the sister-in-law, who had written her affectionate letters and with whom she had spent myriad pleasant hours, now become her reluctant hostess. The looser-tongued Francesco reviled and cursed Cesare, calling him a bastard, the son of a priest. Isabella tried to dampen his fury by reminding him that Cesare was a famous assassin who had not hesitated to kill his own brother and that he continued to press her and Francesco to rid Mantua of Guidobaldo. Elisabetta would not stay without her husband, and together they went off to shelter with her brother Sigismondo in Venice. Isabella, left to take care of the home front while Francesco went to France in the fall of 1502 to consult with Louis, tried to reopen her correspondence with Elisabetta, but the letters were sparse and awkward and stopped with a coarse injury inflicted by Isabella. Her avidity for prized objects impelled her to petition, successfully, of Cesare Borgia two choice objects in the Urbino collection, an antique Venus and the *Cupid* of Michelangelo. When Guidobaldo returned to his dukedom after the death by poison of the Borgia pope in August of 1503 and the rapid decline of Cesare's fortunes shortly thereafter, he asked that the sculptures be returned to him. They never were and the aristocrats of Urbino let the matter go in elegant style. Guidobaldo suggested that Isabella keep the works as a gift; Elisabetta, going him one better, said that her sister-in-law need only have asked and the pieces would have been hers.

It was not until Julius II, patron of Raphael and master and scourge of Michelangelo, became pontiff in 1503 that patient Sigismondo, with the help of Elisabetta, finally became a cardinal, one of the least impressive of the dashing family ecclesiasts. Sigismondo was not exactly simpleminded, not especially acute. A member of a family that had few outstanding beauties, he was one of the least prepossessing to look at. Pasquino, the "speaking statue" of Rome, (a repository of nasty, vindictive notes dropped into a stone figure, usually standing on a popular street corner) dubbed him the "Mantuan baboon," companions spoke of him as a man so weak in his responses, sexual as well as mental, that his erotic encounters were few and unenthusiastic. It was as if his brother Francesco, as lively in sex as behind a sword, had drawn the life and fervor from his sibling to fire his own high heat.

Francesco, now become a coleader with French heads of that army, engaged in attempts to take the kingdom of Naples from Spain, planning to meet with the Este army engaged in the same mission, but attacked by another bout of syphilis, he could not go on.

New in Europe and so virulent that, along with sieges, massacres, typhus, and dysentery, it helped determine the course of campaigns, this "gravest of calamities," according to Francesco Guicciardini, manifested itself "either in the form of the most ugly boils which often became incurable ulcers, or very intense pains at the joints and nerves all over the body. . . . Thus, this disease killed many men and women of all ages, and many became terribly deformed and were rendered useless, suffering from almost continuous torments; indeed, most of those who seemed to have been cured, relapsed in a short time into the same miserable state." After a short rest in Mantua, Francesco tried to make the long, difficult journey to Naples once again, and again was forced by a renewed attack of his disease to return home. Though he took no part in the southern campaign, the house of Gonzaga was honored by Louis, who conferred on Francesco and his son, Federico, the right to use his own heraldic symbols.

The year 1504 was a tired year of comparative peace. A truce was arranged between the king of France and the king of Spain, each to keep his then established territories; free trade was to be reopened in Italy, except in the kingdom of Naples, where unpaid Spanish soldiers were savaging the countryside. Cesare Borgia was under arrest in Spain, no longer a threat to anyone. Francesco took his quiet time to arrange the betrothal of his daughter, Leonora, to Francesco Maria della Rovere, the son of the prefect of Rome and nephew of Pope Julius II. Shortly after, in November of 1505, a second son was born in Mantua, officially named Luigi, in honor of the French king, but recorded in history as Ercole (later Cardinal Ercole), in memory of his mother's father, who had recently died. After an exchange of sharp correspondence with his wife on the matter, the boy's father submitted to the Este Christian name, a name then held in some abhorrence for the bloody brutality of an event in Ferrara, its main protagonist the most distinguished Cardinal Ippolito. It appears that he was in love with a girl in the court, also loved by his bastard brother, Don Giulio. When the girl told Ippolito that she found Giulio's beautiful, warm eyes irresistible, Ippolito tracked his brother through a hunting field, forced him to dismount, and had his eyes plucked out by a set of pages. This especially cruel act in an age rarely shocked by cruelty was never altogether forgotten, and trailed opprobrium for the family through the years.

Francesco could not linger on the matter; he had soon to force his way through yet another perilous swamp of entanglements. Julius II, the warrior pope, was fiercely eager to reconquer as papal domains the lands formerly dominated by Cesare Borgia, some of those lands now claimed by Venice. According to a Medici chronicler, it was "the rash and overly insolent action of the Venetian Senate" that brought down the carnage of the ensuing years. Cesare Borgia, escaped from prison in Spain and then killed in a battle as the head of troops for the king of Navarre, had no longer to be considered. The Pope—inspired by an excess of wine, France said—marched into Perugia, where he met no resistance from her ruler, Giampaolo Baglioni. The *"Papa Terribile"* took over Bologna, another key city, with the same ease, Francesco at that time in his employ as leader of the troops that took both cities. The emperor Maximilian, beset by defeats and insults from Venice, with which he had a pact made of cobwebs, looked to the strength of France to redress his losses and low repute. The Pope also hoped to inspire France to move against Venice. He wanted no part, actually, of Maximilian or of Louis, but his plans dictated a present partnership with the hope of ridding Italy of both at some propitious time. Meetings were set up—in sessions that ran from 1508 to 1510—in the Flemish town of Cambrai, where representatives of the Pope, the emperor, and France met to seal a complexly duplicitous coalition. One of the signators represented Ferdinand of Spain, who had, for his own political reasons, stayed in the background before. The Cambrai League issued clauses designed to explain a concerted attack on Venice, invoking the aid of Christ and God in this crusade against the godless republic, and then spelled out which towns held by Venice were to go specifically to whom: such to the Empire, such to France, such to Spain, such to the Pope. The partners were bound to make no other agreements without the participation of all parties, and should Mantua and Ferrara and others with complaints of Venetian marauding choose, they too might join the league, with full rights to claim lost territories. But the Pope remained uneasy with his detested partners and turned back to bargain with Venice, promising that if she returned Faenza and Rimini to him, he would protect her from the "barbarians." At one meeting of the Venetian senate, an eloquent member of that body persuaded the rest that the league was an unsound structure. Julius was not to be relied on; God would not support so licentious and drunken a pope. Earlier agreements had fallen apart, why not this? In short, there was nothing to fear; Venice would stay magnificently invulnerable without the Pope's armies. In spite of this confidence, by the summer of 1509 Venice was much reduced, and one of those who benefited from her losses was Francesco Gonzaga.

In 1508, Maximilian entered the Veneto with an army destructive enough to force Venice into a treaty, the alignment to become Venice–Empire against France–Julius II. In the meantime, Louis had retaken rebellious Genoa and celebrated the event in the palaces of Milan. Francesco shone among the distinguished guests, while Isabella reached the apogee of her life when Louis asked to meet her. Her reputation as leader of fashion and taste in the arts, her title as "first woman of Europe," had apparently impressed even the king of a chic court.

Whether emboldened by royal compliments, or wine, or the reckless euphoria of her husband, Isabella lost her dignified jewel-and-sable-covered bearings at least once, to act publicly like a fishwife. It was in the court of Milan or Mantua, among a good number of people, that Isabella leaped on a young woman entwined with Francesco, tore at her and pulled her hair, howling at her husband that he conduct his business with his whores elsewhere, in a more private place. The incident was an embarrassment but no serious matter, balanced by the praise and honors shining on Francesco from his sun, the king.

Early in 1509, France declared war on Venice and, to safeguard Milan, assigned Francesco to protect one sector of that dukedom. From Venice came information that she was about to invade the Montovana. In addition to the threat, Venice tried to lure Gonzaga to her side, spreading before him a banquet of flattery and moneys. Francesco refused Venice and borrowed several hundred men from the French to protect his strongholds. To counter his continued resistance, Venice set her agents to broadcast the news that Gonzaga was ready to sever himself from his French allies; the loudest rumor had Francesco in a secret agreement to return to Venice, his reward to be the title Duke of Milan should that city be taken. France was of course informed of Venetian offers and lies, and assured they were actually lies. Venetian soldiers were already dispersed over a number of key places, a substantial army stationed in nearby Verona, while a French army of ten thousand, many of them Italian volunteers, readied to cross the Alps. Francesco stayed at home, providing for the transport of French troops and preparing fortresses for their keep. His citizens and peasants were instructed to devise whatever was necessary for their own defense. He kept his agents sharp, many, and ubiquitous.

Having made all the preparations he could think of, Francesco turned the court over to Isabella and went out to confront the Venetians close to his doors. The encounters were unimpressive at first, the most useful war gains a number of horses and mules to be used for cartage and as food. As he observed the Venetians gathering large bodies of troops, Francesco was additionally disturbed by another piece of troubling news. The agreements he had earlier made with France had specifically promised him the trio claimed by his ancestors—Asola, Peschiera, Lonato. A document sent him confirming his claims omitted Peschiera, a change he protested without success. Whether he was being petulant or actually attacked, he reported a bout of syphilitic pain, which deprived him of the glory of leadership in the decisive battle of Agnadello (near Lodi), won by Louis. His royal ally sent him a letter that, masked in humor, covered him with mild contempt: "If you weren't the poltroon you are, you might have been pleased with yourself in avenging some of the outrages dealt you by the Venetians." Francesco answered humbly, congratulating Louis on his victory, wrested by his own hand from Venice. "As they say among us," Francesco wrote, "you've done it like a real man" (*"l'ha ben facto maschio,"* the essential Italian compliment).

He protests that he is not a lazy poltroon and never was, except that illness temporarily made him one, to his great misfortune. With the help of waters and herbal extracts, he hopes soon to return to His Majesty's victorious service.

On August 7, 1509, Francesco took off for Verona in the hope of preparing there for an assault on Legnano. On the way, he was captured by a Venetian captain and taken to Venice, where he was reviled and imprisoned. In a significant sense, this was the end of Francesco. His career as a warrior, his nimble political minuets, were over. Syphilis was slowing his mind and body, and the humiliation of being captured in his sleep, when he couldn't fight back, the unthinkable role of being a prisoner, sapped his confidence. His wife, who knew all there was to know about administering the affairs of Mantua, was to become the leader of an imperiled state with the help of her brother-in-law Cardinal Sigismondo and with the advice of her brother Cardinal Ippolito d'Este. Fortunately, there was no internal dissension to cope with; Mantuans were confident that Isabella could continue to rule effectively. Both Louis and the emperor offered troops and money for her protection, offers that promised possible entanglements. With many thanks, she rejected their offers and countered the rumors that she might combine her husband's house with that of her brother, the Gonzaga-Este combination to be a fief of France. In the meantime, the furious, bellicose Pope saw large chunks of northern Italy in the hands of France, the kingdom of Naples in control of Spain, and Maximilian in an important Venetian city, Verona—his country overrun by foreign "barbarians." Perhaps it might be useful, Rome said to Venice, that they join forces to rid Italy of France, removing Gonzaga from the French field by reappointing him commander of the Venetian forces and, in order to keep him in line, having his young son Federico held hostage in Venice. Isabella, who had been exploring every possibility of freeing her husband—feverishly consulting with ambassadors, agents, lawyers, priests, and astrologers—refused to send the boy away. Her firstborn son, handsome, adored by the court and especially his mother, was not to leave her side; he was too young and too vital to her very life, now that her husband was not with her. She had her brother Ippolito appeal to Louis of France to release a Venetian commander he had captured so that the Venetians might free Francesco in exchange. The king refused, although Ferrara had done him the service of destroying a Venetian fleet in the Po. When an exuberant letter she had written to her brothers on their Po victory fell into Venetian hands, Isabella was not overly concerned. She had decided that having sustained heavy losses, Venice was about finished; at her fall, Francesco would be released. She also counted on the good offices of her daughter Leonora's husband, Francesco Maria della Rovere of Urbino, to ask his uncle the Pope to arrange the release of his wife's father. Julius, eager to avoid accusations of nepotism, answered with characteristic fury, hurling accusations toward Urbino: The young duke was trying to become a Valentino and to rule his uncle as that Borgia had ruled his father.

Isabella wrote another letter, hoping that it too might be intercepted by Venetians. Addressed to her sister-in-law Elisabetta in Urbino, the letter explained, point by point, that Isabella was not and had never been pro-French. The Venetians were mistaken in their accusations: She had not sent supplies to the emperor's army in Verona; she had not refused to send supplies to Venetian troops; she had not withheld from Venice information she had received from agents assigned to watch the French. Above all, she wrote, it pained her to know that these accusations would reach Francesco, who would be hurt and angered with her and her brother Ippolito. Isabella continued waiting for Venice to collapse, supported in her conviction by Elisabetta, who reasoned that since the republic was doomed brother Francesco was best off not accepting the command of her armies.

Women

The stage on which the Renaissance woman lived is often bathed in the luminous nostalgic glow of a "Golden Age." It was a Golden Age for a few women, very few, and the light was less a broad glow than a spotlight, strengthened by energetic display and the scribblings of ambitious chroniclers and court sycophants. As we know, the Renaissance recorded itself in minute detail, and when there was concentration on one or two figures it was intense and large, pointing up every singularity, every distinction. The ladies who protected courts and fortresses, foiled enemies and placated popes, and who were mythologized in their time and after, though stubbornly strong and bold were not always as effective as some reports would have them. The usually keen Isabella d'Este-Gonzaga, for example, a prototype of the Renaissance Athena, made several serious political mistakes, using a good deal of her energy and cleverness to smooth or explain them away.

The warrior-politician-lady usually came to high responsibility when her husband became a victim of the politics or wars he himself often helped design. In the handsome Renaissance library of the Accademia Lincei in Rome, there is a folio of letters that defined the mature life of Lucrezia Gonzaga of the collateral line of Gazzuolo, a vulnerable territory claimed by various Gonzaga cousins at various times. They are angry letters, servile letters, letters that plead, that grovel, that praise, that beg. Her husband was the prisoner of the duke of Ferrara and his allies. She apologizes for the actions of the spouse, "who was, I think, born a twin of unhappiness," and begs pardon for his grave error. Won't the duke please have him released? His sin was stupidity and nothing more. How can such a flea menace an eagle? What force has a puppy against a lion? There was no response to this flattery; nor did reference to the fact that they were connected by blood and shared honored relatives make an impression on the Este. She also writes for help from the duke of Parma, to the powers of Genoa, Verona, Padua, and to relatives in Mantua. To her sister she writes of the dreadful wariness one has to maintain as a mentor of a court, as a politician, and of the danger and exhaustion inherent in the position. To Pope Paul II and to Julius III she writes letters trembling with piety and humility, and then to her sister she speaks of the unkindness of popes, bishops, archbishops, abbots, as cold as kings and emperors. Nor can she stop the letter-writing in widowhood; it gives her purpose and dimension. We find her groveling gracefully at the feet of Solimano, the emperor of Constantinople, and sending flattering notes to the king of Bohemia.

There were luckier women almost constantly in view. We frequently hear Isabella d'Este dictating to her scribes on a world of matters, and hear her sister Beatrice describing the gold brocade of her vest and the rubies laced into her hair for festivities to celebrate the birth of her first son. The shine of Lucrezia Borgia's golden hair, washed, dried in the sun, and touched with an alchemist's bleach during a day of rest on her progress toward Ferrara to marry Alfonso d'Este, is still refulgent across the centuries. The poetry and letters of devout, learned Vittoria Colonna to Pietro Bembo, to Castiglione, and most famously the sonnets and letters she exchanged with Michelangelo, who wrote a moving poem on her death, still sound for us from yellowed pages. We know of Cecilia Gonzaga's learning, of the cultivated and wise spirit of Elisabetta Gonzaga, of Caterina Sforza's outrageous scheming and courage, and her experiments in magic and medicine that might produce a "celestial water," a panacea for most ills. The intellectual career of Renée of France, who married into the court of Ferrara, where she gathered an "academy" of learned scholars and which she embarrassed profoundly—to the point of being removed to a nunnery by her husband—through her friendship with Calvin and other leaders of the Reformation, is richly documented. The Treaty of Cambria, involving pan-European affairs and often referred to as the "Peace of the Ladies," is praised as a step in the advancement of women. The "ladies," however, were Louise, the mother of the king of France, and Margaret, aunt of the emperor, women in conspicuous positions who may simply have been window dressing in matters actually handled by ambassadors and papal envoys at least as clever and seasoned as they.

Were it not for Leonardo, we might have lost the beauty and the poised, sly charm of such court mistresses as Cecilia Gallerini and Lucrezia Crivelli, painted for Ludovico il Moro of Milan.

Were it not for court chroniclers, we might have lost the translations from the classics, the poetry, and the disquisitions on philosophy written by other court mistresses. Nor did marriage always diminish the gifts of talented and privileged women. Ippolita Gonzaga, the daughter of Isabella's brother Ferrante, continued to study music and astronomy, to write poetry and remain for years "one of the most beautiful and accomplished women of her day." We know of a few polymaths, a few writers, and a few artists, but there must have been many gifted girls lost in anonymity. Large, busy ateliers like those of Squarcione and the Bellini in Padua quite possibly put their daughters to work with the boy apprentices. Who knows what telling passages in which paintings may have been theirs? Who knows what a prospering merchant gleaned from the hints and suggestions of his observant wife (in spite of the fact that, having followed Alberti's injunctions, he kept his papers hidden from her)? Who knows about the management of properties controlled by the wives of Italian bankers who made long, frequent voyages to their branches in Antwerp and London? There are, of course, extant diaries and records, but they touch on comparatively few female lives.

Careers open to women were the three perennials: housewifery and childbearing, the religious life, and whoredom. The little girls of princely houses were, with a few notable exceptions, taught mainly the feminine arts of embroidering, singing, dancing, playing a musical instrument or two, and being able to handle a few Latin phrases. The daughter of a merchant or a well-paid artisan acquired household skills and a knowledge of numbers, while she ate sturdily to achieve the buxom figure that promised fecundity. She was betrothed at about thirteen or earlier, but was not considered of interest until she was ready for childbearing, when her career actually began. The marriage celebration which she had anticipated for years was the fulfillment of a dream with nightmare components. The feasting and dancing were lovely, but how was a fifteen- or sixteen-year-old to react, no matter how sophisticated or well prepared by her female relatives, to heavy practical jokes of attempted rape or being bedded with a proxy, who might go as far as touching her nude leg with his, hardly the *amore* she had heard so much about in stories and carnival songs. Titillating jokes made around the marriage bed, and the display of her bed sheets to prove her virginity and her husband's capability, were familiar customs of her time, yet must have been confusing, even appalling, to a girl who might have been brought up on a blend of piety and romances about gentle knights.

Dowries frequently created problems, particularly in the courts that had inlaid boxes prepared with ingenious mechanisms to safeguard dowries of accumulated pearls and emeralds. Their ambassadors and secretaries rushed back and forth between courts, lawyers argued fine points, scribes scribbled, parents weighed and disputed, grew indignant, melted into acquiescence—acts and scenes that often absorbed protracted lengths of time. Where there was no money or too little, girls were sent to nunneries to weave and embroider, their chastity guarded by nuns who might or might not themselves be chaste and even if chaste, subject to rape—nuns and little girls alike—by gangs of adventuresome young men, who might be severely punished *if* they were caught. When nunneries were overwhelmed with little girls pushed into their doors, they asked for admission fees, spoken of as "dowries." Or a community might gather a dowry fund to distribute to poor girls or design regulations to hold down the size of dowries, always a failure. No one could discourage this prime symbol of upward mobility, particularly flexible among a growing class of prosperous merchants who felt they had the right to buy their way into the ranks of the elite, who often needed the dowry gold.

Among the many pieces of advice and instructions given a girl by her mother was the important matter of being patient and forbearing, of not, by either "learning or magics," attempting to match her husband's accomplishments. Some of the exquisitely painted *cassoni,* wedding chests that held a bride's new finery, presented Mamma's lessons graphically. Although many featured the popular subjects of Hercules' labors and Horatio's defense of his bridge, considerable attention was given the patient Griselda, the heroic Queen Esther, Ulysses' faithful Penelope, and Lucrezia, who stabbed herself rather than live with dishonor after she had been raped.

The rare artifacts that portrayed "woman triumphant" were the birth trays which carried food to women in labor, the most elaborate of them kept and displayed as commemorative pieces. In tempera on wood, a master painter of *cassoni* and trays, taking his theme from Plutarch's *Triumph of Love,* paints a triumphal chariot driven by Cupid. In the foreground, Aristotle acts as beast of burden for his Phyllis; nearby, Delilah cuts Samson's hair. The white-bearded philosopher is made stupid by the bit in his teeth, while Phyllis, young, ravishing, and splendidly dressed, holds the reins that direct and pull the old man. Another variation on the theme has Socrates playing the docile donkey for an exultant Xanthippe.

One tray, luxuriant with gold leaf, Medici symbols, horses, dogs, and armored knights, which compose a bravura display of the miniaturist's art, centers on a winged Fame, holding in one hand a sword, in the other a minute Cupid, bow at the ready. Probably designed by Domenico Veneziano after a passage in Boccaccio, the tray celebrates the birth of Lorenzo de' Medici. One side depicts a birthing-room scene, complete with attendants, visitors, and a lady harpist playing to the swaddled baby. The obverse displays a baby boy with a disconcertingly muscular body, sitting on a rock. He wears a coral amulet and urinates a streamlet of gold and silver, a symbol of the wealth to which he was born and the additional wealth he will achieve.

The same little stream of silver and gold appears in at least one other extant birth tray, decorated with the legend: "May God give health to all women who give birth and to the fathers. May there be no exhaustion or danger. I am an infant on a rock [a symbol of strength and endurance?] and I piss silver and gold." Such prayers, plus the magical amulets, plus the no-nonsense symbol of golden piss, were often accompanied by a weight of religious medals, which the mother of a princeling attached to his swaddling clothes and his cradle. She might also see to it that measures against the power of the evil eye be carefully maintained. (One was a prohibition against cutting the infant's nails for a proscribed time.) When she was no longer fed off the beautiful, flattering trays, when the baby left her care entirely—turned over to a wet nurse or put in the care of members of the court—she returned to being a lesser human being, an enfeebled version of noble man. Frequent literary references point up woman's perfidy and ridicule the barbaric practices to achieve false beauty: filling her wrinkles with unsightly paste, pulling her hair out by the roots to make her forehead taller, wearing wigs made of the hair of corpses.

The daughter of a moneyed family had no hope of inheriting more than a pittance of the family fortune; her dowry was considered her inheritance, and that was secure only if she behaved herself—good behavior frequently meaning her acceptance of her husband's dalliance anywhere, with anyone. If she made her husband a cuckold, a favorite form of fool, or if he merely suspected her and for obscure reasons chose not to have her beheaded or poisoned or shut up forever in a dungeon, he claimed her dowry, never again hers. She was, literally, a chattel of her husband, subject to what one historian called "moral lynching." Should she be maltreated—and many were, and hideously—her family might sympathize, invite her for long cosseting visits, but not rescue her. So notorious was the maltreatment of these golden lambs that Castiglione, an affectionate husband, actually condoned adultery in women and advocated divorce. Occasionally a girl would suffer the humiliation of being repeatedly offered and rejected, like a piece of faulty merchandise. Francesco Sforza of Milan, old enough to have fathered two dozen children, was betrothed to Bianca Maria Visconti when she was seven. The accompanying festivities were attended by nobles, knights, and relations, but not the little fiancée. As time passed, the contract was dissolved and the girl sent to Leonello d'Este for his approval. When he returned her, she was readied for a Gonzaga marriage, which also fell through. Eighteen years after the first marital foray, her long road rounded back to Milan, where she became Francesco Sforza's not too happy duchess.

Annulments were rare, affordable only by those who could make large gifts to the Church and unattainable altogether, as in the case of Henry VIII, by those who scorned papal authority. Leprosy, impotence, and absences of many years were grounds for annulment. Even when armed with such reasons, women were frequently reluctant to avail themselves of annulments; second marriages for women were frowned on by the Church and society, and in any case, chances of improvement might be slim: better the devil one knew.

A woman was eager to produce sons to protect the family and its interests, and happily proud to help arrange consequent jubilation, but her own birth and that of her daughters was rarely cause for celebration. Isabella d'Este owned a magnificent cradle, prepared for the birth of her firstborn, who, however, turned out to be a girl, Leonora, followed by another and yet another girl child. The cradle was kept under wraps for ten years, until Federico, the future marquis and first duke of Mantua, was born. It was then refurbished and shown in its full splendor, appropriate to a son. ("May all your children be sons" is still a common form of "Best wishes" in Italy.)

Should her husband bring home an illegitimate child, as Leonardo da Vinci's father brought him to his stepmother's household, she took care of him no matter how she might feel, among his half-siblings. The humanist tenet that a man's beginnings were of little importance and what a man made of himself, of his own free will, was all that mattered essentially, created a casual acceptance of the illegitimate child. (Illegitimacy rarely caused much inconvenience, except where property and power might be involved, and these matters were carefully settled, frequently by allotting portions of an inheritance to promising bastards. Illegitimate heirs were sometimes needed to continue a dwindling line; at least one pope repeopled his family tree with the help of a number of women. To answer particular problems, formal legitimacy was arranged with the Church, as when the Borgia pope, Alexander VI, established the legitimacy of his son Cesare before he declared him a cardinal.)

* Of the poor, unchronicled woman we know little, her life as unmarked as the vanished hovels in which she and her family lived with their animals and feed. She might not escape the plague by fleeing to a country villa, as her duchess did, but puerperal fever was more democratic, and her children might last longer than princelings did, since the poor woman was likely to nurse them herself rather than have them nursed by hired, not always sound, women. If he survived death in infancy, the peasant child might die of diseases related to malnutrition; drought, famine, and invasions left him weeds, acorns, and grasses for nourishment. When a sharecropper husband was tagged for military service to protect or expand his overlord's holdings, his wife could not apply to an agrarian guild for help. She might ask for help from church confraternities or petition the nuns and monks to take one or two of her young to teach them reading and writing or a useful craft. When taxes, always higher in rural areas, and church tithing became overwhelmingly burdensome, when she realized that surpluses of wheat, oats, millet, barley, and rice were amassed in the city, leaving farmlands scarce of these essentials, she might induce her husband to join the mass that was searching the cities for employment. A son might become an apprentice weaver, a daughter might learn to spin. A boy who could draw or carve might be taken into one of the art ateliers and be fed while he studied and ground colors. A winsome little girl might be taken on as a servant; a dramatically deformed child might become a court toy or a beggar; a blind child might earn a bit more as a street singer. Life in the city offered greater opportunities and, what with frequent guild holidays and theatricals, church and court festivities, considerably more diversion.

A rung below the peasant woman, though not immutably, was the slave. Slavery was a solid institution, waxing and waning with mortality figures and degrees of general prosperity. The busiest slave markets, the concentration mainly on girls, were the ports—Genoa and Venice the most active—where the captives arrived in large numbers from the east, from the Carpathians, from the Black Sea and beyond. These exotics with broad cheekbones and honeyed skin were used as domestics and wet nurses in well-to-do households. A letter dated 1474 written by Barbara of Brandenburg, the wife of Ludovico II, mentions the purchase of a slave arranged for her by Catherine, Queen of Bosnia, a country that supplied slave girls in considerable numbers. The need to ask a highly placed friend to find a slave may indicate a diminished supply that resulted from the fall of Constantinople in 1453 and the consequent collapse of eastern trade. The near disappearance of slaves comforted a few humanists but not householders or the Church, which had found with iterations of dogma—as in the American South centuries later—rationalizations for supporting slavery.

* Vain and courageous girls, and as often the most hapless, found their way to brothels, and with luck, to the "paradise of whores," Venice; two of her ripe, bored, elaborately golden-haired *puellae lupanaris* were forever and wondrously set at rest on their terrace by the Venetian painter Carpaccio. From the ranks of these middle-range prostitutes came the apogee of the Renaissance courtesan, who, like a present-day rock star, had male groupies follow her through the streets as she tottered on her exceedingly tall pattens, supported at each side by a servant. Golden hair, perilous shoes, attentive servants, and adoring admirers frequently enlivened services in churches favored by the aristocracy. Near the crest of the courtesan hierarchy were women like the magnificently dressed beauty painted by Palma Vecchio, who gave her no other name than "La Bella." At the very crest were La Boschetta, to whom Federico Gonzaga was attached most of his life; Vanozza Cataneo, the mother of Lucrezia, Cesare, and

several other children of the Borgia pope; the gifted mistresses of Ludovico Sforza; and an impressive additional list of talented Aspasias, who were the companions and ornaments of cardinals and popes, and frequently the mothers of their numerous "nephews." The ruthless Bianca Capello, who rose from the stews of Venice to become the mistress of Francesco de' Medici, reached the summit of her eventful career by marrying him, to rule and misrule, as the Grand Duchess, in Tuscany and wherever else she could put her troublesome hand.

Among the freest women were the singers and actresses of traveling companies, the most capable groups attached for long periods to one court or another, as in Mantua and Ferrara. England would not have women on the stage, although its throne was held by a woman; actresses were bawds, said the English, and so did Spain, and the Papacy protested their presence as well. The sophisticated Italians countered by pointing out the moral danger of having boys, too many already inclined and encouraged to feminine airs, actually playing pretty nymphs and foul-mouthed old whores. The Church especially loathed the freedom of the commedia dell'arte companies acting lascivious matter, irresistible to the young, who sat in audiences among prostitutes male and female. Some of the actresses, encouraged by their husbands, found "protectors" at court, who supported the husband and often the whole company. But there were a few dedicated professionals who scorned favors and ran their own companies, with distinction, while they also translated classics, studied the learned sciences and the arts of painting and music. Fighting the characterization of "loose women," a universal accusation often justified, they strove to make acting one of the respected arts. One phenomenon still remembered in theater history was Isabella Andreini, a poet, the author of several plays, a member of a learned academy, a musician, a fine actress, the mother of seven, and revered enough to have her head cast—like royalty—in several medals. It was her son's wife, Virginia, who mastered in six days— and sang exquisitely, it was reported—the *Arianna* of Monteverdi and (almost as distinguished an act) never became the sexual property of Duke Vincenzo, preferring to remain the faithful wife of a footloose husband.

* Girls not protected by a court and professional standing had a more stringent time of it. If they had to take to the brothels and streets they were restricted in the hours they could navigate and the areas they might prowl. A vestige of such regulations is still engraved on a wall in Siena, which advises that *meretrici* may not enter the adjoining *contrada* (borough or quarter) under pain of fine or imprisonment. *Donzelle* were, like Jews, required to wear identifying signs in a number of cities and were everywhere taxed, as were brothelkeepers. Taxes were rarely too exigent, not only because the girls were needed to take care of students and visiting tradesmen but because, it was hoped, their availability would reduce the incidence of incest, child rape, and the rape of nuns. Another consideration was the sums that whore taxes brought in; if pressed, the women of Perugia might remove to Bologna and fatten *its* coffers.

Unbelievable Venice had long attracted tourists: artists, engineers interested in its canals, merchants observing the fleets of trading vessels and the signs of prodigious wealth everywhere. More than the city's resplendent churches and marble palazzi and efficient docks, it was the courtesans of Venice who attracted the most attention. A monk of the late fifteenth century, on his way to the Holy Land, blinks briefly at a few of these women and turns away with "I am a priest in the way of pilgrimage and have no wish to inquire further into their lives." He has been pleased with the long, austere gowns of the men; they all look like doctors of law. But the women (not the general run, he hastens to add) wear *pianelle* (platforms twelve inches high); their hair curled down to their eyes makes them look like boys; most of it is false, bought off poles in the piazza. (Would the priest have known that prostitutes often wore masculine articles of clothing and adornments to attract homosexuals?) "They try as much as possible to show their breasts and shoulders, so much so that I marvelled that their clothes did not fall off their backs." Another group of beautiful damsels had on their bared chests, necks, heads, and hands jewels worth 100,000 ducats. (The price of a slave was about fifty ducats.) Thomas Coryat's *Crudities*, published in England in the first decade of the seventeenth century, found the "Nobles' courtesans" entrancing. He wrote and wrote about them, was charmed by their singing, their lute-playing, their graceful discourse. An illustrative engraving he sent his compatriots shows the renowned Margherita Emilia, her blond hair in tight curliness, dressed in a cut-velvet and lace gown, heavy chains of jewelry on a bodice cut deep enough to reveal her breasts.

The whore's haven, everyone's favorite sin city, was also a particular haven for sodomy, for wandering among a generous bounty of pages in clinging hose joined at flowery codpieces, like the pretty boys of the supercilious stare as painted, for one, by Bronzino. The patrons of the boys were often older aristocrats, writers and artists who chose, with varying degrees of discretion, to follow "the Greek ideal," to side with Giovanni Antonio Bazzi da Vercelli, a painter and orator, who at public meetings and as signature to his paintings proclaimed himself "Il Sodoma." Patrons and their boys abounded in the universities, in all centers of learning and pleasure, including those of England and France, whose moralists blamed the Italians for introducing this plague into Europe as they had syphilis. The court of Alfonso II of Naples gave lively parties for charming boys; one need only look at the cherry-ripe lips and velvety eyes of the boys Caravaggio painted for Cardinal del Monte to guess at similar entertainments in Rome; Mantua was a place to be assiduously avoided by young boys, according to Aretino. But no matter what the homosexual activity in other cities, Venice led them all.

Practical and well-organized, La Serenissima took measures to restore some balance in her population. She kept the tax on female prostitutes moderate to increase their already impressive numbers, in the hope that they would reeducate the tastes of the male population, not so much for moral reasons—who was not, at one time or another, a sodomite in the Venice of bisexual Aretino?—but to increase the falling birthrate. Having enjoyed the blandishments and tutelage of the professionals, husbands would return to their wives for rediscovered connubial bliss, an extra reward the annual pregnancy. There was, too, the expectation that in spite of the birth-control tricks of midwives and a few of their own, whores would become pregnant and bear children, investments in the city's future: the bright ones as merchants, the slow as soldiers in the armies Venice was constantly massing to grab lands or protect trade routes. Considering that the city flourished, in spite of setbacks and plagues, for generations on generations, Venice possibly owed her *putane*, her demoiselles, her courtesans, more than a modest tax relief; in justice they might have been acclaimed, with honor, the Mothers of the Republic.

E*I*G*H*T

Francesco, who had in the early days of his capture and imprisonment conducted himself like a madman, was slowly beginning to gather strength and judgment. He had been betrayed by a peasant whom he had paid for protection; he had lost a large sum of money, a heap of jewels, many horses, a cache of arms, their total value twenty thousand ducats, now the property of Venice. The catcalls and imprecations that were bawled at him as he was dragged through the city still tore at his ears. The shame of begging the *signoria* on his knees and in torrents of tears to return to him his two servants (they granted him one) still filled his insomniac nights, but he was again beginning to think politically. He knew a great deal about his captor, her difficulties and her strengths, including the wealth she still controlled. It might make sense to take on the command he was offered; he would be released from imprisonment although he would probably be watched inimically, still in a sense a prisoner. He would, moreover, be generously paid and could again buy the ornaments that had made his court glitter.

While he was sorting out possibilities and undergoing treatment administered by Venetian physicians, he felt seriously deprived of informants and advisers, of visitors in general, although Isabella sent musicians to entertain him. He did receive mail, certainly from Mantua and a good number, expressing sorrow and profound sympathy, from Lucrezia, the wife of Alfonso of Ferrara.

Much has been made of these letters, some historians insisting that there had been an affair between the two, a fact—if it was a fact—difficult to prove or entirely disprove of two such figures, one of them an almost mythical symbol of sexual permissiveness. They had met when Francesco came to her father in Rome to receive the honors due him as the hero of Fornovo. Lucrezia, once a golden girl, was now married to a man who preferred prostitutes, from whom he probably brought home the syphilis that caused her pregnancies to result in abortions and in stillborn children. Ferrarese music and poetry sang about her, her eye constantly met masterly paintings, but she recoiled from the ferocity and hatred among the Este—a father who often hated his sons, brothers who tortured and entombed one another. She much more enjoyed the company of the volatile, affectionate brother-in-law with the odd, entertaining face. In past encounters they had danced and played together and become close enough friends for her to appeal to Francesco for help in freeing her brother Cesare from his Spanish prison. (His petition failed.) After she was delivered of a stillborn child, he invited her to stay with him in a fortress he was inspecting, praising her in a bad poet's terms of gratitude when she accepted. The visit lasted two days, she still suffering the damages of a torturesome delivery and its fruit-lessness. The circumstances were hardly propitious for illuminat-ing high romance, though the visit did serve to cement a strong attachment, which they both valued and idealized.

In time, her husband became more attentive, gave her local commissions, which she executed well, and expressed sympathy when her brother was killed; but he still frequented prostitutes. Meanwhile, the "love letters" continued to travel from Ferrara to Mantua. The names were disguised, the phrases convoluted, the meanings capable of several interpretations. They were writ-ten by Ercole Strozzi, a confidant of Lucrezia, and transmitted to Francesco in Mantua by a close Strozzi relative. The lovers, if lovers they were, had few opportunities to be together, and those hampered by Lucrezia's pregnancies and Francesco's disease. Early in the summer of 1508, Ercole Strozzi was found stabbed to death in his castle in Ferrara, ostensibly killed by an unknown assailant. Francesco made the foolhardy, gallant gesture of offering a reward for information about Strozzi's assailant; Alfonso did nothing. After a pause of silence, several letters arrived from Ferrara via yet another Strozzi, this time clearly requesting a meeting with Francesco. He did not meet Lucrezia; he was too busy, he was too sick; actually, he had become too cautious.

* Ferrara was not concerned with Francesco's imprisonment; Ippolito found it mildly entertaining and Alfonso spread the word that it made no difference to him whether his brother-in-law rotted and died in prison or not. The duke of Ferrara was infinitely more moved by the success of the cannon he helped devise. Lucrezia prayed for Francesco and gave moneys to churches and monasteries for prayer services. When Francesco learned later that the Pope was preparing to take Ferrara, he offered to deliver to Julius his brother-in-law Alfonso—whom he suspected, not without justification, of plotting against him—should Alfonso flee for safety to Mantua. But would the Pope please show kindness to Lucrezia? She was the only one of the family who had been loyal and affectionate during his imprisonment, and in gratitude for her compassion he was making this plea to His Holiness in behalf of the "poor girl."

* From his prison, Francesco let it be known loudly that he profoundly distrusted his wife's pro-French politics. This oblique proof of his loyalty to Venice impressed no one in authority and he remained imprisoned, although he continued to offer Venice his son and his military services in exchange for his freedom. Isabella continued to insist she would not send her ten-year-old boy to Venice nor to France, as had been suggested by the king. Her intransigence caused her critics to hold that it was she alone who blocked Francesco's release. Her repeated boast that all matters passed through her hands when she was the head of the Mantuan state was used as proof that she preferred to remain the ruler of her domain without interference from a debased, diseased partner. (To the epithets she had earned, usually flattering, there was added "Machiavelli in skirts.")

Knowing that nothing escaped the Venetian senate, Francesco let it be known that "my wife, the whore" was the source of his troubles. Pope Julius, also a man with a vile tongue, used the same words to describe the marchesa of Mantua, his hatred inflamed when it was reported to him that Isabella had expressed fear for her son Federico if he was taken to Rome and subjected to the sodomy in the papal court. In spite of the double-pronged vituperation, she held on. The Pope, at this point the friend of Venice, again insisted that the "rebellious whore" send him her son as assurance that she and her brothers would not impede the progress of his troops. He pointed out to the Venetian senate that Isabella, instigated by her brothers, might openly go over to France and, in addition, sabotage his own military operations against Ferrara. Arguing that it might be better to have Mantua as a partner rather than an adversary, the Pope persuaded Venice to free Francesco. But to keep control of the perfidious couple, there was need of a hostage, their most valuable possession, their son Federico. Isabella could no longer fight; with pain and fear, she saw her handsome son, dressed like a prince and accompanied by a princely entourage, leave for Rome.

Francesco Guicciardini offers another explanation for Francesco's release. Venice, he says, had such contempt for the Pope and cared so little about Francesco that he might have been kept a prisoner forever. It was Bajazet, prince of the Turks and an old friend with whom he traded horses and falcons, who achieved Francesco's freedom. The Ottoman prince hit where it hurt most, threatening Venetian commerce. He called before him the commissioner who represented Venetian merchants and charged him with freeing Francesco. When the commissioner asked for time to consult with the senate, Bajazet answered, "Do it and do it now." The senate decided "it was no time to stir up so mighty a prince," and moved to free Francesco, "but in order to hide its dishonor and reap some fruit of the Marquis' liberation the senate lent ear to the Pope's request." On his release, Francesco presented Isabella with a collar of jewels, the sort of lavish ornament she might have received after childbirth, shaping a symbolic pun, much to the Renaissance taste, on "delivery." Back in the world, Francesco was free but not entirely. He was hostage to the Pope, who now held his heir in Rome; obligated to France; living in the dour shadow of Venice; under pressure from the emperor, who kept reminding him that his state was a feudatory of the Empire and consequently it was required that he follow the emperor's uncertain politics. Debilitated by his prison stay, increasingly consumed by his illness, Francesco remained silent and inactive. While Isabella wrote feverishly to Federico's tutors and servants, instructing them about lessons and conduct, demanding full reports on every breath the boy drew, oversolicitous, overanxious while the boy was enjoying himself and learning to be a sleek courtier, Francesco began slowly to reassess his position. Venice and Julius demanded his services against the French—the Pope to design the wars, the republic to pay for them. His own experience and the example of the fate of Ludovico il Moro, not so long before one of the most ruthlessly manipulative and richest of tyrants and now in a French grave, held him immobile. A few months after his release from prison, the Pope offered him the blandishment of a singular honor: He was to be a *Gonfaloniere* of the Church to replace Alfonso d'Este, the former bearer of ecclesiastical honor, now excommunicated in a move to dissolve his dukedom. Francesco was not impressed, no more than he was when the Venetian senate confirmed him as commander of its armies and, in their missives, sent high compliments to Isabella on her intelligent, capable handling of Mantuan affairs during her husband's imprisonment. He was too sick and skeptical, too tired of the confusing political messes in which he had spent his adult life, to leap in response to the flattering offers or to concern himself with the darkening clouds over Ferrara.

Finally forced to take a stand, Francesco agreed to become the man of Venice and the Pope if they increased the offered salary, if they restored to him Peschiera, whose position at the southern end of Lake Garda served to protect the mouth of his Mincio River, and if the negotiations were kept secret, especially from France. The last stipulation was a piece of playacting; he knew better than to think that the agreement would remain a secret or that France would consider him her enemy, with Isabella so passionately a propagandist for pro-French Ferrara and, with the collaboration of her husband, instructing bailiffs and captains of fortresses not to molest the French soldiers who might pass through the Mantovana. The quicksand alliances, the double-dealing, the suspicions heated by the driven Pope, whipped up tensions to add to the constant worries about Federico and the safety of Mantua. The citizens of Mantua, accustomed to being well protected, became thoroughly unnerved as a consequence of one of the Pope's wild orders. He insisted that a bridge be built across the Po so that his army might easily invade Ferrara. That army was to be led by Francesco, who told his wife, who told her brothers, who attacked Mantuan masons, inflicting serious damage. When it became known that Isabella intended to leave for Parma to consult with her brother Cardinal Ippolito, there was terrified protest; it was assumed that she was taking refuge with her brothers, fleeing Mantua, which must be in danger. She was persuaded by her advisers and her husband to stay home, while Francesco removed himself from military action by spreading the news of a severe recurrence of his disease, which would require a long mercury cure. The Pope, who had suffered similarly, seconded the use of mercury, hoping it would speed his commander back to work; this attack was consuming an extraordinary amount of valuable time. One of Francesco's advisers suggested that he ask Julius to send him a trusted physician to find out exactly how incapacitated the marquis was. The physician reported that Francesco was indeed quite ill and earned ten Mantuan ducats for his testimony.

Came the time when Francesco dragged himself to his job and its vagaries, promising King Louis and Ferrara that they would have a week's notice before hostilities against them began.

Venice was hardly unaware of this ploy and insisted that Francesco, still claiming luetic malaise, be more active in her interests. He protested and offered to turn his troops over to the city, knowing that she was temporarily out of money and the unpaid soldiers he offered would become bands of looters. Venice let him be. The status quo held, extended by the illness of the Pope, who was thought by many to be dying. Francesco, a sympathetic soul and not averse to endearing himself to his inimical senior partner should he live, sent him Mantuan cheese, sausage, fruit, and fish. The Pope recovered and was immediately launched on his campaign to take Ferrara and free Italy from the French, with the assistance of Venice and God, expecting enthusiastic cooperation from Gonzaga, who, however, played his waiting game while Isabella, immutably an Este, ran Ferrara's errands, mainly to borrow money for arms and troops.

On January 11, 1511, the Pope entered Mirandola, a defense post of Ferrara, and inspired by his success, felt ready to take the city. Francesco was to send him supplies and, furthermore, not to permit Alfonso to shelter in Mantua. In response, the Este lent themselves to vaulting fantasies of conquest. Since the Pope insisted on leading his own army, like the Crusader kings of old, it should not be difficult to capture him. Furthermore, they might be assisted by a junta of cardinals, backed by Louis XII, planning to unseat the Pope. Julius paused, thought, and decided to treat with France. France was unwilling to join him, deeming Ferrara a steadier ally. To the France-Ferrara link was added Mantua, the trio blessed by the emperor, who still dangled before Francesco the fantasy role of governor of Milan.

The winter of 1511 was extremely severe; the Po froze and remained unnavigable, bridges crumbled, the Pope's planned attack on Ferrara became untenable. It seemed a propitious time for peace talks, which were held in Mantua in March. As a preliminary move, the Pope, eager to soothe the emperor, turned Modena over to him. The rest was failure. The old tunes reappeared: the Pope demanding lands held by Ferrara, the emperor insisting on Venetian territory promised him by the pact of Cambrai. To counter the threat of the dissident pro-France cardinals, the Pope called a large group of conservative, faithful bishops and cardinals for a conclave in Rome, this Sacred League to unite the strength of the Church with that of Venice, Ferdinand of Spain, and Henry VIII of England. As to the role of Francesco: the Pope would free him of the expensive duties of *Gonfaloniere* if he would promise not to help Ferrara. France made broad hints of freeing Federico if Gonzaga would declare himself openly her ally. While Francesco temporized, the clashing armies gathered. The Swiss mercenaries, of the same fearsome reputation as the earlier stradiots but more amenable to discipline, had entered Italy with the French, while the Pope's army had taken on large bodies of Spanish troops.

The French, with the help of Gonzaga information concerning the disposition of Venetian armies, made marked advances in Lombardy. When Venice complained, Francesco responded that the forces she supplied him for holding back the French were inadequate. Yet in spite of his acts of support to the French and the displeasure of Venice, he refused to proclaim his alliance with Louis XII openly. When the emperor Maximilian suggested that he take the governorship of Verona, he slid past that too.

The French and the Ferrarese continued to make impressive advances, routing the papal-Spanish forces almost decisively at Ravenna, but they did not press on as they might have. Old Julius then gathered his troops in an imposing display of strength that dismayed and roused Gonzaga. He decided to sign on with the Pope's *Lega Santa*, offering his services at an inconsequential sum. Something of the spirit of Fornovo returned; he was again eager to rout the French, as fervidly eager as the Pope, who promised Alfonso d'Este, and consequently all Ferrarese, full absolution if they joined his forces. The Este turned their backs on

Julius, but Francesco stayed, adding to his signature in at least one letter, "Long live the Pope." Behind the fervor was a recurrent illusion: Perhaps the Pope would actually see to it that he was promoted from marquis of Mantua to duke of Milan. In the late summer of 1512, the Pope's league held another set of meetings, this time in Mantua. Isabella brought out all her skills and style and the brio of her alluring *damigelle*. In the merry humming and circling among the seductive girls, the entranced delegates agreed that Ferrara was not to be disturbed and that Massimiliano, the son of Beatrice d'Este and Ludovico Sforza, would be named duke of Milan, to rule under the tutelage of his Este uncles. Pleased Isabella was praised and thanked fulsomely for her social and political accomplishments. Isabella's husband was not quite so happy. Milan was not his and the possibility that Ferrara might extend her control over his vulnerable lands presented an uncomfortable prospect.

Francesco appeared to be frequently incapacitated at this time, reduced—and he sometimes rather enjoyed it—to a friendly homebody, the benevolent doyen of his house. He knew that not everything decided by the league would please the irascible Pope, particularly decisions that overlooked the interests of the Church. Francesco tried to appease the raging sick old man, blaming Isabella and her brothers whenever he could: She was a devoted sister, stubbornly firm in her affections and, as everyone knew, not readily obedient to her husband's wishes. To emphasize their political differences, Francesco stayed in Mantua, continuing to explain and soothe, while Isabella went off to Milan with her persuasive ladies to bend the judgment of foreign diplomats toward her brothers and her nephew. Letters between the couple and those directed to other members of the family reported in great detail amusements offered eminent personages, especially by the bold, teasing, high-spirited girl called La Brognina and, to a less active degree, the marchesa herself. Reports of the carnivalesque doings evoked an eruption of rough soldier's words to her from Francesco, and words of shocked refinement—confirmation of his general disapproval of everything Isabella did—aimed at the ears of the Pope. In a more secret voice, he asked Isabella to instruct La Brognina to lure a powerful cardinal, enamored of the girl, into consenting to restore Peschiera to Mantua. Besotted though he was, the cardinal would make no promises, and Peschiera floated away once more.

The Pope, continuing to fire himself up with imprecations, decided once again to go after Ferrara, to take her as the papal state she anciently was. Francesco was concerned that he might try to take Mantua as well, since the papal anger over his own determined inactivity and the perfidy of Isabella had reached a white-heat pitch. Francesco ordered Isabella home, somewhere she was not eager to go for several reasons, mainly that she did not want to leave unresolved a promising situation. The viceroy of Naples had been ensnared by the talented Brognina and among his sighs and sobs of love had uttered promises that he would protect young Massimiliano Sforza of Milan. Isabella was waiting for deeper enmeshment and more solid promises. Then came a grateful breathing spell; Julius II died on February 21, 1513. After his funeral rites were concluded and before a conclave to elect a new pope met, young Federico was declared free. During the pause between popes, Isabella continued politicking, with the help of her girls in Parma, in Piacenza, in Milan, proudly recording their successes, particularly those of La Brognina, not only with the Spanish viceroy of Naples but with Matthew Lang, a leading bishop of Germany and adviser to the emperor Maximilian. (It was the German who "threw himself to the floor, forgetting at the moment the dignity of his position, to make love to her, as much as she liked.") After she returned to Mantua, Isabella continued her appeals to the viceroy in behalf of her Sforza nephew. The viceroy's replies were wails of longing for the missing Brognina, who had suddenly sequestered herself, along with another girl, in a convent. In replying to the Spaniard, Isabella lamented the loss of these girls, to whom she had been as a mother and who had so displeased her. She assured him that his love was misplaced in a girl so cruel, so inhuman, so ungrateful to one who had been as kind as he. He continued to be Isabella's friend, however, and continued to try to extract La Brognina from the cloistered life, in time successfully, with the help of Francesco Gonzaga.

The "Slow Plague"

It was called the "French disease" by the Italians, the "Italian disease" by the French, the disease of the "New Indies" by others; the English strewed blame everywhere but settled on the word "pox" for their affliction. An old nuisance, the disease that was also blamed on the redskins of the New World took on a perverse Renaissance brilliance in the last years of the fifteenth century, unexpected and intensely virulent when it settled on French troops marching on Naples in 1495. By the time the city was taken, it appeared as if everyone had syphilis: soldiers, camp followers, merchants, priests. Among the theories that tried to explain the hideous, rotting look of sufferers, the pain and crippling they endured, and the fumbling, mindless deaths, was a supposition that a man mated to a leper had introduced the disease. Another theory, sponsored by a morality that objected to a common country matter, blamed peasants who lived too intimately with their goats and mares and consequently unleashed this "slow plague," so contagious that the mere touch of a hand would transmit it. (A much later theory, proposed when the disease had abated in frequency and virulence, claimed for syphilis a partnership with genius: a stimulus that produced the works of Nietzsche, of Schumann, of Manet, of Toulouse-Lautrec, and numerous achievements of the Renaissance. Paul Ehrlich, it has been muttered, deprived the world of incalculable greatness with his "606" cure.)

Although Niccolò Leoniceno, a professor of medicine, made several telling observations on the disease when it appeared in its heightened form, it was not until the mid-1500s that the word appeared as the name of an afflicted shepherd in a Latin poem. The author, Girolamo Fracastoro of Verona, an astrologer and a keen scholar of medical matters, did not stop with Latin fantasy, but in a pioneer work, *De Contagione*, wrote of invisible minuscule agents that traveled the air from one body to another. With each encounter the tiny bodies increased, each group carrying its own immutable peculiarities, and the more quickly these evil little spirits could be destroyed, the better a patient's chances for recovery.

Because so many suffered of syphilis, there was a rush of both reputable healers and charlatans to become well-paid "specialists" in the field. The first treatments relied on common Christian and pagan magics: amulets, herbal infusions, strong purges, spells, a written prayer folded in a particular fashion, to be consumed on an empty stomach. Mercury quickly became popular as an ointment and then, mixed with animal fat, was used in injections. Because of the slow, mutable nature of the disease in some patients—witness Francesco Gonzaga's many bouts, and periods of remission when he functioned quite well—mercury was said to alleviate symptoms and quite possibly did. Public baths, sybaritic establishments in the Roman style, which provided relief from muscular pain, were also treatment centers, the effects considerably diminished by the steady presence of prostitutes.

One of the advocates of the use of mercury in ointments came to the court of Mantua specifically to treat the marquis Francesco. Giovanni Battista de Rovere, as extreme a character as his patient, had as a student at the College of Surgery in Venice been involved in two murders, one a knife-wielding students' brawl and the other the death of a patient following the use of a lethal medicament he had sent with a servant. He blamed the servant, apparently convincingly, and was licensed for full medical practice. Moving from court to court as an expert syphilologist and generally skillful practitioner, he ultimately made his way into the court of Pope Leo X, who suffered of an anal fistula. Giovanni Battista did not cure the Pope, nor did he kill him, but he was accused of attempting to inoculate poison into the fistula. He was hanged and quartered in 1517, not so much for malpractice as for his politics: as the friend of dissident cardinals who had plotted, with his cooperation, to kill or at least incapacitate the Pope. There were no proofs, but Leo needed none.

Unusually expert in the nature and uses of mercury was the alchemist-physician Paracelsus, born to the Swiss name of Theophrastus Bombastus von Hohenheim, who knew as much as any man in the early sixteenth century about the properties of metals, to the point of using them, each assigned its specific disease, for curative mineral baths and, conversely, to identify the damage they could do. He scorned the use of general panaceas for most diseases—each, he said, should have its own study and cure—

and was contemptuous of church proclamations that the causes of disease were gaming, theatricals, sodomy, and adultery. Advanced as he was, scorning the ancient authority of the Greek Galen's medicine that his contemporaries followed, battling with them over his conception of "God's knowledge," which led him from alchemy to early pharmacology, he also insisted that he could create incubi and succubi. For his "Satanic" experiments, which included the uses of ether and opium, for his arrogant claims of both supernatural and scientific powers, he was hounded from one university to another, and for his truculence and coarseness, he was killed in a tavern brawl.

In time, sulfur was added to mercury for the treatment of syphilis; to make its odor more acceptable, it was floated in aromatic substances. These were frequently expensive, as Cellini protests in his account of his treatments for the "French disease." More expensive still was a resin brought by the Spaniards from the Americas. It had a pleasant odor and, taken as infusions for several weeks following long periods of starvation and thirst, had curative virtues that lasted a fair while. Those who could not afford the costly resin subjected themselves to immersion in barrels, where they were smoked in the fumes of sulfur and mercury, and along with this suffered the burning of caustic substances placed under their skin.

As the possibility that unseen minute bodies caused contagion became increasingly plausible, regulations for ensuring the public safety were introduced. Syphilitics were forbidden to go to public barbers, and if customers revealed later to be syphilitics had been admitted, the scissors and scrapers used on them were to be discarded. Several cities rid themselves of their prostitutes; other cities had women newly hired by brothels examined for the presence of chancres. By the time syphilis weakened, late in the sixteenth century, giving supremacy in the field to gonorrhea, general medicine had made impressive advances, much of it attributable to enlightenments gathered from observing and attempting to cure the slow plague.

N * I * N * E

The new Pope, elected in 1513, was Leo X, the Medici who virtually owned prosperous Florence and could easily afford the 100,000 ducats he spent on coronation ceremonies that elicited the judgment: "Never since the time of the barbarian invasions had Rome seen so magnificent and proud a celebration." Among the proud lords conspicuous in the procession was Alfonso d'Este, released from papal opprobrium and again carrying the noble standard of the Church. André Maurois speaks of Leo as "His Cautiousness"; Guicciardini said centuries before: "He governed with more prudence but much less goodness than everyone had foreseen." The historian Charles Osman characterizes him as a "patron of all culture . . . entirely destitute of any moral or spiritual enthusiasm, whose contemporaries doubted even if he were a good Christian, but were certain that he was a good art-critic." His interests circled on his friends Raphael, Cardinal Bembo, and a small horde of artistic and literary retainers, including Bramante, who was scheduled to rebuild St. Peter's. Lazy and licentious, wealthy and in general good-natured, Leo much preferred to spend his money and energies on music and painting, on clowns and dwarfs, on "pleasures which are enjoyed with great infamy," rather than on politics and armies. The reform smoldering in the north meant little to him, so little that he fanned the flames by going into the lucrative business of selling indulgences there—to rebuild St. Peter's, he said—thus strengthening Martin Luther's armory of anti-papal accusations.

During his early rule, Leo's Italy settled into a few short years of respite from the wars, soon to recommence, however, because papal ambassadors were arranging the usual almost impromtu pacts, some whispered, some loudly proclaimed, that followed papal policy, obstinately aimed at taking Ferrara, among other coveted cities. Isabella continued touring and politicking, avoiding her husband, one important reason for the long absences strongly suggested by way of a letter from Benedetto Capilupi to Isabella, reporting that a friar with extraordinary medical skills had cured Francesco. He was now ready and eager to return to conjugal love. Considering the ease with which correspondence—except that in code and it, too, often decoded—was intercepted and its contents broadly circulated, the letter might also have been an attempt by Francesco to tell the world in general that he was again in forceful form, again a robust leader of warriors. He was not eagerly claimed at first; occasional feebleness and the straying of his mind were becoming common knowledge. Isabella continued her leisured travels, performing Este tasks and errands for Francesco. And then there was Rome and Leo to explore and if possible find favor with, particularly important in view of the fact that, like his predecessors, Leo had a nephew, this one Giuliano de' Medici, for whom he wanted a state: Ferrara? Urbino? Milan? On Francesco's instructions, Isabella went to Rome in the fall of 1514. She was honorably welcomed and endeared herself to the Pope and his court with her culture and graces. Mantua's productive lands had been despoiled by marauding troops, the exchequer was thin, but these were minor matters, not permitted to sully the pleasant atmosphere of friendship with a cultivated pope, who might, just might, leave Ferrara and Milan and her Este relatives unmolested.

On the first day of 1515, Louis XII of France died ("greedily making use of the excellent beauty and youth of his new wife, a girl of 18, and not considering his own years and weak constitution"), and the young François I became king of France and, on the old claims, the duke of Milan. Dizzied with his new power, boundlessly ambitious, and out of youthful derring-do, he prepared to fall on the Italians, having first sent emissaries to attract the favor of several great powers: the doge of Venice, the emperor, Henry VIII of England, Ferdinand of Spain. With caveats and demurrers, the usual teetery pact was signed to open the next phase of the Italian wars. The French army of over 35,000 men was led by experienced commanders, a number of whom had led Charles VIII's armies twenty years before, who knew how to manage the difficult transport of artillery and horses across the Alps— men who had been and could again be governors of Milan. Gonzaga was approached for two purposes: directly, to fight with France, and indirectly, to arrange a marriage contract between his son Federico and Maria, the daughter of the duke of Monferrato, allied with France. Francesco asked for time; he would like to discuss these matters with his wife, who should soon return from Rome. While he was temporizing, young King François subjected Massimiliano's Swiss troops to a bloodbath at Marignano, southeast of Milan, the Este-Sforza heir becoming a captive of the French as his father had been. Exulting in this victory, François welcomed the ceremonies that pleasured papal ambassadors, now eager to deal with him as an ally.

In the months surrounding the French victory at Marignano, Francesco again fell ill and sent his son Federico to Milan to congratulate François and to present him with four of the choicest horses of the Mantuan stables. Federico caught the fancy of the young king, who shared his extracurricular interests—women, hunting, falconry, dancing, gambling—and he was offered the command of a segment of the French army, at a good salary. As friend and commander, Federico joined the entourage that went to Bologna with François to meet with the Pope. While Federico was marching in the royal progress, his father amused himself with a Boccacciesque plot he devised around Mantua's Circe, La Brognina, who was then not far from his villa at Goito. François had heard of her charms and wanted her. He sent a false bishop with false papers to take her out of the convent and bring her to him. Francesco had a company of Spanish gentlemen intercept the "bishop." They took the girl, probably to deliver to the viceroy of Naples, and beat up the false bishop, who then fled to hide from the wrath of his king.

After the elaborate practical joke, Francesco had to turn to more vital matters: Venice sent legates to Mantua to ask that Francesco return Asola and Lonato. Francesco used the occasion to show the Venetians the magnificence of his court and city. One full Venetian report—and all Renaissance reports were lengthy and, like many of the paintings, wondrously detailed— mentioned sybaritic accommodations in a palace that was exclusively Federico's; one superb meal after another and yet another, all at the expense of the host; then on to the chase and entertainment at Goito, and the pleasures of yet another luxurious villa and *its* unique objects; as a climax to the entertainments, a display of the impressive armory, amassed by Gonzaga generations.

Vis-à-vis the French, Francesco's position, in spite of the uncomfortably close armies, was relatively good. Federico was a friend and employee of François; the son of Chiara Gonzaga and Montpensier was, after all, Charles of the Bourbons, a French commander who might easily be of future use to Mantua. François acknowledged the kind offices of Mantua and, partly as hostage to keep his slippery father in line and because he genuinely enjoyed the companionship of the boy, continued to keep Federico and a train of his gentlemen at his court. Matters were going badly, however, for Federico's sister Leonora, married to the diseased, unwise Francesco Maria della Rovere, duke of Urbino. Francesco Maria had dismissed a number of armed men paid for by the Pope, an egregious error blown up into unforgivable catastrophe by Leo X, who was ready to take Urbino for his nephew, Lorenzo. Their most distinguished *oratore*, Baldassare Castiglione, was sent by the Gonzaga to plead with Leo, to no avail. The respected Elisabetta Gonzaga tried as well and found the Pope adamant. Federico asked François to appeal to the Pope; he too was unsuccessful. Again the troublesome need to shelter relatives who had to leave Urbino. With the cooperation of Florentine and Venetian bankers and Mantuan Jews, Isabella provided the money for the keep of her impoverished daughter and son-in-law and took off once more, ostensibly on a religious pilgrimage. The journey took her and her ladies to France, where the pilgrims awed the natives with their chic, then to Monferrato, to check in on marriage arrangements between Federico and Maria Paleologa, of that nearby dukedom. Isabella's absence, while Francesco stayed to guard his state and his health, was politically useful since she could again be blamed for acts of which, he said, he deeply disapproved. There was also the matter of nudging the Pope in Rome for a favor. With persuasive words and more persuasive sums, amounting to forty thousand ducats dropped here and there among friendly, influential ecclesiasts, Isabella managed to have her bright, sophisticated thirteen-year-old son, Ercole, considered as a cardinal, with the privileges of being schooled in the papal court.

Federico was enjoying his happy, costly sojourn in France. He was invited to royal marriages and baptisms, entered tourneys against the most skillful knights of Europe, took on a French mistress or two or three. His financial needs as a grandee of the French court with a showy entourage to support kept mounting. His stipend as *condottiere* disappeared as soon as he received it, and he needed more from home. Whatever the cost, his situation was worth it; the dynasty was to be in the hands of a son with a remarkable education in court manners and diplomacy—Italian and French—and quite ready to meet as an equal with the crowned heads of Europe, with the masters of Venice and the rulers of Florence. The marriage negotiations with the duke of Monferrato progressed well. The duchess, the mother of the bride, was related to François, who gave Federico leave, early in 1517, to return to Italy to visit with his young betrothed, to get to know her.

As Federico flourished, his father failed. A message to Venice by one of her ambassadors paints a telling picture of the weakened marquis lying near an immense fireplace in one wall of a baronial chamber. Hawks and falcons on leashes surround the patient, while at his feet lies a lean greyhound. The only paintings on the walls are portraits of horses and dogs, the only entertainment is that provided by a favorite dwarf, dressed in gold brocade. As his brain became increasingly affected, Francesco began to reject Isabella's opinions and suggestions, turning for better advice to doubtful impromptu sources—a new doctor, a persuasive friar, a sleek, ambitious secretary. In a letter to Castiglione, Isabella pointed out that she had stayed far from Mantua for so long (nine months) to avoid the humiliations poured on her by her demented husband; but she was in Mantua, and so were the children, when Francesco died, in March of 1519. Whatever his destroyed mind dictated in his last months, his will expressed the respect he had for his wife's capabilities. In the will, he stipulated that the reign of Mantua was to be turned over to Federico and, specifically, that he was to rule under the supervision of Isabella, with the assistance of his uncles Giovanni Gonzaga and the cardinal Sigismondo.

٭ Nineteen-year-old Federico, resplendent in white silk, became the marquis of Mantua shortly after his father's death, and two years later was granted the imperial seal as feudatory to the new emperor, Charles V. His state, depleted by the wars, was yet capable of recovery because of his parents' vigilance: The Gonzaga owned one half of the Mantovana lands and had kept their productivity high by careful maintenance of irrigation canals, the waters of the Mincio kept clear and navigable for the import and export of goods. Through the vicissitudes—the imprisonment and disease of the head of state, the steady thunder of threats, land roughly used by French soldiers—the court flourished, a treasure house of arts and high manners that Europe envied and emulated. Federico, unusually handsome for a Gonzaga, was fully aware of it and dressed with careful appreciation of his own beauty. The fine figure he cut at jousting during the tourneys he staged for his people and his peers, his skill as hunter and falconer, and his derring-do as warrior were bequeathed him by his father. Political enlightenment came from a number of sources—his years in exile, observing and learning in Rome and France; his uncles, his ambassadors, and, markedly, his mother.

Probably pushed by Isabella, uncles Giovanni and Sigismondo slid out of their roles as effective regents and left the job to her veteran expertise. Her most effective support was Castiglione, her ambassador in Rome, who helped her in many delicate tasks, among them the settling of old scores, to be achieved without stirring up Leo's displeasure. Two of her prime enemies were a malicious Mantuan envoy to the papal court, and a perfidious secretary of Francesco, who had twisted her life. It was Castiglione's mission to present as tactfully and convincingly as possible Isabella's reasons for ridding herself of these two irritants, the matter wrapped in condolences to Leo on the death of his nephew Lorenzo, the duke of Urbino. Another of Isabella's concerns was, as ever, money. The spendthrift son of spendthrift parents, Federico, *il bello e amoroso*, needed more money than was provided by the ordinary sources of agriculture, commerce, and high taxation. One of his mother's solutions was that he be given, with the Pope's help, the role of duke of Urbino, although her son-in-law still held legitimate claim to the title. Federico thought differently; he would determine his own politics. Furthermore, the regent Isabella was being pushed into an increasingly obscure corner by another Isabella, La Boschetta, to whom, although he was a libertine, Francesco stayed profoundly attached all his life and through whom newer counselors spoke.

* Since his policies vaguely followed the designs of Julius and since his ego made attractive a self-portrait as a warrior pope, Leo turned to militancy. Once again, the old cry: Take Ferrara, make Mantua impotent by dividing her between France and Venice. Or, better still, offer young Federico command of the armies of the Church, to be used against his uncle Alfonso d'Este. Castiglione, who studied and polished every contract that involved Mantua, suggested that Isabella agree to this development in spite of the recurrent fear for the safety of her brothers. To complicate matters, Mantua was anciently pledged to the Empire, which was now ruled by Charles V, who had come to power at the same time as his contemporary Federico, whom he considered a friend and companion. Charles V was also king of Spain, in control of the Netherlands and Burgundy as well as the Two Sicilies, and was imminently to own the New World—potentially a mighty power. Improvising, signing treaties secret and open, the Pope disturbed the uneasy, temporary peace, his meddling soon to launch France and the emperor into a renewed struggle for Italy. An intricate deal finally worked out stipulated that should the emperor's interests be endangered, Federico would be free to help him, but according to a secret clause, Federico's primary loyalty was to the Pope and his armies. France was of course displeased and increasingly suspicious. (Three of Isabella's sons, the warrior Ferrante, the duke Federico, the cardinal Ercole, were to be conspicuous aides to the Empire.)

In 1521, Charles declared against, and prosecuted, the followers of Martin Luther at the Diet of Worms. This pleased Leo, who then tied himself to the emperor in a secret alliance. (One wonders about these "secret" alliances: secret from whom and for how long?) Pontifical and imperial armies now became one huge force, with Federico to be in charge of the papal sector at a salary of twelve thousand ducats a year. Matters in Mantua were supervised by Isabella, among her tasks the planning of accommodations for German soldiers, servants of the Empire, who might be needed to strengthen local forces.

To the surprise of a few elderly experts, Federico acquitted himself well during a siege of Parma, which the Church had long wanted. After celebrations that offered him churchly honors, Federico ordered a medal struck to immortalize his victory, introducing the significant form of Mount Olympus, which would appear repeatedly among his symbols of glory. He felt Olympian and suggested in a letter to the Pope that he go on, after completing local conquests, to do battle in France proper. The letter, perused by French eyes, invoked threats from French generals, which upset Isabella but not her son. With an army that included dissident Frenchmen, he cut the weak hold of France on Milan, opening the possibility that his cousin Francesco Maria Sforza might take over the dukedom. That matter hung in midair, though, while all interested eyes turned to Rome. Pope Leo, still rejoicing in the victory over Milan, suffered a short illness and died in the winter of 1521. Shortly thereafter, della Rovere and his wife, Leonora Gonzaga, were permitted by the College of Cardinals to return to Urbino from their exile in Venice (where Titian might have painted the tragic portrait of Leonora, which has her richly dressed, her beauty ravaged by unhappiness and illness). The price of their release was not too onerous: Their son was to stay in Mantua under the supervision of his grandmother, expected to be vigilant that her son-in-law not make suspect moves. Court gossip, especially in Rome, was more entertainingly occupied with other Gonzaga matters. In spite of her gifts, Isabella had not succeeded in having young Ercole made a cardinal, and the matter was dropped for a while after Leo's death. Another, more foolish preoccupation took its place: The kindly and un-impressive Sigismondo was, the Gonzaga hoped, to become the Vicar of God, one of the supreme powers, ecclesiastical and po-litical, of Europe. But he too was ill with syphilis, and in spite of his hard-working sister-in-law and his winning sister, Elisa-betta, his attempted ascent became only the butt of jokes dissem-inated by the slanderous voice of Rome's most sardonic of "speak-ing statues." One historian puts the ridiculous attempt down as an early sign of senility in Isabella, others as one of the automatic moves she made ceaselessly to raise the family to greater heights, no matter what the mindless expedient.

The new pope, loathed by the Italians, was the Flemish Ad-rian VI, a pious, pedantic man. He had been tutor to the em-peror, had served him in several capacities and could be counted on to favor him. There was clearly strength in being openly of the imperial party, but the Gonzaga were troubled by a phrase in an earlier contract with Leo: the semihidden clause that claimed Federico as servant of the Church, free to fight the emperor if necessary. There was no immediate threat that the papal and imperial armies would separate, but the clause might at some future time be an embarrassment. His mother found her way into the back alleys and mazes of influence in Rome and succeeded in having the contract pulled out of the papal archives and restored to her. She destroyed it. Free of the hampering clause, Federico eagerly accepted ten thousand French francs of Charles V to lead a segment of his armies. Adrian, as a peace-loving, severely principled man, tried to maintain a semblance of neutrality, but defeated by the contentions and double-dealing of the papal court, he too put on the armor of warrior pope. In the summer of 1523, he signed a pact with Charles V, Archduke Ferdinand of Austria, Henry VIII of England, the republics of Siena, Lucca, Florence, and Genoa, and Francesco Sforza (finally duke of Milan) against France. The hesitant Venetians in time joined the alignment and consented to the appointment of Federico as leader of Florentine armies.

* Between conclaves and battles, Federico considered the question of marriage. After he had been two or three years the marquis of Mantua and had proved himself a redoubtable captain of armies, he set himself a higher goal than the frail Monferrato girl to whom he had been promised. Perhaps the daughter of the king of Poland? Her father was not interested. Federico did not much care. At some point he would have to marry profitably and prestigiously and continue the dynasty. In the meantime, he had Isabella, La Boschetta, who was becoming more and more the marchesa, obliterating her lover's mother, who lived in unaccustomed isolation while she, the mistress, was fawned on by aging Isabella's former courtiers. Federico had early been introduced to the pleasures of sensuality by his mother's lively girls, who wrote him affectionately obscene missives when he was, very young, a hostage in Rome. He took, wherever he was, whatever he liked, but La Boschetta was another matter. His notes to her were extraordinarily fervid and high-flown, even for a florid age. His attachment to her was intense, romantic, and lasted all his life, quite like the more famous liaison between the dauphin of France, later Henry II, and Diane de Poitiers. Henry also took his mistress everywhere with him, and when he was absent, or required to spend time with his wife, Catherine de' Medici, he begged his mistress "to have in remembrance him who has served but one God and one love." Jealous and humiliated, Federico's mother, unaccustomed to sitting in dark corners and scornful of the voluptuousness of her son's court, a voluptuousness she had earlier abetted, removed herself as she had when life with her husband had become untenable.

In 1525, she found herself in Rome, the papal tiara now on the head of the Medici Clement VII, to whom she sent revived petitions that her son Ercole be made a cardinal. In the meantime, France had gathered herself together and again taken Milan, a shocking blow to the Empire. However, in February of 1525, the French army of François suffered a defeat that amounted to massacre, outside Pavia. Eight thousand soldiers were killed, many noble leaders were captured, and the king himself was taken prisoner, all within a day. Federico derived considerable satisfaction from the defeat of his old friend now enemy, François; although he was not a leader, Federico had helped clear the terrain near Pavia of the French and thus impeded the progress of French troops. Praised for his loyalty and valor, he was surrounded by promising suggestions: The duchy of Milan was once more dangled before a Gonzaga, and perhaps the throne of Naples, the latter an idea skeptically discarded by his family, who had a lively appreciation of the swamp of French and Spanish claims he would have to wade through. Uncle Alfonso of Ferrara reexamined his long-standing alliance with France and with the help and urging of his sister began to court the Empire; he was soon under its powerful wing.

The extraordinary young emperor, considered by later leaders the greatest sovereign since Charlemagne—according to Napoleon, a man who should have mastered the world—showed graceful magnanimity. Although he had had limited help in his victory over the French, he wanted all his friends to share in it, but it must not be celebrated too joyously, since it was a victory over Christians and not over the infidels, everyone's enemy. He then turned to the matter of his royal prisoner, François I. A not extraordinary arrangement of keeping French hostages, plus tying in marriage members of the opposing powers, plus a mutual defense pact, served to free François. As cynical about pacts as were his peers, François, no sooner back in France, busied himself summoning allies—several of whom turned him down, while the Pope didn't—to pursue his struggle for supremacy over Spain, in effect synonymous with "Empire" throughout Europe. In the spring of 1526, the League of Cognac emerged, its signatories François, Venice, Sforza (back in Milan), and Pope Clement VII, who carried with him Florence. Having assembled his cohorts, François did nothing about taking up arms against Charles in spite of the importunities of the Pope, who, however, soon had other matters to absorb him.

The Turks had taken Hungary, once considered a border stronghold against them, and Clement declared himself ready to lead troops against the Ottoman warlords. Before he could take action, he found himself in the terrifying confusion that was prelude to the sack of Rome. He had no army, nor popular support, nor respect from his cardinals, and felt forced to shelter in the tomb of Hadrian, which had become the fortress and prison enclave known as the Castel Sant'Angelo. He was running from the dominant Colonna family, among them the fierce cardinal Pompeo Colonna, who was eager to have Clement's life and tiara. The Pope returned to the Vatican and soon ran out of supplies and food, while the Colonna invaders sacked and plundered, carrying off treasures torn from St. Peter's. A truce, a meaningless pause, left the Pope yet vulnerable to the armies the emperor was putting together of experienced, competent German landsknechts and Spaniards under the duke of Bourbon (Chiara Gonzaga's son), who had earlier fought with his king and left him. With the help of Ferrara and Urbino, the imperial armies invaded Tuscany, inspiring a short popular uprising and the diminution of Medici influence. The duke of Bourbon then marched his army swiftly toward Rome, a danger for which the Pope had not been prepared—as he never was prepared, finding too late inept solutions that countered the advice of sounder heads. Although the duke of Bourbon was killed (by a shot from his own arquebus, for which Benvenuto Cellini claimed responsibility in his colorful, apocryphal autobiography) early in the attack of inner Rome, his troops spread through the poorly protected city, scattering the papal court, sending Clement back once more to the safety of the Castel Sant'Angelo. Guicciardini, who was involved in helping keep the peace in Florence, reports the sack of Rome initiated early in May of 1527: "As soon as they entered the city, the imperials began to run about tumultuously in search of booty, respecting neither friends nor the authority, and dignity of prelates, not even churches, monasteries and relics, honored by pilgrims from all over the world, nor sacred things." The historian compares this sack to that of the Goths 980 years before and suggests the impossibility of describing the immense booty, "since such riches were accumulated there, and so many rare and precious things belonging to merchants and courtiers." An even greater source of booty was the large number of important captives who had to buy back their liberty with enormous ransoms. And to bring their misery and infamy to overflowing, many prelates were captured by soldiers, especially by the German landsknechts, who because of their hatred for the Roman Church were cruel and insolent. They contemptuously led priests, wearing the torn robes and insignia of their ecclesiastical dignity, throughout the city of Rome on asses and mules. "Many were tormented and tortured; all prelates were brutalized and nuns were pulled out of convents and led in droves by the soldiers to satisfy their lust," and other women had to hide where they could. "Counting money, gold, silver and jewels, the sack amounted to more than one million ducats, but an even greater sum had been extracted by ransoms."

The Vicar of God held by a Holy Roman Emperor—an arm of the Church in theory—additionally threatened by the plague, which had killed a number of his co-prisoners in the Castel, was forced to sign a shameful treaty in the fall of 1527. Milan and Naples were to be considered the property of the emperor, the control of numerous Italian strongholds would belong to the Empire, and so would 10 percent of ecclesiastical earnings in those places. The Germans were to be given 67,000 ducats and the Spanish half that amount. The Pope would leave Rome (he settled for a while in Orvieto) and later send more money to the Germans, and yet more at a later date. One historian considers it noteworthy "that a Pope, fallen from such power and reverence, is held in captivity, loses Rome and his entire domain falls into the power of others; and that the same Pope, within the space of a few months, is restored to liberty, that which was taken from him is restored, and in a very short time, he is once more returned to his former greatness. So authoritative is the papacy among Christian princes and the respect which all of them have for it." It was Clement's luck, also, to be of the opposition in Henry VIII's suit for divorce from Catherine of Aragon. Legal Church opinion of that time—and into the present—conceded that the Pope's refusal was justified, and he was backed enthusiastically by men who thought Henry stupid for being so tactless, so bombastic, over a matter that might have been solved more smoothly and quietly; divorces and annulments were not unknown in European courts. Spain disliked Henry, so did France; the emperor, closely related to Catherine, certainly loathed him. There was little general sympathy for Henry and renewed respect for the onetime undignified, vacillating Pope. Though the Pope recovered, Italy did not. She lost her élan, her enthusiasms, and her place as a world center.

* Isabella d'Este-Gonzaga, whom we left in Rome, apparently suffered little during the sack. She was determined to get the red hat for Ercole and prepared to sit out any delays, secure in the fact that her French nephew was leader of imperial forces—until he was killed—that her son Ferrante was almost equally powerful and a devoted son, although they had not seen each other for a few years, and that several other Gonzaga *condottieri* would come to her rescue.

Reports vary widely, are often diametrically opposed, concerning her activities during the sack. One devotee says that she fed and housed hundreds of gentlemen and ladies at her own expense in a friend's palace. A more critical report has it that she collected sizable sums of money from her tenants, the profits shared with Ferrante. Perhaps that money was taken by marauding German mercenaries, who left Isabella a pittance, but no one denies that she sent home an impressive number of art treasures, bought from a variety of sources for small sums. Pirates seized a good portion of these, according to Isabella's biographer Julia Cartwright, but Ferrante managed to salvage two Raphael tapestries, Vatican property, which he sold to his mother for five hundred scudi. Her prize possession, the red hat for Ercole, she carried home with her through a difficult journey—escorted by Ferrante and his men to galleys at Ostia, on through storms at Civitavecchia, by horse to Ferrara, and on brother Alfonso's barge to a stop where Ercole was presented with his hat, and then by boat to a clamorous welcome in Mantua. Ercole's cardinalship was not, incidentally, achieved by his mother's maneuvers or Castiglione's. In Clement's search for moneys, he sold five hats, one of those to the Gonzaga for a sum that probably required Isabella to pawn her famous collar of one hundred jewels.

Castiglione and Machiavelli

The Prince and *The Courtier* were written within the short span of two decades, the former in 1513, the latter in 1528. As a primer of courtly ideals, an image of spiritual beauties and exquisite manners, *The Courtier* was quickly picked up in European courts. The French had a version by 1538, the Spanish in 1540, and in 1552, Sir Thomas Hoby translated the book into English, enthralling many Elizabethan writers. By 1566, the book had been translated into five languages; by 1600, there were fifty-seven editions.

Castiglione's land of gentle discourse and exquisite manners became an irresistible magnet for those seeking its somewhat anachronistic "customs and manners." It was recorded by one traveler that Mantua was the richest garden of such refinements. The Englished versions of Castiglione's Utopia did not altogether fade for centuries: Two hundred years after its publication, Dr. Johnson recommended it as "the best book that ever was written upon good breeding."

The Prince cast its darker shadow over a longer period. Early English writers frequently used Machiavelli's name—Shakespeare's "murderous Machiavell," Samuel Butler's suggestion that the name "Old Nick" for the Devil derives from "Nick" Machiavelli—to characterize unscrupulous deviousness and unalloyed cynicism. Later, more reasonable, thought wondered whether *The Prince* was not a diatribe against tyranny and rather a plea for popular government. In the twentieth century, it was used by literary apologists in the courts of fascism.

In spite of occasional bitter plaints that crack its creamy surface, *The Courtier* remains a cherished fantasy, a romantic's Renaissance; *The Prince* remains a hardheaded look at what actually often was, strengthened by a prophetic sense of what was to come. The prophecies were backed by the harsh facts in Francesco Guicciardini's *History of Italy*, written shortly after. Castiglione's and Machiavelli's two portraits of Italy have, through the centuries, melded as one. The susurrus of silks dragging through pools of blood, chivalric elegance living with bestiality in high places, the silver rose boxed with the dagger, fidelity bedded with perfidy, remain a collage whose fascination has never quite faded.

* The portrait of Baldassare Castiglione painted by his close friend Raphael introduces a worn, intelligent face, the patient, tired countenance of a man who had served Ludovico Sforza, two generations of Gonzaga, the court of Urbino, the Papacy as nuncio to Spain, a man who had lived through invasions of Italy by France, the sack of Rome, the domination of much of Italy by Spain, and the eternal quarrels and ephemeral pacts that were the texture of his time. He was of an old Mantuan family, carefully educated and, from his youth, welcome in the Gonzaga court. It was not Mantua but the court at Urbino of an earlier, halcyon era—"the Island of the blest, the abode of mirth and joy and high philosophy," as he remembered it—that became the setting for his *Courtier,* an evocation of lost ideals, of purity of conduct and purpose.

Although the setting is the ivory-tower court under the rule of the frail Duke Guidobaldo, there stands behind him the spirit of his mighty, cultivated father, Federico da Montefeltro. With Guidobaldo's wife, Elisabetta Gonzaga, sits her cousin Emilia Pia, the cleverest and liveliest of Renaissance ladies, equal in witty, spirited exchange to any of the clever men of the court. Another of the women is Margherita Gonzaga, one of Francesco's three illegitimate daughters, an exceedingly bright girl whom the great Sienese banker Agostino Chigi wanted to marry. (He gave up his pursuit when he realized how miserable life with an old man would be for so brightly quick a young woman.) The two dozen men in the circle invited to partake in the discussions are courtier-poets, courtier-musicians, diplomats of noble ancestry; among them sits the cardinal Bibbiena, closely attached to Leo X and frequently spoken of as the real Pope, and the writer of *La Calandria,* an adaptation of a Plautus play that carries the plot of Shakespeare's *Comedy of Errors.* Another among the men of talent, of nimble minds and tongues, is Pietro Bembo, careful guardian of the purity of the Italian language.

The place is the apartments of the duchess Elisabetta, the time four consecutive evenings of repose from hunting and hawking, from dancing and music. On this spring evening of 1507, the entertainment is to consist of consideration of the virtues that mark the perfect courtier and the lady who parallels and enhances him. Before turning to the central matter, Castiglione presents his reasons for writing his book—to put down while it was still fresh "the happiness I had known in the friendly company of those outstanding men and women who used to frequent the court of Urbino," and as a memorial to the members of that circle now dead and especially homage to the duchess, "of even greater worth than the others and I even closer to her than to them."

With praise for Federico da Montefeltro "of glorious memory, who in his day was the light of Italy," and a sad passage about the son Guidobaldo, infirm and unfortunate, and more praise for the duchess, "whose most decorous behavior proved compatible with the greatest freedom, and in her presence our games and laughter were seasoned with the sharpest witticisms and a gracious and sober dignity," the game opens. We reach, after many references to love, the central matter, the courtier. He may be of noble blood or not, he must be modest but not too bashful to sing his own praises (discreetly, however), he must be a competent, brave warrior and, if at all possible, comely, though he must not improve his beauty by curling his hair or plucking his eyebrows or preening "like the most wanton and dissolute creature. He must above all, when fighting, or dancing or speaking, conduct himself with ease and grace, his efforts to appear effortless." The appealingly wayward discourse then turns to the matter of feminine beauty, evoking from one gentleman criticism of the "little agonies"—plucking their eyebrows and their foreheads— that women subject themselves to. Better that a woman wear no makeup or a moderate amount, so that she not be afraid to laugh lest her encrusted mask be disturbed. She must not smile unnecessarily to show off good teeth or gesture extravagantly to display fine hands. Discretion and grace are again the key; affectation is permissible if it isn't too blatant.

We are returned to the courtier again, this time as scholar, reminded that Alexander the Great always kept a copy of the *Iliad* at his bedside and even the brutal Hannibal was something of a scholar of Greek. After some nice teasing about how many gifts one courtier can carry, it is suggested that he be able to read music and play a number of instruments as the ancients did, even the rough Spartans. Music leads to painting, "even if it may appear mechanical and hardly suited to a gentleman," and again the ancients are brought forth as support. Then, deciding after an exchange of graceful witticisms that the next evening's subject would be the uses to which this paragon courtier might be put, everyone retires.

The second meeting gathers up the established virtues of the courtier—the courageous warrior who is gentle, bold yet modest, quiet yet distinctive, virtuous and wise. There follows a debate on dancing and running and wrestling with peasants, a common Lombard pastime. One speaker finds such pastimes permissible only as acts of noblesse oblige, the courtier always to make sure he wins; being bested in a wrestling match with a peasant is unendurably humiliating. Tennis is much more dignified and less likely to include close contact with hoi polloi. The conversation drifts elegantly here and there until it settles on the conduct of the courtier vis-à-vis his prince. He will not be foolishly arrogant, nor the bearer of bad news, nor an idle babbler or a stupid flatterer. If he is especially favored by his lord, he must accept his situation with calm dignity, yet a touch more humbly than his rank requires—unlike the overfamiliar French and the arrogant Spanish. How far does one go in obeying a prince? Kill if commanded to? The evasive answer is that there are evil princes and good, and that the courtier should leave a bad master, not always easy because "in this matter courtiers are like caged birds"—a frequently echoed complaint. The general conclusion seems to be that an unhappy warrior must be extremely agile in his judgments, remain always aware of how perfidious old friends can be, and most important, sit on the sunny side of Fortune.

When woman takes the stage, stories are told of foolishly enamored women who bring dangerous temptation to men. The duchess protests, and a tactful companion offers his opinion that there are as many reasonable women as men, the compliment heightened by contrast with courtiers who use filthy language in the presence of noble ladies and drunkenly launch food across a table into each other's faces. With references to Boccaccio, storytelling is next put forward, and good and varied stories they are, among them tales of the clever tricks of women. With the proposal that the company explore a definition of the perfect lady to match the perfect courtier at the next conclave, that evening closes.

The ideal lady must have "a certain soft and delicate tenderness," an air of feminine sweetness in her every movement. She must be circumspect but not too remote, she must not dance or dress with wild abandon or play any but ladylike instruments, and, repeating the constant injunction for casual grace, "she should avoid giving the impression that she is going to great pains." A faint prophecy of Freud rears its unexpected head: Women are imperfect and without exception want to be men, "by reason of a certain instinct that teaches her to desire her own perfection." Above all, ladies must be chaste, unlike a number of women in Italy, who spend their lives "attending to their pleasure and satisfying their appetites," casting doubts on the paternity of their children and consequently weakening family ties. But what of the dangers to a young girl assaulted by "eloquent eyes," "languid expressions," the dazzle of "festivals, dances, masquerades, and tournaments, all of which she knows are for her benefit"? Following an impassioned monologue which extols the virtues of women and the misery of life without them, there is an exchange of ideas on how careful and wise women must be to welcome or reject amorous advances. The discussion turns to "many to be found whose husbands hate them for no reason at all and do them great injury, sometimes by loving other women, and sometimes by subjecting them to all the annoyances they can think of." Then again, some women are forced by their fathers to marry old men who are in poor health and filthy and disgusting and who make their lives one long misery. The speaker actually proposes divorce when the marriage bed, "which ought to be a haven of concord and love" (Castiglione loved his young wife and deplored his long absences from her), "breeds anger, suspicion and hatred to torture those unhappy souls, cruelly bound together till death by an indissoluble bond."

Unfortunately, the chaste, perfect lady, by her very virtue, often turns men to other kinds of ladies, women so free in their eyes, words, and movements as to "indulge in certain provocative glances, indecent words and utterly shameless acts." The perfect courtier, ostensibly immune to such women, courts his lady mainly with his eyes, "the guides of love, especially if they are graceful and soft," waiting for the response from his lady's eyes, which "wait like soldiers in ambush." Once having won his lady, he must continue to be virtuous and discreet, guarding against emotional vagaries and their excesses.

Evening four opens with a paean in praise of the new duchess, Leonora Gonzaga—the firstborn of Francesco and Isabella, and now the wife of Francesco della Rovere—extolled as a symphony of "grace, beauty, intelligence, refinement, humanity and every other gracious quality." After a blow at effeminacy in masculine dress, which corrupts the young and brings the name of Italy to disgrace, the prince himself is given center stage. He can become drunk with power and corrupt his own judgment with pleasure-seeking or yield stupidly to the false flattery of knavish syco-phants. He might by brute force and hatred, by growing stern and arrogant, move away from his people. One speaker is moved to unusual bitterness when he observes the ignorance of their craft betrayed by rulers who for lack of education and skill bring on death and destruction. They might better leave off some of their present vices and take up the virtues of earlier rulers, who, at the very least, surrounded themselves with wise, respected ad-visers (surely a complaint out of Castiglione's difficult career in several courts). It follows that the courtier's duty is to lead his prince on the stern path of duty, to practice a "healthy deception like a shrewd doctor who often spreads some sweet liquid on the rim of a cup when he wants a frail and sickly child to take a bitter medicine." He should help teach his prince to be honorable and liberal and not allow his rule to become tyranny. With the help of God and his devoted courtier, the prince will be unconquerably valiant in battle and generous in spirit. "He should hold magnif-icent banquets, festivals, games and public shows, and keep a great many fine horses for use in peace and war, as well as falcons, hounds and all the other things that pertain to the pleasures of great lords and their subjects: after the manner of signor Federico Gonzaga, Marquis of Mantua [the brother of Duchess Leonora], in our own day, who in this regard seems more like King of Italy than the ruler of a city."

With this additional bow to his Gonzaga patrons, Castiglione has his characters address themselves to ideal love, and the con-comitant search for beauty, "an influx of divine goodness" that infuses the beloved object with a splendor to which all souls respond. The desire that rises from the sensual only makes for unhappy endings; the rational, who curb their sensuality, are better rewarded. One laughing response mentions that old men, easily reasonable in matters of love, might manage the rational approach better than others. The scholar Pietro Bembo, unde-terred, charges on. Man, he stresses, is a little universe in himself, beautiful in his various pleasing and useful parts. "Beauty is the true trophy of the soul's victory, when with her heavenly power she rules over material nature and with her light dispels the darkness of the body." This enlightenment helps the courtier in love, particularly the man of mature years, like Bembo himself, to quell his fleshly responses and while honoring his lady, exalt the beauty of her soul. He will teach her to be truly chaste in body and thought, in harmony with himself. They will thus be perfectly happy. There is dissent, but Bembo will not be discouraged: Such love, becoming more and more sublime, causes the beauty of one woman to become a symbol of universal beauty. Climbing the ladder of love with the help of philosophy, one discards human passions and enters a purity of true, celestial beauty, "a safe harbor from the raging storms of the tempestuous sea of life."

Bembo is silenced by his own glorious vision, and when urged to continue says he cannot: his inspiration, spurred on by the "holy frenzy of love" has failed. The others exchange bantering words about their own incapacities to follow so difficult a road to perfect love, until someone notices that day has come. The birds are singing in the nearby woods, the dawn, as in Homer, is rosy-fingered, and with everyone off to bed, the book ends.

✳ Niccolò di Bernardo Machiavelli was born in the territory of Florence in 1469 to a family of minor politicians, who saw to it that he was reasonably well educated, especially in the Latin classics provided by the family library. His public career seems to have begun just before he was thirty, as a member of the Florentine chancel, a position he held through a testy time that saw the execution of Savonarola and dramatic shifts in Florentine history. As a member of a council involved in external as well as internal affairs, he traveled several times to France, to meetings with Pope Julius II and the emperor Maximilian, and on one mission he met an impressive new prince, Cesare Borgia, whose conduct matched those of earlier conquerors whom Machiavelli had studied, and whose swift, ruthless swing of conquest he criticized some and admired much.

Machiavelli's political career ended when Giuliano de' Medici and his brother Giovanni, who was shortly to be Pope Leo X, became the rulers of Florence. In the violent roundup of the parties who had supported Paolo Antonio Soderini, a proponent of popular government designed and maintained by responsible citizens, Machiavelli was arrested (1512), tortured, and then released. The Medici, never blind to accomplishment and talent, gave him the harmless task of writing a history of Florence in his forced retirement, which quite suited him. The letters from his country house have earthy humor, warmth, and considerable charm. One famous letter describes the pleasures of wandering in the countryside, reading Dante or Petrarch or the Latin poets, and, after a sparse lunch, spending long hours at cards with the local innkeeper, the butcher, the miller, and two bakers, with whom he argues loudly and with pleasure. Then home to dress in fine clothing appropriate to the company of writers "in the ancient courts of ancient men," making notes on what they have taught him. The letters were grace notes among essays on language and the arts of war and an entertaining anticlerical comedy, The Mandragola. A compendium titled Discourses may have been planned to incorporate The Prince, which flew out of its matrix to become its own significant entity.

Following a dedication to Lorenzo de' Medici, The Prince introduces us to several types of city-states, with parallels culled from history. We are then returned to the present, to the mistakes of Louis XII in his incursions into Italy, his loss of Lombardy, and the relinquishing of the kingdom of Naples to Spain in order to avoid a war. But wars cannot be avoided, can only be postponed, and then to the disadvantage of the hesitant. Here occurs a much-quoted exchange with a French cardinal: The cardinal insists that Italians "understand little of war," to which Machiavelli counters, "The French understand little of politics."

The reasons for the vulnerability or strength of several patterns of state (with always examples from history) lead Machiavelli to the conclusion that some states cannot be secured except by prior annihilation: "anyone who becomes lord of a city used to living in liberty and does not destroy it may expect to be destroyed," because in a republic there is "greater vitality, greater hatred, greater desire for revenge." The ideal situation for triumph and solid rule, according to Machiavelli's formulation, is the meeting of Fortune's impulse to provide the lucky opportunity and the shrewdness of the prince who recognizes her mood and responds to it promptly. A surprising example of just such a successful leader is Moses, powerful, experienced, with the luck to be in the right place at the right time—Fortune's gift—when the Hebrew slaves were oppressed by the Egyptians. Shrewdness and luck cannot, of course, live without each other, an example being the enormously gifted Cesare Borgia, who fell out of fortune when

* * *

A portrait of Isabella d'Este-Gonzaga, now in the Louvre in Paris, as sketched by Leonardo da Vinci and seemingly manipulated by later hands. It is still considered by many as the only authentic portrait of Isabella, although several—vaguely attributed to other artists—exist. A medal by Cristoforo Romano (Kunsthistorisches Museum, Vienna) portraying a middle-aged Isabella is generally considered a truer likeness than the disputed paintings.   (ALINARI/ART RESOURCE)

The facade of the Palazzo Ducale in Mantua which fronts the oldest buildings, once the medieval palaces of the Bonacolsi family from whom the
Gonzaga wrested control of the area in the early fourteenth century. The
present Palazzo Ducale includes not only these early spaces but endless later
additions of halls, salons, apartments, and chapels to create the enormous
present palace. (ALINARI/ART RESOURCE)

RIGHT: The architect Leon Battista Alberti (National Gallery, London) in a medallion he himself designed. He may or may not have been so handsome but considering the high respect he had for his own considerable acccomplishments and virtues, he might have seen himself masterfully beautiful as well.
(ART RESOURCE)

BELOW: One of the nine panels of the "Triumph" of Caesar now in Hampton Court in London, a prime example of Andrea Mantegna's fidelity to classic subjects and modes—of which he was a scholar—strongly marked by Renaissance naturalism and vivacity. The panels were the most coveted treasure of the art and objects the Gonzaga sold early in the seventeenth century. (ALINARI/ART RESOURCE)

ABOVE: A remaining detail of a section of mural by Pisanello in a hall that was apparently totally decorated, but suffered the collapse of walls and vandalism over the years. The painted cycle seemed to have depicted a fierce battle between Lancelot and Tristan as told in Renaissance versions of popular chivalric stories. Among the masterly remains are these two enchanting portraits of (possibly) Guinevere or Isolde and her handmaiden Brangaene.   (SCALA/ART RESOURCE)

RIGHT: Bust of the Marquis Francesco II in the Palazzo Ducale of Mantua, attributed to Mantegna. It clearly indicates his sensual, alert, and impulsive character and the rich, elaborately worked armor emphasizes his role as leading *condottiere* for various forces in his slippery, erratic career.
(ALINARI/ART RESOURCE)

Parnassus (ABOVE) painted by Mantegna for Isabella d'Este's *studiolo* is believed to have been programmed with strict detail by Isabella herself. The lyrical painting of a few happy gods and dancing semigoddesses is thought to include a pregnant and idealized Isabella.　(SCALA/ART RESOURCE)

The Expulsion of the Vices (BELOW) also by Mantegna is one of numerous allegorical paintings that fostered the humanistic concern for the banishment of sloth and ignorance and the rise of higher virtues and thought. Both paintings are now in the Louvre.　(ALINARI/ART RESOURCE)

ABOVE: Detail of a panel in the Hall of Psyche in the Palazzo del Te of Mantua, painted by Giulio Romano and his assistants. The Hall was dedicated to Love as described by the Latin novelist Apuleius in his *Golden Ass*, whose incidents and descriptions were much used by painters and many writers, even as late as Smollett. This detail is a rich example—the drunken Bacchus, the attendant fauns, exotic animals, and ripe nudes—of the pagan soft-porn that characterizes the entire hall. Psyche, incidentally, is said to have been painted in the image (or as the image) of Isabella Boschetti, the woman with whom Federico, the fifth marquis, was profoundly in love for many years.   (SEF/ART RESOURCE)

RIGHT: *Madonna della Vittoria (detail)* by Mantegna, now in the Louvre. The resplendent armor and the blessing gesture of the Virgin commemorate the victory—or at least he claimed it to be—of Francesco II over the French forces at the battle of Fornovo.   SEF/ART RESOURCE)

Baldassare Castiglione as painted by
Raphael (Louvre). A portrait of the patient, homesick, long-suffering ambassador of the Gonzaga in the Papal Court
and the author of the clever, sensitive,
nostalgic book on a departed never-never
land that had been the court of Urbino
in his early years, *The Courtier.*
(ALINARI/ART RESOURCE)

his father died. Borgia's career is sketched out here, with examples of his cleverness and, to sweeten the portrait, of a few gracious acts, which helped him to win "the support of all . . . once the people began to taste the beneficial results of his rule." One of Borgia's commendable acts was to put a "cruel and able man" in authority, the result a province strongly united, where not he, Borgia, was blamed for brutalities but rather his ruthless agent. One of Borgia's serious mistakes was not to oppose the Papacy of Julius II, whom he had offended and who would naturally cause him fear, "For men do harm either out of fear or hatred."

After an exploration of essential severity, to be kept within limits (otherwise a ruler "will always be obliged to keep a knife in his hand"), the writer introduces the "civil principality" achieved with the proper mixture of luck and skill, a state in which nobles and commoners support each other, with wariness on all sides. Basically, Machiavelli champions, to a degree, a system approaching popular government. The desires of the common people, he says, are more honest than those of the plotting nobles, and a prince can easily rule without nobles but absolutely needs his commoners, who ask very little of him except that they not be oppressed. A man of judgment and spirit will never find himself deceived by the common people, who in times of crisis will stand by him. The trustworthiness of the native common man convinced Machiavelli that a citizens' army was infinitely superior to an army of mercenaries, "useless and dangerous," in the writer's opinion. "The present ruin of Italy is caused by nothing other than her dependence for a long period of time on mercenary forces." Such forces helped some rulers for a while, but only princes who were captains of their own forces and republics, like Rome and Sparta, armed with their own citizens, made great military advances. The defeat of Carthage and her mercenaries and the double-dealing of Francesco Sforza of Milan and his hired help are cited as examples of the danger of hiring the cowardly troops of "these *condottieri* [who] have led Italy into slavery and humiliation." "In short, the arms of another man either slide off your back, weigh you down, or tie you up."

The prince himself? His every muscle must throb with war; those who linger with personal luxuries lose their states. Even when not engaged in war, the prince must appear warlike or he will not be respected. He must keep himself in trim and study his surrounding hills, rivers, and swamps for their ultimate defense.

A prince must not be a spendthrift. If he is, he will have to tax his principality to excess and turn his subjects against him. Furthermore, his resulting poverty would make him a contemptible thing. It does not matter if he is stamped "miser." "In our times we have not seen great deeds accomplished except by those who were considered miserly; all other were done away with." Only where there is looting and sacking and ransoms to be gained must a prince be openhanded; these riches are the traditional right of soldiers. Should a prince strive to be both loved and feared? Preferably both, but the safer policy is to rely on fear, if a choice must be made. The author explains in a key sentence that is a dark leitmotiv: "For one can generally say this about men: that they are ungrateful, fickle simulators and deceivers, avoiders of danger, greedy for gain and while you work for their good are completely yours . . . when danger is far away; but when it comes nearer to you they turn away."

The prince should cultivate in himself the presence of the fox and the lion, "a fox in order to recognize traps and a lion in order to frighten the wolves." The fox does not keep his word if it is to his disadvantage. There are countless "modern examples to show how many pacts, how many promises have been made null and void because of the infidelity of princes; and he who has known best how to use the fox has come to a better end. But it is necessary to know how to disguise this nature well and to be a great hypocrite and liar," appearing "to be all mercy, all faithfulness, all integrity, all kindness, all religion." At this point in the book, we reach the key phrase that has made Machiavelli anathema to generations of liberals: "the end justifies the means." His exact phrase, *"si guarda al fine"*—one considers the end—somewhat eases the phrase but does not deny its import.

A subject touched on several times is the fact that "as long as you do not deprive them of their property or their honor the majority of men live happily" and, it is implied, contentedly serve their prince. But he must avoid earning their contempt by being frivolous, effeminate, and vacillating in his decisions, and good at the wrong times, like the effeminate, yielding Alexander, who was too much ruled by his mother and was ultimately despised and killed. Out of Tacitus, Plutarch, and Livy, Machiavelli gives us men who had not kept their foxes and their lions sharply alert. A new prince, in order to acquire prestige, must allow his cunning fox to inspire some hostility and his powerful lion to stamp it out, so that he may continue to be great. Once esteem is established, he arranges his house, gathers his subject army, sees to fortifications, surrounds himself with trustworthy advisers, fosters local trades and agriculture, and—never to be neglected—provides festivals and spectacles for his people.

After yet another reminder that one half of a prince's action is controlled by Fortune and the other half by his own sharpness, the book closes with a dark vision of Machiavelli's Italy, subject to "barbaric cruelties and insolence," plundered by foreigners. Like the Hebrew slaves in Egypt, she is waiting for her Moses, but where is he? The Spanish, the Swiss, the French, the Germans, are not invincible, and with a skillfully organized army and intelligent battle plans, Italy, "after so long a time, may behold its redeemer."

Since Cesare Borgia, earlier praised as the great hope of Italy, had been dead for some years when The Prince was finished, we must assume that the suggested role of "redeemer" and the accompanying flattery were directed at the Medici and their two-pronged potential as rulers of Florence and of the Papacy. But by the time Machiavelli died, in 1527, Leo X was no longer pope, Clement VII, born Giulio de' Medici, was about to be taken prisoner by Charles V during the sack of Rome, Florence was decaying under the weight of intrigue and assassinations, and Italy, increasingly controlled by foreign powers, had little place for the cunning, independent tyrant prince that was Machiavelli's ideal.

T * E * N

Federico, who had been rejected when he applied to the Pope during the convening of the League of Cognac for leadership of the anti-imperial papal-French armies, stayed in his own bailiwick during the sack of Rome, confronted with the matter of settling into a marriage. He promised to take his Monferrato bride to Mantua in late 1527, but by early 1528 was still held by "affairs of State," which might be summed up under the name Isabella Boschetta, who officiated with him at receptions and fetes, helped make court decisions, and bore him children. At this late date, her husband and a congeries of Mantuans whose motives were obscure—prompted by Anna of Monferrato, whose daughter, Maria Paleologa, languished as an unwanted bride?—plotted to poison La Boschetta. (One would wonder why the so long complacent husband, Francesco di Calvisano, rumored also to be planning the murder of Federico, would want to kill his golden geese.) The plot was discovered and Calvisano ran in the wrong direction, to Ferrara, where he was taken by the Este relations and killed. Such unsavory events, involving the marchesa Anna, prompted Federico to try to annul the distasteful connection with Monferrato. The Pope, then in Orvieto (where he had been conducted from Rome, at night and in disguise, by a Gonzaga cousin), was petitioned for an annulment. With a great show of reluctance to disturb the ancient line of Paleologhi, Clement consented to have the marriage dissolved. Now free, Federico had a wider field to graze in. He might endear himself to France by marrying the sister of the king of Navarre; he might move closer to the Empire by marrying the daughter of the duke of Bavaria, kin to the emperor Charles.

On July 7, 1529, one of the many "Peaces," this of Cambrai, was signed, in the main reiterating the restrictions placed on François in the earlier treaty that followed his defeat at Pavia. For Federico, the most attractive result of the Cambrai meeting was the offer from Charles of a large army, a satisfactory salary, and the flattering role of diplomat to negotiate matters between the Empire and the Italian states. When Federico went to Genoa to present Charles with three of the choicest Gonzaga horses and to help escort him part of the way to the second act of his coronation as emperor, there was mention of a possible marriage to the daughter of the German duke of Cleves, maybe the girl who later married and offended Henry VIII by her dullness and was returned by him. A more serious suggestion was the hand of the infanta Giulia of Aragon, the aunt of the emperor. Federico's response was vague; there were more pressing matters to absorb him, as a leader of the imperial armies and as a maker of policy, and since its incumbent was ill, he might yet achieve the dukedom of Milan. But Pope Clement, who had no affection to spare for the imperialist Gonzaga, decided that Milan would not be his, while Venice decided that she would not return to him Asola, Lonato, Peschiera, and Sirmione on Lake Garda, as promised. As if in mitigation of this depressing turn of events, the proposal of marriage to Giulia took on a somewhat promising color. She was at least thirty-eight, near the end of her childbearing years, but she held extensive properties in the area of Cremona and would undoubtedly bring an impressive dowry. The matter rested during the festivities that accompanied the emperor's coronation in Bologna in early November of 1529. Isabella the elder arrived on November 1, as dazzlingly dressed as she had been in her youth, a touch odd, other noblewomen judged, for her years and her expanded figure. With her came her retinue of beauties, the inspirations of jousts and brawls, duels and orgies. Solemnity reigned, though, on November 5, when Charles entered the city with his troops in full armor and an entourage of nobles and pages, which then proceeded to the entrance of the Church of San Petronio, where the Pope was enthroned. Charles kissed Clement's feet and was himself embraced, as churchbells rang and nobles genuflected. (The actual placing of both iron and gold crowns on Charles's head as supreme chief of the Holy Roman Empire was to take place three months later.) The high dignity gave way to masquerades, tourneys, and feasts, marked by fights between Spanish and Italian soldiers for the favor of the Mantuan ladies. Not only for her costume was the dowager marchesa criticized; she had allowed events to reach a heating point that killed several Spaniards and maimed some Italian and German rivals in battles over the ladies' favors. This was for brothels, for bawds and their *putane,* not for the matriarch and ladies-in-waiting of a ranking court. Isabella disdained the criticism, taking her show home only when she was ready, many weeks after the coronation. Federico stayed away from the ceremony and high jinks, although all the princes of Europe attended. His stated reason was the fact that the marquis of Monferrato had been assigned a place in the procession that preceded his. Another reason may have been more subtle, a delicate sign for François to understand that though he worked for the emperor, France and Mantua might at some future time be close friends again. Furthermore, marriage with the princess of Navarre was still a vague possibility.

On March 25, 1530, the Feast of the Annunciation, Charles visited Mantua, an occasion that marked the apogees of two young lives: both only thirty, one newly the master of much of Europe, the other imminently to rise from marquis to duke. Charles came dressed in gold and silver brocade and led a body of thousands to meet Federico and his accompanying knights, lords, and leading ecclesiasts, who brought with them a baldachino covered with brocade picked out in gold. The Mantuan nobles assigned to support the canopy wore gold cloth, slippers and caps of white velvet, and, slung in their belts, golden swords. Surrounding the baldachino under which the emperor strode, there were forty pages in costumes of white brocade and velvet, in their hands golden staffs. The arches and statuary that customarily appeared for festivities were this day many more and grander, to do honor to the most exalted guest yet to arrive in Mantua. One monumental arch flew over eight columns that supported figures of former emperors of the house of Hapsburg, repositories of the seed that had produced this last and greatest flower. Every house, every shop, was hung with vivid drapes adorned with the imperial crests and arms; fronting the Church of San Pietro was an enormous statue of the emperor within a triumphal arch broad and tall enough to frame it.

In the feasting and hunting, among the arches worthy of conquering Caesars, there was inevitably mention of marriage. It was not presented precisely as a quid pro quo but in essence was a clear exchange: the title Duke of Mantua for the hand of the elderly infanta Giulia. Prompted by Federico, Castiglione introduced a clause in the negotiations that would assure La Boschetta's children (there was already one, Alessandro, at the time) the succession to the dukedom if Giulia bore no children. Charles had no objections to the clause, but Alfonso d'Este and especially his sister Isabella objected; she had legitimate sons and grandsons and meant to protect their rights. Poor Giulia was hung back in midair once more when an interesting piece of news arrived from Monferrato. Bonifacio de Paleologhi had fallen from a horse and died, leaving as heir elderly failing Giovanni Giorgio de Paleologhi. Maria, the next in line, again became attractive matrimonial material and Giulia was quickly found wanting. Mantua began to reconsider, most fortunately inspired by a petition purportedly signed by the leading citizens of Monferrato. The petition pointed out that Giulia was beyond childbearing age and that in spite of the earlier annulment, the contract with Maria was valid. Envoys were sent speedily to the Pope and to the emperor, asking that any agreement with Giulia be nullified, that the early contract with Monferrato be recognized as indeed solid. Quick decisions were urged, for fear that Maria might accept one of the marriage offers now pressed on her and on her mother. Charles objected to having his aunt put aside, but the Pope, hemming and hawing, finally declared that Maria Paleologa and Federico of Mantua were indeed man and wife. After years of waiting, since her early childhood, and just about to make the escorted bridal entry trailing coffers of trousseau and dowry into Mantua, the girl died. The court of Mantua went into mourning for the wife of their duke, while emissaries were dispatched, exquisitely discreet but fast, to ask for the hand of Margherita, Maria's sister. Her mother, who had, according to court hearsay, a morbid passion for "Il Bello" (Federico) and was eager for a protective link to the Empire, instantly gave Federico, "while Maria's body was still warm," the living body of Margherita, asking only that her daughter not be injured by La Boschetta, the queen of Mantua.

There was twisting, turning, and appeasing still to be done. Federico commissioned an esteemed abbot to mollify Isabella of

Aragon, mother of Giulia, then living with her cousins in Ferrara. It was to be pointed out to her that Rome was already committed to the renewed Monferrato contract, the name Margherita legitimately substituted for that of Maria. Anyhow, though there might be some airy commitment to Giulia, was there not danger in marrying a relative, no matter how distant a cousin? Anyhow, these lengthy discussions should be closed; he was needed on important business in the wars. To give the matter an indisputable odor of sanctity, a body of clerics, accompanied by ambassadors, went to Casale, the major city of Monferrato, to arrange final marriage details, bearing with them documents signed by Federico, to be confirmed and countersigned. The emperor-Giulia party was not yet appeased. Federico invited Margherita's mother, Anna Paleologa, to take a more active part in the imbroglio, to indicate to the emperor that one of the suitors pressing for her daughter's hand was the duke of Savoy, a staunch friend to France and enemy of the emperor. A more telling gesture was a gift to Charles of fifty thousand scudi (partially in payment for the title of duke), a great help in settling debts incurred in the emperor's purchases of mercenaries, armor, horses, carts, crossbows, and cannon, and in supporting Titian as a nobleman and court painter for the imperial household. Charles reacted with words of indignation but took the money and stepped out of the dispute over brides for Gonzaga, insisting only that Giulia be paid an annual sum, quite like present-day alimony.

The marriage fetes began in Casale in early October of 1531, held to modest limits since the marchesa Anna was ill. A few weeks later, the wedding party went on to Mantua, where brightness, music, dancing, and feasting were organized by the older Isabella and her cardinal son, Ercole. The cost of the celebrations was covered by extra taxes the family had been collecting for a purse marked "Gift for the Marriage of His Excellency." The tax-gathering was meticulously planned and carefully supervised, touching every corner of the state. According to the archivist Davari, letters dated in the late summer of 1531 included a complaint from one commune that due to recent floods, its treasury could not send the five thousand scudi demanded; five hundred was all it could manage. Another letter, from an esteemed old doctor, begs that he be excused; he is sick and poor and the Gonzaga might send him one hundred scudi rather than ask it of him. The jollity bought by the marriage tax did not close off anxiety and intrigue. Margherita's uncle the marquis Giovanni Giorgio, to whom she was heiress, was ill and frequently near death. The duke of Savoy pressed the ailing marquis by every set of influences he could muster to make legitimate one of his natural sons, Flaminio, so that he might become duke of Monferrato and take for his duchess a pro-French Savoy heiress. The French were interested in a legitimized Flaminio to marry into their circles, while the Venetians hoped to get him for the daughter of a Cornaro, a family of doges. Monferrato was worth the contention, for its fertile position in the Po valley, for its proximity to Milan, and for the prestige of the ruling family's antique Byzantine name, a symbol of might before the Turks drove the family across the Adriatic into Italy.

Federico and Anna Paleologa kept after Charles to save Monferrato for themselves, urging that the emperor appoint Margherita his vassal, under obligation to and protected by him, in the feudal style. Charles would only promise to consider the matter and possibly arrange the ritual when he next visited Italy. Charles finally arrived in Italy late in 1532 and was lavishly though testily entertained for a month. Not until after his departure did word come of imperial assurance that on the death of Giovanni Giorgio, Margherita would become officially the marchesa of Monferrato and her husband the marquis. The promise that Federico would control Monferrato was not bought by sumptuous entertainment alone. Charles again needed money, and although Federico depleted the dwindling funds of his dukedom, tapped the Jewish community for large sums, and the private resources of his mother, he continued trading money for favors. A year after his visit, possibly to save face and to tie tight the Mantuan claims to Monferrato, the emperor announced the marriage of Giulia of Aragon to the not quite dead Giovanni Giorgio. The contract was celebrated in Ferrara, the role of the bridegroom, who could not travel, enacted by a Spanish envoy of the imperial court. Some weeks later, the celebrants gathered at the sickbed of the marquis of Casale so that he might sign the document that joined him to Giulia. If, according to the mendacious contract, the couple had no heirs and the dying man expired, Monferrato must go to Mantua. A week later, Giovanni Giorgio, the last of the male Paleologa line, was dead. His wife returned to her mother in Ferrara, to die not long after, "burdened with many misfortunes and pain." Late in 1536, the new marquis of

Monferrato celebrated his shrewdness and luck by inviting Italian, French, and imperial knights to a grand tourney, where Margherita, the new marchesa, ruled as the lady of honor.

Federico was striding the Mount Olympus he had claimed as his. He was thirty-six, duke and marquis, companion of an emperor, diplomat among kings, son of a mother who, in spite of her oddities, was still one of the most respected women of her era. He had a brother, Ferrante, who was an influential member of the inner councils of the Empire. He was the patron of a revered artist, Giulio Romano, and the lover of a mistress who like Cleopatra delighted with her infinite variety. Since no horizon is permanently unstained, however, there were a few clouds gathering for Federico. He was troubled by symptoms of the disease that had killed his father and disturbed by unrest in Monferrato, a prophecy of difficulties to come. To begin with, the nobility of Casale, who claimed descent from Byzantine aristocrats, were scornful of their new Johnny-come-lately ruler, the tricky master of a corrupt court, its subjects matter for scurrilous broadsides and obscene verses. Then, with the help of dissident nobles, the French sacked and destroyed a number of houses in Casale. Spanish-imperial troops responded by sacking much of the rest of the city, etching a pattern that would be followed fiercely by Federico's heir, Guglielmo, against his generation of stubborn rebels. Notwithstanding the *pasticci* of marriage and discontented Monferrato, the Gonzaga family was in a high state of esteem. The new Pope, Paul III, eager for the reconciliation of Rome with Protestant forces, worked with Cardinal Ercole in organizing a council they hoped would meet in Mantua; the papal golden rose with its message of respect and friendship was bestowed on Federico. Capable Ferrante was chosen by Charles to act as viceroy of Sicily, a major position since the grains of Sicily fed the Empire and the man who could have them garnered, stored, and efficiently distributed was invaluable.

The dowager Isabella was delighted with Margherita, not so much for her inheritant charms and her gift of Monferrato but in the expectation—or merely hope—that Federico might be diverted by conjugal duties to his bride and neglect La Boschetta. His gesture to his new bride was a fine set of apartments in the Ducal Palace, designed and decorated by Giulio Romano to include the first formal art gallery, the forerunner of splendid halls that would hold the flourishing Gonzaga collection. La Boschetta,

kept in the background during the marriage festivities, was compensated for the temporary diminution of her position by splendid
gifts and the moneys to entertain lavishly guests like Charles V,
while continuing to rule a court devoted to her pleasures at the
palace at Te.

The queen mother stayed in the old palace, moving farther
from central apartments, almost symbolic of her remove from the
central places of power. When Federico suggested she give him
the space she had used from the time she was a bride as *studiolo*
and *grotta*, she took her paintings, her medallions, her gold-tinted
bronze figures by the sculptor L'Antico, to new, slightly distant
quarters. She soon moved again, claiming that she had grown
too old and fat to negotiate stairs, to a lower level of the Corte
Vecchia, adding to her lutes and intarsias watches and clocks in
large numbers, as if to help her mark the hours left her.

Te

The disquieting, sensual place was built at the edge of the city proper, its name, Te, interpreted in several ways—a shrub, a hut, a dialect word for *teiteo*—a little cut—referring to a canal that helped run off marshy waters. The area anciently held a church and a monastery and areas used by the early Gonzaga for whipping posts and gallows. By the time of Ludovico II, the grounds were cleared for a country retreat more easily reached than the other country villas. Barbara, the wife of Ludovico, wrote: "We keep this place of the Te for pleasure," adding that in the company of Pope Pius II and a train of cardinals and nobles, she and her lord watched the running of a female leopard, an addition to their zoo of rarities, a pleasure of princes and a primitive school of biology. The first buildings at Te were primarily stables, which were expanded and redesigned by order of Francesco to accommodate the greatly increasing numbers of horses he bought, bred, sold, and presented as royal gifts.

It was on these stables that his son Federico decided to build a pleasure palace to celebrate his love for Isabella Boschetta, to give form to a literary conceit that saw Venus in her own inviolable enclave, Mars as her cavalier and slave. An early scheme described a modest place, an apartment and two adjoining salons. But Alberti and Castiglione and many other wise men had said that a prince must build to suit his princeliness, just as a merchant must use the best material in the largest house he could afford to show his worth. Federico's visitors knew his extensive collection of cannon, arquebuses, armor, and lances in the *castello*, and were well acquainted with the stables, the mews for falcons, the well-maintained hunting reserves, the apricot orchards, the pools swarming with fish of Marmirolo. Te was to be something else, an expansion of stables, of course, and in addition a fantasy of caprice, of extraordinary decoration, of gloriously lascivious symbols, a retreat for surprising, with fresh delights. Who to entrust with the design and adornment of a building that must catch the attention of all Europe? Since the death of Luca Fancelli, Alberti's gifted assistant, architecture in Mantua had slowed and dulled in spite of the fact that a few master masons had been sent to Rome to study the new buildings there. Lorenzo Costa, who had succeeded Mantegna as court painter, was expected to decorate portions of Te, but Federico required the most notable of artists, and those were working in Rome. Early in the 1520s, Federico began to press his ambassador in Rome, Castiglione, to bring Giulio Romano with him to Mantua. Giulio, trained in architecture by Bramante, had been Raphael's most valued assistant and, after his death, praised as Raphael's worthy successor. The Pope released the painter, not too reluctant to go since he knew of Federico's generosity and since a diminution of papal patronage promised dark days for painters.

When Castiglione rode into Mantua with the painter and his assistants, they were met by Federico and his gentlemen, who presented Giulio with several lengths of velvet and "smooth cloth" (satin?), then on to the stables in the meadows, where Federico said he wanted, according to Vasari, a place where he could resort for amusement and take refreshment without destroying the old buildings. Giulio's suggestions for reconstruction and "new and extraordinary decoration for the vaulting, and richly decorated interiors, led to the decision to make the present fine palace there from an humble beginning." So pleased was the duke with his imaginative artist that he soon gave him a dignified house, a fine horse, and provisions for himself and his apprentice painters. His stipend of 500 ducats was shortly raised to 850 and then to 1,000, an unusually large fee, increasingly deserved as Giulio became director of all art, architecture, decoration, city planning, and engineering in Mantua. He was dubbed a Mantuan noble and courted as respected adviser in several capacities. Although the court painters Lorenzo Costa and Lorenzo Leonbruno were lavishly praised, it was Giulio who became, in the common Renaissance comparison, the Mantuan Apelles, which inescapably made of his patron Alexander the Great. (Had Michelangelo responded favorably to the polite, flattering invitations to work at sculpture and painting in Te, who would then have been Apelles?)

As the palace and its astonishments grew in spite of plague and disaffections, so did its fame. Guests invited to see Te in the making, and those asked to stay—like Marmirolo and Goito, the new palace had many beds—broadcast its splendors quickly and widely. Pietro Aretino, in his *Stablemaster,* a comedy that plays with the decadence of the city of his friend Federico, suggests that a popular entertainment of the citizenry was to observe the building of the "beautiful edifice" at Te, with its "beautiful paintings." Vasari mentions a Mantuan antiquarian, who rejoiced in the name Cesario Antiquario, summoned to the court of the emperor at Vienna to record, among descriptions of other buildings in Italy, a fully detailed account of the room plans of Te and their decorations. Europe was ripening for new styles like the casual "classicism" of Te architecture and the turbulent paintings on the walls and ceilings, charged with the emotional style that would later be called mannerist. Giulio's fame winged across the waters northward, to appear as "that rare Italian-master, Julio Romano" in Shakespeare's *Winter's Tale,* and decades later we hear that Inigo Jones judged some of Palladio's work to be so closely modeled on Te that he credited Giulio Romano with the design of the famous Palazzo Thiene in Vicenza, which Palladio "merely executed, or it seems so." Later still, we have English writers on the Italian Renaissance kneeling before this "masterwork" that symbolized the warm color and dash the sunless countries sought and found in Italy. It is left to an eighteenth-century Italian critic, Giovanni Cadioli, to write that one needed one hundred eyes to see Te and as many pens to describe it, and then to fly into ecstatic strophes: *"fabrica de delizia," "rarissimo," "maraviglioso."* In the mid-nineteenth century, though, Dickens reported Te as "desolate and neglected as a house could be," in a damp and dreary place.

Vasari, an enthusiastic admirer, recorded the palace in detail and closed his several pages on Te spaces and the mythological figures they held, on ornaments, on plays of perspective, with: "The judgment and art here displayed by Giulio place artists under a great debt to him." Our debt to Giulio and his assistants Benedetto Pagni, Rinaldo Mantovano, Francesco Primaticcio, and their pot boys and brush cleaners is incurred by the pleasures of surprise in the clever architecture, by the fancy that designed dozens of panels on related themes, and by the virtuosity that brought them to vivid though not always comprehensible life.

Buildings Giulio knew in Rome supplied the tall-arched entrances, the rows of columns, the friezes of classical ornaments, but his design, because of the demands of the earlier building, created architectural improvisations that give the palace a certain independence, an unexpectedness close to playfulness. The crowded, hectic merriment of the halls of mythological subjects, the zodiacal symbols, the classical statuary in niches, refer to the conventions of the Renaissance, while overripe bodies disporting themselves in a gentle breeze of soft porn, as well as the stormy apocalyptic rumblings of a Hall of Giants, propel us into a changing mode of painting. The Hall of the Horses, a vast room for receptions, centers on life-size portraits of six horses, distinguished members of the Gonzaga breed. Under the intricately carved ceiling, which features Mount Olympus and the figure of the salamander (which boasts that it can never be destroyed by love no matter how ardently it burns), monochrome panels depict the heroic labors of Hercules: his conflicts with the serpent, with the bull, with the snake. In adjoining small rooms, believed to have been guest rooms: a windiness of plasterworks, ample fireplaces, enormous eagles holding up enormous shells, Julius Caesar in an aggressive stance, and constant reminders that these works were ordered by and belonged to Federico. The heart of this full plenty of the decorative arts is the Hall of Psyche, another large room for entertainments. The square space is introduced by a dedication in bold Latin letters to Federico, "CAPITANEUS GENERALIS" of the Church, who built here to rest from his labors and restore his energies, as, above the fireplace, Hercules rests from his.

The program of paintings here was not Giulio's or Federico's; they had advisers—as Botticelli had relied on Florentine scholars and Isabella d'Este had for the allegorical studies in her *studiolo* the instructions of her scholars. According to E. H. Gombrich, the complexity of arcane astrological references in one ceiling was probably supplied by the noted astrologer Lucas Guaricus, for several years the searcher of the heavens to the Gonzaga. Other planners decided on a panorama of love based on material from *The Golden Ass* of Apuleius, with particular emphasis on the amors of Eros and Psyche, the scheme here to follow Psyche's journey through difficulties in the cave of her flesh to the purer spheres of ideal spirit in marriage with Eros. Along with its Neoplatonic interpretations, the Hall of Psyche is unmistakably a celebration of feasting and sex, of fruits and wine and eternal love, particularly that of Federico and La Boschetta, who, contemporaries said, strongly resembled the image of Psyche. All is sunshine, grape-leaf wreaths, plump fair nudity, graceful draperies and dalliance: on chaises, in shallow bathtubs, among satyrs and goats ruled by a big-horned Priapus and a fat, drunken Bacchus. Pasiphaë stepping into the bull created by Daedalus so that she might give birth to the Minotaur, a woman about to be covered by Triton, a goddess observing preparations for the wedding feast, are all blond, with the small breasts, the wide soft belly, the full buttocks and sturdy legs of many allegorical Venetian paintings. The pretty Saturnalia of blond hair, plump pink flesh, white ribbons, and golden wine vessels is further prettified by babies: human babies, satyr babies, and winged babies who pour bathwater for Venus and wash her earthy legs.

"Rest and recreation" continue on in adjoining salons, which float lovely plaster festoons around scenes of hunting, swimming, and fishing, and then return to mythological nudity, some of it vivacious, some dull, almost constantly featuring the amorous salamander. A stunning tangle of circles, squares, hexagons, makes a zodiacal maze of the ceiling of the Hall of the Winds, the lunettes emphasizing Gonzaga achievements, especially those of Federico, who, to read the insistent Mount Olympus symbol, sits high above the storms that destroy lesser men. On and on the rooms go in their fascinating hyperbole, like one which makes of Federico and his Isabella reincarnations of David and Bathsheba. Then, to the excess of excesses, the Hall of Giants, a swarming, tempestuous room, built not only for its own overwhelming self but as a symbol to flatter the emperor Charles. Opening aerial perspective and erasing wall divisions, Giulio gives us the fall of hideous giants crushed among their crashing, broken temples. The rebellious giants driven forth by Jove represent the enemies of Charles and his triumphs over them, a reference not lost on that honored visitor to Te. For the full effect of the Hall of Giants, one must imagine the appropriate music that accompanied the vision of clouds boiling in endlessly tortured distance, the thunder of cracking pillars, the fierce trumpeting of the wind gods, the shrieks of agony forced out of distorted faces. It is a bravura piece of a pagan Last Judgment, with everyone in extremis except quiet, fatalistic Father Time. (Dickens called it an "apoplectic performance," which had the effect of a "violent rush of blood to the head.")

Halls of giants, heroes, horses, and mythology all designed for astonishing hardly provided intimate space for lovemaking, one of the essential forms of rest and recreation, one might think. At the end of a long garden leading away from the main halls, there are sets of pleasant small rooms decorated with graceful grotesques, at their side a tiny "secret garden" and a damaged grotto. Painted panels deal with the simple subjects of Aesop's fables, and the floors are traced in simple patterns of varicolored pebbles. It must have been a delightful playhouse and quite private, a relief for lovers who sought and achieved brightly spotlighted attention and must, from time to time, have grown tired of it.

A section of the Palazzo del Te is kept alive by its use as a gallery of local modern art, and the broad grounds are often devoted to agricultural fairs and other community activities. Now incorporated in modern, practical Mantuan life, Te yet has forceful impact as a reminder of old profligacy and flash, wonderfully free of moderation.

∗ A literary parallel of Te, of infinitely lesser quality though similar in provenance, was a work by Mario Equicola, "Secretario del Illustrissimo S. Federico II, Gonzaga, Marchese di Mantua," one of the savants who suggested Te themes. He had been secretary to the older Isabella, to whom the book is dedicated and who, he says, had wished that he write his *Libro de Matura de Amore,* which stemmed from his early and constant preoccupation with love. It is an extraordinary work, thoroughly a thing of the time and fashion. Mingled with the required scholarly references to Lucretius, Catullus, and Virgil, and endless lists of the amorous in mythology, appear Dante and Petrarch. The pageant of lovers—Petrarch and Laura, Caesar and Cleopatra, Paris and Helen, Orpheus and Eurydice—halts at discussion of Masilio Ficino's Platonic view of love and what Pico della Mirandola learned of love in his studies of Plato. In great spates of repetitious words woven around Latin, Greek, and Hebrew phrases, Equicola reveals the thoughts of Pietro Bembo and truths that can be found in Hebrew letters, a reference to the Cabala, which had begun to captivate philosophic minds. A second part of the book wanders into an exploration of the emotions that herald the coming of love, how the word *amore* came to be, and another long digression into learned references and citations, including the findings of astrologers, who give Venus, in her various meetings with other planets, supreme importance. For reasons that have lost their clarity over the centuries, Equicola links Venus with the fact that the Hebrews chose September as the time of the creation of the world.

Love in general is then defined and dissected as love of God for man, angelic love, love of man for God, love of man for man, all of which leads us in a convoluted way to physical desire and that power of love which forces the senses to inspire pallor, sighs, and tears. A chapter titled "What Is Beauty" examines minutely details of feminine attractiveness, down to the ideally beautiful sweep of the eyelashes. Then comes the grand tutti, which heaps together Latin poets, Greek writers, Provençal songsters, French romantics, declaimers of poetry (*dicitori*), Tuscan poets, Spanish *trovatori*, all of whom (the subject seems difficult for Equicola to relinquish) wrote of love.

Such love manuals required interludes of wide-ranging pedantry and were abetted, almost as illustration, by suitable paintings, the loves of Jupiter as treated by Ovid much-favored subjects. Where his mother had used the skills of Mantegna to stress virtue and chastity, Federico commissioned of Antonio Correggio several canvases of the loves of Jupiter—as a shower of gold for the love of Danaë, as Leda's swan, as a cloud to take Io—none of them remotely suggesting any virtue but sensuality. The painting of Jupiter as a gentle cloud becoming vaguely human, softly embracing round, eagerly yielding flesh, is consummately seductive and pagan.

Federico's quest for the sensual in art and life was abetted by Pietro Aretino, who lived for a couple of lively years in Mantua and who maintained his on-and-off friendship with the duke from Venice, where he spent the rest of his intense life. There was between them mutual procuring: Aretino recommended that Federico buy a nude Venus of Sansovino that no man could look at purely aesthetically; Federico agreed to try to persuade a Mantuan boy for whom the writer yearned into his house and bed.

The simultaneous presence in Mantua in the years 1526 and 1527 of Aretino and the astrologer Guaricus created stimulating conflicts. The esteemed astrologer wrote a prognostication for the year 1526 that warned Federico to be careful about lovers and horses, but when he presented the completed work to Federico, he lifted him above such ordinary concerns by praising him as a latter-day Achilles, Alexander, Caesar. Aretino replied with a satirical set of prophecies, lampooning the work of Guaricus and astrologers in general. Gombrich suggests that it is not "too fanciful to see the spirits of these two men representing as they do two contrasting aspects of the age, struggling for predominance in the strange, oppressive dream-world of the Palazzo del Te," for which both dictated pictures and symbols.

Painting as painting was, in spite of his tastes for the titillating, of prime interest to Federico. As a captive boy in Rome, he had seen Raphael at work in the Vatican and had actually stood for the painter to appear among the personages of the Stanza della Signatura. Fully aware of the fact that Rome had become the art center of the world, he sent his painter Lorenzo Leonbruno to find out who and what was showing there. In France, he had learned the work of French miniaturists, while his own city surrounded him with the works of Mantegna, Francia, Cossa, Perugino, Caravaggio, Correggio, and now Giulio. His uncle's court at Ferrara had for a long time been collecting Flemish paintings. Federico bought 120 Flemish landscapes, stipulating that they have as little religious matter in them as possible. He also asked his influential friend Aretino (whose raging, begging, threatening correspondence reached Francis I of France, the emperor Charles V, the Medici lords, the Spanish court, Michelangelo, Henry VIII of England, the king of Algiers) to procure for him Raphael's portrait of Leo X. Aretino could not manage that but recommended the works of his friend Titian, who painted the writer as the shrewd powerful presence that now dominates a gallery of the Frick Collection and who painted Federico as the beautiful prince who now shines in the Prado. Titian's paintings became an intense enthusiasm, and from 1528 to 1540, when he died, Federico had amassed thirty Titian works, the largest collection in Italy, and to some degree the stimulant for Charles V's patronage of the painter. One of the Mantuans who sat for Titian, incidentally, was Giulio Romano, who took time out of his harried business of supervising everything artistic in Mantua to pose as a worn, soberly dressed man who points to an architectural drawing, very likely one chosen of his own collection of drawings of antique buildings.

E*L*E*V*E*N

The glory years with Titian, with Giulio, with Aretino, with Charles, faded into lackluster periods of depression and illness. When, in February of 1537, an advisory from the Pope, enthusiastically seconded by Cardinal Ercole, declared that Mantua was looked to as host for a council of Church reforms and reconciliations with the Protestants, Federico objected, advising the Pope and his uncle that he could not be responsible for the costs of the projected conclave, nor the care for public order it would require. The council was held elsewhere, to the disappointment and displeasure of both prelates.

On February 13, 1539, Federico's mother died, at the age of sixty-five, an extraordinary age for a time when the populace in general, and women in particular, died quite young. He may have loved her, at times hated her, diminished her, used her, plotted with and against her, and had he been inclined to mourn her, hadn't the energy for it. A crippling flare-up of his syphilis drove him to the quiet of Marmirolo, where he died fifteen months later, at the age of forty.

* "Show was power" is a constantly reiterated phrase in matters of the Renaissance (and not yet ready to be discarded), and certainly was in the consciousness of Federico. An element of the drive for show was the ancestral responsibility of keeping Mantua a handsome community. Giulio and his well-paid assistants laid out streets, rebuilt old churches, erected new ones, while they

also reorganized and embellished old spaces in the Palazzo Ducale. Scores of engineers and masons, under the supervision of Giulio, erected bridges and strengthened ramparts. Horizons of learning in the small university were broadened by new professors, and by a committee of physicians called to teach other physicians and to dissuade the public from resorting to charlatan itinerants for cures. Homeless children were gathered into a new orphanage, where they were taught work skills. The fury of improvement slowed when Federico's earnings as *condottiere* diminished, but it revived with sales of crops and land in Monferrato as well as Mantua and a steady if unjust system of taxation and free labor. In spite of his proclamation that the burden of taxes would be evenly distributed, it was palpably not. The ownership of oxen, even by a marginal farmer, required that a tax be paid, but not by land-owning members of the aristocracy, who were also free of property tax. Workers on Gonzaga farms and orchards paid no taxes but were pulled out, in threatening times, to strengthen bastions along with the peasants who had nothing to tax. The very young, the very old, sick and wounded veterans, heads of large families, fishermen, barbers, and doctors were taxed lightly. The essential millers, often corrupt and monopolistic, and bakers, often accused of skimming off unbaked dough entrusted to them, flourished tax free.

✳ The Jewish community had been for some time an entrenched part of the financial and cultural life. When the archduke Ferdinand had need of someone who could read and write Turkish, he wrote Federico, asking that he send one of his multilingual Jews. Jewish loan banks increased in number, and individual Jews like the highly respected physician Abramo lent the court impressive sums of money at the then moderate interest of 30 percent. The right to build a second kosher slaughterhouse and a new synagogue indicated that traditional restrictions on the purchase of property by Jews had been relaxed. For favors needed of Jews, and on the example of his mother, who tried to protect them, the atmosphere in Federico's Mantua was unusually generous. Particularly respected were the Jewish doctors, as they were elsewhere in Europe. (Erasmus mentions being attacked by an illness that was diagnosed as plague. With his usual balanced skepticism, he made it his business to find a Jewish doctor, who assured him that he suffered of a minor disorder which would shortly clear up. It did. Montaigne, whose journeys were marked with frequent intestinal discomfort, sought out Jewish doctors.) Among Aretino's voluminous correspondence, there is a letter of thanks and praise to a Jewish doctor, extolling his skills and kindness: "And even if your skills did not give me cause, I should do so in order that from you who are a Jew people can learn how to be a Christian." From Aretino we also find, according to lines in his *Stablemaster*, that Mantuan Jews were permitted wider latitude than was common elsewhere. He mentions "a Jewish specialist of hats, fans and perfumed gloves," introduces a Jewish peddler of trinkets, perfumes, and toothpowder, and has one Christian character, bested in bargaining with the peddler, deplore the fact that he is not permitted to punish him.

✳ In short, Federico left a thriving state: protected citizenry, properties accounted for and taxed, money value stabilized, and, for new complexities in accounting and census taking, a growing body of treasurers, estate managers, and scribes, ready to turn to the service of sixteen-year-old Francesco, who became duke in the midsummer of 1540, the rites of imperial investiture to come three years later. The regents who ruled with him were his mother, Margherita, and his uncles Ferrante and Ercole. Ferrante, described as "learned and brutal" and *"splendido,"* was close to the emperor, while Ercole continued to remain on good terms with the Papacy, and the family was spared, for a time, its customary nervous political dilemmas. Gonzaga were aware of, though seemingly undisturbed by, the rise of a strong merchant class, financially outreaching the aristocracy; the hordes of Protestants in the north; and the renewed ambition and drive of the king of France. Ferrante continued the peripatetic life he was trained for: from his command of imperial armies in Tuscany in his twenties, to leadership in the sack of Rome, to assignments in Tunis, to Sicily as viceroy, to Milan as governor, to heading armies in the Netherlands. Ercole was left to manage the court and its expenses, and to direct further public works by Giulio Romano. It was his function to ask for a show of religiosity, from time to time, of Mantuans and otherwise he did little to disturb the peaceable status quo. The brothers were constantly in touch with each other, exchanging information about conditions in Mantua, about political moves of cohorts and enemies, about the adventures of Ferrante, whose letters came from a diversity of places as far apart as Palermo and London. Like his mother, he wrote voluminously about everything he thought and experienced, including the process of building a fortress, recorded in precise detail. While the brothers informed, consulted, and advised each other, Margherita faded into the background.

Inevitably, there were ominous developments from the near north: The much-contested duchy of Milan had been given by the emperor Charles to his son Philip II, a bitter zealot, the most active royal sponsor of the Inquisition when he later became king and ultimately despoiler of Spanish power. Seeing the prize torn from him and angered by the murder of his leading agents, François approached the Protestant Germans and the infidel Turks to join him against the emperor. The Pope, Paul III, afraid of France and eager to carve an Italian state for his son Pier Luigi, applied to Charles for help, offering his nephew Ottavio in marriage to a natural daughter of the emperor. While negotiations were going on, France invaded. As her Turkish allies pillaged Italy's Adriatic coast, French troops routed imperial forces in the Piedmont. It was at the opening of these Franco-Ottoman raids, which went on through 1543 and 1544, that young Francesco Gonzaga met with the emperor for his investiture as duke of Mantua and marquis of Monferrato, and to negotiate a marriage with Caterina of Hapsburg, niece to Charles and daughter to Ferdinand of Austria, who would succeed his brother as emperor. The marriage not only would mean increased glory and security for Mantua but was yet another stamp of influence for the Empire, whose policy it was to amass potential territories and income by careful marriages, less costly than bribes and wars.

While Ferrante fought to regain Luxembourg from the French and even planned to march on Paris, thus forcing French troops in Italy to return to defend their city, there were French armies threatening the borders of the Mantovana. Ercole, the sybarite and arts connoisseur of "Olympic serenity," suggested that fortresses and walls be checked and did nothing else. He was not naturally given to politics, but by force of his position as regent, became highly competent in civic and economic matters. Taking time out from cultural and artistic interests, particularly the pursuit of antiquities, he saw to the improvement and regularization of the silk-weaving industry and the craft of embroidering in silk, a Mantuan skill then famous throughout Italy. For the silk, he encouraged increased cultivation of mulberry trees; for the profitable distribution of objects made of silk, he gave special permissions and protection to Jewish merchants, a breed he did not particularly like. As an ecclesiast, he watched for symptoms of Protestantism but hoped those he noticed would go away in spite of a storm of papal bulls thundering for strong measures. Ercole's calm and confidence appeared well founded—or it may have been the Gonzaga luck—when a truce was declared between France and the emperor, both menaced by the religious upheavals in Germany in the fall of 1544, the same situation that drew Charles and the Pope together, urging them to organize the Council of Trent, established in 1545. Ercole continued to be buffeted by the Counter-Reformation, the Papacy's response to accusations by Protestants and Catholic reformers that the Roman Church was a pit of pagan depravity. To decorate his image as reformer and enhance his chances for being elected pope at some future time, he increased his fulminations against the widespread concubinage among priests, and let float the rumor that he was a flagellant, scourging himself for the sin of having produced three or four bastards.

There were other excesses criticized by the reformers, which Ercole had to try to control. One area was Gargantuan banqueting. His new rules called for severe restrictions in the consumption of peacocks, pheasants, and other game birds; only two kinds of roast and poultry were to be served at one time; no fish or oysters were to be offered with meats; dishes were not to be ornamented with figurines, fine inlays, bits of gold, as was the court custom; only one type of dessert was to be served, and for late-night snacks, fruit rather than elaborate sweets. The next area for reform was dress and jewelry, particularly the latter; only one conspicuous gem might be worn, although women were allowed more than one ring.

The aristocracy of Mantua vigorously protested these shackles on their freedom. They, whose ancestors had helped build and glorify the court, and who now worked devotedly in its service, were not to be restricted; such hobbling had better be visited on the vulgar nouveau-riche merchants. Thus the oysters continued to arrive in big tubs rimmed with fried frogs' legs ("curiously dressed" and good, according to Thomas Coryat, the English reporter on things Italian); peacocks continued to sit resplendently on marble mosaic tables blazing with gold tableware, jeweled condiment dishes, and platters from Faenza and Persia. Noblemen and their wives and mistresses continued to glitter in jeweled collars and caps. Ercole himself was the owner of distinctive gems, and when he became a representative to the Council of Trent in later years, was noted for the abundance and variety of the dishes his servants offered his guests.

Another of Ercole's major civic occupations was paring down the spendthrift court and the debts left by Federico. Allotting money for the building of churches and their adornment (one such embellishment was a vessel for Mantua's Sacred Blood, to be designed by Cellini) and paying a large force of workmen to widen streets and improve the water supply to peasants and urban workers, he cut and cut other expenditures. He dismissed a large number of useless court sycophants and undeserving pensioners, thus reducing Federico's court of eight hundred by more than half, each remaining man required to take on a specific responsibility. Part of the savings went into general charities, including the care of fallen women, and to the purchase of grain to feed the poor in dire times. Monopolies of merchandise, which had flourished in Federico's time, were dissolved and lower, competitive prices established.

Economies in the entertainment of nobles were unthinkable, almost denying the existence and purpose of the court. One display of hospitality in the accustomed grand style was occasioned by the visit of Prince Maximilian, son of Ferdinand I, on his way to Spain to arrange a royal marriage. It was the midsummer of 1548, the Mincio waters rang with song and the fields echoed with hunting calls. For the next visitor, the city was made even more decorously splendid. The visitor was Philip, son of the emperor Charles V. Under a triumphal arch that swarmed with allegory and mythology, there appeared a large statue of Philip holding a figure of Dame Fortune, whom he, unlike most of humanity, apparently controlled. Descriptions of the welcome of the prince by the duke seem to echo passages in a Benozzo Gozzoli painting: pages in green velvet trimmed with black and white velvet; fifty gentlemen in white velvet studded with gold buttons, wearing medallions on golden chains, carrying staffs and golden swords. An equally glorious group held a canopy of cloth-of-gold over the Hapsburg scion, whose family controlled sizable sectors of the Western world and owned the newfound silver and gold pouring in from the Americas.

Shortly after Philip's visit in 1549 came the marriage of Francesco to his Hapsburg princess, Caterina. She was met at Verona by a cortege of knights led by uncles Ferrante and Ercole, who escorted her to Mantua and its pleasures. Within the year the girl was a widow. Her seventeen-year-old husband had fallen into the lake that edged his castle and died of a resulting fever shortly thereafter. When she was found to be not yet pregnant, the girl was given generous gifts, escorted by Ercole and his entourage to the border, and sent home. Her husband's successor was his twelve-year-old brother, Guglielmo, one of the Gonzaga unfortunates, with a pronounced hump and an ugly disposition. His mentors were still Ercole and Ferrante, the latter less and less available as he pursued his restless career. A year after the boy reached his title, Ferrante was again off to the wars in the interests of the emperor, to counter the renewed thrusts of the French. Ferrante's successes were few, hampered by a lack of arms and money the emperor had promised him. His unpaid soldiers deserted and, as usual, preyed on the peasants. France marched on aided by locals, who attacked the marauding, disorganized imperial forces. When Mantua appeared immediately vulnerable, Ercole destroyed those fortifications that could not be successfully defended and placed troops in key positions to protect the inhabitants from looting.

Amid the dangers created by the lack of promised supplies and soldiers and the devastations of the ravaging gangs, small lords became embittered and chose to cast their lots with the French, who already held Mantua's annex, Monferrato. Commanders quarreled, strategies strayed, and then it was once more time for a breather, a two-year pact signed in April 1552, which stilled most of the combat between the Spanish-imperial armies and the French. Although calumnies against Ferrante when he was governor of Milan had been officially stopped, the position was never again his. He journeyed to Spain, then came back to Guastalla, his small principality by inheritance, and, in fear of the French, fled to Molfetta on the Adriatic, his holding by marriage. Leaving his large family—twelve children, the records say, in spite of his long absences from home—he responded to the call of Philip II of Spain to lead a sector of his troops in Flanders. He was better supplied with men and arms than before, but the Gonzaga luck did not this time support him. He died in battle in 1557, at the age of fifty, an impressive life span for a man almost from birth an ardent warrior and a politico in sticky places.

Theater and Music

In 1513, while Baldassare Castiglione was in the service of the court of Urbino, he reported with his usual meticulousness on what must have been a most remarkable theater spectacle (for its time; a century later, Bernini produced costumes, scenery, and effects on a broader, more astonishing scale, including rain that threatened to become a biblical deluge). The hall itself was richly decorated with great branches of foliage covering the ceiling; two towers on the stage held pipers and trumpeters. Rows of wire high up in the hall held rows of candelabra that shaped letters spelling *Deliciae Populi,* each letter large enough to hold seven or eight torches for bright illumination.

Below, a fine city with various buildings painted in "admirable perspective." Among them, a temple that had taken four months to complete, for good reason. It was "covered with beautiful stucco reliefs, the windows were made to imitate alabaster, the architraves and cornices were of fine gold and ultramarine blue, with glass jewels here and there, looking exactly like real gems; there were roundels of marble containing figures, carved pillars, and much more that would take me too long to describe." Although he takes the time to marvel at a group of amazingly skilled child actors, much of the rest of the letter deals with a series of intermezzi, sometimes more important and attractive than the plays: A *moresca* (a Moorish dance-song tempered in Provence) is danced by Jason in full armor; approaching him from the other side of the stage are two bulls, "so lifelike that several of the spectators took them for real animals, breathing fire through their nostrils." The warriors he has sown as dragons' teeth spring to the stage in a fiery dance, trying to kill him. Jason reappears, after the warriors are routed, at first looking truly fallen and slain, then recovering, to dance gracefully with the golden fleece on his shoulder.

The second interlude presents Venus seated in a beautiful chariot. "The car is drawn by two doves, who certainly seemed to be alive, and who were ridden by two Amorini with lighted

tapers in their hands and bows and quivers on their shoulders."
More *moresca* dancing is performed, by Amorini carrying torches
and nine gallants, whom they have freed from behind a burning
door.

The third intermezzo brings on Neptune in a carriage drawn
by two sea horses with wonderfully made scales and fins. The sea
god and his trident are accompanied by eight monsters, who perform a sword dance while the carriage flames. Juno appears next
in a chariot that seems to be floating in a cloud surrounded "by
numberless heads blowing the winds of heaven." Her car was
drawn "by two peacocks so beautiful and lifelike that I could not
believe my eyes, and yet I had seen them before, and had myself
given directions how they were to be made. In front were two
eagles and ostriches, behind two sea-birds and two large parrots,
with gaily colored plumage." These animals also dance a most
graceful "sword" dance. At the end of the performance, one of
the Amorini explains the intermezzi, feeding the Renaissance
love of multiple meanings: Jason's story tells his audience to live
in peace with kin; Love and Concord, accompanied by the hidden
music of four viols and four voices, sing a tuneful hymn to Love.
The show is over, after long hours of viewing and admiring the
amazements provided by the scene painters and the effects men,
the costumers, the performers, and the deep purse of the prince
who paid for it all.

∗ The performance Castiglione describes was not quite the peak
of Renaissance theater but came close, following a long line of
development. The Renaissance theater had old, wide, and deep
roots. The Roman comedies, especially of Plautus, and adapta-
tions of Greek comedy provided matter spiced by ageless panto-
mimic scenes. The Church shaped the essential drama of its
services as dialogues and choral responses, on Easter morning as
the emotional spectacle of one feeble light moving from candle
to candle, swelling to a great mystical radiance. The trade guilds
of the Middle Ages trundled their "mystery" plays on biblical
themes from square to square, running a gamut from primitive
lament to noble portrait to lewd wit. Wandering acrobats, jug-
glers, medicine men, pipers, and singers provided their own free-
form entertainment. Not to be altogether out of the lively world,
some convents staged plays, nuns playing men when assigned such
roles. (The Counter-Reformation put an end to that unseemli-

ness.) On this fertile mélange, plus its love of oratory, of duels of elegant verbalism, and the masques and "scenes" staged in the court, the Italian Renaissance theater flourished brilliantly, producing several impressive innovations, among them the wily, ribald commedia dell'arte, whose characters and mischief live on vividly.

To house a burgeoning of theater and to feed its love of building and the absorbing games of perspective, the Renaissance put men like Bramante, Peruzzi, Sangallo, and Vignola to designing theaters and stage sets. When he was not devising lyres, war machines, and engineering projects for Ludovico Sforza of Milan, Leonardo da Vinci designed costumes and ornaments for theatricals. The busy biographer and painter Vasari was assigned to theater crafts in Florence, while Giulio Romano, equally busy as general art factotum in Mantua, continued to astonish with his theatrical inventions. The earliest theaters, however, were decorated courtyards, gardens, palace halls—any attractive space large enough for performers and audience, and for jousting and feasting.

The building that was exclusively theater was not, even in the beginning, altogether simple. Elaborations in size and decoration, like the theater built by Scamozzo in Sabbioneta and the more imposing Teatro Olimpico in Vicenza, built by Palladio (each claiming the right to call itself the first covered theater), were generally worked on one crowded ornate set, most commonly arranged as a group of streets retreating in sharp perspective among houses, churches, arches, and towers: for comedy, cozy clusters of houses; for tragedy, an emphasis on classical pillars and broader, larger temples. The static effect of one set was later relieved by devices that could turn a section of scenery to reveal a new street and stage effects that appeared to alter the light in the sky to suggest changing hours. Sets soon began to reproduce actual city streets: the Piazza della Signoria of Florence for one play, Pisa and its leaning tower as arranged by Vasari for another. Renaissance ingenuity increasingly concentrated on effects so variedly stunning that the play itself was often overwhelmed, its story and eloquence lost to the audience, which did not always care. Children winged as cherubim flew through the air as centuries later Peter Pan would, evoking the same astonished joy. The Virgin and Child and their saints were not left enthroned on wobbly chairs, as on the crude street wagons of il popolo; the court theater pulled them up to refulgent heavens in breathtaking ascensions.

* The court itself was theater, surrounded by the dramas of mythology. The tapestries that hung on the walls, the surrounds of fireplaces, paintings, and sculpture, were the small stages for that favorite subject, Jove, to disport himself on in his several seductive guises, the favorite being his appearance as Leda's swan in a pretty, lascivious entwining. Hercules and his muscles performing his labors, fat Bacchus instructing his salacious fauns, the languid adventures of Venus, all provided impromptu playlets on salvers and ewers. When awesome, remote Byzantine Virgins and saints gave way to the naturalism, the emotional evocation of biblical events, as painted by Giotto, by Masaccio, by the artists who followed, there was an added echo of theater in the church.

For a theatrical civilization that liked to think of itself as the new Rome, "bread and circuses" was not a remote concept. Bread was sometimes provided, sometimes not, but the circuses were constant. The main *"vivicissime, allegre"* piazze, the cathedral, the roads surrounding a town, offered wondrous theatrical processions. The casts numbered hundreds when a pope, his cardinals, his lawyers, and falconers and horsemen, traveled on matters of state. An emperor on his way to his coronation might bring a brilliant entourage of thousands. An act of charity, staged as a procession of nobles to accompany the duke Ercole d'Este, on his search for Ferrara's poor that he might offer them alms, was something of a theatrical event. A baptism of a royal baby, the funeral of a court notable, a public execution, the arrival of a new bride in a jeweled chaplet, accompanied by her glossy ladies-in-waiting and liveried guards, all made exciting theater. For its most important visitors—an emperor, a pope, a foreign prince—a city would dress its nobles and knights in their most magnificent costumes and place them among the stunning props that made their city a stage. Chariots that recalled the progress of Roman heroes were driven through the streets by groups of young nobles meant to be Jason and his cohorts, one of them draped in an animal skin to reenact Hercules. Another chariot might carry a court favorite gorgeously dressed as Juno and surrounded by a bubbly swarm of Cupids.

Hospitality inside the palace took on more than a tinge of playacting; a mock tourney in a palace courtyard presented blooded horses and fine armor over velvet brocade and lances festooned with green branches, meant to harm no one. In one of the long galleries, an interval for lighter entertainments: the capers of buffoons and clowns perhaps, or the cavorting of a tribe of court dwarfs, one of whom could (at least in Mantua) release flatulence on order. Isabella and Francesco had one dwarf dressed as a bishop to amuse the visiting Duke of Milan. A dwarf named Nanino frequently dressed as a priest to conduct garbled masses. (Thus hints of anticlericalism were taken from the patrons to become the responsibility of their human toys.) As background, music of voices purring courtly dalliance, a voice singing an old rueful tune of Provence to a lute, the strains of learned discourse in Latin spotted with Greek phrases.

High feasting was theatrical, an extravaganza of gold and silver plate, of damask and brocade tablecloths (changed frequently because their edges were used as napkins), of endless hours through a progress of two dozen courses. Not only the fervid eating and drinking and the leisured pace imitated Rome, but the utensils themselves: ewers of crystal shaped like mythical birds, bowls painted in grotesque designs surmounted by harpies' heads and studded with breasts. Pottery from Faenza and Urbino told the cherished old stories: of Diana turning Actaeon into a stag; Apollo in his sun chariot; Daphne becoming a laurel tree—characters who often came to actual life in the pageantry of the banquet itself. A fanfare of trumpets and the flare of torches introduced a live Diana leading off platters of venison and hare. Juno ushered in the display of peacocks, deplumed, stuffed, reassembled. Ceres appeared with the highly prized Mantuan cheese and sausage; Mercury flew before trays that carried the dessert, hundreds of figurines of dough, sugar, and gold dust.

Like the medieval baron, the Renaissance host made the rounds of his great eating hall, greeting each honored guest, sharing with him a choice tidbit that was plucked out of the communal bowl with a silver fork, one of Italy's innovations soon picked up by the rest of Europe. Another refinement (avidly imitated by the nouveau wealth of early-twentieth-century America) was the costly little gift that appeared at the place of each guest. All this—the sumptuous new dress and ropes of gems ordered for the distinguished occasion, the gifts, the profligacy of viands, the accompanying theatricals and balls—depleted the treasury and sent agents to the moneylenders of Venice and the Jews closer at hand. The spending for these luxurious shows, the borrowing, the settling up, as when Francesco Gonzaga received his stipend from Venice, followed a lively, constant rhythm, which marked much of a nobleman's life.

 * The late fifteenth-century popes Paul II and Sixtus IV, enthusiasts of Roman antiquities and the beautification of Rome, made attempts to revive the antique theater, but much of the actual rebirth of the old abundance took place in Ferrara. When Isabella d'Este married Francesco Gonzaga, she brought a passion and knowledge of the theater with her. A childhood lived in a fervor of selecting, planning, producing plays both religious and profane was as much part of her dowry as her jewels, her Latin, her lutes, and her books of chivalric romances. Her father had spent a prodigious sum of money to build a theater, mainly for the plays of Plautus, when she was twelve. Not as sophisticated in its scenic machinery as those built by the Medici, it was yet imposingly large, with a capacity of five hundred, the choice seats reserved for visiting foreigners and the rest for local knights and their ladies, seated in separate sections. During one of her frequent visits to her family as marchesa of Mantua, Isabella wrote that her father had shown her the costumes for five plays to be presented shortly, over twenty costumes for each play, no outfit to appear in any but its specifically designated play. Anything but the full luxurious gesture for his theater was scorned by Duke Ercole of Ferrara.

Not that Mantua was totally devoid of distinction in the field before Isabella's time. The young Poliziano had written his landmark *Orfeo*, a prophecy of opera, in the time of her husband's grandfather. The court had distinguished musicians and dancers, as sought after and prized as a popular painter might be. One spill from Mantua's cornucopia of archives speaks of Ascension Day festivities of the late fifteenth century when a Gian Pietro della Viola, poet and musician, is preparing to stage scenes he had devised as a "Laurel Festival." He cannot continue, however, without the services of "*Lorenzo ballerino*," apparently in demand elsewhere. *Lorenzo ballerino* must have been threatened or exceptionally well paid to appear, since the Festa da Lauro was ultimately performed several times for visiting dignitaries. We shortly lose the dancer, but the musician-poet's life is recorded as following the peripatetic path of many artists. Gian Pietro was taken to France by Clara Gonzaga when she married into the house of Montpensier, then returned to Italy to write and make music for the Sforza of Milan. After Ludovico Sforza was taken by the French in 1499, Gian Pietro reappeared in Mantua and remained there under the patronage of Francesco and Isabella.

Francesco Gonzaga, who particularly enjoyed *Orfeo*, called for a revival of the play, whose presentation became a family tradition. Among his cast of actors and singers we find artists of multiple capacities, very much like the painters who were also architects, goldsmiths, decorators of wedding chests and furniture. One famous singer, Filippe Lapaccini, wrote scenes for acting and miming and composed dance songs. Another distinguished performer, Ercole Albergati, put his hand to designing triumphal arches, banners, and room decorations, and served as assistant to court engineers and architects. For his contributions to the court and the city he was rewarded with a grant of land by Francesco.

Isabella was more literary than her husband and eager for a broader collection of plays. She wrote frequently to Ferrara and its literati (reputed to be more numerous than frogs in Ferrara), requesting translations into the vulgate of classical comedies and copies of those plays already translated and adapted. She had a broad field from which to make selections. While Ariosto was weaving his multicolored *Orlando* tapestry, his contemporaries were feverishly writing plays, not only those hung on Roman models but dramatizations of the stories Boccaccio recorded and entirely new inventions. One of the earliest purely Italian comedies, the *Formicone* of Publio Filippo, emerged from Mantua. Gian Giorgio Trisino, with a bit of help from the Greeks, wrote *Sofonisba*, one of the earliest of Italian tragedies. Ariosto balanced his praise of the Este in *Orlando* with a comedy, *Lena*, which pricked with its wit the ineptitude and corruption of his court, Ferrara, which did not seem to mind. Machiavelli's *Mandragola* took on the clergy in bright, robust thrusts, while Aretino put his wits to the sexual corruption, the lumpish horseplay and practical jokes that absorbed his Mantuan friends. The numerous salacious plays, produced at times in courts, at times performed by amateurs in "academies," did not hamper the appearance of chivalric fantasy, or of lyrical pastorals like Torquato Tasso's appealing *Aminta*.

Once in usable scripts, favorite plays were kept in a repertoire that supplied frequent and long performances, interrupted with intermezzi of dance, mime, and music. In a letter to her husband in Mantua from Ferrara, Isabella mentions the performance of several plays during *carnevale* and describes the extra material woven into the last of the series. At the end of the first act, she writes, Fortune appears with a cortege of young men and women, who enact a playlet of the "sadness and desperation" a Madman causes them. The second act offers at its conclusion gaggles of young women and men of several ages, who complain of the complications love suffers when money matters interfere. The third act introduces five musicians, who sing and play the lute. The fourth leads into the popular *moresca* which is performed by twelve people carrying torches; the wonder, Isabella says, is not only the elegance with which it was danced but the fact that no one was injured. The fifth act finished with a highly moral recitation. It wasn't until she was considerably older that Isabella complained of boredom with these interminable entertainments. (The play of the five intermezzi was, incidentally, called *The Eunuch.*)

Isabella's son Federico turned to his master builder, Giulio Romano, when particularly staggering effects were wanted. Romano, described by Vasari as "profound, spirited, fanciful, various, prolific and universal," used his rich imagination and practiced skills to make the triumphant arches that welcomed Charles V to Mantua in 1530 and to design "curious costumes for jousts, feasts, tournaments, which excited great wonder in the emperor and all present." Among the many items devoted to Romano in Mantuan correspondence, there is a reference to an entertainment staged for fifty of the most beautiful and noble gentlewomen of Mantua. Eight pages of the court were dressed as shepherds, animal skins over flesh-colored tights, laurel garlands on black curls, and masks so devised that they did not interfere with the singing of the *moresca*, which was a "pleasure to the eyes and ears." Besides the eight shepherds, the letter goes on, there was their god, Pan, played by a skillful harpist, the Jew Abramo dell'Arpa, mentioned several times in Mantuan theater annals. A few days later, Romano is again praised for the wonderful costumes he designed for a performance of Plautus's *Captives*, in Latin. Since, we are told, not too many in the audience understood Latin, the action was explained in a number of intermezzi in Italian, that they not be bored.

Later in the files concerning theatricals, we witness once more the eternal conflict of impatient patron and recalcitrant artist. Vincenzo Gonzaga, a most fervid aficionado of plays, stage effects, female singers and actresses, presented Guarini's *Pastor Fido*—five acts of lengthy speeches and very long in the writing—as a "beautiful ornament" in the celebration of his marriage to Eleonora de' Medici. The request for the supposedly completed play was made in the spring of 1584. Guarini's expected answer arrived promptly: In spite of three years' work, the play is not yet finished. The author has been under the care of physicians for four or five months and is not yet at all well, and an unwilling brain produces only unsatisfactory poetry. He is worried about those in the audience who have no understanding of playcraft, who require intermezzi full of showy stage inventions. Among his complaints he includes his hatred and fear of perfidious courtiers. Vincenzo tried again in 1591 and in time was given the news that Guarini was on his way to Mantua to supervise the production of his play. A cast was assembled, including among the dancers Angelo, the son of Giuseppe Sacerdoti, *ebreo* (Hebrew), rehearsing under Isaachino, *ballerino* and also *ebreo*. After a long delay, Guarini did arrive, still worrying. What about artificial light, which would enhance dramatic effects, rather than daylight, which flattened them? What about refining the ballet, a tricky pause in the work? Finally, the full cast went into rehearsal and the tragicomic pastoral was performed, to be performed at least twice again in Mantua, where it was viewed enthusiastically by large audiences of foreign nobles, one of them a royal princess on her way to a marriage in Spain, her entourage an unbelievable seven thousand.

* Abramo dell'Arpa, and Isaachino, choreographer and dancer, and Angelo, the dancer son of Giuseppe Sacerdoti (whose name strongly suggests that he was a rabbi), were members of a seminal core of Mantua's theater, the Università Israelitica. The word *Università* was often used for the whole Jewish community but more frequently for its writers, actors, and stage craftsmen, who lived under the protection of the court. Mantua's tolerance of its Jews over long periods may have been motivated not only by its own profligacy, for which it needed quick, large loans, but also by its love of the theater. The community was an accomplished, culturally alert group; in 1476, an Abramo Conato had already established a Hebrew press. A century later, the court maintained as engineer and mathematician and bewilderingly adroit performer of card tricks (which he attributed to occult secrets in his special possession) Abramo Colorni. Some of the physicians of the community were in the employ of the Gonzaga, and there were, of course, the essential bankers.

The theater company performed in private palaces initially and in time asked for permission to use a hall in which to perform for a period of ten years, the rental to be annual gifts to the poor. No records of such a theater, if it was ever established, remain, but the name of the petitioner, Leone de Sommi, lasts as the writer of plays and poetry and of informed material concerning theater techniques. Well thought of and aware of his prestige, Sommi petitioned the authorities for exemption from wearing the circlet that appeared on all Jewish cloaks and for permission to buy property, prohibited to Jews. It isn't known whether these requests were granted him, but it was a mark of his stature and a measure of the court's relatively relaxed attitudes that he had the confidence to ask.

Sommi's *Dialogues,* written in the mid-sixteenth century, introduces three savants of the theater, Verdico, Massimiano, and Santino, who discuss at great leisured length such theater matters as costuming, revealing in the process the expectations of the audience. "I insist that all the actors be as nobly dressed as possible, but that there be distinctions among them on the understanding that sumptuous clothing (especially important in these times *when pomp is at a maximum stage*) be used; it would seem that sumptuous dress greatly increases the worth and appeal of comedy and even more, that of tragedy." The discourse continues with the injunction that before they utter a word, a group of similar characters—pages, shall we say—suggest their different characters by the colors they wear, by a feather in a cap, or none. Of course, a play whose setting is Constantinople, for instance, would be costumed in dress unlike Italy's and yet as rich. Should a play reproduce a tragedy of ancient times, classical sculpture and painting must be followed; the proud helmets of captains, the metal and leather armor of soldiers, the trappings of gladiators, always make a splendid presentation. But, says one speaker, these are expensive things and require an enthusiastic patron and an open hand. Third speaker: There is no prince who cannot find something suitably splendid in his wardrobe, to which he must only add a mantle, a stole, a broad centurion's belt. As for the ubiquitous shepherds of the popular pastoral plays, they were to appear as described in Homer: a simple sleeveless garment, legs nude, feet in rustic sandals, on the chest and shoulders an animal skin (leopard preferred for its dramatic effect), on the head a laurel or ivy wreath. Nymphs follow the descriptions of the classical poets, adorned in gossamer silks and bright ribbons of gold, a "sumptuous mantle" fastened at one shoulder. The hair must be blond, full and loose, held only by a simple ornament, suggesting a natural creature of the woods, an evanescent wraith.

There were *ebreo* actors and dancers in other Italian cities, Milan and Venice, for example, but it was Mantua's Università that produced a Leone de Sommi and, it is claimed by some scholars, the first modern Italian comedy. The Università's odd way of life was carefully observed and respected: Theater lovers were reminded that Friday performances had to be scheduled early, not to interfere with the *festa del sabbato* (Sabbath). During high holy days, performances were suspended because it was then forbidden Jews to light torches, set off fireworks, and put in motion stage-effects machinery, at which they were singularly skillful. Vincenzo Gonzaga, who loved magic effects, whether on the stage or in an alchemist's alembic, commissioned the company to perform during the celebrations of his birthday and to add their arts to carnival merriment. For the festivities that surrounded his first marriage, to Margherita Farnese, he ordered a comedy to be written and staged by Sommi. The fame of the Mantuan players spreading throughout Europe undoubtedly stemmed to a considerable degree from the talents of the Università; Elizabeth I of England watched a Mantuan group perform in 1577; Spain was entertained by Mantuans ten years later, and soon after, France was enjoying and imitating them.

✳ The duke Guglielmo and, to a greater degree, his son Vincenzo were, as mentioned, deeply involved in theatricals, constantly improving the quality of presentations, Vincenzo so possessive and protective of his players that he would not follow the common practice of giving permission for wandering companies to perform in Mantua. He housed his favorite actors, settled the jealous quarrels that arose among them, saw to the care of their children, and humbled himself before the stars he urged to his court, signing one letter to a popular diva, "Yours to do your pleasure." To appear with a favored actress, star-struck Vincenzo himself frequently pantomimed, danced, sang, and recited in masques and stage scenes. Benefactor almost constantly, he could also be destructive, separating the members of two or three well-functioning companies, selecting the best performers to regroup as his own company, letting the rest go to find work where they could. For those who were kept on, there were substantial rewards: besides the promise of fairly long-term employment, gifts as tokens of praise and often the gift of an exalted name for a baby born to a performer. One actor and writer on the theater, Niccolò Barbieri, reported that "many princes and princesses, kings and queens, emperors and empresses, held the babies of players at the baptismal font and as godparents honored the infants with their names as spoken and written."

In 1587, Guglielmo Gonzaga died and theatricals were suspended for a year. Ten years later, a similar long pause followed the death of the last Este duke, Alfonso II. Leone de Sommi died in 1590. There is mention of the Università several times in the last decade of the sixteenth century, and notice, in 1602, of a Simone Basilia, *ebreo*, who had the distinctive capacity to create many characters in his own person, his own voice. After 1605, silence from the Università. A guiding genius of Italian stagecraft for some time thereafter was Giambattista Andreini, the son of the gifted Isabella and husband of the equally gifted Virginia. His troupe, the renowned Fedeli, worked in France and Ferrara as well as in Mantua. From these patron courts he received moneys for inventions that advanced stagecraft in all of Europe. One of his most innovative productions was *La Maddalena*, the "most beautiful mixture of comedy-drama-tragedy-melodrama-pantomime-dance" (see *Hamlet*). A connoisseur of music, Andreini had his text set to music by Monteverdi and Salomone de' Rossi, both Mantuan composers. Born into the theater, Andreini spent all his years acting, directing, and writing for and about the stage. His strong and authoritative tendency was to naturalism and simplicity, novelties in a mannerist age. He advocated frequent changes of scenery to create a sense of realistic changes of place and time; as director, he moved his actors about the stage so that they appeared emotionally related to one another rather than isolated, oratorical figures; in short, he was the first of modern directors.

* Neither as gifted musically as the Este nor as avid in collecting musicians and composers, the Gonzaga were sufficiently interested to make a good showing in competition with their relatives and even outshone Florence, at times, in the splendor of their musical productions. The earliest singular musical event in the court was, as mentioned, the use of accompaniment to Poliziano's *Orfeo*. French and Flemish music were favored at the time, the services of composers like Josquin des Prez energetically sought. (Ferrara very much wanted him until the duke was warned that he was overly temperamental and independent.) In 1498, a book of *frottole*, precursors of the madrigal, was published in Venice. Using various verse patterns, among them Petrarch's sonnet form, and combining them with rhythms of traditional song, the *frottola* composer shaped a work that had a leading vocal line entwined with three or four instrumental lines. An attractive innovation, readily capable of variations, the *frottola* swept Europe and made it almost imperative for gentlemen and ladies to learn to sight-read. Isabella, an Este with a pleasing singing voice, a lutenist of some skill, knowledgeable about music and always in the forefront of all fashions, hired a good number of court musicians and ordered an impressive number of new instruments. She also sponsored two leading *frottola* composers, Marchetto Cara and Bartolomeo Tromboncino, who sang and instructed in the general singing frequently mentioned by Isabella. It was the role of her husband to see to liturgical music. With the loan of a few singers from Ferrara to add to his Mantuan group, Francesco established a chapel choir, expanded it with singers from Venice, and ordered an organ built to accompany their voices. Since there were not yet resident composers of liturgical music in his court, the choir sang material borrowed from Venice and Ferrara, becoming so skillful in its execution that Leo X ordered that several Mantuan singers be shipped to Rome for his chapels.

Francesco and Isabella's son Cardinal Ercole enjoyed madrigalists, but it was his role to concentrate on church music, for which he commissioned a composer of great repute throughout Europe, Jacques Colebault, who would in time be known as "Jacquet of Mantua." The two successive generations of Gonzaga were ardent aficionados of music. Guglielmo concerned himself mainly with church music, commissioning masses and motets of Pierluigi da Palestrina, with whom he carried on an extensive correspondence which included discussions of his own works, soliciting from the composer suggestions for their improvement. Repeatedly urged to come to Mantua, Palestrina demurred. He dispatched a few masses but preferred to stay in Rome with Julius II, conducting papal choirs and writing litanies and magnificats for them to perform. Instead, he sent a gifted pupil, Francesco Suriano, remembered in the history of music as a leading composer of liturgical music. For the position as composer and master of the choir in his ducal chapel of Santa Barbara, Guglielmo hired the prestigious Netherlander Giaches de Wert, who, it is said, helped Guglielmo write settings to Petrarch sonnets—works which have disappeared or never actually existed.

Vincenzo, in opposition to his father in all matters, changed the color of Mantuan music as well. His relatives in Ferrara entertained with performances of versatile singing groups, largely female, whose charms and gifts as instrumentalists moved Vincenzo to establish a similar Concerto della Donne. To Guglielmo's displeasure, de Wert, tired of his liturgical tasks, wrote music for these accomplished ensembles, as did other court composers. Expanding, growing ever more complex and sophisticated, secular music was soon to reach an apogee in Mantua with the maturation of one of its young musicians. On the list of court violists of 1591 there appears the name of Claudio Monteverdi. He was twenty-four and had already composed numerous pieces of vocal music for the church and court of his native town, Cremona, the cradle of violin and cello making. Monteverdi remained a violist in Mantua for five years and then, in spite of rivalries and intrigues among other musicians and composers, was elevated to a position that recognized his talent for writing vocal music. A companion composer supported by Vincenzo was a member of the Università, Salomone de' Rossi, who wrote madrigals for the court, along with sonatas and theater music; for his synagogues he brightened the dark Hebrew chants with the more worldly modes of the outer Mantuan world.

In spite of Monteverdi's litany of being passed over in appointments by intriguers, of not being paid enough, of being made ill by the bad airs of Mantua, the composer did not do too badly in Vincenzo's time, nor in the court of his sons Ferdinando and Francesco. Vincenzo granted the composer a generous annual wage—never enough, according to the recipient—and the honor for himself and his children of Mantuan citizenship. Genuinely fond of music and as fond of the spotlight, Vincenzo took Monteverdi as head of a martial band on the crusade against the Turks organized by the emperor Rudolph II. They played and marched into what is now Austria and Czechoslovakia and finally into Hungary, where the duke picked up a skin disease and the troops various ailments, mainly dysentery. They crawled back to Italy. Four years later, a more pleasurable trip to the Netherlands, where the duke took the waters and Monteverdi listened to the works of Flemish and French composers.

When he was not traveling or supervising court musicians, Monteverdi was writing and publishing an astonishing amount of music, madrigals primarily. It was a fertile time for secular music; Palestrina's conservative modes had begun to die before his death in 1594, while in Florence a *camerata* of musicians and literati were preparing to produce the first known opera, *Dafne*, the libretto by Ottavio Rinuccini, a dramatic poet, the music by the singer Jacopo Peri with the assistance of a musical nobleman, Jacopo Corsi. Shortly after, Florence presented two operatic versions of the Eurydice story, the composers Peri again and another singer, Giulio Caccini, the librettist Rinuccini. A short time before, Orazio Vecchi's *Amfiparnasso*, a madrigal comedy, was published in Modena. It was quickly followed by similar works, which became popular as *melodramme* but were not quite opera, limiting themselves to polyphony, which left no room for the emotional solo aria. Nor were the Florentine works, for that matter, especially expressive, being constrained in their imitation of what they imagined the Greek theater had demanded. Opera had to wait for Monteverdi to bring it to fuller, more evocative development. It has been suggested that both Monteverdi and Vincenzo attended a performance of Rinuccini's *Eurydice* in Florence, the principal singer a Mantuan. This performance may have spurred the duke to confer on Monteverdi the title Maestro della Musica and suggest that he compete with the Florentines, that *he* write an opera. But there were ballets to prepare, a heavy schedule of court music to supervise, and the inexhaustible flow of madrigals—a fifth volume dedicated to the duke in 1605, a great success that quickly went into several editions.

Finally, in early 1607, Mantua witnessed the full genius of Monteverdi in a performance of his *Orfeo*, frequently referred to as a "milestone," a "great leap forward" in musical history. The uncanny sensibility to voice and instrument, the richness of invention, the artist's need to venture beyond the accepted confines of his craft, prophesied opera as we know it now. The tragic low strains with which Verdi accompanies Otello's despair parallel those to which Monteverdi's Orfeo sings his lamentations. The tremulant tones that Monteverdi used to elicit sorrow from his listeners still sound in the deaths of Aida and Violetta. Melding the capabilities of his instruments, he used them for a richer polyphony than had been heard before. The role of Orfeo was sung by a castrato, Giovanni Gualberto, whose early emasculation had produced a voice of strength and flexibility, capable of coping with high florid passages. He was lauded both for having memorized the role and for the profound emotion with which he sang it. Dedicated to Vincenzo's son Francesco, also an opera buff and then the head of the local aristocratic Accademia, in whose meeting hall the first performance took place, Orfeo was enthusiastically received and repeated twice in the court, while the libretto, by Alessandro Striggio, was immediately published and distributed widely.

Later that same year, the composer's singer wife, Claudia, died in Cremona, where she and her two young sons had spent much time, cared for by Monteverdi's physician father. The composer returned to Cremona, to help take care of his children and because he, as always, felt that the respect and compensation the Mantuan court offered him was not commensurate with his contributions to its glory. He was still its servant, however, on a life stipend, and was recalled to Mantua to write an opera in celebration of the wedding of Francesco to Margherita of Savoy. The opera was Arianna, to be performed with four works of other composers (three of them also premieres), the whole an extraordinary blossoming of the new musical form, presented in what was probably the earliest opera festival. Although the libretto remains, nothing is left of the Arianna score (probably lost with other treasures during later invasions of the city) except the famous and infinitely affecting "Lament," which moved its first audience to tears as it has moved listeners through the centuries, to become a prototype for lamentation as written by many composers—most notably matched, perhaps, by the wrenching beauty of Dido's lament in Purcell's Dido and Aeneas.

Because of his own irritable nature, or because his payments were delayed while the Florentines whose operas were performed at the Mantuan opera festival were courteously treated and promptly paid, or because he was actually ill, Monteverdi returned to Cremona. He still had obligations in Mantua, though, and there he worked again, with ill will, while he searched elsewhere—Venice, Rome—for situations, with no success. Three years later, the same Francesco to whom the *Orfeo* was dedicated dismissed the composer, although he scheduled a performance of *Arianna* a few months later, while its creator sat in Cremona, gazing bitterly at a dim future.

In August 1613, Venice offered a good house, a generous salary, the title Maestro di Cappella, and the esteem that Mantua, he felt, had not given him, and there Monteverdi stayed, with occasional visits to Mantua and Cremona, until his death, at seventy-seven. It was for Venice that he wrote at an advanced age the brilliant *L'Incoronazione di Poppea*, the first historical opera, and the innovative *Ritorno d'Ulisse*. Although his connections with Mantua became increasingly tenuous, Monteverdi wrote at least two long vocal works for the Gonzaga, probably destroyed in the sack of 1630. He dedicated a new book of madrigals to the wife of Duke Ferdinando, who urged that he return to Mantua. He responded that he found Venice, in spite of its weather, thoroughly agreeable and its people eager to listen to his music, secular and religious. He allowed himself, however, to be persuaded by his old collaborator, the librettist of *Orfeo*, Alessandro Striggio, now an esteemed adviser in the Mantuan court, to write yet another ballet and opera for Mantua, the score of those also gone.

With the loss of Monteverdi to Venice and the termination of a short stay by Girolamo Frescobaldi, music of any significance in this place that had for decades been a creative center dwindled to insignificant sounds. The last Gonzaga admirer of Monteverdi was the youngest daughter of his first patron, Vincenzo I. As the empress Eleonora, the wife of the emperor Ferdinand II, she sponsored a church work and an eighth book of madrigals, dedicated to her husband, and, scholars believe, staged a performance of *Il Ritorno d'Ulisse* in Vienna.

By the time of Monteverdi's state funeral in 1643, the opera Mantua had nurtured flourished elsewhere. Like his contemporary Shakespeare, Monteverdi faded from the public ear for a long period and, like the Elizabethan, was later revived, both to remain in the repertory of the world's masterworks, still performed, still awesome, still, as Ben Jonson said it, "for all time."

T·W·E·L·V·E

Giulio Romano died in 1556, leaving Ercole more sincerely moved than by possible French invasions or a drought that starved his mulberry trees. There was pressing distraction in continuing to teach Guglielmo, who took readily to Uncle Ercole's lessons concerning the economics of their state, to remain, all his life, a capable, watchful administrator of moneys collected and moneys spent. When not guiding Guglielmo and assiduously avoiding political entanglements, Ercole kept his eye on Rome. His contacts there and his connections with the emperor helped him formalize quite specifically all Gonzaga privileges for Guglielmo; in addition to the dukedom of Mantua and the marquisate of Monferrato, he had control of Luzzara, a short distance south of Mantua, acquired by purchase from a Gonzaga relation. In his watchfulness for the prosperity of the state, Ercole had the port of Mantua made more efficient, and because he was a balanced, just man, he instituted a court of appeals, to establish a reasonable judicial system. The apex of his life, in a role of high esteem, came when he was appointed as one of the presiding heads of the Council of Trent, which had been several times moved from place to place and from date to date. Under the aegis of Pius IV, it was once again called in 1562 and sat until 1563; it was in these sessions that Ercole served. One historian who thinks less of him than did Alessandro Luzio, who praised fulsomely the high quality of his learning and wisdom, points out that he was not gifted in theological reasoning and, moreover, was quite deaf. He was, though, elegant and tactful and, as was his inclination, managed to find a quiet corner in hot disputes. Digging into doctrine and reexamining canon law left him indifferent. In March of 1563, while the council was still in session, he died, a loss less significant in Trent than it was in Mantua, where he had managed to rule rationally to the profit of the state.

Guglielmo was then twenty-five, knowledgeable, highly disciplined, severe, humorless, and enamored of money, not so much for what it could buy—as it had bought talent, palaces, gems, and paintings for his father—but for its own shining presence in his coffers. One historian sees him as very clever and enlightened, another as of ordinary intelligence and a tyrant and bigot; all speak of his avarice and greed. Nor are his capacity for work and his unremitting devotion to his state, his political adroitness, his organizational skills, ever questioned. The fact that he was cruelly, implacably tyrannical is often attributed to his physical weaknesses, a tendency to frequent attacks of gout and arthritis, and his fury with his humpback. It was said that Guglielmo never danced because he had once tried and felt himself ridiculous and ugly. He was, they said, not a frequenter of women because his deformity made him self-conscious and afraid of painful comments. There is no mention in reports of his life of the syphilis that killed his father and grandfather, a fate he was spared, ironically enough, by way of the detested hump and his avoidance of extracurricular sex.

Much of the Italy of Guglielmo's maturity was in the hands of either the Papacy or Spain. Milan had become a branch of the Spanish court, Florence and her Tuscan satellites were diminished, near exhaustion; Venice survived, Mantua survived. The somber colors and solemn rigidities, the new joyless religion, the dark presence of the Inquisition, fostered by suspicious Philip II in his grim Escorial, obliterated gaiety in once-exuberant Italy, an atmosphere that suited dour Guglielmo. It suited him, as well, to prove and keep proving his right to rule the Monferrini with the harshest measures he could devise. In spite of the legitimate Gonzaga claim to Monferrato, her leading citizens still held with the pro-French house of Savoy and its esteemed ruler, Emanuele Filiberto. Their own debility kept them from joining him, as well as the fear that a strengthened Savoy might elicit attack from armies stationed in Spanish-governed Milan. The impotent Monferrini chose Guglielmo as their most hated symbol and focus for fury. They proposed that his brother, Ludovico, who had gone to France to claim as his inheritance the titles Duke of Nevers, Count of Rethel, return to rule Monferrato instead of Guglielmo. The notion was rejected on several scores, one of them Guglielmo's intransigence; another the fact that with Ludovico at its head, the territory would become too distinctly French. Whatever hopes the Monferrini had of amelioration of their prospects under Guglielmo (and Ercole, then alive) disappeared when the French and Spanish in the area withdrew, leaving Monferrato entirely to the Gonzaga. In 1561, Guglielmo married Eleonora of Austria, daughter of the emperor Ferdinand I. Whether it was out of the pleasure of having made the most prestigious marriage yet among the Gonzaga, or the need to supervise Mantuan managers of commerce and agriculture and to direct his architects and painters, Guglielmo decided not to be troubled with Monferrato. He suggested that it be exchanged for Cremona, closer to Mantua and more docile. Uncle Ercole and Spain disapproved, and Guglielmo had again to deal with an angry people, on whom he imposed increasingly heavy tax burdens. Reluctant to appear among the Monferrini and searching for a threatening local presence to keep them in line, he dispatched his sister, Isabella, as regent, powerfully shadowed by her husband, the marquis of Pescara, then governor of Milan. Her solution to the lack of fealty to Mantua was more taxation and refining a system of informants, who nosed out the names of citizens with friends and relatives in Savoy. When, in 1563, the marquis of Pescara finished his term as governor of Milan and took his wife home with him, her job went to her mother, Margherita. Margherita's first act was to abolish the autonomy of the city of Casale, granted long before by her ancestors the Paleologhi. By sending the head of Casale's commune into exile, she effectively weakened the frail remains of citizens' rights. While the women of his family fostered virulent enmities, Guglielmo went off to Innsbruck to pay his respects to the emperor and to attend to the death of his uncle, Cardinal Ercole, in Trent, a loss balanced by the recent birth of his first son, Vincenzo. Back in Mantua, he raised taxes and altogether obliterated traditional liberties; still extant documentary proofs of the rights of the old Mantuan Commune were destroyed during his marriage celebration. Somehow the heated merriment had turned to riot, somehow the Jewish quarter was attacked, somehow the archives were burned, leaving citizens' rights in ashes.

The people of Casale declared war on Guglielmo, actually a series of gallant futile gestures. They fortified the main gates of their city against a Mantuan incursion; Guglielmo sent agents to warn them, as before, of the danger of showing pro-French leanings. Assured of backing by Spanish troops, he shook his mailed fist at Casale, which agreed that it would tolerate his entrance into the city as its ruler if he would grant them their communal rights again. He promised, and after entering the city, canceled those rights and demanded greater revenues. In response to ensuing uprisings, Guglielmo ordered the local militia dissolved and put in its place Mantuan soldiers, to be paid by Casale. The property of exiles was gathered up as his own, protesting priests were arrested and punished, with the consent of the Pope. In broader politicking, Guglielmo promised the emperor fifty thousand scudi for a campaign against the Turks, the money to be pressed out of Monferrato. His mother, who was becoming a nuisance with her protests that this and other demands he made were impossible to fulfill out of an impoverished people, did not send the money, and the honor of presenting the scudi to the emperor went to Emanuele Filiberto, the duke of Savoy, "a famously noble and generous warrior, courteous even with his enemies." It was time to take Margherita out of Monferrato; she wasn't fulfilling her required tasks and furthermore was ill. When she died soon after, the bolder of the court gossips attributed her death to the wear and tear of being her son's mother.

The limited controls Margherita had exerted on Guglielmo disappeared altogether and life for the Monferrini became an ordeal of ceaseless oppression. One exile from Casale ran a gamut of spies and ambush to present charges against the tyrant before the Pope. To the message from Rome that he lighten his hand, Guglielmo answered that he had sent his own version of matters to the emperor and would therefore, for the time being, put aside the Pope's request. Having pulled money from the Monferrini to their very skins, he ordered an armed incursion into an area in the Savoy where influential exiles might be found. He found no one and commanded, in his frustration, that Casale hand over an exorbitant sum, ostensibly to improve its fortifications. At about the same time, he sent to a representative of the court of Spain, asking that she pay for the same fortifications, since the cost might be difficult to obtain from the Monferrini. Spain refused and instead gave pleasing Emanuele Filiberto the sum needed to build protective new walls in his Savoy. The event did not sweeten Guglielmo's temper, and he avenged himself by tightening the screws, particularly tight when he heard, or thought he heard, rumors of a plot to kill him during the investiture of the new bishop of Casale.

Infuriated and apprehensive, he returned to Mantua, leaving the governing of Monferrato to an appropriate man for the job, his cousin the cruel, imperious Vespasiano Gonzaga of Sabbioneta, a man who was reputed to have killed his own son for an act of minor disobedience. More fines were imposed, more tributes demanded, Casale was put under curfew, patrols were everywhere watching to see that no more than two people gathered together—and that under bright illumination—at night. Many were arrested and tortured to confess to plotting; the exile who had made his way to the Pope, Oliviero Capello, was tracked down and murdered. The arrest that raised the most clamorous protests in and outside Casale was that of the last Paleologa, the natural son of the marquis Gian Giorgio and cousin to Margherita. He was old and ill, and though he had probably once been a conspirator against the Gonzaga, was now too feeble to be in any way effectual. Spain requested that he be liberated; so did the emperor. Guglielmo's response was that he was awaiting advice from the Pope and could not yet free his prisoner. Turning uneasily under the criticism poured on him from every side, he had the Paleologa poisoned.

Sniffing out plots, whipping off messages to all the major powers to declare himself a victim, Guglielmo found himself confronted by a new, shocking development. Vespasiano turned against him, taking on as supporters several Gonzaga cousins who hoped for help from Spain—where Vespasiano was well known and his capacities respected—as well as that of the duke of Savoy, in an attempt to oust Guglielmo. Searching for plausible justification and to keep their minute states safe from claims that Guglielmo might make on them, the cousins proclaimed the duke of Mantua illegitimate, born of the questionable semimarriage of Federico with Giulia of Aragon. While their agents were conveying this information to Spain and urging her to act on their behalf, Emanuele Filiberto, the duke of Savoy, let it be known that he had no faith in the success of their efforts and would not lend a hand. The plot dissolved before it could ripen to action.

This difficulty set aside, Gonzaga returned to his pressures on Monferrato, alternating that with lighter pressures on Mantuans.

Though its citizens complained about high taxes and the fact that the portion of agricultural earnings that had traditionally been set aside for the Commune was now privately Gonzaga, theirs was one of the richest cities in Italy, thanks, in a considerable degree, to the acumen and sharp accountant's eye of their duke. Mantua's population of over forty thousand included more than two thousand weavers of prized silks and woolens, which were widely exported. Rural lands were carefully administered and yielded well. Citizens could rely on an enlightened judicial system instituted by Ercole and supervised by respected jurists; for the indigent and ailing, the Ospedale Maggiore was expanded and improved medical services were instituted. Guglielmo had records of everything that was going on everywhere. From the records of his time, going back to Ercole's regency, we have a sound idea of what the word *villa* meant as it pertained to Marmirolo, Castiglione, Pietole, and Goito. We are told of hordes of guests and the contents of their rooms by inventories kept in categorized bundles in the Gonzaga archives. A notary named Stivani has left us, in ink that is now a gentle, tired brown, lists of the furnishings of Marmirolo. The inventory mentions each room by its descriptive name—the French Room, the Room of the Wolf, the Room of the Falcons—and the objects it held. A similar inventory lists broken and worn objects which need replacing, the most common of these by far beds and mattresses. No detail lacks: We are given listings of pots and pans, spits for roasting meat, mortars of marble to grind spices and nuts, tables and small tapestries to cover them, chairs and benches, painted and inlaid, house altars, credenzas, and chests. Each villa functioned as well as the center of a farm, which included barns, stables, granaries, dovecotes, gardens, orchards, and boats and docks for waterfronts. In addition to the country villas, there were small *corte*, each surrounded by gardens and vineyards, which, from descriptive details, suggest tenant farms that held several houses, a number described as "tenements" of several rooms, including space for winepresses and vats. Some of them concentrated on raising sheep, others on horses, yet others on cows and oxen. Every building and its furnishings carried price tags, down to the mounds of hay in a hayloft, the value of beasts in "good shape," and that of equipment "between good and sad." Guglielmo received daily reports from the managers of his estates, informing him how much hay had been baled, how much wine had been pressed, which cows had calved, the cost of the feed for his animals. One exquisitely lettered broadside in the archives, headed *"Affari della Caccia"*—Matters of Hunting—bears Guglielmo's name and the date 1576, and declares that hunting is reserved for princes (an old ruling that had constantly to be reiterated), that care had to be taken not to kill hunting dogs, and that citizens and gentlemen were not to kill hare, pheasant, grouse, or boar, apparently a princely prerogative.

Since the brutalities of ruling and profiting were essential and not to be weighed by ordinary religious morality—witness the "warrior popes"—Guglielmo could yet consider himself more consistently religious than most of his forebears. The *avaro* in him had little difficulty in paying six thousand gold scudi for the building and decorating of the basilica of Santa Barbara in the old *castello* and ordering of Veronese, at the peak of his popularity in Venice, a painting of the Temptation of Saint Anthony. There sprang up in his time churches and the seats of several religious orders, a number of them in the suburbs and in the vicinity of the villas. This church-building fervor, and the concomitant flurry of religiosity it inspired, sat well with the Pope; religion never quite dispelled politics, but churchly show usually bought favor, worth the money. A stunning secular display was provided by Tintoretto, called from Venice to paint a set of eight "Triumphs," the subjects programmed for the painter by a literary courtier.

Among Guglielmo's avocations, when there was a leisured moment, was the reading of detailed, colorful reports of life in other places. An agent stationed in England described for him gentlemen dressed in the Italian style who are addressed "Milord." "Le Miladi" are dressed in the French style, wear linen cloths on their heads, and ride horses. The agent comments on the odd system of inheritance, creating a lord of the eldest son and servitors of the younger. He is amazed at the freedom of English women, who are not watched inside or outside their houses although they are "beautiful in flesh and manner." The Irish he reports as a strange, incomprehensible people. London is an interesting place, with a cathedral called St. Paul's (meticulously described) and riverfront houses that keep big dogs to fight bears, wolves, and bulls. Trained to note everything, the Italian lists principal ports, rivers, and communities, and makes careful travel notes of places called Cornovaglia (Cornwall), Nortuaglia (North Wales), Bristo (Bristol), Cantuaria (Canterbury), and Coventria (Coventry).

One enthusiasm Guglielmo sustained all his life was music. We are not sure which of an anonymous mass of musical material found later was of his composition, but it is taken for granted that he set music to poems and probably pieces of liturgical prose. And ceaselessly there was the building and rebuilding of the apartments in the Palazzo Ducale, where he rearranged the distinguished family collection and the pieces of antique marble that were of special interest to him, fired by rivalry with his cousin Cesare Gonzaga. The son of Uncle Ferrante, Cesare had, in fact, a superior collection, and it was his tapestries Guglielmo was forced to borrow when he readied apartments in the palace for a visit from King Henry III of France. When the king arrived (in 1574), he was greeted by a procession of more than five hundred men-at-arms in black and yellow velvet, and one hundred white-clad knights. Broad, ornamented arches were built for the king's delight and a bridge of boats was placed to ease his descent from the barge that brought him from Venice. After refreshments and a hunt, at the Palazzo del Te, the king and his entourage returned to the ducal apartments, accompanied by attendants blazing in cloth-of-gold.

As duke of a brilliant city and host to the ruler of a major kingdom, Guglielmo felt additional honor was due him. Papal decree had granted Cosimo de' Medici the right to call himself the Grand Duke of Tuscany, to be addressed as "Most Serene Highness," as "Serenissimo" and "Altezza." The present duke of Tuscany, Ferdinando, insisted that the practice be maintained. Guglielmo petitioned the emperor Maximilian II for the same privilege, which was rejected, the rejection made gentler by the promotion of Monferrato to a duchy, an event celebrated with grave rituals. No matter how the emperor felt about it, a suggestion here and there in the courts of Mantua and Monferrato evoked the sounds of "Serenissimo" and "Altezza," and woe to him who forgot to use them. With what one of his biographers calls his "vulpine astuteness," Guglielmo sent to the emperor to assure him that he never intended using the title of Grand Duke since the emperor did not approve, but there was no way to discourage his subjects, who preferred the terms of address that accompanied the title.

✳ Guglielmo and Eleonora had two daughters and one son, and stopped there with solemn vows of spiritual love. She was intensely religious and uneasy with matters carnal; she might have been afraid of disease and the perils of childbirth. His consent is less comprehensible; one son was not protection enough for a dynasty at some risk from contending Gonzaga, especially brother Ludovico of Nevers and Rethel.

Shaped by one of life's malicious designs, that son, Vincenzo, was in every way the opposite of his father, the differences sharpened by hatred. According to the archivist Giuseppe Coniglio, *"Quanto era malfatto, avaro, calcolatore e perfido Guglielmo, tanto era bello, generoso, impetuoso e spontaneo Vincento. L'uno era introverso, l'altro estroso, rubacuori e brillante cavaliere."* Vincenzo was straight-backed, generous, impulsive, and merry, and probably exaggerated these aspects of himself when they most annoyed his severe father. The youngster was a spendthrift libertine, a sword flasher, fervidly fond of women. As heir of a lustrous house with imposing connections, the potential possessor of a wealthy state, he felt he had the right to costly pleasures. His jealous, sickly father, infuriated by his son's capers, by his very existence, kept him short-reined by doling out a meager allowance. To one of his teachers, he wrote—speaking of his father as *"Sua Altezza"*—that his father treated him like a child although he was nineteen, a mature age, and capable of being respected and making his own unhampered decisions. Even the lower classes, he said, provide decent clothing and means to their sons, while he himself lives like the lowest, borrowing from his servants. And God knows what the world has to say of a young man of his quality living in this ignoble fashion. It makes him bitter in the stomach, he adds, to think of how little affection and trust his father has for him, that their communication is through an intermediary, never direct.

Vincenzo wrote from a villa in Viadana, not far from the home court, where, the young man said, some liberties were available. It was these liberties, and not only their cost, that made his father breathe fire. Vincenzo was well launched on the career that set him incontestably at the front of dissolute Gonzaga, his friends as loose and carefree as himself. He enjoyed boys but not quite as much as he enjoyed women of advanced talents; he loved wine and spirited horses. His straight comeliness deserved the flow of silks, the softness of velvet, the brightness of gold cloth, and the glitter of jewels. When his time came, he proved to be a competent ruler, a decent strategist, and exceedingly popular with his people, to whom he showed unusual generosity and for whom he provided endless entertainments in the time-honored bread-and-circus combination. His tendency to be amiable and sympathetic (except when he was drunk and murderous) lightened the onerous tax load on the Monferrini and restored a measure of their civil liberties. It was his open hand that supported the young Rubens, hired and promoted Monteverdi, sponsored the writer Guarini, and pulled Torquato Tasso out of a madhouse in Ferrara to comfortable shelter in Mantua, from which the poet issued sonnets and songs in praise of his patron's beauty and the loveliness of his mistresses. From early youth, Vincenzo supported talented actors and actresses. Both he and his father were patrons of the liveliest theater in Italy, but Guglielmo often ordered performances stopped when Vincenzo suggested hiring a prestigious company and supplying it with elaborate costumes and scenery. The son occasionally won out and was undoubtedly responsible for one presentation that roared gleeful vengeance: All the characters in the play were humpbacks. Guglielmo, in the audience, laughed politely during the performance, and at its end shrieked torture and beheading, then, having threatened the worst, banished the actors from Mantua.

Vincenzo met one of the most influential women of his early life during the festivities in Ferrara that celebrated the marriage of his sister Margherita to Alfonso II of the Este. Among the bevies of pretty, accomplished, and acquiescent women, several of them Este and Gonzaga nobles, there appeared the well-known, supremely confident Barbara Sanseverino Sanvitale, the countess of Sala. To her and her imaginative friends, whose orgies were widely praised for their originality, he stayed attached for a long time, though never to the total exclusion of other gifted ladies. Barbara, one of the most radiant of Italian courtesans, a paragon of learning and wit universally admired and courted, was still extraordinarily attractive at thirty, when Vincenzo met her. She was then the wife of an elderly, compliant nobleman and the "protégé" of the duke of Parma, who had made her a gift of the fiefdom of Colorno, where Vincenzo visited frequently. Always his good and instructive friend, she encouraged him to defy his father, whose serious faults included a lack of interest in women. When Barbara had to give her attention to other absorbing commitments, she turned Vincenzo over to her friend Hippolita, the countess Torelli, who pleased him quite as much as Barbara had.

With Hippolita still very much in his mind and life, he joined his parents in arrangements concerning a marriage with Margherita Farnese of Parma. There was no reason for protesting; he had to marry someone, and the choice of this particular girl was a sound political move. Furthermore, his mother had established a fragile peace between her husband and son, and Vincenzo preferred to maintain it, with the expectation that, as a married man and maybe soon a father, he would earn greater respect and a more seemly allowance. While the negotiations went on between the families in Parma and Mantua, Vincenzo wrote impassioned letters to Hippolita, addressing her as "Andromeda"—the supreme beauty who became a star in the heavens. Barbara found the time to arrange the secret flow of letters between the lovers, assisted by a Mantuan dwarf who was a trusted friend of Vincenzo. Through the flurry of marriage preparations, he found time to disappear from Mantua for a week of pleasure with Hippolita.

Margherita's family was anciently important. Her unpleasant mother had been a princess of Portugal and her frequently absent father, Alessandro (Barbara's patron), acted as governor of Flanders for Philip II. Margherita was a romantic, music-loving girl of fourteen when she was married, in the spring of 1581. Perhaps she was physically ready for marriage, perhaps not; it never comes quite clear in the ensuing bizarre and sad farce of her adolescent years. There were questions quite early: It had been mentioned to Guglielmo that she was not ready for sex and childbearing and that, being impaired, she might never be. Parma's most prestigious physician declared her capable of intercourse and childbearing; all she needed was treatment he prescribed. She acceded eagerly and soon returned to Vincenzo, who took her with him to the carnival festivities in Ferrara, treated her with kindness, and gave her little gifts. That she provided little sexual pleasure was of no moment; he had friends. It was not her role, though childbearing was.

Vincenzo's dark side prowled the night streets, looking for trouble in the company of dangerous friends. One of the people he killed was a Scotsman, Chrichton, an unusual presence in Mantua but not a rarity; many young men came down from the north for the sun, the art, the theater, the gaming, the stimulating life of the Italian university. Others came on official missions as ambassadorial trainees, to learn the Italian language, manners, and customs, and to keep an ear open for what was being said of political significance in Milan, Venice, Genoa, and an observant eye on fortifications in the making. A few disliked the adventure, complaining about the loose morals, about the inedible raw greens they were served (salads were not in favor in the homelands), the threatening aura of Catholicism avid for converts while, at the same time, the Church was held in ribald contempt. Others never recovered from the pleasures of Italy; they came home in foreign clothes of ebullient color and finer texture than the native homespuns. They were perfumed, handsomely coiffed, used forks as the Italians did, and readily drew their swords over an imagined insult, like the Italians. They could not forget the glorious Italian cities and their painting and architecture, complaining of the dullness and dirt of their own. Roger Ascham's verdict on these Italophiles was that they returned with "less learning and worse manners" than they left with.

This particular northerner known as "Critonio" would have been quite safe if he had not been a favorite of father Guglielmo. Guglielmo had had a well-rounded education under the guidance of his uncle Ercole and had developed a taste for letters and learning, for which he was willing to pay. The young, attractive Scotsman had brought from Venice to Mantua a formidable reputation: He knew languages modern and ancient, could discuss philosophy, mathematics, theology, and the arts. Guglielmo enjoyed speaking with him and appointed him one of his counselors at a decent stipend. Vincenzo could not brook the fact that a man no older than himself was treated with respect by his father and members of the court. Since he could hardly kill his father, a favorite would do. It was the summer of 1582, and Guglielmo had retired from Mantua's heat into the villa of Goito. On the evening of July 3, Vincenzo sallied out with Ippolito Lanzani, a vicious parasite of whom Guglielmo especially disapproved. They tracked down Chrichton, a scuffle ensued, and Chrichton stabbed and killed Lanzani, upon which Vincenzo killed Chrichton. Vincenzo later claimed that the Scotsman had attacked him and his companion without provocation. Guglielmo, on hearing of the murder of his scholar, tore back from Goito to heap blame and anger on Vincenzo. Marcello Donati, Vincenzo's mentor-secretary-doctor, persuaded the young man to be humble and apologetic and to submit to a hearing. He was absolved and immediately removed himself from his father's wrath and the frowns of the court by going to Ferrara and on to the solace of Barbara and her beauties in Colorno. There he hunted, acted in lively theatricals, sang, and danced. Among the sparkling women, he favored the ballerinas, a species for whom he had a particular fondness since they, he claimed, had initiated his sex education. It was a good place to forget the obscene jokes about his sword being shorter than the Scotsman's, one of the reasons invented for exonerating him and, in a double entendre, suggesting the reason for his fruitless marriage.

After two years, there was no promise of an heir with Margherita; her screams of pain in the night were no more heard; attempts at cohabitation seemed to have stopped. The Farnese were embarrassed, discomfited, annoyed; the Gonzaga wanted to be rid of the girl. It appeared that whatever correction was made, she still found sex painful; as she explained to an elderly relative, Cardinal Farnese, dean of the College of Cardinals, the plug and socket did not fit each other. While the girl was undergoing examinations and interrogations, Mantua was searching for another, more physically reliable princess. Florence had just such a one, Eleonora de' Medici. Her father was Francesco, the grand duke of Tuscany, and her mother had been Giovanna, daughter of the emperor Ferdinand I. The ruling woman of the court in which Eleonora had been raised was, however, the second grand duchess, Bianca Capello, a Venetian courtesan-magician with an eventful history, on whom Francesco had settled a title and great wealth. At first Guglielmo expressed only disdain for the immoral, Satanic Tuscans, but with the failure of Margherita to produce heirs, and reexamination of Francesco's immense wealth of trade and banking throughout Europe, he decided to reconsider. He shipped Margherita back to Parma as tactfully as he could, assuming that her elders would send her to a favored order of nuns. Her father was willing, eager to convince the girl that she was not made for fleshly matters and to consider the whole matter closed. Her brother Ranuccio, deeply wounded in his family pride, preferred to shout accusations at Vincenzo: He was an adulterer, a sodomite, impotent and syphilitic. The second grand duchess of Tuscany, resentful of the disdain earlier shown her by the Gonzaga, also let it be known that she and her husband doubted Vincenzo's virility. Guglielmo placed all the blame on Margherita, who, in one set of examinations, was judged to have an abnormal "architude," an anatomically vague diagnosis which was possibly a euphemism for an obdurate hymen. Doctors with Farnese leanings said it was a condition that could easily be corrected. Marcello Donati argued for Mantua that were she to choose the required surgery and die, the girl would be considered a suicide and forbidden a Christian burial. Other adolescent girls were examined to check possible similarities to Margherita's condition, research that produced no conclusions. Accusations new and old, outpourings of delighted gossip, detailed reviews of Vincenzo's dissipations, and opposition reviews of the duke of Parma's extracurricular activities created a storm that soon reached the Pope.

"The Prince's Person"

There then ensued a year of events that, were one to forget sad young Margherita, make an extraordinary opera buffa. The matter of investigations of Vincenzo's *membro virile* (also referred to as "the prince's person") involved cardinals, princes, ambassadors of several states, physicians, midwives, ladies-in-waiting, a few orphan girls, lawyers, scribes, and innkeepers. Accounts of the events that fed many entertained courts are, some of them, like that of the French writer of our day, Roger Peyrefitte, filled with laughter. Some of the accounts are solemn, lumpishly serious. The editor of a tome of letters dealing exclusively with "A Proof of Matrimony" describes the events as material for a remarkable picture, in all its strata—inept medical research, intense sexuality, unabashed vulgarity—of the Italian Renaissance in the sixteenth century. He adds, "One leaves from a base of materialism that is almost repugnant in its excess, a profound lack of modesty and discretion, to arrive [the reference is apparently to Vincenzo's later flamboyant court] at a dazzling pinnacle of beauty and art."

After an overture of insults and accusations back and forth, the first act opens in Rome, where Cardinal Carlo Borromeo (later Saint Carlo Borromeo), a man respected by all parties, has been appointed by the Pope to study and adjudicate the shameful matter. He calls a conclave of cardinals and they agree that if judgment goes against Vincenzo, if he is found to be the deficient partner in the fruitless marriage, Margherita's dowry is to be returned to her, and the "counter-dowry" paid by the Gonzaga will also remain hers. Borromeo then meets with doctors, midwives, lawyers, churchmen, and finally, in Ferrara, with Vincenzo himself, who states his case clearly and firmly. Cardinal Borromeo considers this imbroglio no longer a simple affair since it involves Church considerations of the suitability of marriage partners, legitimate reasons for annulment and divorce, and careful accounting of dowries kept and dowries returned. He orders that prayers be said in several holy places and himself retreats for a while to make his own strict observances. Margherita uses the interval for masques and music and dancing into the dawn.

Margherita, now sixteen, meets with the cardinal, who repeats the judgment of Donati that surgical intervention might kill her and her consent to such treatment would be considered suicide. She was ready to take the risk, but it was impressed on her by her family that there was no point in such a sacrifice; the Gonzaga didn't want her, and in any case, she was not made for motherhood. The music and dancing stopped, and with the permission of Borromeo, she entered a nunnery. (It is probably of this time that we have a portrait by an anonymous artist that shows a frail, big-eyed girl staring sadly out of a heavy weight of jewels.) Her retirement did not stop the Farnese, particularly brother Ranuccio, from slandering Vincenzo and spreading the word of his physical deficiencies to Florence.

Developments of the story of La Prova—The Test—elicit from a later editor of the many letters that flew among the involved personages a judgment that it is a "modern" novel, that it undoubtedly would have interested students of the "Don Juan" character and certainly Sigmund Freud. The ground bass for the arias in many voices of the bizarre show, more salacious and imaginative than the most raffish of commedia dell'arte inventions, was the constant deep-voiced rumble of canon law: Was impotence—the main charge against Vincenzo—not a now-and-then thing? Doesn't the attractiveness of a wife play a role? Might it not discourage a husband if his wife stank? Black magic and other Satanic forces were known to make a man incapable; was Vincenzo a victim of evil spirits? Another concern was the delicate problem of examining the virgins who appear and disappear in the course of the plot: Such an act injured modesty and might even appear as rape if the girl were not delicately handled. The cardinals questioned and debated and met for long sessions with witnesses, one of them Vincenzo's cousin Don Cesare d'Este, who said they were frequently together in sexual adventures and he had seen Vincenzo perform ably through all the essential stages: erection, entry, and emission. In the intervals between his meetings with church fathers and physicians, Vincenzo played with Barbara and Hippolita and wrote to Margherita, whom he liked and pitied.

The Farnese bonds dissolved, earnest negotiations began between the Medici and the Gonzaga, the letters loaded with precise figures and caveats. Guglielmo stipulated a dowry of 300,000 crowns, to which the grand duke consented. The first payment of 100,000 crowns would be made immediately on the signing of contracts; the rest in two yearly installments. If the bride died childless before her husband (assuming he had clearly consummated the marriage), he would keep half the dowry, the rest to be returned to the Medici. Or Guglielmo might accept a smaller sum to begin with and return nothing if the girl died childless. If Vincenzo died earlier than his wife, both the dowry and the counter-dowry would be hers. Guglielmo, who entrusted Vincenzo with no serious moneys, would be responsible for Eleonora's general expenses, to be discussed with her father. The grand duke would pay for the bridal party in its progress from Florence to Mantua, and the costs of the celebration in Mantua would be paid jointly by both fathers.

One great stumbling block: All arrangements were contingent on proof of Vincenzo's potency—no easy task, as it turned out. Bianca Capello took malicious pleasure in expressing frequently and loudly her grave doubts. The subject became a fervid campaign for the Farnese, especially Ranuccio and particularly after the Gonzaga accused him and his henchmen of burning the Gonzaga armory and theater. Protesting their innocence and their disgust, the courtiers of Parma spread into every amused corner of Europe their highly moralistic view that sexual pleasures were private and public examinations of such matters were abominations; carryings on of this kind would be a joy to heretics, who already had enough to feed on in these corrupt times. Vincenzo was impotent and that was that. While the French relatives and the German and the Spanish and their friends in England giggled, contractual discussions went on, with stubborn bargaining between the duke and the grand duke, but there could be no final signing of contracts until Vincenzo had been tested and proved.

While Vincenzo was acting and gambling in his sister's court in Innsbruck, Ferrara was setting up a scene for a proof of his virility. First the search for the appropriate orphan girl, who was then to be examined by a committee of physicians, ladies, midwives, and representatives, lay and clerical, of both families. When Vincenzo returned to the crowded scene, he was told he must perform in the view of eight women and a set of guards, priests, and agents, and that one trusted man might view closely and even touch him while he was in the act, and that act to be performed within three hours (according to one account, longer according to another, but in any case a limited time). As anyone's might have been, Vincenzo's performance was deplorable. Tired of the obscene jokes that danced like leering fauns in every salon and alley, tired of defending himself against accusations of immorality in consenting that his son rape a virgin, and frantically eager to conclude a lucrative marriage contract before someone else claimed the desirable Eleonora, Guglielmo insisted and kept insisting that Vincenzo had proved himself virile.

Reluctantly, he was soon forced to agree with the grand duke Francesco that the test be repeated, this time in Venice, three attempts permitted in one full day. The heads of the witnessing committees were to be Dr. Donati of Mantua and, for Tuscany, Belisario Vinta, who had the right to "put his hand between the two buttocks until he felt the member well inside the vaginal cavity." The chosen girl, a Florentine named Giulia, was good-looking—Vincenzo had insisted on this—and not too young, about twenty, and well-mannered. She was carefully examined by all hands, scrubbed clean by female attendants, and finely dressed. Vincenzo was scrutinized in every detail, judged by the Florentines to be well formed and healthy. Then there were delays. Some of the many reports that papered Italy said that Giulia was exhausted by her trip from Florence to Venice and had begun to menstruate or feigned menstrual malaise. Donati and Vinta made the girl handsome promises, Mantua offered money, Florence offered a husband and a dowry, if she cooperated nicely.

On an appointed later night, the girl was again washed, dressed seductively, and put to bed. Vincenzo stripped, allowed his genitals to be examined once again, and joined the girl on newly laundered sheets. The witnesses waited behind a screen while three hours passed. Suddenly Vincenzo bounded out of the room, his body contorted in pain, his outraged face holding back vomit. Between gasps, he explained that he had eaten too much rich Venetian food. The girl reported that he had kissed and stroked her and had gone off to sleep. Vinta immediately fired off a letter to Tuscany, expressing his astonishment that a young man who appeared so well endowed might in truth be impotent and that his family was so stupid as to submit him to tests he could not meet. Donati pointed out to Vinta that they had witnessed only one test of the agreed-upon three, and most of the twenty-four hours granted Vincenzo still remained. No longer as good-naturedly amused as he had been all along, the young man tried to beg off, but his father's injunction included the reminder that should he lose the Medici bride and settle for the daughter of the duke of Lorraine, a marriage in which France had shown considerable interest, the French family would insist on the same proofs of his manhood as the Medici did. In some quarters Vincenzo's impotence was blamed on an attack of syphilis, but one witness who had been called by Borromeo said that with the help of herbal juices, a quick cure had been effected. Guglielmo blamed Vincenzo's debility on sorcerers employed by Margherita's brother and insisted that his son be exorcised. Donati, accustomed to handling Vincenzo, took matters into his own hands. Cajoling and flattering him, titillating him with erotic phrases, he convinced Vincenzo to try again with Giulia. Again he was examined, showing himself nude and unarmed, bearing no device other than his "person" with which to deflower the girl. When he was ready and inside the girl, he called to Vinta, who exercised his right to deep examination and was dismissed. Many hours later, Vincenzo emerged rosy and happy, claiming at least three successful attempts. The girl had a different story; she came out crying and claimed that the blood on the sheets was the result of deep scratches her partner had inflicted on her. Vincenzo answered blithely that she was crying because she wanted more, and he was quite willing to comply. Giulia, after a discussion of the purported scratches, changed her mind; she really liked and had enjoyed lying with him. (Her earlier lie might easily have been an attempt to force another test and additional rewards. Everyone of normal intelligence was an adept plotter, and why not Giulia?) She submitted to examination and question. Yes, she had been deflowered. No, not with any instrument but his penis. He hadn't threatened her at any time. He was a fine specimen of manhood, praise she repeated when they had another long, more private encounter. Promises made Giulia were kept. She was soon married off, the ceremonies blessed by no less than an archbishop. The grand duke gave her a dowry of three thousand scudi to add to the generous gift sent by Vincenzo. The child she claimed as the fruit of the Venetian test was sent to Mantua but was not included in the list of Vincenzo's other illegitimate children.

Vincenzo danced out of the Congress of Venice, as the divertissement was called, in triumph, while his father continued disputing details of the Medici marriage contract, although the banns were already published and Eleonora's ladies busily placing in painted *cassoni* the jewelry, velvet gowns embroidered in gold thread, brocades strewn with gems, silver and gold flatware, and singular objects provided by her father as proof that he esteemed not only his daughter but the house to which she was now joined.

T·H·I·R·T·E·E·N

One large problem solved, there were others for Guglielmo to cope with in the webs he himself made and those foisted on him by his times. By accommodation and temporizing, he had managed to hold off the major fires of the Inquisition, burning all over Italy. At first it showed pallidly in Mantua, until Rome sent a fervid inquisitor who busied himself arresting a conspicuous number of "heretics," among them high functionaries of Guglielmo's court, and inevitably Jews. The duke protested to the Pope, while other Mantuans killed two inquisitorial friars. Again the duke petitioned Rome to remove its inquisitors, but since consent would mean condoning the assassination of the friars, the Pope refused, sending the influential Cardinal Borromeo to explain. With no choice, Gonzaga decreed the right of the Dominicans, the champions of the Inquisition, to carry on their campaign, set aside a building for their offices, and tolerated the fumes of autos-da-fé that clouded his piazzas. Above all a pragmatist, Guglielmo set his legal aides to a search of old—or newly improvised—rulings that gave half the properties of proved heretics to the Commune, half to himself. He found it profitable, as well, to cooperate with those who denounced enemies and Jewish bankers, accumulating great quantities of money and heating wild flames of anti-Semitism. Toward the end of his life, for fear of death and God's judgment, he turned the inquisitors on a few old madwomen who had been declared witches, and the inquisitorial fervor abated.

Neither the Medici marriage, nor troubles with the Inquisition, nor the birth of a grandson, Francesco, in 1585, softened Guglielmo toward his son. In spite of Vincenzo's amorous flights, he and Eleonora got along reasonably well. They often collected paintings and worked at theatricals together. Although fidelity was out of the question, he respected her judgment and taste, and she was too worldly, the product of a particularly malodorous court, to complain or criticize, except in correspondence with her sister, Marie (in time queen of France), whom she urged to avoid the cruel pains of marriage. The couple had six children together and she helped raise, as was expected of her, four of his natural children. As long as he lived, though, Guglielmo treated his merry, careless son as an irresponsible child, not to be trusted with money. The money to mount plays and other entertainments came from friends and relatives and often usurers. On rare occasions, Vincenzo was invited to attend a decision-making court council, where his advice, usually sensible, was invariably overlooked. The hatred was monumental, in the larger-than-life Renaissance style, as reflected for us in plays like *The Duchess of Malfi* and *King Lear*. Vincenzo did not always sweeten the atmosphere; he permitted his frustration and furies to explode as knifings, of course reviled by his father, of course exonerated by the court. Others took his night encounters and the spilling of blood—out of drunkenness, for possession of a girl, for a show of violent manliness not permitted him in daylight hours—as decorations of their lives, supplied by a colorful, virile prince. When his pride was scraped to the bone, Vincenzo thought seriously to remove himself from Mantua and, like his ancestors, amass money and fame as a *condottiere* in regions where he might gain some stature, unlike the "neither honor nor regard" that faced him at home. Guglielmo objected, not unexpectedly, and Vincenzo continued pressing until his father became seriously ill. An empty formal reconciliation, a deathbed ritual inspired by Vincenzo's devout mother and his wife, took place in Goito, where Guglielmo died in August of 1587.

* Vincenzo was twenty-five when he was crowned duke of Mantua and Monferrato. He emerged from the ceremonies in the cathedral wearing a crown of large stones set on a cap whose gems included a priceless ruby. Carrying an ivory scepter, like an anointed king, he led off a procession of men-at-arms in black velvet stiff with gems, adorned with chains of precious metals, each man flourishing a carved and ivory-inlaid arquebus. The total sum spent for the coronation and for entertaining guests from reigning houses can only be guessed at; we are told that the ruby in Vincenzo's cap was worth over fifteen thousand scudi and that his ensemble of satin and ermine cost well over thirty thousand scudi. Such expenditures would appear niggardly when he came into his full spending power, when his household would support one thousand servants, when he wallowed happily among the strongboxes of gold coins amassed and hidden from him by his father.

The state he inherited was by the tenacity and avarice of Guglielmo an exceedingly prosperous one. A riches of grain burst out of its lands; meat and milk products were plentiful and of high quality; Mantuan currency was sound; the judicial system Ercole and Guglielmo had devised and Guglielmo's effective hospice-hospital for the poor were admired and imitated in other states. The extraordinary machinery of Gonzaga diplomacy reached its highest efficiency under Guglielmo. Constantly complaining—as almost all ambassadors did—of being too long from home, of being underpaid and leading the lives of beggars, Mantua's agents worked diligently and well. The full, carefully organized accounts of everything they observed, heard, and negotiated afforded detailed background matter for new agents and left the present refulgence of archival material.

As for the Inquisition, Vincenzo as duke made some concessions to the Dominicans but otherwise avoided it as well as he could. It is difficult to see through the density of years and the mists of amour and gold just how much time and attention Vincenzo gave to religious devotions. His religious surrogate was his cousin Luigi, of the Castiglione delle Stiviere line, who entered hagiography as Saint Luigi Gonzaga. Affected by the pietistic mysticism of Philip II's court, where he had been a page, Luigi later joined the order of the Jesuits, after having turned over his goods and land to his brother, Rodolfo. He died, still in his twenties, serving the stricken in a Roman pesthouse, and was canonized for his holy work and death early in the eighteenth century. Vincenzo was genuinely fond of Luigi; a matter of the attraction of opposites and a handful of religious security by way of osmosis and affection.

Eleonora de' Medici relied more on iron controls and shrewdness than on religion. She handled the many amours—singers, ballerinas, prostitutes, and court ladies "with stretched-forth necks and eager eyes," as the Old Testament might have described them—protecting her house and her children. She learned to know the women who were more than passing fancies and warned Vincenzo when he might run into the sword of an irate protector. Selecting with care, she occasionally pandered for her husband along with the master panderer Pietro Aretino and trusted servants. When she had more than she could handle with poise, she retired into illness, into the malaise of pregnancy, and confined her outbursts against her situation, and that of other women, in letters. Her illnesses were very likely, like Isabella d'Este's travels, a retreat from contact with Vincenzo, a prime candidate for syphilis, and to avoid yet other pregnancies.

One of the duke's steadiest suppliers was still his friend and mentor Barbara Sanseverino, who had under her tutelage a choice Neapolitan morsel of good family to substitute for the Andromeda-Hippolita who had slipped off Vincenzo's horizon. This southern Agnese, ready for her debut as polished courtesan, was brought, as Isabella Boschetta had been fifty years before, to the inspirations of the Palazzo del Te. She was given a husband, lands, a title, splendid gifts, and at least one child by Vincenzo. Like La Boschetta, she held court among languid gentlemen and literati, who played with chivalric thoughts of love. With companies of actors always at hand—Vincenzo liked their raffish, colorful ways and they his—she busied herself with play productions, one of them an attempt to stage the popular *Pastor Fido* by Battista Guarini, a confection of Arcadian lyricism and pagan sensuality. While Vincenzo's mother, like Gonzaga mothers before her, avoided Te as a pit of iniquity, sensible, disciplined Eleonora spent considerable time there, helping with sets and palace decorations.

Although he fervently tried, Vincenzo could not always wander in pleasure groves. For one thing, the heightened struggle, which included assassinations, for land and succession in the minor Gonzaga courts—Sabbioneta, Bozzolo, Castiglione delle Stiviere, Castelgoffredo, Medole—required interception by a careful, even hand. It was Vincenzo who established at least a temporary peace among them and managed to settle an old recurrent quarrel over water rights with Ferrara. When floods and famine hit Mantua, its duke gathered a number of capable advisers, who helped him arrange decently paid work projects, distributed rice and wheat to the needy, and kept a punitive eye on hoarders and profiteers. In spite of his civic works, his participation in religious processions to dispel the plague, and the occasional favors he showed ecclesiasts, the Papacy sent harsh messages warning the duke of the hideous consequences of adultery. Nothing much changed except the names and bodies of willing beauties. Barbara now had in tow three exquisite young women to dangle before Vincenzo. She herself, though no longer young, was still fascinating. In her early forties, she was courted not only as mistress but as wife. She preferred her freewheeling life and was tied completely to no one. When he was in Italy, the duke of Parma took care of her, but when he was abroad, as much of the time he was, his son Ranuccio, the blackhearted brother of Margherita, mistreated her and forced her to find shelter in Mantua, where she was warmly welcomed.

Although they had been defeated at the battle of Lepanto in 1571, the Turks were still making terrifying headway into Europe. They did not fight in the refined anachronistic manner that still clung to European warfare: a nobleman for a ransom, exchanges of loot and prisoners, courtly gestures between princes. Like the stradiots of Francesco's time, the Turks beheaded their victims and were reputed to flay them for the pleasure of it. The emperor Rudolph II called among the princes of Europe for help against the infidels. Italian response was feeble; the Turks were in Hungary, a great distance from Italy and not her concern. Vincenzo thought differently. In spite of suggestions, mainly from his wife, that he do as others did—send the emperor several thousand scudi and a gang of mercenaries and let his contribution remain at that—Vincenzo, eager to prove himself in battle and in the eyes of amused, skeptical Europe, to become an Orlando beating back the Saracens, prepared himself for war. He gathered several hundred foot soldiers and horsemen, armed them with arquebuses and pikes, had arcane little mottoes under a half-moon embroidered on their sleeves, and by mid-1595, considered them ready to march forth under his gallant banners. After ceremonious blessings and the gathering together of cooks, surgeons, priests, and muscians—who would play both martial music and gentler strophes for resting hours—Vincenzo marched forth. He had hoped that he would lead the Pope's armies, but that expectation soon collapsed. The fantasy and fervor faded, and the journey to join with other imperial troops took on a leisured pace. He spent a number of entertaining days at Innsbruck with his sister Anna Caterina, and after a pause to check supplies and to allow his soldiers rest and diversion, visited with Prince Maximilian of Bavaria. Then on to Prague, where Vincenzo was greeted with expressions of respect and gratitude by the emperor, a man who had little faith in his own military skills (gathering art was his forte) and was pleased with his eager Italian warrior. Laden with gifts from his sister, riding a velvet-lined carriage and trailing lines of Mantuan horses, Vincenzo rode on to Vienna, where his army stopped for religious observances, and then to meet with the archduke Matthias of Austria and his nobles, who were entertained with feasting and music. The Austrian troops were in wild disorder because they had not been paid, and it was Vincenzo who calmed them with money and reorganized them as companies ready for battle. The first military action resulted in a victory at Plintenburg, an approach to Budapest, which the Turks ceded to the Grand Seigneur from Italy. Immediately after, confusion and dissolution. Too many high nobles vied with each other to lead these armies, too much money and time was wasted in acrimonious shows of hubris and accusations of cowardice. Plans to fill the enemy's wells with lice, thus to foster typhoid, failed. Poisons to lay the Turks low were as ineffectual as the lice. Whether Vincenzo actually suffered of the neuralgia and arthritis (a common Gonzaga affliction) he complained of or not, he gathered his men and, without the leave of the emperor or the commander of the moment, folded his tents and took his army and its accoutrements back to Mantua.

After warm rejoicing and treating with Ferrara in another of the constant quarrels over border taxes, he prepared for the war against the Turks once more. The march of this campaign, of 1597, was, as before, at a handsome, sybarite's pace, with long pauses for ceremonies and fetes to celebrate meetings with Austrian dukes and plan for an allied march. The first major action was the seige of Javarino (in Czechoslovakia), led by Vincenzo and two Austrians, one of whom was killed. The replacement was a captain Vincenzo thought inadequate for the job, so again he left for home, stopping at Prague for courtesies exchanged with the emperor, and thus lost the opportunity to be a hero when Javarino was taken from the Turks a few months later.

While he was fighting the infidels in his vainglorious and generous way—providing rest areas, physicians, and conveyances for his wounded, by no means a common practice at the time—several pots of trouble were coming to a boiling point. Sabbioneta was ready to sell itself and its incomes to vengeful Parma, which had offered, as well, to supply troops for an uprising against the mainline Gonzaga by the ruler of Castiglione delle Stiviere. A mischievous, wild-tongued friend of Vincenzo, the marquis del Vasto, pushed himself to the front line of the Parma-Mantua vendetta by issuing a public statement to the effect that the Farnese of Parma had become rich and powerful only because a member of the family, Giulia Farnese, had been the mistress of the Borgia Pope Alexander VI. Ranuccio Farnese picked up the gauntlet and began again to attack Vincenzo's virility. The delectable strands of this fading fabric were augmented by testimony from court and theater ladies who swore to Vincenzo's sexual talents. Eleonora's uncle, now grand duke of Tuscany (having, they said, poisoned his brother and sister-in-law), insisted that she have her shameless husband imprisoned and take the rule of Mantua to herself, with the implied assistance of her devoted uncle. Papal legates of various degrees of tact and hellfire were sent from Rome to induce the duke to silence the marquis del Vasto. Vincenzo said that was impossible; nearer the possible was his pleasure in the excitement of constant notorious stardom.

His not too private life took a couple of its common turns. Agnese, who had been his confidante, even in matters she should have known nothing about, and briefly the one star in his sky, was gradually replaced by two women, who played dichotomous roles. One was a holy woman, a substitute for his cousin Saint Luigi, with whom he spent hours in prayer, and the other a court lady, who presented him with a daughter, for whom he provided responsibly. He also had a new son, by Agnese, Silvio, who would be raised with all the advantages and cosseting given his legitimate siblings. The women, the children, the brouhaha with Parma, the lures to warfare that offered no glory, began to trouble and bore him. The cure, as often, was to escape from Mantua in an alternation of religious pilgrimages and visits to courts of pleasure. He gamed for exorbitant stakes in Innsbruck, in Genoa, in Venice, in Rome, pawning his father's jewels and the produce of some of the richest lands in the Mantovana. His debts were so large and many that he was incessantly pressed for long-delayed payments. Yet he gambled, and he bought a stack of paintings, cartloads of objects to illuminate his palaces, gifts for his friends and lovers and the abbots of holy shrines. Wherever he was, Vincenzo lived with the boundless luxury of a Nero and appeared, like Maecenas, to be a fountain that poured gold.

In the last years of the 1500s, a voice came from the distant east, that of a Polish marquis, offering Vincenzo the rule of Poland. Although he was easily seduced by almost any vision of exotic adventure, and particularly himself in an exalted role, Vincenzo hesitated; unbridled and impulsive, he was yet not altogether a fool. He dispatched a group of agents disguised as grain merchants to assess the economic potential of the country, among them, according to the historian Maria Bellonci, a number of Jews, whose experience and judgments were respected and whose reports, written in Hebrew, still exist in Mantuan archives. The results of the investigation proved, as had been suspected, that Vincenzo would have to pour huge sums of money into untrustworthy hands for misty results. Having spent prodigiously on his gorgeous futile forays against the Turks, Vincenzo forgot about Poland, to concentrate on exigent matters nearby.

* As we know, Rome had wanted Ferrara for a long time, eager to absorb it among the papal states. When Duke Alfonso II died in 1597, he left Margherita, Vincenzo's sister, a young and wealthy widow but childless, a promising state of affairs for the Papacy. The Este put forth a desperate claim that there *was* an heir to the dukedom, Don Cesare d'Este, Alfonso's illegitimate son and a sporting companion of Vincenzo—who made no strong effort to help him, realizing that the determined Church would inevitably take Ferrara. Refusing to consider him a legitimate heir, Clement VIII and his Curia mollified Don Cesare by giving him Reggio and Modena, long controlled by Ferrara, and the right to call himself Duke, but not of Ferrara. Headed by the Pope, a long procession of ecclesiasts and noblemen formally took over the ancient dukedom, its formidable castle and luscious pleasure palaces, its paintings and musical instruments, its echoes of song and poetry. By 1598, the splendor that had begun to shine in the thirteenth century dimmed and faded, and Ferrara became a backwater controlled by a Church now more interested in power and piety than in the arts. The wake that marked the loss of the dukedom absorbed days of feasting and roistering, enlivened by Vincenzo and his company of hundreds of knights, who were greeted warmly by the triumphant Pope.

Soon after, Eleonora, the last of the children of Vincenzo and Eleonora de' Medici—the child who was to be consort to the emperor Ferdinand II—was born, and although it was not customary to celebrate extravagantly the birth of a girl child, her father could not let such an opportunity for gaiety go by; he invited everyone to the dancing and the clashing of swords and lances. From neighboring states came the most attractive women, dressed in the stiff jeweled magnificence of the now fashionable Spanish modes of plumed headdresses and skirts like pearl-studded fortresses. Guarini's *Pastor Fido* was performed for three princely audiences, its innate majestic length prolonged by intervals of ballet, song, and displays of startling stage effects. Festivities over, Vincenzo took his arthritis to Flanders for a cure, also for casting around proofs of his influence and for smelling out how things were going with Spain now that its mighty armada had been blown to shreds by English strategy and malevolent winds. The jubilee year of 1600 brought everyone to a Rome befogged with gossip and occasional bits of sound information. The marriage ceremonies of Maria de' Medici to Henry IV provided yet another informative agora where Vincenzo, accompanied by his wife, who was to take her young sister as far as Marseilles, could dispense hauteur and coins.

* A useful tool for dispelling the judgment that Vincenzo might be somewhat pro-French, especially after his sister-in-law became queen of France, offered itself in a renewed crusade against the Turks. The Pope and the emperor were begging for help to stay the Turkish advance, and again Vincenzo stepped before the footlights to pace out Act III of his performance as a Christian knight. He informed the emperor that he would act only if he was given unquestioned total command, that he required extra pay for his special guard and standard-bearers and the cost of transporting supplies. This would run high but no more than was due a prince who never traveled, in war or peace, without a splendid entourage. A few minor requests were denied him, but he was appointed chief of staff and in July of 1601, entering his fortieth year, he rode forth to do battle once more. After a pause for an exchange of compliments and light entertainment with the archduke Ferdinand, he reached the field, where a humiliating surprise awaited him: The grand duke of Tuscany had appointed Giovanni de' Medici chief of the Tuscan and Spanish armies, an appointment that should have been Vincenzo's to make or veto. The fury of insults and blistering hatreds approaching mayhem was moderated by calmer members of both families. In the meantime, the crusade remained paralyzed because the other European armies were reluctant to pursue their barbarous foe without the arms of the Medici and Gonzaga. Ultimately they all set out, stopping when one commander gave orders that were countermanded by the other. While the leaders roared and fought, the troops wandered aimlessly. Pulling his own Italians together, Vincenzo managed to conquer but one Turkish stronghold; replacement of supplies and men continued to come too slowly; those in the field usually refused to fight. Vincenzo could stage only feeble imitations of military encounters. He turned to his alchemists for more dramatic measures and bolder effects. In their search for the philosopher's stone, several alchemists—Paracelsus most notably—had observed the effect of certain noxious gases on the human body. It should be possible, Vincenzo instructed his experimenters, to produce a gas that might put a whole Turkish army to sleep or kill it outright. No success, no more than he had had with earlier measures.

After one concerted attempt against the Turks ended in a bloody defeat for the Europeans, the emperor's war council sent out a German commander to accuse Vincenzo of ineptness and cowardice. Vincenzo returned the insults, and since it soon became obvious that the German considered himself absolute leader, with no need to consult the duke, the Italian took his soldiers and umbrage home. There he found a spate of Venetian gossip sheets spreading calumnies: He was a coward and lacked any of the skills essential to a leader of armies. As best he could, he disregarded the humiliation and busied himself with arranging new music rooms, new art galleries, ordering new windows of Murano glass, and setting to work as copyist an attractive, poised young Fleming, Peter Paul Rubens, whose artistic, social, and linguistic skills he would soon use in matters of diplomacy.

Rubens

Carrying a passport testifying that Antwerp was free of the plague, Peter Paul Rubens took off for Italy, the Mecca of northern painters. He had served several apprenticeships since early adolescence, perfecting his skills in catching the light of a gem, the dash of a plume, the whisper of lace, and was, at twenty-one, admitted to the Guild of St. Luke as a master painter. But there was the lure of Italy, its painters, sculptors, and architects living in a seductive world glowing with genius, and, unlike the Netherlands, crowded with art-intoxicated, free-spending dukes and princes.

In the spring of 1600, Rubens landed in Venice, the mother of Giorgione, the Bellini, Titian, Tintoretto, Veronese—the keen portraitists and lovers of pearls, satins, and sentient flesh, from whom he learned some of the luscious buoyancy we call "Rubenesque." Through an acquaintance who worked in Mantua and showed the duke examples of Rubens's work, the painter was invited to work in the Gonzaga court as copyist of the large, choice collection. Since few famous fifteenth- and sixteenth-century paintings were available for purchase, collectors exchanged copies or used them as gifts. The work may have represented a drop in position for a master painter of St. Luke's Guild, but it did require high, precise skills and offered the opportunity to live with some of the best of Italian painting. There was a decent stipend to enjoy and the optimistic expectation that the duke would start collecting his copyist's original paintings—which rarely happened. There were difficulties, Vincenzo being Vincenzo, and among his idle sycophants intrigues to discredit the handsome and talented foreigner. But the young master painter of Antwerp, clever and confident, began to cultivate powerful friends, whose language he quickly mastered, and although he chafed under the duke's exigencies and assignments, he found life at Mantua's court lively and endlessly entertaining. In his grayer years, Rubens recalled his "delightful residence in Mantua," which offered him, along with other gifts, an education in court manners and politics, and the combination of subtlety and persuasiveness that made of him a skilled ambassador in the courts of England and Spain when he became the preferred painter of Europe.

Pricked by boredom, by reports of an irresistible woman in a distant town, by the reputation of a Neapolitan alchemist, the restless duke went anywhere, everywhere. With him, as part of his lordly processions, went his gaggle of painters. In Florence to attend the wedding of Maria de' Medici to a proxy standing in for Henry IV of France, Rubens may have struck up an acquaintance with the girl who, as Queen Marie of France, would much later commission him to commemorate her life in large, sententious panels that absorb commanding space in the Louvre. As apprentice court painter, Rubens must have been required to posture and charm through many formal occasions, but there was always time to examine and sketch local Italian wonders.

Still a copyist, Rubens also became art adviser to Vincenzo, helping him expand and arrange his collection. In early 1603, his Italian, his manner and style of address, were considered ready for him to undertake an ambassadorial mission to the court of Spain, where he was to present gifts to Philip III and to the king's favorite, the duke of Lerma, the actual head of state. A small court like Mantua had to keep proving its adulation for the mighty Spaniards, and building up, gem by gem, painting by painting, horse by horse, a tower of Spanish goodwill. Dozens on dozens of letters—Rubens was almost as prolific with his pen as with his brush—written to his friend Annibale Chieppo, Vincenzo's secretary of state and a very decent man in a trying situation, give us the exasperations and shocks inherent in the mission. Rubens gives full accounting of his expenditures and complains of the contemptuous treatment given him by Mantua's representative in the Spanish court. "As for the money His Highness has given me, to the great displeasure of the critics of the voyage, it will not be sufficient for expenses from Alicante to Madrid. . . . No one can accuse me of negligence or extravagance; my clearly balanced accounts will prove to the contrary," in spite of "all the crowd of busybodies and pseudo-experts." "The expenses for the horses are large but necessary, including wine-baths. . . . I beg you to favor me by informing His Highness freely of everything . . . in order that he banish from his mind every other vain persuasion concerning the expenses of my voyage." In a letter directed to Vincenzo, he asks that judgment of his expenditures be postponed for later explanations. "In the meantime I console myself in the thought of your boundless judgment, commensurate with the greatness of your heroic spirit, before the serene splendor of which I bow in reverence and humbly kiss your noble hand."

Three weeks of rain and mud had ruined a number of the copies of masterworks to be presented. Rejecting the "incredible incompetence and carelessness of painters here" (Zurbarán and Velázquez were infants at the time and El Greco was sequestered in decaying Toledo), Rubens reworked the paintings himself. Still obsessed with possible accusations of "carelessness and fraud," and maltreatment by the ambassador from Mantua, he found compensating satisfaction in meeting with the duke of Lerma, who was sufficiently impressed by the quality of Rubens's restorations and improvisations to consider them originals. Lerma commissioned an equestrian portrait of himself and arranged that a few court ladies sit for the Gonzaga "gallery of beauties." Pleased with the favor of Lerma and intimations that Vincenzo was satisfied with the manner in which he had accomplished his mission, Rubens returned to Mantua.

It had been an extraordinary experience and invaluable in reconfirming his judgment of himself as a singular painter, with increased courage to tell his duke so. He refused to go to France to expand the "gallery of beauties" there, suggesting that the French court might already have such works and certainly had artists capable of painting the ladies. "Then I shall not have to waste more time, travel, expenses, salaries upon works unworthy of me." Assuring the duke of his eagerness, "like a good servant," to obey, he begs for employment at "works more appropriate to my talents."

Not too long after, he asks the duke to maintain him in studies in Rome so that he will not have to "turn elsewhere for resources—which would not be lacking for me in Rome." They did not lack; there was a commission to paint an altarpiece for the Chiesa Nuova and during its execution a call to return to Mantua, which elicited a request for permission to stay until the completion of the work: "personages of such rank are interested in it that I could not honorably give up a contract obtained so gloriously against the pretensions of all the leading painters of Rome." The altarpiece, *Virgin Adored by Saints*, was highly praised, but when it was put in place it could hardly be seen.

Rubens offered to copy it on slate, which would better reflect the limited light, and proceeded to change it considerably, offering the original to "Their Highnesses" of Mantua. Their Highnesses rejected it because, their secretary wrote, they needed their money for a progress to Turin with the "largest [yet] and most brilliant of entourages" and for additional paintings to arrange— with the help of Rubens, now their Keeper of the Ducal Collection—in the long new Galleria della Mostra. Although there are records of mythological ceiling and wall decorations in the Ducal Palace executed by Rubens, gone or dispersed, and the existent patched-up sections of a church work now gathered as "The Dukes Guglielmo and Vincenzo Gonzaga with their duchesses Eleonora of Austria and Eleonora de' Medici adoring the Most Holy Trinity," there was never a Rubens painting in the grand gallery. He managed, however, to persuade them to buy Caravaggio's moving *Death of the Virgin*, rejected for its disturbing naturalism by the church fathers, and he protected the painters he commissioned for Mantua, as witness a reproof to the Most Serene Madame, Eleonora, complaining that she dealt with the painter Pomarancio in the manner of Mantua (tight-fisted) rather than Rome (open-handed) when she complained that the work was excessively priced.

That letter was dated February 1608. Before the year was out, Chieppo had a letter saying that Rubens was returning to Flanders because his mother was very ill there, but he would return to Mantua. His mother died before he reached her, and he never returned. He took Italy to Flanders in the shape of old medallions and bronzes and bookfuls of sketches of ruins, arches, and columns, which he would use as illustrations for his brother's book on antiquities. He took with him memories of the work of Michelangelo, of Mantegna, of myriad painters. Of the numerous sketches of palaces in Genoa which he gathered during a gambling season there, he later made a book of architecture, hoping to free his countrymen from their stolid house designs. Carrying with him a high reputation and sophistication gathered in Mantua and the courts it dealt with, the thirty-one-year-old Rubens was in shining readiness to become a distinguished art adviser and the painter who was chosen by England's Charles I to enliven the banqueting and entertainment salon of Whitehall with merrily turbulent flashes of color and shapes that bounce along its ceilings.

F·O·U·R·T·E·E·N

Vincenzo did not use Rubens's judgment or expertise in their first years together. There was hardly need to, since the duke dealt with many agents in many parts of Europe, expressing to them some boredom with religious painting. Like his grandfather Federico, he preferred "not so much of sacred matters as poetic and lovely to look at"—serene Flemish landscapes, perhaps. Other agents offered him other goods: A truly small dwarf was available for import from Poland and another from Hungary, ready to be shipped if the duke wished. He almost always wished. From the mysterious East, pearls and the rare medicaments into which they were to be melted for aphrodisiac effects; from the North, potable gold, also a fine stimulant; from everywhere, books—on the new science of physiognomy, on mathematics, on Hebrew and the Cabala, on the latest medical findings. His ambassadors reported that he had spent "a million in gold" on the huge fortress at Casale, that he "spent on all matters so profusely that it was to marvel at." Taxes, fines, and duties became increasingly exigent; the pawning of land and crops covered increasingly large areas in the Mantovana and Monferrato. Though Mantua had codes of fair trade practices and a system of commercial checking, she also had controllers who manipulated money into their own coffers and those of a heedless prince. His subjects tolerated the wild uses of their tax money because it was a prince's due and because he saw to his poor and kept the debtors among them out of prison. In spite of the tottering wool trade, which was being taken over by the Netherlands and England, the city still seemed to flourish under its entertaining, profligate prince.

＊ Vincenzo's profitable relationship with the large community of Mantuan Jews suffered disturbing changes, however. By Church order, foreign Jews were exiled and the Mantuans subjected to the violent anti-Semitic preaching of a friar, Bartolomeo Cambi, whose words were especially authoritative because he was reputed to be a miracle healer. Among the aroused, hysterical population, rumors swelled that the godless Jews had, in their arrogance, reviled the holy friar and even the duke. Vincenzo had seven Jews hanged. It was an impractical act, which he soon regretted, yet not as much as he feared the threats of violence inspired among his citizens by the thunderous messages of the friar. On an appeal to Rome, Cambi was removed, but in accord with papal rulings, Vincenzo let it be known, near the end of 1602, that Jews must always wear their identifying disks in public, that they were to sell their houses and gather together in one tight area held by gates. One family was exempted, apparently to save court treasurers the embarrassment of entering the ghetto to borrow money.

In spite of shows of fealty to the Church, Vincenzo had to wait through a long series of pressures here, threats there, Byzantine maneuvers, and always gifts, to procure a cardinal's cap for his second son, Bishop Ferdinando. The young man was then twenty and neither robust nor sharp, showing no aptitude for becoming a Gonzaga power. Instead, Ferdinando and his gangs chose to enliven the Roman nights by searching out Spaniards to beat and stab. The education and polish for which he had been sent to Germany and later to Pisa left him with a few impressive areas of knowledge, but little of the political wisdom he might have picked up stayed with him. While he was disporting himself in Rome, the family found itself busy with the marriage of the heir, Francesco, to Margherita, the daughter of the duke of Savoy. The tumult of celebrations stilled, Vincenzo returned to a favorite dream, this time inspired by heads not always as quixotic as his, to achieve a kingdom of his own. He was forty-six and generally in robust health and vigorous; his good humor and generosity and his enthusiastically sustained interest in his subjects and his city earned him solid support. (This flattering description was written not, as one might expect, by a court chronicler but by a Venetian ambassador.) By way of his ancestral Paleologa connections, he had a claim to the crown of Byzantium (the Balkans) if it could be taken from the Turks. Trying for an unreal kingdom on unreal claims was an irresistible challenge to Vincenzo, who was encouraged by many of the Gonzaga clan. The invitations and promises by deposed Balkan overlords became increasingly pressing and persuasive, enhanced by rumors of competition—or was it cooperation?—from other princes. Prince Maurice of Nassau-Orange was interested enough, an agent reported, to have already gathered and outfitted a Flemish army and the ships to transport it to Ragusa (Dubrovnik), the entrance port to the ephemeral kingdom. Before ships crossed the Adriatic, informants were instructed to assay the Balkan situation and pave the way for Vincenzo to treat with the leader, Baron Stefano Vulatkovich, and his satellites. The agents reported the barbaric lay of the land to be unwelcoming, the Balkan leaders eccentric and clearly not trustworthy. They would not be reliable allies against the forceful Turks, who had first to be conquered, and they obviously expected Mantua to carry the financial burdens of their campaigns. Advisers suggested that Vincenzo forget the Balkan kingdom and he did, with some reluctance.

He died not too long after the conclusion of this subplot in an opera buffa, the year 1612, Vincenzo fifty. He left a court of eight hundred personages, who ranged from savants to whores; he left theater and music of an extraordinary level, he left a distinguished collection of paintings, bronzes, tapestries, jewels, laces, and objects in rare metals. Having spent over twenty million ducats, which his alchemists, among them the Jewish court physician, Abramo Portaleone, could not restore, he left immense debts, and a legend. Who else provided his people with weekly concerts of high caliber? Who else bought an unfurnished villa for 100,000 scudi? And there was certainly no other prince who had given a fiefdom worth 50,000 scudi for a Raphael painting, a truly princely gesture. After the passing of "l'ultimo cavaliere di casa Gonzaga" the light faded.

* Francesco Gonzaga became duke of Mantua on the tenth of June, 1612. Like the sons of other zesty fathers, he was pallid and remote where his father had been gaudy and ebullient. Politics interested him minimally, as little as heroic fantasies did. His immediate concerns were reducing his father's debts and coping with the inexhaustible rage of the Farnese, who continued to stir up quarrels whenever and wherever they could find a chink for a belligerent wedge. Though he enjoyed the theater and music his father had provided, he found it necessary to curtail casts and performances drastically. Because he needed money, he feigned loosening the strictures imposed on Mantuan Jews, mainly by a long decree (in the fashionable writing style of one or two nonstop sentences) that insisted Jews not be molested. Notwithstanding the decree, life for the Jew in Mantua remained as harsh as, possibly harsher than, before. Whether Francesco would have become more flexible with maturity and experience will never be known. Smallpox invaded the area in December of 1612. First, young brother Ludovico died, and three weeks later, Francesco, six months the fifth duke of Mantua, and twenty-six years old, died. He left a young child, Maria, and her mother, Margherita of Savoy, who was also mourning the death of an infant son.

Francesco's successors were his two brothers who had escaped smallpox: Ferdinando, the cardinal, and the younger Vincenzo, shards of a once sturdy line that began to follow "a frantic road towards catastrophe" (according to Coniglio), themselves the early blows that would ultimately help annihilate the long-lived dynasty. Their dukedom was still extraordinarily handsome, still burdened with mounting taxes and old debts. Jewels were steadily pawned and so was the court silver, but the proceeds did not necessarily go to the creditors. A recrudescence of theater and music—Cardinal Ferdinando wrote bits of music and was very fond of female singers, especially of the singer Adriana Basile, who had been Vincenzo's mistress—and a court reglorified with actors, ballerinas, alchemists, charlatans, and sycophants, absorbed forty thousand ducats in one year alone. When Ferdinando attempted to establish a bank, hoping to attract Mantuan money, he found no investors. They were disturbed by the wars to the north, which might spill into Italy, as had happened before, and they were uncertain about the durability of the Gonzaga and their financial acumen. The sizable Mantuan army had dwindled, and Ferdinando was forced to hire outlanders, mainly Swiss mercenaries, to flesh out his troops. Concern for the care of citizens disappeared; the court moved farther and farther away from its people and lands except as sources of taxes and fines. The constant, shrewd Gonzaga surveillance of what other states were doing and might be planning melted away. The politics of Mantua became a concentration on court intrigue. "The state," as one historian puts it, "became more and more head without body." So conspicuously incapable and heedless were the brothers, and so vulnerable, that the duke of Savoy insisted his granddaughter Maria, the child of his daughter Margherita and the dead Francesco, be sent to him so that she might be guarded as the legitimate heiress of Mantua and Monferrato should her uncles die without heirs—implying homosexuality and disease. Monferrato was of especial importance to Savoy because it was earning more than debt-ridden, half-pawned Mantua earned; there were obvious advantages in being regent for his granddaughter should events move in his direction, and he pressed vigorously to have the child. Cardinal Ferdinando bestirred himself to appeal to the Pope in Rome for support against Savoy. Suppressing his gluttony and intemperance, he showed well. His extensive command of languages, especially Hebrew and Greek, and his knowledge of philosophy and law, all of it stored in a prodigious memory, were astonishing. He discoursed interestingly on literature and music, as had his cardinal ancestor Ercole. It was altogether an impressive display. The Papacy ruled that he could hold on to Maria, whom he placed in a nunnery under the supervision of his aunt Margherita, the widow of the duke of Ferrara. His sister-in-law Margherita of Savoy was sent to the villa at Goito to await possible signs of a pregnancy that might produce an indisputable Gonzaga heir. Savoy hammered at Ferdinando to give him the child Maria. Her unhappy and not pregnant mother was sent back to Savoy, while Maria was held. After an attempt by Savoy to enter Monferrato, backed by Spanish forces, and on the urging of the emperor, the child was sent to join her mother in Savoy.

For the further protection of the enfeebled line, it was time to look for wives, once cautiously and cleverly managed by Gonzaga ancestors. The stupidity here was awesome. Though Ferdinando stayed attached in his bloodless way to his father's aging musician-courtesan, Adriana Basile, marry he must. He chose seventeen-year-old Camilla Faa, daughter of one of his ambassadors, Count Ardizzino Faa. He may have liked her, he may not have; it was difficult for him to express great personal interest, much less passion, and there were still the distractions of troublesome Monferrato. Aunt Margherita of Ferrara was put in charge of the contentious state. Like the women governors before her, she was unsparing of the Monferrini, spraying harsh, unjust edicts. When a revolt she inspired seemed to be coming to a head, she was returned to Mantua, where she continued to exercise her despotic rule in the court, interfering, plotting, making life extremely uneasy for her languid nephews.

To become a husband and sixth duke of Mantua, Ferdinando took off his cardinal's cap and placed it on the head of his brother Vincenzo. In early January, there was a great ringing of bells and splashing of moneys to celebrate the combined coronation of the duke and his marriage with Camilla, who was charmed to be a duchess and innocent of the knowledge that she was neither wife nor duchess legally. The contract devised by Ferdinando and a friendly ecclesiast was declared invalid; one year later, the duke married a rich Medici heiress under a less assailable contract. The bride's father questioned and scrutinized the matter of the earlier marriage, but a series of inventive rationalizations seemed to content him, and the matter rested.

Vincenzo, considerably less intelligent than his brother, was better at inept deviousness and the irresponsibility that never measured the consequences of any act. He was a dissolute brawler, troublesome beyond his brother's lax tolerance. As a result of a particularly perverted mess, the ensuing scandal too much even for his freewheeling court, Ferdinando sent Vincenzo away to the relatives in Bozzolo. Here he met the attractive widow of the prince of Bozzolo, the mother of several children, forty years old to his twenty-one, and offered to marry her without asking the approval of his brother or the permission of the Pope. Shortly after, in 1615, he became a married cardinal. Ferdinando disapproved of the marriage beyond its ecclesiastical prohibition, and besides, Isabella of Bozzolo might still be fertile, possibly victorious in a childbearing rivalry with Ferdinando's Medici wife. Furthermore, she was a member of a branch of the family suspect in its loyalty to Mantua and could easily, should she become the mother of a mainline Gonzaga heir, present a serious threat. Vincenzo fought his brother's anger in Mantua and in appeals to Rome. Ferdinando retaliated by forcing his brother into house arrest in the palace stronghold of Goito. Imprisonment impelled Vincenzo to agree to his brother's judgment, and together they petitioned for an annulment of the marriage with Isabella. In spite of the pronouncements of three savants of jurisprudence the Gonzaga imported from Paris, the Pope would not arrange an annulment. It was a valid marriage, he ruled, and bored with

Gonzaga embroilments and ensuing importunities, he ordered Vincenzo to stop trying to be a cardinal, whose duties and disciplines he found, in any case, onerous, and continue his life with Isabella. Vincenzo responded with a letter that was arrogant, idiotic, and futile. He then removed himself from Pope, brother, and wife by entering the military service of Spain, where he managed not to make an utter fool of himself. In the meantime, Ferdinando attempted a perfidious peace with Isabella, inviting her to enjoy the ease of one of his country retreats for the duration of a pregnancy; he was sure she was pregnant. She refused; she was not pregnant and was afraid that his servants in the villa might poison her. Almost as a reflex, her brother-in-law then accused her friends and relations at Bozzolo of trying to poison Vincenzo and himself.

Difficulties for which the brothers were totally unprepared closed in on several sides. Bozzolo remained a threat, while the Guastalla Gonzaga, the heirs of valiant Ferrante, found grounds for claiming the dukedom. At the same time, the French Nevers Gonzaga put forth their strong claim. France and Spain were lining up for battle to take Italy, and no one was much interested in helping Ferdinando fight off his several relatives. He struck at Bozzolo in the person of Isabella, hoping to free Vincenzo at the same time, for a better marriage and progeny. The brothers found an old woman who testified that Isabella had fed Vincenzo an aphrodisiac whose ingredients included bits of the Host and of a skull, a powerful brew that impelled him to rush into marriage. Although it was a worn plot, accusations of witchcraft and the use of black-magic potions were frequent and readily prosecuted. Isabella came close to being burned at the stake. A clever, controlled woman, she rushed to Rome and asked to be tried for witchcraft there. Ferdinando wrote his usual high-and-mighty letter, casting blame on the woman, which did not endear him to the papal judges. Nor was his Medici wife much help in calming troubled waters. Afraid that Camilla Faa's son, Giacinto, might be considered heir to the dukedom while she remained childless, she had the boy removed to a small marquisate, which became his, and had his mother enclosed in a nunnery.

Ferdinando had difficulty coping with the Nevers and Guastalla threats, both branches increasingly prepared to take over the dukedom in the struggle that was to become known as the Mantuan Succession. Nor could he have Isabella burned as a witch.

She was safely in the Castel Sant' Angelo, near the Vatican, persuading Church jurists of her innocence. In the course of their hearings, they discovered that the woman who had testified to Isabella's black magic had first been imprisoned and brutalized, the duke himself among several gentlemen who maltreated her, and freed only when she consented to tell the story they invented. By the time Vincenzo's marriage was annulled, in early 1627, not without its trail of nuisances, brother Ferdinando had died (1626), at the age of thirty-seven. Vincenzo II was now the seventh duke of Mantua, a role for which he had little talent, although its privileges were much to his taste. His matrimonial difficulties were not yet over; Pope Urban VII considered Isabella blameless and victimized and therefore entitled to damages. Her ex-husband poured bribes into the papal court to have the judgment against him reversed, and simultaneously tried to have Isabella murdered. Between loud outpourings of vengeful hatred, he journeyed to miracle shrines, a practice that stopped when he died at thirty-three, the fine owed Isabella unpaid.

Collections

As poison-making and the manufacture of cosmetics and perfumes contributed to early pharmacology, curiosity about animals and plants led toward zoology and botany. Often, one field was stimulated by one particular interest. As the passion of the Hohenstaufen emperor Frederick II for falconry led him to observations on the falcon that are still valid seven centuries later, the Gonzaga interest in the breeding of horses for entertainments and war matériel produced fruitful studies, including the treatise on the diseases of horses written by the head blacksmith for Ludovico II in the fifteenth century. An increasing number of illustrated volumes described several hundred animals, from quadrupeds to worms, from fish to birds. The illustrations repeated some of the mythological oddities that were the matter of medieval bestiaries: the ever-present basilisk, whose stare could turn a man to stone, and the fearsome manticore, who had the head of a man, the body of a lion, and a scorpion's sting as tail. By and large, however, the drawings are naturalistic and informative. With the animal sketches of such artists as Pisanello, Mantegna, Carpaccio, and Dürer widely disseminated, the public eye became more knowing, aided by the availability of living subjects in court zoos. Often encompassing gifts from foreign potentates—an ostrich for Ludovico, a lion for Francesco—the zoos provided places for studying anatomy and behavior. Isabella d'Este's whim to cross a domestic cat with a civet cat might, if successful, have led to other experiments in cross-breeding. The elephant that Pope Leo X cherished and mourned broadened a bit the field of zoology, as did the giraffe earlier presented to his father, Lorenzo de' Medici. The irrepressible alchemists made their own contributions to the study of animals. Into which zodiacal house, dominated by what humors, would one put an elephant? Was he sanguine or phlegmatic? And there were rumors steadily coming from the East that a rhinoceros horn had aphrodisiac powers. Shouldn't one try to find such an oddity, study it, and extract from it, if possible, the elixir that assured enhanced sexual might?

The earliest zoos were private hunting preserves. From their beginnings as lords of Mantua, the Gonzaga raised prized falcons and prestigious hunting dogs, their lean elegance adorning several paintings. As hunters, they knew the habits and anatomy of wolves and boars, deer and rabbits, and from their surrounding waters the lives of aquatic birds. Falcons and other birds of prey were of particular interest to Francesco II, who kept as many as one hundred fifty in the aviaries of his hunting villa at Marmirolo, honoring their noble deaths with marble sepulchers.

One aspect of "zoo" incorporated miscellanies of the rare and bizarre, the "cabinets of curiosities" or "natural history," proofs to their owners and their guests that they truly inhabited and partially owned a world of marvels. Displayed with rare precious stones, with illuminated books, with recently discovered Roman medallions, were the huge tusk of an elephant, the plates from the back of an armadillo, the horn of a rhinoceros.

As libraries grew to thousands of books and art collections expanded prodigiously, as botany, mainly derived from old herbal studies, and zoology began slowly to define themselves, there were attempts at compartmentalization of collections, not yet in the sixteenth century clearly defined. Isabella d'Este-Gonzaga's famously omnivorous collection included seashells, branches of coral, the ubiquitous unicorn's horn, and the teeth of strange fish. Her son Federico II, who paid agents in port cities to buy animals from foreign traders, requesting a leopard to be trained for hunting and racing; a mongoose to kill snakes; ostriches; and whatever else was rare and exotic, added to the collection larger fish teeth, the sword of a swordfish, and several alligators. His consuming interest in animals gave way at times to a knowledgeable enthusiasm for gardens and plants and then to monsters, in the actuality when possible, and when not, in pictures and engravings like Dürer's two-headed baby.

Along with the essential unicorn horn and its wondrous combination of rarity and holiness—only a virgin could capture a unicorn, and from there other virtues flowed, including the unicorn's role as the savior of mankind—the Renaissance court often held a variety of repellent mythological animals. The powerfully evil basilisk turned up as the property of Medici in the earlier-mentioned exhibition in Florence: a smallish thing with distorted bat wings, a long curly tail, many sharp teeth, and huge exophthalmic eyes. (According to Vasari, playful Leonardo, on being given a peculiar lizard, "made wings pulled off other lizards which he filled with mercury so that they moved and trembled when it walked; he then made for it eyes, a beard and horns, tamed it in a little box and terrified all his friends with it.") One wonders how a shrewd, hardheaded sixteenth-century tyrant like Cosimo de' Medici could accept such a fraud, skillfully made as it was, possibly by Leonardo himself. He lived in a universe that was a melding of here-and-now commercial expansion and a new world of boundless astonishments no less strange than the familiar basilisk. Monsters, however, made fine shockers to add to collections. Always lively furnishings of the human mind, the chimera of fancy and terror from time immemorial, they were explained by ecclesiasts as the hideous get of witches who coupled with devils, a conviction that stayed as firm truth for centuries.

The emotive freedoms and exaggerations of the High Renaissance that produced the monumental earth mothers of Pontormo's *Visitation* and the disturbing swan-necked *Virgin* of Parmigianino might have in some degree reflected an intensified interest in the abnormal, in monsters made more monstrous by word of mouth and graphic illustration. Ravenna produced an engraving of a monster early in the sixteenth century that had the sad head of the baby Christ who sensed his tragic destiny, a rhinoceros horn in the middle of his head, wings instead of arms, and the genitalia of both sexes, reflecting early alchemy's androgynous ideal. The monster's torso ends in feathers, a large eye in the knee and one huge claw in place of feet. It was claimed to be a prophecy of the destruction of Italy by the French; yet the letter Y and the cross inscribed on the body promised ultimate peace and harmony. This sad-faced monster and others like it were used as anti-papal caricatures by Protestants, the repellent features emblematic of the decadence of the Church. The distorted, incomprehensible bodies were also sources of steadier study and led to tentative investigations of primitive genetics, of early questionings in gynecology and obstetrics.

In the mid-seventeenth century, Guglielmo Gonzaga built the palace of Goito, whose woods held an abundance of animals for the hunt and an aviary of unusual birds. Historians claim that Guglielmo became an avid collector of other matter to rival a cousin, whose gathering of curiosities included a blood-red clump of earth capable of curing gonorrhea and counteracting poisons. Whatever the stimulus, Guglielmo added to the accumulation of his ancestors a singularly large unicorn's horn, a beautiful specimen, to be coupled in perfection and elegance only with the horn owned by King Sigismund of Poland.

Guglielmo's son Vincenzo added to his notable varied collection leading scientists. He sponsored Gaspare Tagliacozzi of the University of Bologna, an innovator in plastic surgery, who used the skin and muscles of arms and legs to rebuild torn, broken faces, dedicating a book on his work to Vincenzo. (The practice of plastic surgery disappeared for centuries, under the condemnation of the Church.) When Galileo Galilei came to Vincenzo's attention, he was invited to work for him as military mathematician-engineer. It appears that Galileo met with the duke in Mantua two or three times, and that he might have taken the job were there not a difference over the salary offered. In spite of his disappointment, openhanded Vincenzo sent Galileo a fine collar, which supported a medallion of the ducal image.

Among the waves of information and misinformation that flew to Europe from the New World, there was frequent mention of a gusano (a cactus larva, still considered a delicacy in Mexico), from which a powerful aphrodisiac could be extracted. (The mode of extracting the special virtues of the worm required that Indian women apply the gusano to the genitals of their men, whose bite would make them more vigorously sexual.) So Evangelista Marcobruno was sent by Vincenzo to Peru to collect gusanos. The worms were disappointingly ineffective, but the expedition brought back plants that were medically promising, to be added to Mantua's pharmacopoeia, one of the first to be compiled. What Vincenzo could not stimulate in medicine he hoped for from his carefully educated sons, Vincenzo and Ferdinando. Along with the social graces of manners and music, along with mathematics, Latin, and training in war games, they were encouraged in scientific studies, Vincenzo, like his father, especially an enthusiast for plants and their medicinal possibilities. With the assistance of the court *speziale*—the spice master, the pharmacist—he produced "a noble medicament," an antivenom serum, in large enough quantities to offer at no charge to "poor people oppressed by poison."

The numerous gardens in the city palace and the country villas were, for many years, supervised by a Florentine monk, Zenobio Bocchi, widely respected as a botanist and an extractor of simples from his medicinal plants, raised with attention to the dictates of the zodiac. Bocchi kept careful records of his plants and the cures supposedly derived from them, including flowers that counteracted poisons and stomachaches, and when Ferdinando established a *studio* that taught law and medicine, Bocchi lectured on botany and its linked branch, primitive pharmacology. The aging botanist, also responsible for the yield of the orchard, was reluctantly pressed into trying his arts at making gold, along with the other court alchemists, and, as supervisor of the Gonzaga collection of objects and natural phenomena, into searching for additional wonders for this early museum.

A German architect who lived and traveled in Italy during Ferdinando's time leads off his description of the "natural" curios, quite expectedly, with the spectacular unicorn horn. Among the crocodiles, an armadillo; a seal with four huge curved teeth; the mummified corpse of a Bonacolsi killed centuries before, a portion of his viscera left visible, curtained so that it might not appall the ladies; an embalmed human head on a salver, many pretty branches of coral, the corpses of two dogs who died of starvation, a petrified elephant tusk. There was also a fetus with a large head, four eyes, and two mouths, and, "curious to see," a hydra with seven necks and heads and handsomely marked skin. Uncut jewels and veins of gold in the matrix, and next to a garden of beautiful plants, more princely objects. (To describe all of them would take many days, says the German, and he can mention only a few.) Columns of gold; columns of lapis; a horse cut of one piece of crystal; boxes full of other objects of crystal, itself a marvel since it was a substance that was a solidified fluid of the earth; daggers and belts covered with rubies; tables of gold; horses' cloaks ornamented with rubies, pearls, gold; numerous bits of antiquity, artistic clocks—and then the patient reporter runs out of breath.

A contemporary physician from Verona also tries, after paying his respects to Mantua's dukes, its superb buildings and celebrated art collection. He then systematizes his observations to accord with the scheme of the museum, which was divided into four sections that represented the four humors. The first category, he says, is devoted to minerals, among them gold, silver, and stones that included diamonds, sapphires, amethysts, and an emerald. Of major importance among these is a compact piece of the famous earth from Lemnos, the color of flesh, its astringent properties useful in stemming hemorrhages. The second category comprises marine plants, many of them brought from the New World: sea birds, a large variety of bivalves and conches, mother-of-pearl, shell fossil, and not-quite-ready pearls in their shells.

The third category concerns itself with fruits of the Americas, including the extraordinary hairy coconut, petrified wood from England, ancient inscribed bark, gums and syrups from rare trees. The fourth category holds the only armadillo in Italy and goes on to birds' eggs, that of the ostrich amazingly huge and paper thin. A vase made of the dorsal spine of a whale, the exquisite design of a fossilized fish skeleton, the size of an elephant's tusk, the peculiar nature of the skins, teeth, and tails of odd animals, greatly impress the visitor. Most impressive, and of great value, is the cup ornamented in gold and jewels that had been cut from a bezoar stone (actually a gallstone emitted by cows), which was believed by the ancient Arabs and Hebrews to have highly curative effects against almost any disease. This observer, Benedetto Ceruti, also winds down in time, explaining that he chose only a few things to describe, and gracefully closes his account with compliments to the collection, the collector, and the renowned expert in botany and the natural sciences, the Florentine Zenobio Bocchi, of the order of Franciscans. The awed reports—except for the listings of dealers—stopped altogether when the bulk of the collection was taken to Venice to be sold in the 1620s, the rest subjected to the looting of Mantua by the Austrians in 1630, leaving dusty space and disorder where there was once glitter and wonder.

F*I*F*T*E*E*N

The lack of direct heirs remained a pressing problem. Before he died, in late 1627, Vincenzo married off the French Carlo (Charles of Rethel, son of the duke of Nevers and grandson to Ludovico Gonzaga, the founder of that line), to his niece Maria, the daughter of his dead brother Francesco and Margherita of Savoy. It was a marriage in macabre tones, the traditional merry festivities replaced by funeral services for Vincenzo. The young Frenchman, not yet aware that the dissolution of Mantua was well advanced, that he and his line would fall into dreadful straits and ultimate destruction, found himself appalled and frightened by a disordered, depraved court and the war threats that further darkened it. His father, more clearly aware of the European conflicts that would choose Italy as their stage of action, came to his aid. To bring Mantuans to his son's side, he relieved them of the excessive taxes that Vincenzo and Ferdinando had imposed and lightened their debts to the city. Controlling difficulties imposed by forces outside Mantua was another matter. The pan-European Thirty Years' War with its complexities of aims dynastic, religious, and territorial, a war of indescribable cruelty, which broke the power of the Holy Roman Empire, was in its full destructive swing. The uneasy French succession in Mantua, challenged by the Guastalla Gonzaga, who were sponsored by the opposing force, Spain in collaboration with the Empire, must ultimately be involved. The older Nevers played for time, trying to hold a stance of neutrality while he was pinned between demands for definite commitment to one side or the other. To protect his son's doomed dukedom, he sent for his French army, which was stopped and assaulted by the Savoyards while Carlo was in Vienna, the seat of the empire, to plead for support. He got none and, with no other choice, declared himself with the French, having been promised help, help that was actually limited to futile meetings.

Skirmishes in northern Italy and endless, fruitless negotiations were halted by a plague and the consequent flight of those soldiers and peasants who had escaped death. (An English letter from Mantua describes the city as a corpse, her population reduced to seven thousand, the fields turned to weeds, her court and aristocracy ruined.) Nevertheless, Nevers managed to achieve his son's investiture as duke of Mantua, a duke with no means, no army, no confidence from his decimated populace. The investiture was a short-lived, meaningless honor. Though the French had made military advances here and there, the imperial troops thrust the ducal family out, unprepared and penniless, to find shelter in Ariano, a papal enclave, where they were sustained by moneys from Maria's Hapsburg aunt Eleonora. Young Carlo was reconfirmed, probably through the intervention of the Hapsburg aunt, as duke of Mantua by the emperor, who demanded, in return, that the governorship of Monferrato be turned over to the Gonzaga of Guastalla, the Empire's friends. After the agreement was arranged, the young duke made his reentry with modest ceremony; there was no longer gold for extravagant displays. Shortly after the ceremony, he died, still quite young. His father took on again the rule of the exhausted land, whose people chanted: "France wins, Spain wins—we must be contented with a morsel of food if we can get it." Appeals to Tuscany and the Venetian republic brought financial relief, which Nevers might have handled with acumen if he hadn't been absorbed by a renewal of old problems. The Savoyards demanded that his daughter-in-law Maria and her baby son, Carlo II, be given them. The hostage boy might serve as instrument for claiming Monferrato in time and possibly Mantua later. Maria was to remarry, preferably a prince who would strengthen Savoy. Her father-in-law, Nevers, urged her to marry him instead, so that her child might stay where he belonged, in the court that was indisputably his as the next duke of Mantua. Pope Urban VIII vigorously opposed such a marriage, with its odor of incest. Nevers went back to running from the path of one arrow to meet the flight of another. He conferred, he signed, he contracted, he promised an army to fight Spain—with what moneys and troops? Exhausted, he contracted a fever, which was followed by a fatal heart attack in the fall of 1637.

* Maria, regent for her young duke, who was eight years old when his grandfather died, was twenty-eight. No longer young, she had probably never been young, thrown as she was into dynastic struggles and war from early childhood. She had observed and learned a good deal and now directed those insights to the protection of her son's rights with a shrewdness and tenacity that recalled an earlier Gonzaga regent, Isabella d'Este. She dispatched agents in every direction: to her aunt Eleonora and the new emperor, Ferdinand III, to Venice, to the court of France, to Rome. She tried to arrange that everyone protect her son from everyone else. Her leanings were definitely slanted toward the Empire, attached as she was to her sympathetic aunt and her emperor cousin. She was a shrewd woman, as a fierce mother-regent had to be; she was a capable administrator, handling the shaky finances of the impoverished city with more order than had existed for decades. She nosed out Francophile plotters and swept them and their spies from her court. Her one serious mistake was to be so fond and foolish about her boy that he became a replica of his uncle Vincenzo II. A willful, spoiled dolt, uneducated and vulgar, skillful only, according to one biographer, at whipping up carnival riots, the youth "was without any sense of measure and of any virtue of heart and brain." His mother, clear-sighted except for the rosy mist that cloaked her son, turned the government over to this wilderness of unreined impulses when he was eighteen, in 1647, and ready for marriage, which, it was hoped, might tame and mature him. With the help of Aunt Eleonora, his mother found a bride among the Hapsburgs. She was Isabella Clara, the daughter of the archduke Leopold. Once again triumphal arches rose in the streets, knights-at-arms once again pranced and shone, the indispensable splendid canopy again set off and shielded the bride. Under the pennons and the heroic mottoes, the city was a shambles, depleted of its paintings and rarities, the heir not inclined, had he the means, to supplant them. The brawling, the carousing that filled his life left no room for art or politics or trade or agriculture. His discouraged mother removed herself from the dissolute court but not from her son's interests. In Germany, she was assured of his investiture as Carlo II, duke of Mantua, by the emperor and also extracted a promise that he would be nominally ruler of two minute duchies, which stayed, however, with the Guastalla Gonzaga.

Hard-pressed, durable Maria lasted until she was fifty-one. After she died, in 1660, Carlo II was entirely free of the few strictures his mother had tried to impose on him. No longer could she banish Margherita della Rovere, Carlo's favorite courtesan, from Mantua, as she had repeatedly done. Following a common, sensible tradition, the favorite was given a husband, a man who cared less about the woman than the sums he earned for her lease. The husband, anciently connected with the Gonzaga, lived in Casale. Margherita settled herself there and so did Carlo. For the baubles he gave Margherita, for the carnival costumes, the wines, the entertainers he hired, for the bags of gold given to the count della Rovere and the rest of Margherita's numerous family, Carlo bled more and more taxes out of Monferrato and Mantua. In addition to throwing thousands of ducats in several directions, he subsidized mysterious ambassadorial missions, complete with imposing retinues, headed by Margherita's husband. To no one's surprise, the complaisant cuckold disappeared in Poland, never to appear again. His presumptive widow and her duke returned to Mantua, to a stimulating state of affairs which colored and spiced court gossip throughout Europe. Isabella Clara, of a house of rigid imperial-Spanish decorum, was lost and isolated in the raffish gypsy camp of a court, and deprived of the consolation and pleasure she might have derived from the birth of a boy child, Ferdinando Carlo, who was kept from her, carefully guarded by court servants and functionaries. One of the few speakers of German in the court was a Count Bulgarini, who, though a convert, was still considered a member of the Mantuan community of Jews. In addition to being a linguist, he was intelligent and well educated (he is credited with having established the first newspaper to be published in Mantua), a valued adviser, stimulating companion, and, inevitably, lover. It was in no way a secret liaison, but it was conducted with a degree of the discretion and decorum that Isabella Clara tried to impose on Carlo and his sycophants, to no avail. The historian Giuseppe Coniglio, who writes of the last despoilers of his city with poisoned ink, tells of several incidents that point up the infantilism of the penultimate duke.

Invited to attend formal state festivities in Bologna, Carlo brought along his Margherita, with whom he disported himself in his usual unleashed fashion. The Bolognese elders, particularly Bologna's papal legate, expressed their disgust openly and volubly. Carlo as loudly and volubly expressed his disgust with them and, to punctuate his displeasure, had a body of Mantuan soldiers shoot out the windows of the legate's palace as he left the city. A visit to Genoa, with Margherita and friends in tow, inspired two monks to plead with Carlo to modify his outrageously sinful life. He had them thrown out bodily. Among the scurrilous pamphlets that papered his time, there appeared one titled *Il Puttanismo*— whoring. It named the duke "prince of whores, keeper of brothels," and contrasted him with other Italian rulers, praising them highly whether they deserved it or not. The reading public was additionally informed that this well-known "Mantua nobleman" provided lavishly for the sisters, cousins, nieces, and a long etcetera of relatives of his mistress-procuress, who were "capable of anything, everything," their orgies justly dubbed, therefore, *puttanismo.*

While Carlo was disporting himself in his fun houses, Casale was once again contested in blood, this time taken by the Spanish from occupying French troops. "Spanish infantry died for him on the hills of Monferrato while he was stretched out with his concubine awaiting news that Casale was his again." Although Spain was his protector, there was no harm in going to France, where he was cordially received in 1655. General information had it that he was there to sell portions of Monferrato—some said all of it—to help support his harem and the extravaganzas he staged to impress visiting dignitaries. Whether the matter was seriously considered or not, France had other concerns, and a few alarmed advisers forced Carlo back to Mantua, to recognize that the European wars were threatening his borders. He gathered an army.

French troops pierced the borders of the Milanese, long under the aegis of Spain. Here they were joined by the pro-French army of the duke of Modena, and together they besieged Pavia, near Casale and no great distance from Mantua. At this point, Carlo, roused to a show of militancy and because the salary was irresistible, offered his services to the emperor, who, amazingly, appointed him general of the imperial armies in Italy at a salary of thirty thousand scudi a month plus a generous bonus per annum. It soon became obvious that the emperor had made a serious error, and Carlo was dispatched to oversee maneuvers in a remote part of the battle area. Inept, confused, a subject of contempt, he wrapped himself in illness and called for the ministrations of his Margherita. After *"boccaccesche"* adventures—including capture by the Spaniards, whom she was forced to service—and disguised in masculine attire, she reached her charge and master. During Carlo's short, inept attempt at being a military man, French forces tore the Mantovana apart and remained—French, Italian, Swiss mercenaries—looting, stealing, ravaging throughout the winter of 1658.

The only way Carlo could see to remove the French was to call to Venice for help. She elicited a firm promise that Mantua would stay absolutely neutral in the French-Spanish conflict, and treated with the French for a removal of their troops. The departure provided no peace. The emperor, considering Carlo's declaration of neutrality the defection it actually was, fired the duke from his generalship and declared him no longer a friend or responsibility of the Empire. Carlo blamed the loss of income, glory, and protection on councillors and advisers, whom he hounded to ruin.

His capable wife and her count, appraising realistically the danger into which Carlo had put his dukedom, appealed to Venice for men to guard its major fortress (Mantuan troops were either not available or too demoralized), their pay to be the responsibility of Mantua. According to Carlo, the expense was a waste of money. He sent the Venetians back and spent the amount that might have supported the garrison for several months on a show of nobles, emissaries, secretaries, horsemen, all splendidly dressed, who marched into Venice to show their glory as Carlo's men and to thank the senate for its earlier help.

Three years later, in 1665, Carlo was dead at thirty-six, his foolish body having succumbed, it was said, to malaria. (An Italian historian says he died of *dissoluzione*.) His only recorded achievements were the enrichment of jewelers, pornographers, and Margherita della Rovere's relations, and the removal of the few supporting pins that might have held together his collapsing dukedom. It may all have been, in a remote way, not his fault at all. His father had died of syphilis, and the son's lack of quality in body, mind, and spirit might have been attributable to congenital syphilis. Whatever the actual cause of his early death, suspicion was automatically turned on his wife and her unacknowledged consort, Count Bulgarini. The usual accusations of poisoning did not hold, and Isabella Clara, now feigning a more formal relationship with her lover, who continued to function as adviser, became regent for her thirteen-year-old son, Ferdinando Carlo.

Isabella made it her business to mend the breaks with the Empire, not too difficult in view of her familial ties. She assured her son's rights to inherited French holdings as a Rethel-Nevers, and arranged a marriage for him with Anna Isabella Gonzaga, the daughter of the last duke of Guastalla, some of whose properties would be hers and therefore her husband's on her father's death. This arrangement agreed on by the emperor, the wedding contract was signed, sealed, and celebrated. But Ferdinando Carlo proved no more husband or statesman than his father had been; he followed the same gaudy, mindless paths. It was his mother and Count Bulgarini who devised modes of increasing land productivity, who strengthened borders, who persuaded Spain that Mantua would help her protect Milan from the French if she expanded Mantuan fortresses and manned them at Spanish expense.

When her son reached his majority, in 1669, and ceremoniously took on the rule he could not manage, his mother retired to Goito. There she was visited by an agent of the emperor, who persuaded her to enter a nunnery, Count Bulgarini to remove himself to a monastery. She had lived with the man for a long, useful time in a court of infinitely more decadent liaisons; why should this connection, the most solid of her life, be severed now? The actual reasons remain vague. In the ploys of vicious attacks and mendacious treaties that led to the War of the Spanish Succession, Mantua was always considered useful as a wedge into Italy. Isabella Clara was clearly too independent, too dedicated to the Mantuan dukedom; she might make difficulties for potential invaders. It would be infinitely easier to treat with her libertine son, away from the strengths of his mother and her consort.

With his mother and the count gone, Ferdinando Carlo was defenseless, unprepared for the overwhelming events in which he would drown. He absorbed himself in collecting money and more money, wherever he could find it, for his long, curly wigs, his jeweled medallions, the Mars-like armor he chose to strut around in, for his favorite courtiers and his ceaseless debaucheries. The ledgers of his time show that Gonzaga villa farms were satisfactorily producing vegetables, wine, hay, straw, and horses. The Università degli Ebrei occasionally added to the large annual payments it was traditionally required to make. The largest monthly sum, steadily the same, was sent by the *salaro*, who collected the salt tax, a ducal monopoly. But weaving had long before decayed as a profitable craft, and export of other goods was hampered by the destruction of roads and bridges.

In spite of Mantua's decline from past riches and the threat of events around her, Ferdinando Carlo was able to continue hiding in revelries and court intrigues until the turbulent outside world pierced his sybaritic safeties. In 1678, the duke of Guastalla died and the dukedom was claimed by Vincenzo Gonzaga, the next in line. To strengthen his claim there and possibly to other Gonzaga territories, he married the younger sister of Ferdinando Carlo's wife, Anna Isabella. Since Spain backed Vincenzo, Ferdinando Carlo sped his minister, Ercole Mattioli, to France for advice and help. In a secret treaty, Mantua granted Louis XIV the right to station men in the fortress of Casale, "the key to Italy." As compensation, Ferdinando Carlo was given 100,000 scudi, ostensibly for services, never performed, as head of French armies in Italy. At the same time, a Mantuan minister let himself be persuaded by a solid sum of money to reveal the details of the French-Mantuan agreement to the Savoyards, who had for a long time claimed Monferrato and its fortress city. Prepared by the Mantuan agent, Savoy was able to impede the French takeover of Casale for a period. The double agent Mattioli then retracted his promise to turn the fortress of Casale over to the French. He was flattered, coaxed, and tricked into returning to French soil, where he was imprisoned and held in various dungeons for forty years. (His death in the Bastille became the death of a legend rather than of an ambitious functionary. Under the mask he wore constantly, there was the face, it was conjectured, of the French king's twin brother, or an older brother. Or was it the duke of Buckingham, taken during his exile from England? Alexandre Dumas later studied the long, mysterious imprisonment, laced it with conspiracies to displace Louis, and left us the immortal *Man in the Iron Mask*—neither French nor English, but in actuality a greedy, careless agent from Mantua.)

In spite of the efforts of the Savoyards, the French finally settled into Casale in 1681, about the time that Ferdinando Carlo made another pact with France, which would remain, according to his judgment, the greatest of the European powers. The agreement stipulated that if Ferdinando Carlo left no heir, Monferrato would belong to the French crown in perpetuity, as would French territories held by Gonzagas. In turn, he was to be reconfirmed as general of the French armies in Italy, with—and this was of prime importance—"all the honors, graces and privileges" such a general merited. For the city of Casale he received 50,000 doubloons, and for other areas he controlled, 200,000 doubloons. And again, all "honors, graces, immunities and privileges," like those enjoyed by princes of the blood in France, were to enhance him. The grapevine, the thick cable that ran from Rome to Milan, to Naples, to Florence, to Vienna, to Paris, to Madrid, to Venice, spread the news that Ferdinando Carlo had sold Mantua's future. He denied the accusation, explained awkwardly, lied, and then, to find favor with the emperor, traveled eastward to visit the front, where imperial forces were battling the Turks. He looked around for a while, expressed his admiration of the valor he observed, and took his resplendent following back to Mantua. The next year, 1688, he increased his entourage and took them to observe the assault by the Austrians on Belgrade. On his return to Mantua, he busied himself preparing big fetes in his city and in Venice, both cities brightened by his attractive populace of singers and dancers. The French money that kept them singing and dancing was augmented by gold exchanged for a promise that Louis might fortify Guastalla, which Ferdinando Carlo considered legitimately his as the husband of its putative heiress, Anna Isabella. Spanish Milan disapproved, and descended on Guastalla to dismantle the French fortress. With the French money melting rapidly and the emperor demanding 500,000 scudi for his war against the Turks, Mantua's duke worked out another stratagem: He petitioned for French engineers and masons to strengthen the fortifications of his own city. Again Milan disapproved, and its wrathful Spanish governor told him so forcefully. With France busy elsewhere in Europe and no one to fight his battles, Gonzaga turned over his rule to his wife and fled to his Eden, Venice.

Like Gonzaga women before her, intelligent and maltreated Anna Isabella performed valiantly in doomed circumstances. European events informed against her. A coalition of European powers led by the Empire and Spain halted France's ambitious drives, and the Italian footholds Ferdinando Carlo had prepared for Louis could not be held. Bands of Spanish soldiers swaggered through the streets of Mantua, terrifying the citizenry, until Anna Isabella prevailed on a new, more reasonable Spanish governor of Milan to withdraw his troops. Her duke returned from Venice, only to be confronted by a proclamation issued by the emperor, which reaffirmed Vincenzo Gonzaga's right to Guastalla, the claim open to negotiations if Ferdinando Carlo compensated Vincenzo for the moneys drawn from Guastalla as produce, taxes, and sales of estates. Without waiting for long parlays, Vincenzo, accompanied by Spanish troops, settled in as duke of Guastalla with the emperor's blessings. Ferdinando Carlo howled and pleaded, sending representatives to the imperial court in Vienna to hear his cause. No one listened.

Mired in his own muddy spirit and influenced by courtiers and advisers in the pay of France, Ferdinando could do nothing but maintain his stubborn position. On the call of the emperor that he rid his court of French agents, he made the gesture of expelling one French diplomat. Unable to accept the loss of Guastalla, he continued bombarding Vienna with indignant letters and wordy emissaries. Out of pique and contempt, the emperor markedly reconfirmed Vincenzo Gonzaga in his dukedom of Guastalla and again decreed that back moneys owed him by Mantua, 24,000 scudi, be paid forthwith. The cries of self-pity and hatred poured more loudly than ever out of the Mantuan court. Again, to no avail.

* The War of the Spanish Succession was coming to its monstrous head. A treaty of 1698 had acknowledged Joseph Ferdinand, the great-grandson of Philip IV, the heir with the soundest claim to the Spanish throne. It was proposed that the French crown control Naples, Sicily, and Tuscany; Milan and the immediately surrounding territories were to go to the Hapsburg archduke Charles, later the emperor Charles VI. The Spanish, angered by the proposals, which would take much of Italy from them, nevertheless accepted Joseph Ferdinand as heir. While arguments chased back and forth across Europe, Joseph Ferdinand died. Another treaty was written, with France as recipient of even more extensive territories. The emperor, pressing for the rights of his son, the archduke Charles, to the Spanish throne, would not sign the treaty. While heated negotiations spun on, the French managed to reach the ear of the dying Spanish king, Charles II, and induced him to name as his heir the grandson of

Louis XIV—Philip, duke of Anjou, who would become Philip V, king of Spain. With France about to hold the coveted plum, treaty discussions collapsed, to be supplanted by warfare, one of the battlegrounds northern Italy. The war then moved northward, into the Low Countries, into Germany, back to Italy and Spain and into the New World, a phase Americans know as the French and Indian Wars. It ended after fourteen fierce years, with the strength of the Empire dramatically reduced and France with a considerably lesser empire than Louis XIV had dreamed.

While he was pressed between French and imperial forces, Ferdinando Carlo was urged by Rome and Venice to take a position of neutrality, but he clung to France, the only viable offer he could now make her being the famously strategic position of Mantua. In April of 1701, French troops entered the city, and for this boon Louis gave Ferdinando Carlo 60,000 scudi down and 36,000 to come in each of many following months. Mantua finally *had* been sold. Its duke explained the sale by saying that he was clearly in no position to impede or do combat with the powerful forces menacing him. A month later, the emperor Leopold denounced Ferdinando Carlo as a traitor to whom his subjects owed no fealty, no moneys or services. While Ferdinando Carlo howled his usual plaints and accusations, the capable Prince Eugene of Savoy moved toward the borders and on to the gates of Mantua as an ally of the Empire. Besieged and battered, the crippled dukedom was soon utterly destroyed. The duke turned the broken bits over to his wife and fled to Casale, which had been abandoned by the French and now was comparatively quiet. When, in 1703, his wife sickened and was at the point of death, he did not return but sent, instead, suggestions for a body of regents who might rule after her death. Where now to find a second wife of political and financial value? His patron, Louis, helped him to Susanne Henriquette of Lorraine. Again happy in this strengthened tie to France, which, he was sure, would always protect him, he returned to Mantua to prepare a glorious welcome for his bride. She arrived in the spring of 1706, the bright opening of a singularly dark year. The warrior prince Eugene of Savoy routed the French from Italy in the battle of Turin, a humiliating defeat paralleled by the duke of Marlborough's triumphs in the Low Countries. Licking her wounds, France was obviously no longer to be relied on, unwilling and incapable of shaking her sword at the new emperor, Joseph I, who ruled that Milan, Mantua, and their territories were to be annexed to the Empire. Disregarding advice that he flee with his wife to Rome, to the protection of the Pope, who might conceivably persuade the emperor to restore his dukedom, Ferdinando Carlo abandoned his French wife, to lie in the warm arms of Padua in the Veneto. He took with him fifty horses and over nine hundred works of art that had escaped a 1627 sale, two hundred fifty of them of stellar quality. Susanne Henriquette left for Paris and the court of Louis, who supported her until her early death in 1710, two years after her husband's death. Before he died, in Padua, Ferdinando Carlo was again declared a traitor and was stripped officially of all rights to the dukedom of Mantua. The Götterdämmerung staved off by a few capable women now closed into night. Mantua, the survivor of three centuries, was no longer a dukedom, no longer a state, only an exsanguinated fief of the Empire, washed by tired waters.

Sale, Farewell

Although there was little money in the declining years of the dynasty, there was great value in a collection, considered the greatest in Europe, of paintings, antiquities, and objets. As they had for centuries, artists, antiquarians, and goldsmiths pursued the court, pressing their wares, confident, even in hard times, of an eager reception from the traditionally omnivorous Gonzaga. However, Ferdinando and Vincenzo II bought art sparsely and in a desultory manner; the money was needed to pay singers, mimes, and those with the capacity to offer especially exotic pleasures. (One report of a meeting with an important official has Vincenzo incapable of concentrating on the matter at hand; he was too absorbed in describing his intense love of a court dwarf.) Here we might consider the "dwarf's apartment one sees on a visit to the Ducal Palace. Several theories confuse its actual origins. It was supposedly built by Guglielmo to effect a shortcut to the ducal apartments. Vincenzo, his son, improved and decorated them. Another theory has Ferdinando building them in 1615 to resemble the Santa Scala in Rome. Or it is possible that the enamored Vincenzo II had the apartments built for his favored dwarf.

∗ A growing breed of collectors and dealers—Italian, Dutch, English, German—had been looking with covetous eyes on the Gonzaga treasures, freely displayed during court celebrations, and judging them, considering the flaccid character of the dukes and the decay of the land, not too far from available. From time to time, rare works had disappeared from the court, as when Isabella gave France a group of her *studiolo* paintings to win political favor with the French powers. But there were always valuable replacements, like the *Madonna of the Pearl*, painted by Raphael and bought by Vincenzo I. The collection was rarely diminished but grew and grew until the rule of Ferdinando and Vincenzo II.

As it became increasingly apparent throughout Europe that Mantua was in a desperate state and possibly ready to be persuaded to sell her major asset, one ruler, especially, kept an eager eye on the developing situation. Henry VIII of England had had as court painter Hans Holbein the Younger, mainly to glorify his large image. Elizabeth, who had ordered many portraits of herself and supported a few gifted miniaturists, was not generally interested in art. It was Charles I who was the first royal collector of enthusiasm and keen taste. Mantua was not unaware of Charles's intense interest and, in its convoluted way, made tentative approaches to the countess of Arundel, the wife of Thomas Howard, earl of Arundel, a knowing collector who shared his expertise with his wife. Mantua sent Count Alessandro Striggi, its grand chancellor, to meet with her and explore her interest in Mantua's gems of art. She asked only for a model of the Palazzo del Te and a detailed description of all it held, preferably the creations of its famous architect and decorator, Giulio Romano.

Nothing happened for some years, and then, in the mid-1620s, began the negotiations for an actual sale, an entanglement of rivalries and duplicity. Alessandro Striggi remained one of the protagonists of the complicated affair, and with him in the dealing and wheeling were Nicholas Lanier, Charles's master of music, who was also an astute judge of drawings, and Daniel Nys, a Dutchman, some say (or French, or even English). Long a resident of Venice, Nys knew a great deal about art—himself a sharp merchant in the field—and about impoverished and weak-minded houses that were ready to sell soon and cheaply. Lanier came to him in Venice to discuss a potential Mantua sale and after a short visit to Mantua to look at the merchandise, returned to England and continued to communicate with both Nys and Striggi, while Charles waited impatiently. At this point, Duke Ferdinando died, leaving his treasures in the incapable hands of his brother, Vincenzo II, whose major concern was that the collection not go to Italian courts, especially to the Medici. That would be a major humiliation. On the promise that the works would be sent out of the country, Nys was able to make a deal, for fifty thousand scudi, the original cost of Raphael's *Perla,* to buy that same *Perla,* eleven "Caesars" by Titian, the *Death of the Virgin* by Caravaggio, among a good number of other masterworks. After the boxes were opened by Nys in Venice, he declared the shipment short of some promised objects. As that news came to Mantua and was spread along the streets, the shocked public presented Vincenzo with an offer of twice the sale amount if he would recall the works already shipped and stop the sale. In spite of Mantuan outrage and the offer of Mantuan money, additional merchandise left Venice aboard an English ship. She was hit by a fierce storm but managed to survive and continued on her voyage. However, the careless placement of freight and buffeting by the storm caused large quantities of mercury to wash over a considerable number of canvases and ruin them. Lanier managed to save several Correggios by carrying them with him overland.

The duke Vincenzo had held on to other paintings, with which he could not bear to part. When he died, the dealers again descended in an avid contest for the nine "Triumph of Caesar" panels by Mantegna. Every collector wanted them, and Nys, who gained control of them, began to offer them surreptitiously to the Medici, to France. To Charles he sent off inconsequential objects of antiquity, hoping that these would elicit at least some of the money that Charles owed him on earlier transactions. Turning here and a crooked there, Nys, still in debt for the Mantua art in which he had invested, opened his house to creditors so that they might take what they liked and reduce his debt to them. Much to his own surprise, he said, someone turned up three Titians, a Cupid attributed to Praxiteles and another by Michelangelo—among other distinctive works—all once of the Mantua collection. Nys's act was a mistake, a giveaway of what he might be withholding. Charles insisted and threatened, and Nys was forced to yield the "Mantua pieces," including Mantegna's "Triumph," to the king. Not all the art was worth the keeping, but in the main it was an incredible collection, a wonder of Europe and a great source of pride to elegant Charles. However, this disbursement of thirty thousand pounds on art, moneys needed to equip soldiers, troubled his already threatened career. The arrangement of the new glories in his various palaces was disturbed when he left London in 1642 and the palaces were occupied by Parliament. Shortly after his execution, in 1649, much of the collection was sold abroad, but Mantegna's "Triumph of Caesar" were too much admired by Cromwell to let them stray, and they stayed a treasure of England still displayed in Hampton Court, the palace of Henry VIII.

* The original inventory is gone and later lists are not altogether accurate, or are confusingly contradictory, but it is generally estimated that the Mantuan art and objects sold numbered two thousand, among them seven hundred paintings. To the continued plaints of Mantuans, court functionaries replied that the palace was still full of treasures, though certainly not as replete as it was before the sales. But the imperial sack of Mantua in 1630 carried off more fine furniture, objects of semiprecious stone, and silks and velvets from the court, from gutted churches and gentlemen's palaces. The final assault was made by the later duke, Ferdinando Carlo, who sent his remaining fine works by Caravaggio, by Van Dyke, by Veronese and Raphael, to the Veneto when he fled Mantua in 1707. He gave some to church institutions; the rest became a source of contention among several claimants: his wife in France, his sisters and cousins in France and Germany. He chose as his heiress the duchess of Lorraine, the daughter of his sister the empress Eleonora. Not much was then left but the decaying walls of the Camera degli Sposi and what may then have been visible of the Pisanello frescoes.

The rest, the original Charles I collection? Some were bought back by Italy, some retained by England, where a number appear in the National Gallery (except a jester painted as a naked Bacchus, destroyed by order of Queen Victoria). A few great houses bought a number, and there is the collection at Hampton Court, drawings at the British Museum, and tiles and medals at the Victoria and Albert Museum.

The Hermitage owns Gonzaga paintings, as does the Prado and the Louvre and museums in Vienna. The Metropolitan Museum in New York and the National Gallery in Washington also share Mantua. It has been suggested by scholars that almost every famous museum has a piece of Mantua in it—some of it as distinguished paintings, from Sienese primitives on, some of it as medallions, reliquaries, vessels of Venetian glass, tableware of silver and iron, of ivory and bone, mosaics, laces, tiles. And in almost any "Renaissance furniture" museum area or another, one comes on a great chest with panels of inlaid marble, in which Guglielmo might have kept his gold, or a great table made entirely of multicolored semiprecious stones, at which Vincenzo might have dined with a few actress friends. It seems a curious irony that small, striving Mantua achieved little of the historical importance for which she once struggled and yet left her mark on the whole of the Western world as an incomparable source of magnificences achieved by that same ambitious striving.

Lacking art and power, Mantua came to some small importance as a possession of the Austrian empire after 1707, strongly fortified to protect that corner of imperial holdings. She was also a citadel of prime importance to Napoleon Bonaparte, who assaulted and besieged the city for six months, to take it over completely in 1797. When his whirlwind campaigns and consequent misadventures left him in Elba, Mantua again returned to Austria, as an adjunct to Milan.

As early as 1830, there were sporadic Italian attempts at uprisings against the Austrians. They increased in number and ferocity, arousing the imperial forces to arrest thousands and execute countless numbers, seven of the rebels hanged in Mantua. Led and urged on by heroic leaders—Mazzini, Garibaldi, Cavour—Italy finally became its own united kingdom, ruled by the house of Savoy, in 1870.

* There might be a few farewell words written concerning the states with which the Gonzaga were for so long involved as hirelings, as allies, as adversaries, and at times all three. Milan flourished under the Austrians, profiting from a number of enlightened rulings, which helped create a jaunty social life that surprised Napoleon and his forces. Savoy, after its endless struggles with the Gonzaga over Monferrato, finally achieved that territory and became an increasingly important state. As Savoy rose, Naples sank into poverty and decay. The brilliant Ferrara and Urbino had long ago faded, to become the dulled property of a diminished, debile Papacy, whose states were incorporated as part of the French empire in 1809.

Venice, La Serenissima, suffered a long, slow decline, a continuous dimming of her once supreme power. She had been forced by the Ottoman Empire to give up Cyprus, later Crete, and large areas of the Levant. Newer competitive trade routes had enfeebled her commerce. The Jesuits and their insistence on adherence to the prohibitions of a papal Index diminished her as an intellectual city—one hundred and more printing presses reduced to a few dozen. The Inquisition and the Council of Trent, with its strong Counter-Reformation tenets, frowned on the exuberant paganism that illuminated Venetian painting. (Paolo Veronese, for one, was called before an Inquisition tribunal and told to remove buffoons, dwarfs, halberdiers, and other "vulgarities" from a holy painting. They were judged symbols of heresy that "mock, vituperate and scorn" the True Church. The painter made the required changes.)

As long as she could, however, Venice held on to her splendid, defiant shows. Carnival danced for four months at a time. Canaletto and Gaudi painted her allure and Goldoni enriched her fading theater. But as shuttlecock between the swift destructive games of Austria and France, Venice underwent considerable battering to remain a city of magnificent churches, golden, silken paintings, decaying palaces, and silenced docks. She contents herself with being the world's most seductive city, never quite a solid presence, a dream living in the susurrus of a magnificent past.

BIBLIOGRAPHY

* * *

Ackerknecht, E. H. *A Short History of Medicine.* Ronald Press, 1955.

Alberti, Leon Battista. On Architecture; On the Family; On Virtue; etc. Several translators and editors in many editions.

———. *On Painting.* Translated by John R. Spencer. New Haven: Yale University Press, 1956.

———. *Ten Books of Architecture.* Translated by James Leoni. London: Tiranti, 1955.

Amadei, F. Crònaca Universale della città di Mantova, II. Mantua, 1955.

Ancona, Alessandro d'. *Il Teatro Montevano nel Secolo XVI.* Vol. 2, *Le Origini del Teatro Italiano.*

Aretino, Pietro. *Selected Letters.* New York: Penguin, 1976.

Ariosto, Ludovico. *Orlando Furioso.* Translated by Barbara Reynolds. New York: Penguin, 1975.

Aston, Margaret. *The Fifteenth Century: The Prospect of Europe.* New York: Harcourt Brace Jovanovich, 1968.

Avermaete, Roger. *Rubens and His Times.* Translated by Christine Trollope. South Brunswick, N.J.: A. S. Barnes, 1968.

Bandello, Matteo. *Tragical Tales.* New York: E. P. Dutton, 1924.

———. *Twelve Stories.* Translated by Percy Pinkerton. London: George Routledge, 1895.

Barolsky, Paul. *Infinite Jest: Wit and Humor in Italian Renaissance Art.* Columbia, Mo.: University of Missouri Press, 1978.

Baron, Hans. *The Crisis of the Early Italian Renaissance: Civic Humanism and Republican Liberty in an Age of Classicism and Tyranny.* Princeton, N.J.: Princeton University Press, 1955.

———. *Humanistic and Political Literature in Florence and Venice in the Beginning of the Quattrocento.* Cambridge, Mass.: Harvard University Press, 1955.

Bates, Lowry. *Renaissance Architecture.* New York: George Braziller, 1954.

Beck, James. *Italian Renaissance Painting.* New York: Harper & Row, 1981.

Bellonci, Dell'Aqua, Perogalli. *I Visconti a Milano.* Milan, 1977.

Bellonci, Maria. *The Life and Times of Lucrezia Borgia.* New York: Harcourt, Brace, 1953.

————. *Segreti dei Gonzaga.* Milan: Mondadori, 1947.

————, ed. *L'Opera Completa del Mantegna.* Milan, 1967.

Bentley, Eric. *The Genius of the Italian Theater.* New York, 1964.

Berenson, Bernhard. *The Italian Painters of the Renaissance.* London: Phaidon, 1959.

Bertolotti, Antonio. *Artisti in Relazione coi Gonzaga.* Modena, 1885.

Bistici, Vespasiano da. *Lives of Illustrious Men of the Fifteenth Century.* Translated by William George and Emily Waters. London: George Routledge, 1926.

Blunt, Anthony. *Artistic Theory in Italy, 1450–1600.* Oxford: Clarendon Press, 1952.

Boas, Marie. *The Scientific Renaissance, 1450–1630.* New York: Harper & Row, 1962.

Bocazzi, Franca Z. *Mantegna.* London: Thames and Hudson, 1971.

Boccaccio, Giovanni. *The Decameron.* Translated by G. H. McWilliam. London: Penguin, 1972.

Boulting, William. *Woman in Italy: From the Introduction of Chivalrous Service to the Appearance of the Professional Actress.* London: Methuen, 1910.

Bowers, Jane and Tick, Judith, eds. *Women Making Music: The Western Art Tradition.* Chicago: University of Illinois Press, 1986.

Braudel, Fernand. *Capitalism and Material Life, 1400–1800.* New York: Harper & Row, 1973.

————. *Civilization and Capitalism, 15th–18th Centuries.* 3 vols. New York: Harper & Row, 1982.

————. *The Mediterranean and the Mediterranean World in the Age of Philip II.* 2 vols. New York: Harper & Row, 1972.

Brinton, Selwyn. *Lords of Mantua.* London, 1927.

Brosio, Valentino. *Francesco II, Marchese di Mantova.* Turin, 1938.

Brown, C. M. "New Documents for Andrea Mantegna," *Burlington Magazine.* Manchester, Vt., 1972.

————. "New Documents on Isabella d'Este's Collecting of Antiquities," *Burlington Magazine.* Manchester, Vt., 1976.

Browning, Oscar. *Age of Condottiere.* London: Methuen and Company, 1895.

Burke, Peter. *Culture and Society in Renaissance Italy.* New York: Charles Scribner's Sons, 1972.

————. *Popular Culture in Early Modern Europe.* New York: New York University Press, 1978.

Burkhardt, Jacob. *Civilization of the Renaissance in Italy.* New York: Harper & Row, 1958.

Burkhardt, Titus. *Alchemy.* New York: Penguin, 1971.

Cabanne, Pierre. *The Great Collectors.* New York: Farrar, Straus, 1963.

Cage, John. *Life in Italy at the Time of the Medicis.* New York: G. P. Putnam's Sons.

Cairns, Christopher. *Italian Literature.* New York: Harper & Row, 1977.

Carnevali, Luigi. *Il Ghetto do Mantova.* Mantua: Sartori, 1973.

————. *La Tortura a Mantova.* Mantua: Sartori, 1974.

Carpi, Attilio. *Vespasiano Gonzaga, Duca di Sabbioneta.* Cambridge, Mass.: Harvard University Press.

Carriere, Raffaele. *La Danza in Italia.* Milan: Editoriale Domus.

Cartwright, Julia. *Isabella d'Este: Marchioness of Mantua.* London, 1903.

Cassirer, E.; Kristeller, P. O. and Randall, J. H. *The Renaissance Philosophy of Man.* Chicago: University of Chicago Press, 1948.

Castiglione, Arturo. *Adventures of the Mind.* New York: Alfred A. Knopf, 1946.

Castiglione, Baldassare. *The Book of the Courtier.* Translated by George Bull. New York: Penguin, 1976.

Cellini, Benvenuto. *Autobiography.* New York: Penguin, 1956.

Chamberlin, E. R. *Everyday Life in the Renaissance.* New York: G. P. Putnam's Sons, 1965.

Chambers, D. S. *The Imperial Age of Venice, 1380–1580.* New York: Harcourt Brace Jovanovich, 1970.

Chambers, D. S., ed. *Patrons and Artists in the Italian Renaissance.* Columbia, S.C.: University of South Carolina Press, 1971.

Chapbooks. Sixteenth Century Italian, British Library.

Chiarelli, Renazo. *Pisanello.* Florence: Sadea Editore, 1966.

Cipolla, Carlo M. *Public Health and the Medical Profession in the Renaissance.* New York: Cambridge University Press, 1971.

Clark, Kenneth. "A Failure of Nerve." Lecture. Oxford: Oxford University.

———. "L. B. Alberti on Painting." London, 1944.

Coniglio, Giuseppe. *I Gonzaga.* Milan: Dall'Oglio Editore, 1967.

Coryat, Thomas. *Coryat's Crudities.* England, 1611; 2 vols., 1905.

Dampier, Cecil. *A Shorter History of Science.* New York: Meridian, 1957.

Davari, Stefano. *La Musica a Mantova.* Lombardo: Arch. Storico, n.d.

———. *Il Palazzo di Mantova.* Lombardo: Arch. Storico, 1895.

Dennistoun, J. V. *Memoirs of the Dukes of Urbino.* London: Longman, Brown, Green, and Longmans, 1851.

DeWald, Ernest T. *Italian Painting, 1200–1600.* New York: Holt, Rinehart and Winston, 1962.

Dickens, Charles. *Pictures from Italy.* New York: Coward-McCann, 1960.

Ehrenberg, Richard. *Capital and Finance in the Age of the Renaissance.* Translated by H. M. Lucas. New York: A. M. Kelly, 1963.

Einstein, Lewis D. *The Italian Renaissance in England.* New York: Franklin, 1962.

Equicola, Mario. *Chronica di Mantova.* London: Warburg Institute, University of London, 1521.

———. *Di Nature d'Amore.* Venice, 1583.

———. *Istituzioni di M. Equicola.* Mantua: Archives, Biblioteca Communale, late 16th century.

Erlanger, Rachel. *Lucrezia Borgia: A Biography.* New York: Hawthorn, 1978.

Evelyn, John with Arundel. *Diaries in Mantua.*

Ferguson, Wallace. *The Renaissance in Historical Thought: Five Centuries of Interpretation.* Boston: Houghton Mifflin, 1948.

Fochessati, G. *I Gonzaga di Mantova.* Milan, 1930.

Franchini, Dario A. et al. *La Scienza a Corte.* Rome: Bulzione Editore, 1979.

Freud, Sigmund. *Leonardo da Vinci.* New York: Random House, 1966.

Friedlander, M. S. *On Art and Connoisseurship.* Oxford: Oxford University Press, 1946.

Friedlander, Walter. *Mannerism and Anti-Mannerism.* New York: Columbia University Press, 1957.

Garin, Eugenio. *Italian Humanism: Philosophy and Civic Life in the Renaissance.* Translated by Peter Munz. Westport, Conn.: Greenwood Press, 1976.

Garrison, F. H. *History of Medicine.* Philadelphia: W. B. Saunders, 1914.

Gleadow, Rupert. *The Origin of the Zodiac.* New York: Atheneum, 1969.

Gombrich, E. H. *In Search of Cultural History.* Oxford: Phaidon, n.d.

———. *The Story of Art.* Oxford: Phaidon, 1950.

———. *Symbolic Images.* London: Phaidon, 1972.

Gonzaga, Ferdinando. Cinque lettere di Don Ferrante Gonzaga a suo fratello. Mantua Archives.

Gregorovius, Ferdinand. *Lucrezia Borgia.* New York: B. Blom, 1968.

Guicciardini, F. *History of Italy.* London: Collier Macmillan, 1969.

Gundersheimer, Werner L. *Ferrara.* Princeton, N.J.: Princeton University Press, 1973.

Gundersheimer, Werner L., ed. *The Italian Renaissance.* Englewood Cliffs, N.J.: Prentice-Hall, 1965.

Hale, John Rigby. *England and the Italian Renaissance.* London: Faber and Faber, 1954.

———. *Renaissance Europe: Individual and Society, 1480–1520.* New York: Harper & Row, 1971.

Hartt, Frederick. *Gonzaga Symbols in the Palazzo del Te.* Thesis. London: *Journal of the Warburg-Courtauld Institute,* vol. 13, 1950.

———. *Giulio Romano.* 2 vols. New Haven: Yale University Press, 1958.

———. *The Palazzo del Te.*

Haskell, Francis. *Market for Italian Art in the Seventeenth Century.* Past and Present, 1959.

———. *Patrons and Painters.* New York: Alfred A. Knopf, 1963.

———. *Rediscoveries in Art.* Ithaca, N.Y.: Cornell University Press, 1976.

Haskins, Charles Homer. *Studies in Medieval Culture.* New York: Frederick Ungar, 1965.

Hauser, Arnold. *Renaissance to Baroque. The Social History of Art,* vol. 2. New York: Random House, 1957.

Hay, Denys. *The Age of the Renaissance.* London: Thames and Hudson, 1967.

———. *Europe: The Emergence of an Idea.* Edinburgh: Edinburgh University Press, 1968.

———. *Italian Renaissance in Its Historical Background.* Cambridge: Cambridge University Press, 1961.

———. *Italy and Barbarian Europe.* Italian Renaissance Studies.

———. *The Renaissance Debate.*

Haydn, Hiram. *The Counter-Renaissance.* New York: Harcourt, Brace and World, 1950.

Herrick, Marvin T. *Italian Comedy in the Renaissance.* Urbana: University of Illinois Press, 1960.

Hibbard, Howard. *Metropolitan Museum of Art.* New York: Harper & Row, 1985.

Hibbert, Christopher. *House of Medici.* New York: William Morrow, 1975.

Holt, Elizabeth G. *Documentary History of Art.* Princeton, N.J.: Princeton University Press, 1947.

Horizon Book of the Renaissance. New York: American Heritage, 1961.

Howard, Clare. *English Travelers of the Renaissance.* London, 1914.

Huizinga, Johan. *Men and Ideas.* New York: Meridian, 1959.

———. *Waning of the Middle Ages.* New York: Doubleday, 1924.

Hunt, Leigh. *Stories from the Italian Poets.* London: Chapman, 1856.

Intra, Gian B. *Il Castello Gonzaghesco di Goito.* Mantua: Sartori, 1976.

———. *La Reggia Montevana, Nazze e Funerali.* Mantua: Sartori, 1974.

Jacobs, E. F., ed. *Italian Renaissance Studies.* New York: Barnes and Noble, 1960.

Kamp, Martin. *Leonardo da Vinci.* Cambridge, Mass.: Harvard University Press, 1981.

Kay, George, ed. *Italian Verse.* London: Penguin, 1958.

Kinsman, R. S., ed. *Darker Vision of the Renaissance.* London, 1974.

Kristeller, Paul. *Beyond Their Sex: Learned Women of Early Modern Italy.* Edited by P. Labalm. New York: New York University Press, n.d.

———. *Iter Italicum, A Finding List of Uncatalogued or Incompletely Catalogued Humanistic Manuscripts of the Renaissance in Italian and Other Libraries.* 3 vols. completed. Leyden: Brill, 1963, 1967, 1983.

———. *Mantegna.* London and New York: Longmans Green, 1901.

———. *Studies in Italian Thought.* Rome: Storia e Letteratura, 1956.

Larousse Encyclopedia of Renaissance and Baroque Art. London: Paul Hamlyn, 1950.

Leicht, P. S. *Operai, Artigiani, Agricultori in Italia.*

Levey, Michael. *Early Renaissance.* London: Penguin, 1975.

———. *High Renaissance.* London: Penguin, 1975.

———. *Painting at Court.* New York: New York University Press, 1971.

Longhi, Giuseppe. *Le donne, i cavalieri, gli'amori,* etc. Bologna, 1968.

Lopez, Robert S. *Hard Times and Investment in Culture: The Renaissance.* New York, 1953.

———. *Three Ages of the Italian Renaissance.* Boston: Little, Brown, 1980.

Lucas, John, ed. *The Oxford Book of Italian Verse.* Oxford: Clarendon Press, 1952.

Luzio, Alessandro. *Gli Arazzi dei Gonzaga, La Galleria dei Gonzaga.* Mantua: Archives, Biblioteca Communale, 1913.

———. *Chroniche del Marchese di Mantova.* Mantua: Archives, Biblioteca Communale, n.d.

———. *La Galleria dei Gonzaga Venduta d'Inghilterra.* Mantua: Archives, Biblioteca Communale, n.d.

———. *Guerrieri Gonzaga.* Mantua: Archives, Biblioteca Communale, 1915.

———. *Isabella and Elisabetta Gonzaga.* Mantua: Archives, Biblioteca Communale, 1893.

———. *Pietro Aretino.* Mantua: Archives, Biblioteca Communale, 1888.

———. *I Precettori d'Isabella d'Este.* Mantua: Archives, Biblioteca Communale, 1887.

Luzio, A. and Paribene, F. *Il trionfo di Cesare di A. Mantegna.* Mantua: Archives, Biblioteca Communale, n.d.

Luzio, A. and Renier, R. *Buffoni, Nani, Schiavi ai Tempi di Isabella d'Este.* Mantua: Archives, Biblioteca Communale, n.d.

———. *Delle Relazione di Isabella d'Este con Ludovico e Beatrice Sforza.* Mantua: Archives, Biblioteca Communale, n.d.

Machiavelli, Niccolò. *Portable Machiavelli.* Translated by Peter Bondella and Mark Musa. New York: Viking Penguin, 1979.

———. *The Prince.* Translated by George Bull. New York: Penguin, 1961.

Maclean, Ian. *The Renaissance Notion of Women.* Cambridge: Cambridge University Press, 1979.

Mallet, Michael. *The Borgias.* New York: Barnes and Noble, 1969.

Marek, George. *The Bed and the Throne: The Life of Isabella d'Este.* New York: Harper & Row, 1976.

Martines, Lauro. *Disorder in Italian Cities, 1200–1500.*

———. *Lawyers and Statecraft in Renaissance Florence.* Princeton, N.J.: Princeton University Press, 1968.

———. *Power and Imagination: City-States in Renaissance Italy.* New York: Alfred A. Knopf, 1979.

Masson, Georgina. *Courtesans of the Italian Renaissance.* New York: St. Martin's Press, 1975.

Mattingly, Garrett. *Renaissance Diplomacy.* Boston: Houghton Mifflin, 1971.

Maulde, La Claviere R. *The Women of the Renaissance.* Translated by G. H. Ely. London: Sonnenscheim, 1901.

Maurois, André. *History of France*. London: Jonathan Cape, 1949.

Mause, Lloyd de. *The History of Childhood*. New York: Alfred A. Knopf, 1974.

Mead, William E. *The Grand Tour in the Eighteenth Century*. Boston: Houghton, 1914.

Meiss, Millard. *Andrea Mantegna as Illuminator*. New York: Columbia University Press, 1957.

————. *Painting in Florence and Siena After the Black Death*. New York: Harper & Row, 1951.

Monter, William. *Ritual, Myth and Magic in Early Modern Europe*. Athens, Ohio: Ohio University Press, 1984.

More, Sir Thomas. Biography of Pico de la Mirandola.

More, Sir Thomas, trans. *Works of Pico de la Mirandola*.

O'Kelly, Bernard, ed. *The Renaissance Image of Man and the World*. Columbus, Ohio: Ohio State University Press, 1966.

Oman, Charles. *The Sixteenth Century*. New York: E. P. Dutton, 1937.

Origo, Iris. *The Domestic Enemy*. Speculum, n.d.

Paccagnini, Giovanni. *Palazzo Ducale di Mantova*. Turin, 1969.

————. *Pisanella e Il Ciclo Cavalleresco*. Electra Editrice, 1972; London, 1973.

Pagel, W. *Paracelsus*, 2nd ed. S. Karger, 1982.

Panofsky, Erwin. *Studies in Iconology*. New York: Harper & Row, 1972.

Parks, G. B. *The English Traveler to Italy*. Vol. 1. Rome, 1954.

Pazzini, Adalberto. *La Medicina alla Corte dei Gonzaga a Mantova*. Rome: Academia Linceo, n.d.

Penman, Bruce, ed. *Five Italian Renaissance Comedies*. New York: Penguin, 1978.

Penrose, B. *Travel and Discovery in the Renaissance*. Cambridge, Mass.: Harvard University Press, 1952.

Pevsner, N. *Academies of Art Past and Present*. Cambridge: Cambridge University Press, 1946.

————. *Studies in Art, Architecture and Design*. New York: Walker, 1968.

Peyrefitte, Roger. *The Prince's Person*. Paris, 1963.

Pizer, William F. "Isabella d'Este and Lucrezia Borgia as Patrons of Music; the Frottola at Mantua and Ferrara," *Journal of the American Musicological Society* (Spring, 1985).

Plumb, J. H., ed. *Renaissance Peoples*. New York: Harper & Row, 1965.

Pope Pius II. *Autobiography*.

————. *Miseries of Courtiers*.

Pope-Hennessy, John and Christiansen, Keith. *Secular Painting in Fifteenth Century Tuscany*. New York: Metropolitan Museum of Art Bulletin, 1980.

Prescott, Orville. *Princes of the Renaissance*. New York: Random House, 1969.

Pullan, Brian. *Rich and Poor in Renaissance Venice*. Cambridge, Mass.: Harvard University Press, 1971.

Quazza, Romolo. *La Diplomazia Gonzaghesca*. Mantua: Archives, Biblioteca Communale, n.d.

Redlich, Hans F. *Claudio Monteverdi*. Oxford: Oxford University Press, 1955.

Rosmini, H. *Vita di Vittorini da Feltre*.

Ross, James B. and McLaughlin, Mary M., eds. *Renaissance Reader*. New York: Viking, 1953.

Rubens, P. P. *Letters*. Translated and edited by Ruth Saunders Magurn. Cambridge, Mass.: Harvard University Press, 1955.

Rugoff, Milton. *The Great Travelers*. New York: Simon & Schuster, 1960.

Saslow, James M. *Ganymede in the Renaissance*. New Haven: Yale University Press, 1986.

Smith, Winifred. *Commedia dell'Arte*. New York: Coward-McCann, n.d.
———. *Italian Actors of the Renaissance*. New York: Coward-McCann, 1930.
Smith, W. J., ed. *Poems from Italy*. New York: Thomas Y. Crowell, 1974.
Splendours of the Gonzaga. Catalogue of exhibition. London: Victoria and Albert Museum, 1981–1982.
Stokes, Adrian. *The Quattro Cento*. New York: Schocken, 1968.
Stoye, J. W. *English Travellers Abroad, 1604–1667*. London, 1952.
Symonds, John A. *Renaissance in Italy: The Fine Arts*. London: Smith, Elder, 1897.
———. *Short History of the Renaissance in Italy*. New York: Cooper Square Publishers, 1966.
Taylor, F. H. *The Taste of Angels: A History of Art Collecting*. Boston: Little, Brown, 1948.
Tietze-Conrat, Erika. *Pisanello e Il Ciclo Cavalleresco di Mantova*.
Todorow, M. F. "Pisanello at the Court of the Gonzaga," *Burlington Magazine*, Manchester, Vt., 1972.
Van Dyke, Paul. *Renaissance Portraits*. New York: Charles Scribner's Sons, 1905.
Vantaggi, R. *Mantua and Her Art Treasures*. Narni-Terni: Plurigraf, 1978.
Vasari, Giorgio. *Lives of the Painters, Sculptors and Architects*. London: J. M. Dent and Sons, 1927.
Venturi, Leonello, ed. *Sixteenth Century Painting*. Switzerland: Skira Books, 1956.
Verheyen, Egon. *Paintings in Studiolo of Isabella d'Este at Mantua*. New York: New York University Press, 1971.
———. *Palazzo del Te*. Baltimore, Md.: Johns Hopkins University Press, 1977.
Waagen, Gustave. *Treasures of Art in Great Britain*. 3 vols. London: John Murray, 1854.
Waley, Daniel. *Italian City-Republics*. New York: McGraw-Hill, 1969.
Walker, D. P. *Spiritual and Demonic Magic*. London: Warburg Institute, University of London, 1958.
Weiss, Roberto. *Renaissance Discovery of Classical Antiquity*. Oxford, 1969.
White, T. H., trans. *Book of Beasts*. New York: G. P. Putnam's Sons, 1954.
Wightman, W. P. *Science and the Renaissance*. New York: Hafner, 1962.
Wilkins, Ernest H. *History of Italian Literature*. Cambridge, Mass.: Harvard University Press, 1974.
Wind, Edgar. *Pagan Mysteries in the Renaissance*, rev. ed. New York: Norton, 1969.
Wittkower, Rudolf. *Architectural Principles in the Age of Humanism*. New York: Norton, 1971.
Woodward, William H. "Studies in Education During the Age of the Renaissance," in *The History of Education*. Cambridge: Cambridge University Press, 1897.
Zolla, Elemire. *The Androgyne*. London: Thames and Hudson, 1981.
Artisti in Relazione coi Gonzaga. Series III, vol. 3; collected essays. Modena, 1885.
Guida Breva alla Mostra dei Codici Gonzaghesci. Among collected papers. Mantua: Biblioteca Communale, 1966.
La Medicina alla Corte dei Gonzaga a Mantova. In collection of essays and pictures on a variety of subjects. Milan: Academia Virgiliana/Mondadori, 1977.
Una Prova di Matrimonio. Letters dealing with the testing of Vincenzo Gonzaga. No one author. Rome: Canesie Editore, 1961.
La Scienza a Corte: collezionismo eclectiso natura e imagine a Mantova fra Rinascimento e Manierismo. Several essays. Rome: Bulzoni Editore, 1979.

INDEX

* * *

INDEX